Syntax of the SQL SELECT Command

   In the following command syntax, square brackets ([]) enclose optional parameters, braces ({})
enclose alternatives where a choice is required, and vertical bars (|) separate the alternatives. Italicized
words are placeholders for actual entries. (The SQL SELECT command is discussed in Chapter 5.)

SELECT   [ALL | DISTINCT] {[*table.*]* | *expression* [*alias*],...}

FROM   *table* [*alias*] [,*table* [*alias*]]...

[WHERE   *condition*]

[CONNECT · BY *condition* [START WITH *condition*]]

[GROUP   BY *expression* [,*expression*]... [HAVING *condition*]]

[ORDER   BY {*expression* | *position*} [ASC | DESC] [,{*expression* | *position*} [ASC | DESC]]...]

[{UNION | INTERSECT | MINUS} *query*]

[FOR UPDATE OF *column* [,*column*]... [NOWAIT]];

UNDERSTANDING ORACLE

UNDERSTANDING ORACLE®

James T. Perry, Ph.D.
Joseph G. Lateer

SAN FRANCISCO ★ PARIS ★ DÜSSELDORF ★ LONDON

Cover design by Thomas Ingalls + Associates
Cover photography by Mark Johann
Book design by Ingrid Owen
Illustrations by Jeff Giese
Screen production, Sonja Schenk
Copy editor, Deborah Craig
Technical editor, Dan Tauber
Proofreader, Kristen Iverson
Typesetter, Winnie Kelly
Word processors, Jocelyn Reynolds and Bob Myren
Index by Anne Leach
Screen reproductions produced by XenoFont

ACKNOWLEDGMENTS

A GREAT DEAL OF TIME AND MUCH EFFORT HAVE gone into researching and writing this book. The thousands of hours we have spent with Oracle have reaffirmed its power and utility.

Several special people and organizations have contributed significantly to this effort. We wish to publicly recognize and thank them. Oracle Corporation has graciously supplied us with several copies of Oracle software. We especially appreciate timely assistance from Rich Schwartz and from John Rockeman of Oracle's San Diego office. The person who helped us pull this book together and gave so much to the whole effort is our Sybex editor, Lyn Cordell. She has been an absolute joy to work with. She cheerfully (and firmly!) guided us through the sometimes frustrating process leading from idea to finished book. When we needed a dose of encouragement, she somehow sensed that and provided it at just the right time.

We appreciate the patience demonstrated by our families during this entire project. The Perry children, Jessica, Stirling, and Kelly, have been exceptionally generous in allowing their father to be away from them on many weekends. Both of our Nancys have been remarkably understanding while we spent countless hours planning, writing, editing, and typing. Without their support and cooperation, we would not have attempted to write this book.

James T. Perry   San Diego
Joseph G. Lateer   1988

TABLE OF CONTENTS

3   INTERFACING WITH ORACLE: SQL AND SQL*PLUS

4 DESIGNING A DATABASE, CREATING TABLES, AND ADDING DATA

85

5

QUERYING
THE DATABASE

6 DEFINING AND USING VIEWS

161

7 OPERATORS AND FUNCTIONS

199

8 UNDERSTANDING SQL*FORMS

11   MAINTAINING DATABASE SECURITY

12 OPTIMIZING SYSTEM PERFORMANCE: INDEXING AND CLUSTERING

389

13 PROGRAMMING WITH ORACLE: USING PRO*C 415

14 ORACLE UTILITIES: EXP, IMP, ODL, AND SQL*LOADER 449

15   ORACLE FOR 1-2-3   495

16   USING THE SPREADSHEET: SQL*CALC

541

INTRODUCTION

ORACLE IS ONE OF THE MOST EXCITING PROGRAMS for microcomputer systems on the market today. First created and marketed for large mainframe computers and minicomputers, over more than ten years the Oracle relational database management system has matured and improved as a full-featured, SQL-based database system.

Prior to SQL, there was no standard data access language. The SQL relational database interface was developed by IBM in the late 1970's. The American National Standards Institute (ANSI) and the International Standards Organization (ISO) have adopted SQL as the standard language for relational database management system access. The United States Department of Defense will probably require a SQL interface for database systems that are part of future software procurements.

The 1990's will undoubtedly see SQL widely accepted as the standard language for data manipulation, definition, and control. Applications written with SQL can easily be moved from one computer platform to another. Software vendors have added their own, non-standard extensions to the SQL language, which fill gaps in the SQL definition. Oracle has followed the ANSI standard painstakingly, and they have also provided SQL*Plus extensions to the standard language.

The Oracle family of database products includes several powerful applications development and generation tools. These tools provide complete facilities that systems designers and developers can use to design, develop, and test software products whose engine is the Oracle relational database management system.

WHO SHOULD USE THIS BOOK?

This book can serve both as an Oracle RDBMS tutorial and as a reference to the SQL standard RDBMS language. You can use this book if you plan to use a microcomputer, minicomputer, or main-frame computer version of Oracle for the first time, if you have used other SQL products such as DB2 and wish to brush up on the SQL language, or if you are a software developer who wishes to design and develop applications using Oracle's RDBMS as the engine. Whether you have no relational database experience or you are an experienced database user, this book will help you. There are numerous ways Oracle's relational database system can save you time, help organize your information, and provide a sound, structured approach to systems design and implementation with the SQL language interface. Chapter 15 is for Lotus 1-2-3 users who want to learn how to use Oracle's powerful database management system. It shows how to install and use the Oracle add-in database commands to manage vast amounts of data easily and efficiently.

WHAT IS IN THIS BOOK?

Many chapters of *Understanding Oracle* are organized around a comprehensive database application. Each application shows you how to use highlighted SQL and SQL*Plus commands as well as the Oracle systems development and generation tools. Seeing what Oracle can do in practical examples enhances your understanding and demonstrates Oracle's usefulness in various business situations.

Chapter 1 is an overview of the entire Oracle suite of software, including the relational database management system, SQL and SQL*Plus, and system developer's tools. It presents general requirements for running Oracle, and outlines the advantages Oracle has over other database management systems.

Chapter 2 contains step-by-step instructions on installing Oracle. This chapter is a must if you are installing Professional Oracle for the first time. On the other hand, you can skip this chapter if you have access to an Oracle system.

Chapter 3 is an overview of the SQL and SQL*Plus Oracle interface commands. You will learn how to log on and off of Oracle, obtain on-line help, and save often-used SQL statements. A SQL Primer teaches you how to formulate, execute, and edit SQL commands and describes the syntax of major SQL commands. You will learn the SQL commands for creating tables, deleting tables, and querying tables, among others. Sections on The SQL*Plus extensions to the SQL standard describe how to format query results. Finally, you will learn how to leave Oracle and remove its Protective Mode Executive from memory.

Chapter 4 details the fundamental SQL commands that create and query database tables. The chapter highlights SQL commands CREATE TABLE and INSERT and introduces the SQL*Forms systems design and generation tool. You will find many valuable hints about how to create tables that follow good database design criteria in this chapter.

Chapter 5 discusses the SELECT command in detail. You will learn how to display tables, select rows, project certain table columns, and use table aliases. The chapter describes subqueries in detail. It also describes the SQL operators EXIST, ANY, ALL, IN, UNION, INTERSECT, and MINUS. The ORDER BY and GROUP BY clauses will help you to organize returned query results. You will learn how to join related tables and display those results. Chapter 5 also discusses correlated subqueries, equijoin JOIN operations, joining a table to itself, and query optimization.

Chapter 6 is devoted to database views. You are shown how to define views, how to formulate queries that use views, and how to INSERT, DELETE, and UPDATE tables through views. You learn database protection and query simplification using views. You also learn about the important views that are stored in the Oracle data dictionary.

Chapter 7 describes the many SQL functions, operators, and SET system variables. Many examples illustrate string functions, numeric functions, date functions, and aggregate functions. The chapter presents logical, relational, arithmetic, and character operators. Collectively, the functions, operators, and system SET system variables help you to expand the information that you can display and insert into the Oracle relational database management system.

Chapter 8 covers SQL*Forms, an extremely powerful Oracle system developers tool. You will learn how to create a form, copy and rename a form, and how to create screen-driven applications for adding, deleting, querying, and updating information. SQL*Forms is a vehicle for designing complete systems for use by non-experts.

Chapter 9 explains Oracle's powerful SQL*ReportWriter. A tool complementary to SQL*Forms, SQL*ReportWriter provides you with an easy-to-use, fill-in-the-blanks format for creating reports. You will learn how to use SQL*ReportWriter to create comprehensive reports that display database tables in a clear and informative manner.

Although not available for Professional Oracle at the time of this writing, SQL*ReportWriter has been available on other Oracle platforms for quite some time. Because it is expected to be available for Professional Oracle in early 1989 and to replace the cryptic SQL*Report as principal report-writing tool, we base Chapter 9 on the current Vax implementation of SQL*ReportWriter.

Chapter 10 presents the powerful, high-level SQL*Menu interface and describes how to use SQL*Menu with other Oracle products, such as SQL*Forms and SQL*Plus. This program can be especially helpful for novice users learning to work with various application programs. Program designers can use SQL*Menu to rapidly develop complete menu-driven applications. SQL*Menu is a versatile tool that can simplify and organize your work.

Chapter 11 is devoted to database security and auditing. You will learn how to grant and revoke individual user's access to the Oracle system and to tables. Several SQL commands allow you to list existing user system and table privileges. Database auditing is described. You are reintroduced to views as a method of enforcing security. The SQL commands highlighted include GRANT, REVOKE, and AUDIT. System privileges of CONNECT, RESOURCE, and DBA provide the first level of protection, and each one is described fully.

Chapter 12 is of particular interest to database administrators and Professional Oracle users who want optimal performance from the Oracle system. You will learn fundamental database design techniques for optimizing performance. The SQL commands INDEX and CLUSTER are discussed in detail.

Chapter 13 is important for those creating complete software products that use the Oracle relational database management system. The chapter focuses on SQL and SQL*Plus system interfaces to the C programming language. It shows examples of high-level language interface statements that call Oracle RDBMS SQL statements to combine the power of Oracle with the versatility of programming languages.

Chapter 14 provides an in-depth description of the Oracle utilities Export, Import, Oracle Data Loader, and SQL*Loaders. With the Export utility, you can back up all or part of your database. Import loads database tables from backup copies. The ODL and SQL*Loader utilities provide the interface between Oracle and non-database software products. You learn how to backup and restore your database and how to incorporate data from outside, non-database sources into your Oracle database management system tables. The ODL and SQL*Loader utilities are convenient tools for loading your database tables with digitized information from other files in your computer.

Chapter 15 describes the Lotus 1-2-3 add-in product Oracle for 1-2-3. Users familiar with 1-2-3 may wish to read this chapter before reading other chapters. The chapter illustrates the full set of Oracle capabilities and shows all examples as 1-2-3 spreadsheet screens.

Chapter 16 discusses the Oracle spreadsheet tool, SQL*Calc. If you want to interface with the database system through a spreadsheet, this chapter is a must. Users familiar with Lotus 1-2-3 or similar spreadsheets may find this tool the easiest way to use the powerful Oracle database system. You will learn spreadsheet basics and all of the database manipulation and query commands provided by SQL*Calc.

You should carefully examine the appendices and endsheets in this book. The appendices list several important tables that you will refer to frequently. These include the SQL and SQL*Plus commands and functions, a SQL*Forms reference, and SQL*Calc functions and function keys, as well as useful command trees for SQL*Forms and SQL*Calc.

PRODUCT CONFIGURATION VARIATIONS

Oracle is flexible enough to run under PC-DOS 3.1, VAX/VMS, Unix, and IBM VM/CMS. To offer an identical package for each of these platforms is no easy job, but Oracle does it. The core RDBMS utilities, are identical regardless of the environment; an application and database built on an IBM-AT can be run on the largest mainframe. Product packaging does vary somewhat depending on which hardware platform you are using.

In some cases, product configuration varies because a product is not necessary. For example, the product called *Networkstation ORACLE* is for loading onto a PC that is running as a node on a network. Because the network server will have the RDBMS product, it is not necessary to indlude it in the network node version of Oracle. In another instance, the ODS utility program is used to monitor multiple-users on a system; because *Professional ORACLE* is for a single-user computer running under DOS, this utility is not necessary.

On the other hand, with the DOS version, although it is complete with all of the core RDBMS utilities, some of the ancillary products such as SQL*ReportWriter Easy*SQL are not currently available. This should not affect the development or use of an AT-based Oracle installation. The programs that are available in the *Professional Oracle* product configuration work identically to their counterparts residing on any DEC VAX, which is all that is necessary.

Except for SQL*ReportWriter, this book is based on Oracle RDBMS version 5.1B of Professional Oracle for AT-class microcomputers with version 5.1.22.6 of the RDBMS, version 2.1.12.3 of SQL*Plus, version 2.3.16.1 of SQL*Forms, and version 4.1.7.2 of SQL*Menu.

ORACLE:
THE RIGHT TOOL
FOR MANY JOBS

PROFESSIONAL ORACLE IS A COMPREHENSIVE operating environment that packs the power of a mainframe relational database management system into your microcomputer. It provides a set of functional programs that you can use as tools to build structures and perform tasks. Because applications developed on Professional Oracle are completely portable to other versions of the program, you can create a complex application in a single-user environment and then move it to a multiuser platform.

You do not have to be an expert to appreciate Oracle, but the better you understand the program, the more productively and creatively you will use the tools it provides. This chapter will introduce those tools, but first, let's look at the wide range of jobs they are designed to accomplish.

WHAT A RELATIONAL DATABASE MANAGEMENT SYSTEM DOES

A modern relational database management system (RDBMS) can perform a wide array of tasks. In general, it acts as a transparent interface between the physical storage and the logical presentation of data. In practice, it provides a set of more or less flexible and sophisticated tools for handling information. You can use these tools to

- Define a database
- Query the database
- Add, edit, and delete data
- Modify the structure of the database
- Secure data from public access
- Communicate within networks
- Export and import data

Because it gives you so much control over your data, a relational DBMS can also serve as the foundation for products that generate applications and extract data.

Which of these abilities you consider most important depends on the job that you need to do. You might be in charge of creating and maintaining a database; you might be a casual user who primarily works with existing applications to accomplish specific tasks; or, you might be a system developer who creates such applications. If you are using Professional Oracle version 5.1 or later, you will probably combine aspects of all three roles in your work, so let's take a closer look at each of them.

THE DATABASE ADMINISTRATOR

To avoid chaos in any complex system, someone has to be in charge. The person responsible for a database is called the *database administrator* (DBA). The DBA has a special set of privileges that give him or her complete control over the database. Any system with more than one user should have a DBA. For single-user systems, such as Professional Oracle, the user has multiple roles, sometimes acting as the system DBA and sometimes as an ''ordinary'' user with limited database privileges. The DBA's job includes

- Creating primary database storage structures
- Modifying the structure of the database
- Backing up and restoring the database
- Monitoring database performance and efficiency
- Monitoring and reestablishing database consistency
- Transferring data between the database and external files
- Controlling and monitoring user access to the database
- Manipulating the physical location of the database

The complexity of these tasks for the system and for the DBA dictates that a *central documentation system* be incorporated into any relational DBMS. Oracle's data dictionary, discussed later in this chapter, is such a system.

THE END USER

End users have less complex but equally important needs. They must be able to

- Query the database
- Generate printed output
- Share data with or secure data from others
- Use nonexpert methods to update the database
- Define applications from a user's point of view

THE SYSTEM DEVELOPER

System developers create applications ranging from simple data-entry forms to comprehensive multiuser applications. Depending on the level and complexity of the task at hand, the system developer must

- Present understandable screens with which users can access data

- Edit and control user input within those screens
- Secure and present data based on the user login
- Lock data at the row or column level
- Process data using conditional logic
- Access the database from traditional procedural languages
- Access peripheral devices
- Interface data with other packages
- Move to other hardware platforms as an application grows

A system developer need not be a programmer, but those who are will find that their productivity is greatly enhanced by the tools a modern relational DBMS provides. Just as electronic spreadsheets have transformed the accountant's task from labor-intensive cross balancing to high-level analysis, so modern database management systems eliminate many repetitive and time-consuming programming tasks. Hours previously spent creating lines of code for adding, updating, and displaying data can now be spent designing more comprehensive and effective information systems.

New tools, such as fourth generation languages (4GLs), allow developers to concentrate on the significance of data rather than on its location. Nonprocedural forms generators and data manipulation languages make it possible to develop more effective applications in less time. It is the quality of these tools that differentiates the various relational DBMS products on the market. The more advanced the tools a product provides, the easier the developer's job becomes.

It can be difficult to select the right combination of tools for an application, but doing so will ensure that the remainder of your project goes smoothly. One thing is certain: a successful implementation must go far beyond traditional, inflexible programs that simply add, update, display, and report on a file of data. It is no longer enough to provide massive amounts of data in one fixed structure. The ultimate goal is a flexible system that makes information available to management in a form compatible with each individual's decision-making style.

It is also important to create applications that can be modified quickly in response to change. Converting outdated systems is expensive. By storing data in easily altered structures and using flexible tools to present data, you can do much to control such costs.

Also, no matter how limited in scope an application seems, it should be capable of growth. The single-user commercial application is a thing of the past; more than one person will always want access to a database. For this reason, applications need to provide access for multiple users with appropriate security, and a clear and extended hardware growth path.

A modern relational DBMS must be able to meet all these needs and perform all these tasks in order to handle today's multiuser database applications. Oracle provides an outstanding set of tools for data management and applications development, as well as a versatile working environment for end users. With version 5.1, Oracle has grouped its functional programs into products that provide various ways to enter and use the system depending on what a person needs, or is qualified, to do.

Before you are introduced to the components of the Oracle system, you should have some basic information about how Oracle organizes and accesses data.

HOW ORACLE ORGANIZES DATA

In Oracle, all data is stored and displayed in *tables*. A table consists of *columns* (also called *fields*) and of *rows*. A single row of data is called a *record*. From a table, you might select a subset of rows or columns but the result always appears on screen or in print as another table. Figure 1.1 shows the basic structure of a table.

Emp. #	Date	Time in	Time out	Task
9041	9/22	8:05	11:59	ASSEMBLY

Columns, or fields

ASSEMBLY ◄──── One record

Figure 1.1: A simple table

A *view* is a derived table that you can create for purposes of display. Although it looks like a "real" table, within the database a view is only stored as a definition. For this reason, views are referred to as *virtual tables,* while the tables they are derived from are called *base tables.* A view can be a combination of two base tables or a subset of one base table. You can use views to restrict access to your tables and to make certain database chores easier, as you'll discover in Chapter 6.

Because Oracle is a relational system, you can connect the data stored in various tables to increase its usefulness and to avoid duplication. *Selection* is the process of producing a new table consisting of a set of rows from another table that match certain specified criteria. *Projection* is the process of creating a table from a set of columns from another table that match certain specified criteria. A *join* produces a new table that is the union of all rows in two tables, less any duplicate rows.

Chapter 4 provides an in-depth discussion of tables and how they are used in Oracle.

HOW ORACLE ACCESSES DATA

At the core of Oracle (as well as a growing number of competitive systems) is SQL (pronounced "see kwul," or sometimes "ess que el"), which stands for structured query language. SQL is the language that you use to communicate with Oracle. It consists of a set of common English words, such as *select* and *create,* which you can arrange in highly structured commands and statements in order to access and manipulate data stored in a relational database.

The standard set of SQL commands falls into four categories. Data Definition Language (DDL) commands are for creating and altering the structure of the database. Data Manipulation Language (DML) commands are for adding and modifying data. Data Control Language (DCL) commands are for controlling access to the database. Finally, query commands are used to extract information from the database.

Although it is not the only data language for accessing relational databases, SQL has emerged as the standard. Implemented by IBM in their main database product (DB2) in 1982, SQL was adopted by the American National Standards Institute (ANSI) as the standard data access language in 1986.

To grasp the importance of standardization, think of life without the QWERTY keyboard, parallel communication standards, ASCII and EBCDIC, 110-volt, 2-plug outlets, and driving on the right side of the road. Costs skyrocket without standards.

Typically, it takes a major vendor or product to begin the standardization process. The IBM-sponsored research in relational theory that resulted in Structured Query Language has been a giant step forward in the area of database management and querying. Within five years, a user familiar with the simple but powerful SQL command set will be able to sit down at practically any size or type of machine with any brand of database manager and query the database using SQL.

Oracle uses SQL to access, modify, and display data. Additional tools are also included, but this base set of commands is the foundation upon which Oracle is built. You'll learn more about SQL in Chapter 3, and throughout this book.

THE ORACLE ENVIRONMENT

Oracle is a modular system that consists of the Oracle database and several functional programs. As stated at the beginning of this chapter, these components can be viewed as tools; each has a special purpose and can be accessed and used independently. Oracle's tools do four major kinds of work:

- Database management
- Data access and manipulation
- Programming
- Connectivity

DATABASE MANAGEMENT TOOLS

This category (called the RDBMS by Oracle) includes the core programs of Oracle's database management system: the Oracle database with its associated tables and views, which are stored in Oracle's data dictionary, and a group of helpful ''housekeeping'' utilities, listed in Table 1.1. All of these are essential to the DBA's job.

Table 1.1: The Oracle Utilities

Utility	Use
IOR	Starts, stops, and initializes an Oracle system
SGI	Provides system global memory usage information
ODS*	Displays system use for each user
AIJ*	After image journaling logs changes to the system
CRT	Adjusts screen display characteristics
EXP	Exports data from the database to a file
IMP	Imports data from a file to the database
ODL	Loads data from external file formats
CCF	Creates a file to store database information

* not included in *Professional Oracle*

The data dictionary is Oracle's central documentation system. It stores information related to every facit of the database system. User names, user access rights, table names, table attribute names, table storage information, and auditing data for disaster recovery are all stored in the data dictionary. It would be impossible to manage a DBMS without this tool.

A data dictionary can be either *passive* or *active*. Oracle's data dictionary is active, meaning that the system automatically updates the dictionary in ''real time''—that is, as changes are made. The Oracle database programs then reference the data dictionary as required. This is preferable to the passive method, in which the system does not use the dictionary, and the DBA is responsible for updating its contents. Not just the DBA needs the data dictionary, however; all users access it to gain information relating to their own activities.

DATA ACCESS AND MANIPULATION TOOLS

All of Oracle's data access and manipulation tools have one vital thing in common: they are firmly based on ANSI standard SQL. These programs are your gateway to Oracle, the tools that you will use to access and manipulate data, as well as to design or use applications. Each provides a separate point of entry and a unique approach to the Oracle system. SQL*Plus allows direct access to the database with SQL commands. SQL*Forms offers a user-friendly way to create and use forms. SQL*ReportWriter lets you create formatted output. SQL*Menu provides a way for you to integrate your application using menus. Table 1.2 lists the Oracle data access tools and the commands that you'll learn in later chapters to invoke them. A major part of *Understanding Oracle* is devoted to these four programs.

Table 1.2: Oracle's Data Access Tools

PROGRAM	COMMAND (from DOS prompt)	PURPOSE
SQL*Plus	C>SQLPLUS	To use SQL to define, manipulate, and query data
SQL*Forms	C>SQLFORMS	To design a form
	C>RUNFORM	To use a form
SQL*ReportWriter	C>SQLREP	To format a report
SQL*Menu	C>SQLMENU	To create menus for integrating applications

SQL*Plus

SQL*Plus is the main direct access interface to the Oracle relational DBMS. For DBAs, high-level system developers, or others who want to go straight to the heart of the Oracle DBMS, SQL*Plus is the right path. The program provides a full implementation of ANSI standard SQL, plus an assortment of extensions you can use when strict standardization is not required.

Typing **SQLPLUS** and pressing Enter at the host prompt loads the SQL*Plus program and presents the SQL> prompt, which is similar to the dBASE dot (.) prompt. From this prompt, you can access the database directly using standard SQL commands and Oracle-specific SQL*Plus commands. With SQL*Plus, you can query your database and perform data definition, data manipulation, and data control operations. Extensive on-line help is also available. You'll learn more about SQL*Plus in Chapter 3.

SQL*Forms

SQL*Forms provides a convenient and easy method for nonexperts to query a database and update, delete, or add information. Its forms-driven, query-by-example approach is a boon for users not familiar with the SQL language.

For more knowledgeable users, SQL*Forms offers applications building software, that is a must for those building screen-driven applications or using a forms-driven interface to Oracle. With this advanced tool, you can convert, design, generate, and run sophisticated forms for accessing the database. You'll learn about SQL*Forms in Chapter 8.

SQL*ReportWriter

SQL*ReportWriter is a menu-driven formatting tool that uses SQL to create professional-looking reports and other merged specialty output, such as form letters. Chapter 9 covers SQL*ReportWriter.

SQL*Menu

SQL*Menu is an advanced, nonprocedural tool for integrating different Oracle functions and forms into a menu-driven system. With SQL*Menu, developers can focus on what features to include, instead of on how to create menus. SQL*Menu is discussed in Chapter 10.

Additional Access Tools

There are a few additional means of accessing an Oracle database that are either packaged separately from or are not yet available for Professional Oracle. Remember, the tools that come with Professional Oracle work identically to their counterparts residing on any mainframe or mini. An application and database built on an IBM-AT can be run on the largest IBM mainframe, so users of Professional Oracle are part of that larger world.

Two packages provide an alternate user interface to Oracle for those who prefer a spreadsheet environment: SQL*Calc and Oracle for 1-2-3. Either product lets you directly access an Oracle database using SQL commands. SQL*Calc has the advantage of portability to a variety of hardware and software environments. Oracle for 1-2-3 is discussed in Chapter 15; Chapter 16 covers SQL*Calc.

SQL*Graph is a graphics support tool that translates your SQL database queries into graphic representations.

Easy*SQL provides a quick and simple method for getting "up and running" on Oracle data access. With this program, users can build queries or reports one step at a time without learning SQL.

SQL*QMX is an optional report writer that lets you enter queries by example.

PROGRAMMING TOOLS

One of the most important categories of tools available from Oracle is its series of Pro* programming interfaces. These precompiler software tools provide a convenient and easy-to-use method of incorporating Oracle SQL statements in high-level programming languages. Using these products, you can run a supported high-level procedural language merged with SQL data language statements through a precompiler, which converts the SQL statements into that language's native code so that they can be compiled normally. Currently, users of Professional Oracle can interface with Cobol and C. Fortran, PL/1, Ada, and Pascal are available for other implementations, and additional interfaces are being added.

This product gives you the flexibility to write your application in the language you prefer and to access the relational database (using the Oracle interface syntax) directly from compilers for that language. Chapter 13 covers Oracle's programming tools.

CONNECTIVITY TOOLS

Connectivity tools make Oracle available to networks and to other database managers. SQL*Star is a group of products including

SQL*Net and SQL*Connect that allows you to use data stored on remote machines as if they were available locally. With a micro-based version of Oracle called Networkstation Oracle, you receive SQL*Net, instead of a resident version of the Oracle RDBMS. This product consists of a set of device and protocol drivers for handling the Oracle asynchronous protocol, DECnet over the 3COM or the MICOM local area network, and IBM's 3270 protocol. You can load one of these devices to handle the network protocol interfacing for your situation. You can purchase SQL*Net as an option for Professional Oracle if you need to hook into a network or access a remote database.

SQL*Connect lets you access IBM DB2 and SQL/DS databases directly using normal Oracle commands. SQL*Connect does the translating interactively without any prior modification or translation.

Although the components of the SQL*Star product line are only available as options for some implementations of Oracle, the optional components are easily added and implemented when your application requires them. The connections necessary to use these optional tools are included in the base software and can be activated easily when you acquire the connectivity tools.

A detailed discussion of Oracle's connectivity tools is beyond the scope of this book, but it is important to know that these tools exist as you gain expertise with the system. Although Professional Oracle makes Oracle available on single-user systems, anyone who is using Oracle to develop applications may eventually move them to a multiuser platform such as XENIX or UNIX.

WHY CHOOSE ORACLE?

Its track record is often the best reason to consider buying a software package. Choosing a proven product increases the chance that you'll get a system capable of meeting all your needs—even those you can't anticipate now.

Oracle has had many years in the relational market to fine-tune their offering on large, complex applications. Although the functionality and interface of microcomputer-based systems like dBASE IV are appealing, their multiuser capabilities, access controls, and SQL compatibility have been added on. Although Oracle demands greater expertise on the part of the application developer, an application developed on Oracle will be able to keep pace with growth and change—in your company and in the world at large.

ORACLE GIVES YOU SECURITY AND CONTROL

Disaster recovery can be extremely problematic. Oracle has several features that ensure the integrity of your database. If an interruption occurs in processing, a rollback can reset the database to a point before the disaster. If a restore is necessary, Oracle has a rollforward command for recreating your database to its most recent safe point.

Oracle provides users with several functions for securing data. Grant and Revoke commands limit access to information down to the row and column levels. Views are a valuable feature for limiting access to the primary tables in the database. As you can see, there are many ways to control access to an Oracle database.

ORACLE PERFORMS COMPETITIVELY

Through years of experience in the mini and mainframe market, Oracle has been constantly improved to perform competitively on the largest database. Because relational database systems have been hampered by a reputation for slow access times, Oracle has had to prove itself continually. The result is routines that quickly and automatically calculate the best path to the data, and sophisticated, fast indexing routines. Oracle's unique clustering techniques for storing data on the disk are another performance gain.

Additional functions help control complex database installations. The active data dictionary, which automatically updates and logs modifications to the database, provides documentation. A variety of auditing commands and journaling ease error detection and tracking tasks. Database table, partition, and space altering "on the fly" eliminates cumbersome data offloading and loading from the modification process.

Finally, Professional Oracle stores the DBMS kernel in extended memory, so more main memory is available for other applications.

ORACLE SUPPORTS
APPLICATIONS DEVELOPMENT

SQL*Forms is an excellent user-friendly tool for quickly creating forms. You can start with extremely simple default forms or use the full screen painting function to create detailed screens for accessing and updating multiple tables and for controlling and editing data as it is entered.

In SQL*Forms, Oracle provides unique control devices called *triggers* to influence user action on a field before, during, and after data input. These triggers can execute SQL commands, native SQL*Forms commands, or external procedural language subroutines from within a form. SQL*Forms is an advanced fourth-generation tool that will adapt to your requirements extremely well.

Rather than forcing you to program in the procedural language that comes with the product, Oracle provides precompilers that enable you to incorporate SQL commands into your favorite procedural language.

With SQL*Menu, you can link all of your forms, programs, and queries in an easily maintained, secure menu structure. You can include other packages and operating system commands, too.

ORACLE USES THE SQL COMMAND SET

Oracle provides a SQL command set that is close to the ANSI standard. It is highly compatible with IBM's DB2 and DS/SQL. Using SQL*Connect, you can even access these two competitive databases through Oracle.

If a high degree of standardization is not critical to your application, however, you can take advantage of Oracle's numerous improvements to the SQL standard. Oracle has added extensive report-formatting commands to extend the direct SQL language output capabilities and to delay the need for alternative report formatting techniques. Statistical, arithmetic, string, and date/time functions are also included.

Like any other product, Oracle has its limitations. The single-user package does not include all of the tools available on other hardware platforms. Some of these tools can be purchased separately; a few are not yet available for single-user systems. Also, Oracle is relatively expensive and more complex than most single-user, PC-based database managers. As a result, however, Oracle delivers a comprehensive package that allows for unlimited growth.

This chapter described the wide variety of tasks a modern relational DBMS must be able to handle. It touched on the way Oracle organizes data, and discussed SQL, the ANSI standard data access language that is at the heart of the Oracle system. Next, we explored Oracle's structure and components—its rich set of tools for database management, database access, programming, and connectivity. Finally, we considered how these tools contribute to Oracle's overall performance.

The next chapter walks you through the simple installation procedure for Professional Oracle. If Oracle is already installed on your system, you can go on to Chapter 3, where you'll learn more about SQL and SQL*Plus.

INSTALLING
PROFESSIONAL
ORACLE

THIS CHAPTER DESCRIBES HOW TO INSTALL
Professional Oracle on a microcomputer. If you have already
installed Oracle or if you are working on a mainframe or minicomputer (once installed, Oracle's components work identically on any system), you can skip ahead. Here, those who need
them will find detailed, step-by-step instructions for preparing a
microcomputer and installing Professional Oracle.

WHAT COMES WITH ORACLE

Professional Oracle comes with three slip cases containing twenty-two manuals, five reference cards, and fourteen 5¹/₄-inch or nine 3¹/₂-inch disks. Because this collection may seem overwhelming at first, ignore the manuals for now and concentrate on the installation procedure described in this chapter. Installing Oracle is actually quite simple. Before proceeding, however, let's look at Oracle's hardware and software requirements.

WHAT YOU NEED TO RUN ORACLE

Your microcomputer hardware must meet these minimal requirements to run Oracle:

- A central processing unit equivalent to that of an IBM PC/ AT or Oracle-certified compatible (that is, an Intel 80286 or 80386 CPU)

- 640K of random access memory and an additional 896K of extended or enhanced memory for a total minimum memory of 1.5 million bytes

- A fixed (hard) disk with at least 8.5 megabytes of available storage for real mode, and an additional 1.5 megabytes for protected mode

- A monochrome or color monitor

You need version 3.0 or later of PC-DOS or MS-DOS to run Professional Oracle. You can also run Oracle using OS/2 (version 1.0). If you are using OS/2, you will see the Program Selector screen instead of the DOS prompt when you start up. Use the arrow keys to highlight "MS-DOS Command Prompt," which appears in the second column. Press Enter and you'll see the DOS prompt. From there you can proceed as though you were using DOS.

PREPARING FOR INSTALLATION

You must follow a few simple procedures before installing Professional Oracle. These steps, which you need perform only once, will ensure that your system is correctly prepared to run Oracle.

CREATING BACKUP
COPIES OF YOUR ORACLE DISKS

It is always best to create backup copies of your Oracle software and use the copies to install Oracle. The disk copying procedure described next applies to both 3½-inch and 5¼-inch disks. There is one method for single-floppy systems and another for double-floppy systems. Both methods assume that you also have a hard disk—Oracle requires a hard disk to run.

To create backup copies of the original software, you must use the operating system program DISKCOPY. The DOS COPY command will not work. During installation, Oracle checks each disk label to ensure that you have inserted the correct disk. COPY just copies individual files; DISKCOPY copies entire disks, guaranteeing that your backup copies of Oracle are labeled correctly.

Making Oracle Backups on a Single-Floppy System

If you have a double-floppy system and a hard disk, skip to the next section. Otherwise, follow these steps to create backup copies:

1. Type **DISKCOPY A: A:** and press Enter. DOS will display the message:

```
Insert SOURCE diskette in drive A:
Press any key when ready . . .
```

2. Insert the original Oracle disk in drive A and press Enter. DOS will display the message

```
Copying 40 tracks
9 Sectors/Track, 2 Side(s)
```

3. When DOS prompts,

```
Insert TARGET diskette in drive A:
Press any key when ready . . .
```

insert the unused backup disk in drive A and press Enter. When the original disk is completely copied to the backup disk, you'll see the message

```
Copy another diskette (Y/N)?
```

4. To backup the remaining Oracle disks, press Y and repeat steps 2 and 3 until the complete set of Oracle disks is copied.

Making Oracle Backups on a Double-Floppy System

If you have a double-floppy system, making backups is easy. The steps are as follows:

1. Type **DISKCOPY A: B:** and press Enter. DOS displays the message:

```
Insert SOURCE diskette in drive A:
Insert TARGET diskette in drive B:
Press any key when ready . . .
```

2. Place the original Oracle disk in drive A; place the backup disk in drive B, and press Enter. When the disk has been copied, DOS prompts:

```
Copy another diskette (Y/N)?
```

3. To copy more disks, press Y; when all your backups are made, press N.

MODIFYING YOUR AUTOEXEC.BAT AND CONFIG.SYS FILES

You must slightly alter two DOS files, AUTOEXEC.BAT and CONFIG.SYS, before you can install Oracle. If you do not, Oracle will halt the installation process until you make the required changes and reboot the system. Changing AUTOEXEC.BAT and CONFIG.SYS in advance will save time during installation.

Place AUTOEXEC.BAT and CONFIG.SYS in the root directory of your hard disk (C:\). The DOS device driver file called ANSI.SYS must also be in the root directory. If one of these files is not in the root directory, copy it to that directory. Here is a sample DOS command that copies ANSI.SYS from a subdirectory called C:\DOS to the root directory:

```
C>COPY C:\DOS\ANSI.SYS C:\
```

You must always press Enter to execute a DOS command.

Changing the Config.Sys File

Once the three system files are in the root directory, you can use any word processor (EDLIN, for example) to modify the CONFIG.SYS file. These four lines must be added:

```
FILES = 40
BUFFERS = 16
BREAK = ON
DEVICE = ANSI.SYS
```

The order of these lines is unimportant, nor will they affect the rest of the CONFIG.SYS file.

Changing the Autoexec.Bat File

For Oracle to find its programs and utilities automatically, the AUTOEXEC.BAT file must contain a PATH command that locates them. If you do not have a PATH statement in your AUTOEXEC.BAT file, enter the line,

```
PATH C:\ORACLE5\PBIN;C:\ORACLE5\BIN
```

(assuming that you are installing Oracle on drive C) with your text editor or word processor. If you already have a PATH statement, add C:\ORACLE5\PBIN;C:\ORACLE5\BIN to the existing PATH expression. Your placement of this statement affects the speed of your computer. If you plan to use Oracle a great deal, type the Oracle path near the beginning of the PATH expression. For example:

```
PATH C:\ORACLE5\PBIN;C:\ORACLE5\BIN;C:\;C:\DOS;C:\DOS\UTILITYS
```

On the other hand, if you will use Oracle infrequently, you can type the expression in the middle or near the end of the PATH statement.

```
PATH C:\;C:\DOS;C:\DOS\UTILITYS;C:\ORACLE5\PBIN;C:\ORACLE5\BIN
```

Once you have made any requisite changes to AUTOEXEC-.BAT or CONFIG.SYS, reboot your system by pressing Ctrl-Alt-Del (hold down the Ctrl, Alt, and Del keys simultaneously). After rebooting, you are ready to install Oracle.

INSTALLING ORACLE AND ITS SUPPORT TOOLS

You can install all of Oracle's programs and utilities in a few simple steps. Or, you can install only the main Oracle database and selected support software. During the installation process, you can choose to continue installing additional Oracle products, skip installing a particular product, or cease the installation process altogether.

The sections that follow show you how to install each component of Professional Oracle. Installing the complete system—the Oracle database and all support tools and programs—takes approximately 40 minutes. The time required will vary, depending on the speed of your hard disk and CPU.

The steps in the installation process correspond to Oracle's major components (called *bundles* by Oracle). Oracle 5.1B software consists of:

- The Oracle relational database and initial tables
- SQL*Plus
- Oracle utility programs: Import, Export, SQL*Loader, and CRT definitions
- SQL*ReportWriter
- SQL*Forms
- SQL*Menu

You can purchase and install other Oracle software. These extra-cost options include SQL*Calc, Oracle for 1-2-3 (to interface the Oracle RDBMS with Lotus 1-2-3), and the precompiler software for interfacing to languages such as C (Pro*C) or Cobol (Pro*Cobol).

The remaining sections of this chapter assume that you are installing only the "base" Oracle 5.1B software—SQL*Calc and precompiler software are not covered. (Installing Oracle for 1-2-3 is described in Chapter 15).

INITIATING INSTALLATION: ORAINST

To start the Oracle installation process, establish drive C (the hard disk drive) as your logged drive by typing **C:** at the DOS prompt and pressing Enter. Next, place the disk marked "ORACLE Installation" in drive A and type **A:ORAINST** (in upper- or lowercase). Then press Enter. Here is what you'll see:

```
C>a:orainst
```

The ORAINST program initiates installation of Oracle. The banner shown in Figure 2.1 is displayed, indicating that the installation process has begun. To continue installing Oracle, press C. Otherwise, press Q to abandon the installation process.

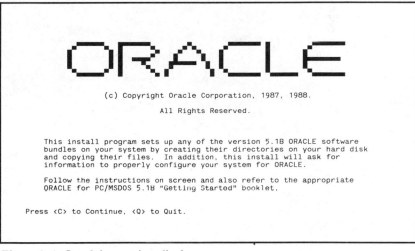

Figure 2.1: Oracle's opening display

Creating Oracle's Home Directory

Once you press C to continue installing Oracle, the opening display disappears and the installation software establishes the default directory structure to contain all of the Oracle software. You are prompted to select the drive and directory in which you will install Oracle (see Figure 2.2). Your response determines where the Oracle database and its associated software will be placed on your hard disk. If you press Enter, the proposed default of

```
C:\ORACLE5
```

will be defined as the home directory for Oracle, and the Oracle installation software will create the directory name ORACLE5 under the root directory. To place Oracle in a different subdirectory on your hard disk, type a new subdirectory name. For example, typing

`C:\DATABASE\ORACLE`

places Oracle in a subdirectory called ORACLE located in another subdirectory called DATABASE. Accept the proposed default of C:\ORACLE5 by pressing the Enter key.

```
          Enter the drive and directory where you will install ORACLE.
                  Press <ENTER> to accept the default.

          Oracle's Home Directory ──▶ C:\ORACLE5
```

Figure 2.2: Establishing Oracle's home directory

If you do not have sufficient hard disk space to store all of the Oracle software and database files, an error message is issued:

```
WARNING - The full ORACLE product line requires over 7 megabytes of storage.
          Your current disk drive has fewer than 8 megabytes available; so you
          may wish to limit the products you install. You may press CTRL-BREAK
          to TERMINATE this procedure and use CHKDSK to check disk storage.

          Press <C> to Continue, <Q> to Quit.
```

If you see the preceding message, press Ctrl-Break (hold down the Ctrl key and press the Break key). Remove any files you can to make available the requisite seven megabytes of fixed disk storage. Then, begin the Oracle installation process again.

After you have selected the home directory for Oracle, the installation software builds the main Oracle directory and the subdirectories that will contain database utilities and tools used with Oracle. Three subdirectories are built initially: BIN, PBIN, and DBS. Programs and data are loaded into each of these subdirectories at various times during the installation process. The BIN and PBIN subdirectories contain executable programs and batch files. DBS, the largest of these subdirectories, contains disk operating system files, the Oracle database, and several types of related tables and Oracle configuration files. Figure 2.3 shows this default directory structure.

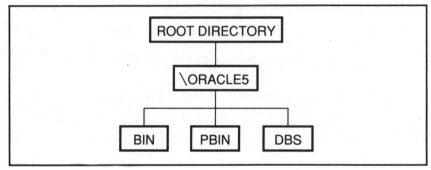

Figure 2.3: The default directory structure

After you select the home directory, the screen is cleared and this message appears:

```
Making ORACLE's home directory...
```

This indicates that the directory structure shown in Figure 2.3 is being established.

After the directories are established, the message shown in Figure 2.4 appears. This indicates that you can choose any of the Oracle products. Perhaps the first product you should install is the Oracle RDBMS and SQL*Plus. Remove the installation disk and place the disk labeled RDBMS disk 1 in drive A and press C to continue with the installation process.

Checking the AUTOEXEC.BAT and CONFIG.SYS Files

Once the Oracle directory is built, the installation process continues. The installation software checks the AUTOEXEC.BAT and CONFIG.SYS files to ensure that they contain special statements required to run Oracle. The screen clears and the display shown in Figure 2.5 appears.

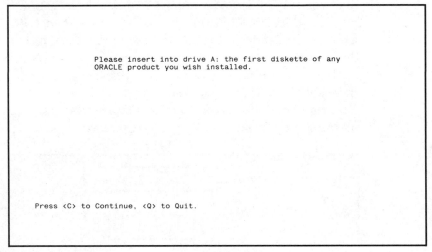

Figure 2.4: Product installation message

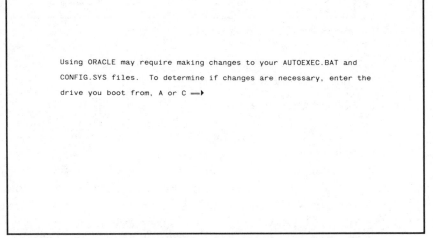

Figure 2.5: Checking the AUTOEXEC.BAT and CONFIG.SYS files

Press the letter corresponding to the disk drive from which you always boot your computer (normally drive C). If you have altered these DOS files before installing Oracle, as described earlier in this chapter, the installation program proceeds immediately to the next step. Otherwise, AUTOEXEC.BAT and CONFIG.SYS are changed automatically.

The following message is displayed while Oracle checks the AUTOEXEC.BAT file:

```
Checking file C:\AUTOEXEC.BAT :
```

If the file must be altered, Oracle automatically displays this message:

```
Changes are needed in C:\AUTOEXEC.BAT :
Do you want these changes made automatically? (y/n): Y
```

When you see this message, press Y or Enter to have Oracle alter your AUTOEXEC.BAT file. If you do not see the preceding message, your AUTOEXEC.BAT file is correct and will not be changed by Oracle. If Oracle's installation software makes changes, the following message appears:

```
Your original "C:\AUTOEXEC.BAT" has been renamed to "AUTOEXEC.BAK"
You have a new "C:\AUTOEXEC.BAT" with modified parameters.
```

Next, Oracle's installation software checks your CONFIG.SYS file. The message

```
Checking file C:\CONFIG.SYS
```

appears when Oracle examines the CONFIG.SYS file. If this file requires changes, the message

```
Changes are needed in C:\CONFIG.SYS;
Do you want these changes made automatically? (y/n): Y
```

is displayed. Press Y or Enter to change the file if the preceding message appears. The message

```
Your original "C:\CONFIG.SYS" has been renamed to "CONFIG.BAK"
You have a new "C:\CONFIG.SYS" with modified parameters
```

signals that CONFIG.SYS has been appropriately altered. If you already changed your AUTOEXEC.BAT or CONFIG.SYS files, neither of the change messages appear.

If either the AUTOEXEC.BAT or CONFIG.SYS file was altered, the following message reminds you to reboot your computer before proceeding with the Oracle installation

```
You will need to reboot the machine in order to reconfigure your
system for ORACLE.  Do this by pressing <CTRL>-<ALT>-<DEL>.

You will then need to rerun ORAINST by typing : ORAINST <ENTER>
```

Be sure to remove the Oracle disk from drive A before rebooting your computer. Then, place the Installation disk back into drive A and type **A:ORAINST** to resume installation.

If neither AUTOEXEC.BAT nor CONFIG.SYS required changes, the product in drive A is automatically installed.

INSTALLING THE DATABASE

Having placed the RDBMS disk 1 in drive A, you are ready to install the Oracle database and its associated tables and views. A series of messages is displayed as the RDBMS is being installed:

```
ORACLE RDBMS installation Procedure

This procedure installs the ORACLE RDBMS executables, and a "seed"
database that contains the views and tables that make up the ORACLE
data dictionary, and also the SQL*Plus help facility.

Copying dba Utilities into C:\ORACLE5\BIN...
Copying DBA Utility Message Files into C:\ORACLE5\DBS...
Copying Initial Default Database into C:\ORACLE5\DBS...
```

This message tells you that the ORAINST installation program is building the database on the hard disk from data and files on the disk in drive A. After a short time, the following message appears:

```
Insert the disk labelled "RDBMS Disk 2" into drive A:
Press <C> to Continue, <Q> to Quit...
```

Remove the previous disk and insert the requested disk into drive A. Press C to resume. The message

```
Copying Initial Default Database into C:\ORACLE5\DBS...
```

will appear at the top of the screen. A third disk is requested with the message:

```
Insert the disk labelled "RDBMS Disk 3" into drive A:
Press <C> to Continue, <Q> to Quit...
```

After you press C at the previous prompt, a new message appears:

```
Copying Initial Default Database into C:\ORACLE5\DBS...
Copying the ORACLE Kernel Software into C:\ORACLE5\BIN...
```

Then, the screen clears and the message

```
Initializing the database...
```

appears, indicating that the database is being initialized and loaded. When the database is initialized, Oracle displays the following prompt:

```
Insert the disk labelled "SQL*Plus Disk 1"
Press <C> to Continue, <S> to Skip, or <Q> to Quit.
```

Pressing Q stops the installation. Pressing S skips the SQL*Plus installation step. Press C to install SQL*Plus.

INSTALLING SQL*PLUS

SQL*Plus is the main interface between you and your databases. Consisting of ANSI standard Structured Query Language (SQL) and extensions to that standard, SQL*Plus permits you to perform data manipulation, data definition, and data control operations. You can also install on-line help in the database during this step of the initialization process.

When you press C to continue, the screen clears and displays the SQL*Plus installation message, shown in Figure 2.6.

You have three choices: real mode, protected mode, or both. If you select real mode, whenever you invoke SQL*Plus it will be loaded and run in your lower 640K of memory. If you choose protected mode, SQL*Plus will be loaded into *extended memory,* located above the 640K memory block. In this case, you will have more

```
                Do you want to install SQL*Plus to run in

                    <R>eal mode?
                    <P>rotected mode?
                    <B>oth Real and Protected modes?

                Enter R, P, or B : B
```

Figure 2.6: Choosing real or protected mode for SQL*Plus

memory available for other programs, since SQL*Plus is not occupying the real memory block in which most programs must run. If you choose Both, SQL*Plus will be stored in two subdirectories, BIN and PBIN, under subdirectory ORACLE5. Press B to choose Both.

Next you will see a message regarding SQL*Plus help, as shown in Figure 2.7. Because the database already contains help files, you will

```
SQL*Plus Installation Procedure

This procedure installs SQL*Plus, which is used to manipulate both
the data within the database, and the database itself, using SQL,
the industry standard database query language.

Do you wish to copy the files necessary to generate the SQL*Plus help
    system?  Note that the default ORACLE version 5.1B database already
    contains the SQL*Plus help information, so this operation is useful
    only if you anticipate having to regenerate the database at some
    future time, and would want to install SQL*Plus help in it at that
    time.  Note also that these files require just over 300 K bytes of
    disk space.

Do you wish to copy the SQL*Plus help files (Yes or No)? N
```

Figure 2.7: Installing SQL help

probably want to press Enter to accept the default value of N (No). If you choose Y, you can install help if you should ever *regenerate* the database (empty it out completely and start from scratch). To invoke help at a later time you can simply type **help**.

When you choose N, these messages are displayed one after the other:

```
Copying SQL*Plus executables into C:\ORACLE5\BIN...
Copying Protected mode executables into C:\ORACLE5\PBIN...
Copying SQL*Plus Message files into C:\ORACLE5\DBS...
Copying Demo scripts into C:\ORACLE5\DBS...
```

The last message indicates that the SQL*Plus installation process is going smoothly and will soon be completed. When Oracle installation is finished, you will see the message

```
Please insert into drive A: the first diskette of any
ORACLE product you wish installed.
```

Remove the SQL*Plus disk from drive A, place the disk labelled "Utilities Disk 1" in drive A, and press C to continue with the installation.

INSTALLING THE UTILITY PROGRAMS, SQL*REPORTWRITER, AND SQL*FORMS

After you have installed SQL*Plus, you will want to install the Oracle Utilities. They include the following programs

- Import, Export, and SQL*Loader
- CRT definitions
- SQL*ReportWriter
- SQL*Forms

This section shows you how to install SQL*ReportWriter, SQL*Forms, and the database utilities ODL, IMP, EXP, and SQL*Loader. ODL, IMP, EXP, and SQL*Loader allow the database administrator to interface Oracle with external software products and files. The ODL (Oracle Data Loader) loads files produced by other software (such as Lotus 1-2-3 files or dBASE IV-produced flat files) into Oracle databases. IMP (import) and EXP (export) provide an interface between two distinct Oracle databases. SQL*Loader can move data into Oracle from a large variety of external operating system files.

You install these utility programs in the order listed; the installation software prompts you to insert the appropriate disks.

Installing the Utility Programs

After you press C to continue with the installation process (be sure Utilities Disk 1 is in drive A), this message appears

```
Do you want to install Utilities to run in

    <R>eal mode?
    <P>rotected mode?
    <B>oth Real and Protected modes?

Enter R, P, or B: B
```

Press Enter to choose B, the default. This choice offers the greatest versatility, allowing the utility programs to execute in either your low 640K memory block or in extended memory where most other programs cannot execute. Once you choose either R, P, or B the message shown in Figure 2.8 appears.

```
ORACLE Utilities Installation Procedure

This procedure installs the ORACLE utilities, IMPort, and EXPort for
importing ORACLE RDBMS data from backup media or other ORACLE sites,
and exporting data for backup or distribution to other sites.  This
procedure also installs the ORACLE Report Text Formatter, Report
Generator, SQL*Loader, and CRT definitions.

Please select the CRT definition that you wish to install as the
    default.  The CRT definition determines the key mapping and
    screen attributes of most of ORACLE's screen-oriented products
    (for example: SQL*Forms and SQL*Menu).

CRT Driver to be installed ──▶ BIOS

Use :    ↑      for previous driver
         ↓      for next driver
      <ENTER>   to accept selection.
```

Figure 2.8: Selecting the default CRT definition

Oracle's screen-oriented products such as SQL*Forms and SQL*Menu make use of the full-screen features of your monitor. Consequently, this installation step requests that you to select one of several full-screen display *drivers*. These special files, called "CRT files" in the Oracle manuals, are incorporated into the Oracle products that take advantage of your console's full-screen capabilities. Products with full-screen display forms include SQL*Forms, SQL*ReportWriter, SQL*Forms, and SQL*Calc.

At this point, you can choose a default CRT file that matches the characteristics of your display. Depending on your monitor and display adapter card, several CRT files may work with your system. The choices available are described in Table 2.1.

Table 2.1: Default CRT File Choices

FILE	DESCRIPTION
BIOS.CRT	Key definition designed for PC use; can be used with CGA, EGA, and VGA monitors
BIOSBLUE.CRT	For any color card with a color monitor; same key definition as BIOS.CRT; displays a form with blue background
BIOSBW.CRT	For systems with a CGA or equivalent card and a monochrome monitor; same key definitions as BIOS.CRT
BIOSMONO.CRT	For systems with an MDA or equivalent card and a monochrome monitor; same key definitions as BIOS.CRT
BIOS43.CRT	For 43-line mode of EGAs; same key definitions as BIOS.CRT
BIOSOLD.CRT	Pertains to Oracle version 4.1.4 key mapping
ANSI.CRT	Same as BIOS.CRT
ANSIOLD.CRT	Same as BIOSOLD.CRT
VT100.CRT	VMS VT100 CRT definition

To select a CRT definition, press the ↑ or ↓ key until the double arrow appears to the left of your choice, and then press Enter to install it as the default.

Once you select a CRT driver, the screen clears and the following message appears:

```
Copying the Oracle RDBMS Utilities...
Copying the Report Text Formatter and Report Generator...
Copying SQL*Loader and its example cases...
```

Then the screen clears and you are prompted to insert the next Oracle Utility disk:

```
Insert the disk labelled "Utilities Disk 2" into drive A:
Press <C> to Continue, <Q> to Quit...
```

Remove the first utility disk from drive A and replace it with Utilities Disk 2. Press C to continue.

The next group of utilities is copied from the installation disk to your hard disk, and a series of messages is displayed as each product is copied:

```
Copying SQL*Loader and its example cases...
Copying ORACLE's CRT Utility...
Copying CRT definitions into C:\ORACLE5\CRT...
```

Installing SQL *Forms

SQL*Forms provides an easy way for nonexperts to query databases, update records, delete records, and add records. Its forms-driven, query-by-example approach to interfacing with databases is a must for users not familiar with the SQL language.

The next message instructs you to insert the appropriate disk to install SQL*Forms:

```
Insert the disk labelled "SQL*Forms Disk 1"
Press <C> to Continue, <S> to Skip, or <Q> to Quit.
```

As with previous installation steps, you can skip this product (press S), halt the installation process completely (press Q), or continue with this step (press C). To install SQL*Forms, place the indicated SQL*Forms disk in drive A and press C.

You will see the following familiar message:

```
Do you want to install SQL*Forms to run in

    <R>eal mode?
    <P>rotected mode?
    <B>oth Real and Protected modes?

Enter R, P, or B : B
```

Again, you may wish to choose the default, B, by pressing Enter. Oracle will ask you whether or not you want to install the SQL*Forms applications-building software (see Figure 2.9).

```
SQL*Forms Installation Procedure

This procedure installs SQL*Forms, which can be used to both
generate and utilize sophisticated data entry forms.

Operators only using existing forms for data entry and data query
    do not require all SQL*Forms software.  If you plan to design forms
    and develop applications, you will need to install SQL*Forms
    application-building software.

Do you want to install SQL*Forms application-building
    software (Yes or No)? N
```

Figure 2.9: SQL*Forms installation procedure messages

Because SQL*Forms is a must for building screen-driven applications or a forms-driven interface to Oracle, you should include it. Press Y to install the application-building software. Additional messages will appear on the screen asking whether or not you wish to include customized Runform user exit files (see Figure 2.10).

Press Y if you want to call user exits from Runform files (see Chapter 8) The application-building software is copied to your hard drive. The message

```
Do you wish to use MicroSoft, Lattice, or Both (M, L, or B)? M
```

```
SQL*Forms Installation Procedure

This procedure installs SQL*Forms, which can be used to both
generate and utilize sophisticated data entry forms.


Operators only using existing forms for data entry and data query
    do not require all SQL*Forms software.  If you plan to design forms
    and develop applications, you will need to install SQL*Forms
    application-building software.

Do you want to install SQL*Forms application-building
    software (Yes or No)? Yes

Included with the application building software are files necessary
    to build a customized Runform containing user exits, which may be
    written in a MicroSoft 'C' environment, or a Lattice 'C' environment.

Do you wish to have these files installed at this time (Y or N)? Y
```

Figure 2.10: Additional SQL*Forms installation procedure messages

is displayed at the bottom of your screen. Press M if you have Micro-Soft C, L if you have Lattice C, or B if you will be using both programming languages for user exit routines.

The screen clears and the following messages are displayed:

```
Copying SQL*Forms executables into C:\ORACLE5\BIN...
Copying Protected Mode executables into C:\ORACLE5\PBIN...
```

The screen clears again and you are instructed to insert the next SQL*Forms disk:

```
Insert the disk labelled "SQL*Forms Disk 2" into drive A:
Press <C> to Continue, <Q> to Quit...
```

Press C to continue installing SQL*Forms. After the screen is cleared, the following messages indicate that SQL*Forms is being loaded to your hard disk:

```
Copying Protected Mode executables into C:\ORACLE5\PBIN...
Copying Message files and SQL scripts into C:\ORACLE5\DBS...
```

When this step is completed, you are instructed to insert the third and final SQL*Forms disk:

```
Insert the disk labelled "SQL*Forms Disk 3" into drive A:
Press <C> to Continue, <Q> to Quit...
```

Remove SQL*Forms Disk 2 from drive A and insert SQL*Forms Disk 3 in its place. Press C to continue with the installation. Additional messages indicate that the remaining SQL*Forms software is being loaded to your hard disk.

```
Copying Message files and SQL scripts into C:\ORACLE5\DBS...
Copying Demo forms into C:\ORACLE5\DBS...
Bringing up the database...
```

Oracle installation software next asks whether or not you want to load special SQL*Forms tables called *designer tables*. Because you need these tables to design forms and store their definitions in the database, press Enter or type Y to accept the proposed default of yes. If you press N, the designer table information is not loaded.

```
The SQL*Forms Designer tables need to be added to your database
    before the SQL*Forms Designer can be used. Do you want this
    done automatically at this time (Y or N) ? Y
```

If you press Enter, the designer tables are added to the database. The following messages are displayed as the tables are being loaded.

```
Adding SQL*Forms Designer tables to database.
The output of this operation is being spooled to \ORACLE5\DBS\SQLFORMS.LOG
```

This completes the SQL*Forms installation step. Oracle installation software automatically proceeds to the next step—SQL*Menu installation.

Installing SQL*Menu

The SQL*Menu utility program provides a full-screen, menu-driven interface between you and all Oracle products as well as all host operating system commands. You can use SQL*Menu to develop elaborate, forms-based systems through SQL*Menu's nested, tree-structured menu system.

As with the preceding installation steps, you can continue (press C), skip (press S), or halt the installation process (press Q). The prompts are

```
Insert the disk labelled "SQL*Menu Disk 1"
Press <C> to Continue, <S> to Skip, or <Q> to Quit...
```

Press C to install SQL*Menu.

You can install SQL*Menu to run in protected memory, real memory, or both by pressing R, P, or B in response to the prompt

```
Do you want to install SQL*Menu to run in

    <R>eal mode?
    <P>rotected mode?
    <B>oth Real and Protected modes?

Enter R, P, or B : B
```

Select B if you want to run SQL*Menu in either real or protected mode (you choose which mode SQL*Menu actually runs in later).

Once you make a choice, the screen clears and you see the following display:

```
SQL*Menu Installation Procedure

This procedure installs SQL*Menu, ORACLE's menuing utility, which
supports the creation, use and maintenance of an easy, menu-driven
interface to virtually any application, simple or complex.

Copying Real Mode Menu Executables into C:\ORACLE5\BIN...
```

Insert the second SQL*Menu installation disk when the screen clears and the following message is displayed:

```
Insert the disk labelled "SQL*Menu Disk 2" into drive A:
Press <C> to Continue, <Q> to Quit...
```

Press C to continue installing SQL*Menu. Several messages indicate the progress of this installation step. They are

```
Copying Real Mode Menu Executables into C:\ORACLE5\BIN...
Copying Menu Libraries into C:\ORACLE5\DMU...
Copying Forms used by Menu into C:\ORACLE5\DMU...
Copying Menu's SQL scripts into C:\ORACLE5\DMU...
```

Like SQL*Forms, SQL*Menu requires several special database tables to operate correctly. After the message ''Bringing up the database...'' is displayed at the top of the screen, the following messages allow you to decide whether or not you want the installation software to load the requisite tables now.

```
The SQL*Menu database tables need to be added to your database
    before SQL*Menu can be used.  Do you want this done automatically
    at this time (Y or N) ? Y
```

Select Yes by pressing either Enter or Y. The message

```
Adding SQL*Menu tables to database.
The output of this operation is being spooled to \ORACLE5\DBS\SQLMENU.LOG
```

appears at the bottom of the screen. This completes the installation of SQL*Menu and the suite of utility software. The last prompt displayed is the customary one

```
Please insert into drive A: the first diskette of any
ORACLE product you wish installed.

Press <C> to Continue, <Q> to Quit.
```

INSTALLING OTHER ORACLE PRODUCTS

If you don't want to install other Oracle products, press Q to halt the installation process. However, if you have other products such as SQL*Calc or high-level language precompiler software such as PRO*C or PRO*Cobol, you may want to install these at this time. As should be familiar, insert the product disk in drive A and press C to start the installation. Follow and respond to the prompts.

SUMMARY

Installing Oracle is a simple and straightforward process. The description in this chapter is longer than the installation process itself. You've learned how to install

- The Oracle database and data dictionary
- SQL*Plus
- The utilities SQL*Loader, ODL, IMP, and EXP
- SQL*ReportWriter
- SQL*Forms
- SQL*Menu

Once Oracle is installed, you can invoke and create databases, query databases, insert records, update records, delete records, and use the rich set of tools that Oracle makes available. Application developers will be especially pleased with SQL*Menu, SQL*Forms, SQL*ReportWriter, and the high-level language interfaces. All of these are Oracle-supplied tools that make building and testing applications relatively simple tasks.

The next chapter describes how to log on to Oracle from SQL-*Plus, and illustrates some of the SQL*Plus language interface features that allow you to create, manipulate, and query one or more databases. In the process, you'll also get a closer look at SQL itself. Because Oracle fully implements ANSI standard SQL, you can apply much of what you'll learn in Chapter 3 in any environment that uses SQL.

INTERFACING
WITH ORACLE:
SQL AND SQL*PLUS

SQL IS THE INTERFACE LANGUAGE BETWEEN YOU and the Oracle database. The American National Standards Institute (ANSI) has accepted SQL as the standard access language for relational database management systems, and all of Oracle's access tools are based on this standard. Oracle's implementation of SQL is fully compatible with IBM Corporation's SQL/DS and DB2 database management systems, and with most other SQL-based systems.

Of all the programs included in the Oracle system, SQL*Plus provides the most direct access to data. SQL*Plus includes a full implementation of ANSI standard SQL, the lingua franca of relational systems. Commands written in SQL*Plus using the ANSI standard command set are portable to any SQL-based system. For this reason it is frequently desirable to remain within this standard when you use SQL*Plus, and most of the examples in this chapter consist of ANSI standard commands that apply to SQL-based systems in general, as well as to Oracle.

Although the ability to operate entirely within standard SQL is fundamental to Oracle, the program also provides a rich set of extensions to SQL, which are called SQL*Plus commands. Although these extensions cannot be used with all SQL-based systems, they are extremely useful when standardization is not an issue; they fill in some gaps left in standard SQL and provide a variety of excellent development aids. In this book, as in the Oracle documentation and SQL*Plus on-line help, extensions to the SQL standard are always called SQL*Plus commands. Unless specifically identified as a SQL*Plus command, any command mentioned in this book is ANSI standard SQL.

This chapter introduces you to SQL and gets you started using SQL*Plus, Oracle's implementation of standard SQL. You'll begin by logging on to Oracle with SQL*Plus and using your first SQL statements to enroll users and assign user privileges for your system. The database administrator (DBA) of every system must perform these essential database tasks, even in a single-user system such as Professional Oracle, where one person is both user and DBA.

Then, you'll learn a few fundamentals about the components and structure of SQL to prepare you for a tour of basic SQL operations, which will provide a foundation for more detailed discussions in the chapters that follow. When you have finished, you will be able to write a wide variety of SQL statements, including statements to query a database, update rows of a database, create a new database table, insert new rows into a table, and delete table rows. A brief discussion of useful SQL*Plus extensions to SQL follows, and, finally, you'll learn to log off of SQL and leave Oracle gracefully when your work is done.

LOADING THE ORACLE PROTECTED MODE EXECUTIVE

The first step in using Oracle is to place a small part of it into memory. This memory-resident portion of Oracle is called the *Protected Mode Executive* and must be present before you can use SQL or any of Oracle's development tools. If you attempt to invoke SQL without the Oracle Protected Mode Executive, Oracle displays this error message:

```
ERROR: Error during Connect - 3121
```

To correct this error, merely return to the DOS prompt and place the Oracle Executive in memory.

Place the Protected Mode Executive into memory and start Oracle by typing **ORACLE** at the DOS prompt and pressing Enter. As the Oracle Executive is loaded, a series of messages appears on the screen. Because Oracle is portable to many computers, the content of these messages varies depending on which computer platform you are using to run Oracle.

Once Oracle has been loaded into extended memory and started, it is *transparent;* there is no visible evidence that it is running. Other applications programs that you use once Oracle is loaded will not be affected by its presence.

Now you are ready to log on to SQL∗Plus, the SQL interface to Oracle, so that you can use SQL commands to accomplish various database tasks.

LOGGING ON TO ORACLE WITH SQL∗PLUS

In Oracle, invoke the SQL prompt by typing **SQLPLUS** and pressing Enter. Before the prompt will appear, however, you must respond to Oracle's requests for a username and associated password.

Because you do not, at first, have an established username and password, Oracle provides a predefined username and password that you can use to log on to SQL for the first time. The special username built into Oracle is SYSTEM; the associated password is MANAGER. Type **system** and **manager**, respectively, in response to Oracle's prompts. Here is the screen display that appears after you type SQLPLUS, press Enter, and type the username (also called a *user ID*) and the password:

```
C:\ORACLE5\DBS>SQLPLUS

SQL*Plus: Version 2.1.12.3 - Production on Sun Jun 4 09:31:00 1989

Copyright (c) 1987, Oracle Corporation, California, USA.  All rights reserved.

Enter user-name: SYSTEM
Enter password:
Connected to: ORACLE V5.1.22.6 - Production

SQL>
```

Notice that the username is displayed, but the password does not show on the screen. Passwords should always remain confidential. For this reason, any user can change his or her own password.

CHANGING THE "SUPERUSER" PASSWORDS

The passwords used with the special usernames SYSTEM and SYS are called *superuser* passwords, because they have database administrator (DBA) privileges. A user with DBA privileges can alter virtually any table in the entire system. Once you successfully log on to the system, you should change the passwords so that only you can log on to Oracle via the special username SYSTEM and SYS. It is critical that you change the passwords to protect your system.

Although a password can be from one to thirty characters long, you should specify one that is at least five or six characters long to prevent a "hostile agent" from easily guessing it. Also, choose a password that you are positive you will remember.

To change the default password for username SYSTEM, you'll use your first SQL command, GRANT. At the SQL prompt, type the following, substituting the password that you have chosen for *newpassword:*

```
GRANT CONNECT TO SYSTEM IDENTIFIED BY newpassword;
```

Remember to terminate the GRANT command with a semicolon and press Enter to submit the command to SQL for processing. SQL records the new password and then displays a message and redisplays the SQL prompt:

```
Grant succeeded.
SQL> _
```

Again, remember the new password you have chosen; write it down and place it in a secure location where you can find it later.

Change the SYS password by issuing this GRANT command while logged on under the SYSTEM username:

```
GRANT CONNECT TO SYS IDENTIFIED BY newpassword;
```

Now that you have secured your system by creating your own superuser passwords, there is a shortcut you can use to log on to SQL*Plus. Instead of typing SQLPLUS at the DOS prompt, pressing Enter, and responding to Oracle's requests for your username and password, you can simply type

```
SQLPLUS username/password
```

substituting SYSTEM for *username,* and your superuser password for *password.* (Remember to type a slash between the two, as shown.) When you press Enter, you will be logged on to SQL*Plus immediately.

GRANTING USER PRIVILEGES

You typed in a GRANT command to change the superuser password. GRANT is the SQL Data Control Language statement that establishes users' specific privileges on the Oracle system. The previous example shows how to change a password. In addition, you can use GRANT to create usernames, assign passwords, and grant users access to database tables.

There is an obvious need for several usernames, or user IDs, in a multiuser database environment (such as Oracle on a mainframe). It may be less obvious why you would establish several user IDs on a microcomputer running Oracle. However, you will find that multiple user IDs are indispensable to logically separate distinct databases and database applications. For example, you might want to create a user ID called REALESTATE to establish and maintain real estate database records. Another user ID such as PROJECTMGMT might hold tables associated with project management information.

As you know, any system with more than one user should have a designated DBA. For single-user systems, the "ordinary" user also serves as the DBA. The username SYSTEM allows the DBA to create new user IDs and passwords. This is called *enrolling* users. The DBA can also remove users from the system. Enrolling and removing users are two of the most important functions that a database administrator performs.

Enrolling Users

Once the database administrator has logged on, he or she can add new users to the system with the SQL GRANT command. The syntax for enrolling new users is

```
GRANT privilege TO username [IDENTIFIED BY password]
```

(Note that in Professional Oracle the user password is a requirement rather than an option.)

There are three major types of database privileges. Listed in increasing order of capability, they are:

CONNECT

RESOURCE

DBA

To give you a sense of each of these three privilege levels, let's look at some GRANT commands that add users to the system.

A command to create a new username LATEER with the CONNECT privilege might look like this:

```
GRANT CONNECT TO LATEER IDENTIFIED BY LAZARETTI;
```

This command establishes the new username LATEER with an associated password LAZARETTI. User LATEER has only CONNECT privileges. LATEER can log on to Oracle and display database tables to which he has been granted access, and, like any other user, he can change his own password.

The next command gives username PERRY more privileges than LATEER was granted:

```
GRANT CONNECT, RESOURCE TO PERRY IDENTIFIED BY TILDEN;
```

In addition to CONNECT, PERRY has RESOURCE privileges; he can create his own tables and views, and can allow other users to manipulate his tables. User PERRY's password is set to TILDEN by the DBA executing the GRANT command, but again, PERRY is free to change it.

The next command gives user SYBEX a full set of DBA privileges:

```
GRANT CONNECT, RESOURCE, DBA TO SYBEX IDENTIFIED BY KING;
```

Besides CONNECT and RESOURCE privileges, SYBEX's DBA privilege permits her to enroll other users, change existing users' passwords, perform database audit activities, remove users from the system, and perform additional DBA duties.

Once these GRANT commands have been executed to enroll users LATEER, PERRY, and SYBEX, they can log on to Oracle using the method described and perform database operations according to their individual privilege levels. Here is what users LATEER, PERRY, and SYBEX, respectively, would type at the DOS prompt to log on to Oracle:

```
SQLPLUS LATEER/LAZARETTI
SQLPLUS PERRY/TILDEN
SQLPLUS SYBEX/KING
```

Listing Enrolled-User Information

Once multiple users (or usernames) are enrolled on a system, the DBA needs a way to keep track of them. Information about usernames, privileges, and user enrollment dates is stored in a special table called <u>SYSUSERAUTH</u> that is created and maintained by Oracle. Only a DBA can display the contents of this table. Given the users enrolled in this chapter, relevant portions of the SYSUSER-AUTH table would look like this:

```
USERNAME        PASSWORD                TIMESTAMP C R D
------------    --------------------    --------- - - -
LATEER          PM[Q^ME5c               14-AUG-88 Y
PERRY           5WQKM26>                14-AUG-88 Y Y
SYBEX           :Q[aU                   14-AUG-88 Y Y Y
PUBLIC                                  12-JUL-87
SYS             <3ZKR8BV                12-JUL-87 Y Y Y
SYSTEM          <3H;W8BV                24-JUL-87 Y Y Y
```

The USERNAME column lists users who have at least a CONNECT privilege. The PASSWORD column displays the encrypted password (actual passwords are never displayed). The Y indicator below C, R, or D means that a user has CONNECT, RESOURCE, or DBA authority. User SYSTEM has all three privileges, whereas user LATEER has only a C (CONNECT) privilege. SYS, like SYSTEM, is a predefined username provided by Oracle. PUBLIC is a predefined username that grants table access to all users.

DROPPING USERS AND ALTERING PRIVILEGES

Only a user with a DBA privilege can remove users from the system. To remove users from the system, log on to SQL*Plus with a username that has a DBA privilege. Remember, initially the only users having that privilege are the two predefined usernames provided with the system: SYS and SYSTEM. The SQL command REVOKE removes users. Its syntax is

```
REVOKE CONNECT FROM username;
```

where *username* is the user to be removed. Because CONNECT is the lowest privilege level, revoking that privilege removes a username from the system. To remove user PERRY, type

```
REVOKE CONNECT FROM PERRY;
```

SQL responds with the message ''Revoke succeeded.'' If you attempt to remove a nonexistent user, Oracle displays the error message ''user does not exist.''

To alter a user's privileges you can either add them with the GRANT command or remove them with the REVOKE command. For example,

```
REVOKE DBA FROM SYBEX;
```

removes the DBA privilege from user SYBEX without affecting her CONNECT and RESOURCE privileges. Similarly,

```
GRANT RESOURCE, DBA TO LATEER;
```

adds RESOURCE and DBA privileges to username LATEER.

You've learned to log on to Oracle with SQL*Plus and you have already used a few SQL commands to establish user privileges. Before you add additional commands to your repertoire, let's step back for a quick overview of SQL.

A SQL PRIMER

SQL—Structured Query Language—consists of a basic vocabulary of English and English-like words. These are called *keywords* or *reserved words* in Oracle because they cannot be used to name tables or other objects that users create. Some reserved words are used frequently in SQL, others far less often. As you read this book, you will become familiar with most of them. Table 3.1 lists Oracle's reserved words (for convenience, they are also listed in Appendix A). With these words and a few familiar punctuation marks you can create endlessly varied SQL statements.

In SQL, as in English, different words serve different purposes and there are rules for combining different kinds of words. Many of the words in Table 3.1 are SQL command words—GRANT, CREATE, and DROP, for example. These are action words, like verbs in English. Every SQL statement begins with a command word or phrase that determines its basic purpose. Incidentally, the words *command* and *statement* are often used interchangeably to mean both isolated command words and complete SQL statements. For now, however, we'll use *command word* specifically to refer to the word or phrase that begins a SQL statement and determines what kind of statement it is.

TYPES OF SQL STATEMENTS

SQL statements can be grouped into three general categories: Data Definition Language (DDL), Data Manipulation Language (DML), and Data Control Language (DCL). Table 3.2 describes some of the important SQL commands in each of these categories. You'll find a complete alphabetical listing of SQL commands in Appendix C.

Structuring the Database: Data Definition Language

You use the Data Definition Language statements CREATE, ALTER, and DROP to create new objects, alter the structure of existing objects, or completely remove objects from the system.

Using the Database: Data Manipulation Language

Once a database is established, data manipulation statements are the most frequently used of the three kinds of SQL statements. You use them to extract records from a database or to alter it in some way.

SELECT statements are used to query the database. You can construct a variety of SELECTs to retrieve and display rows from one or

Table 3.1: Oracle's Reserved Words

ACCESS	CREATE	FROM	LOCK	ORDER	SPACE
ADD	CURRENT	GRANT	LONG	PAGE	START
ALL	DATAPAGES	GRAPHIC	MAXEXTENTS	PARTITION	SUCCESSFUL
ALTER	DATE	GROUP	MINUS	PCTFREE	SYNONYM
AND	DBA	HAVING	MODE	PRIOR	SYSDATE
ANY	ABLINK	IDENTIFIED	MODIFY	PRIVILEGES	SYSSORT
APPEND	DECIMAL	IF	MOVE	PUBLIC	TABLE
AS	DEFAULT	IMAGE	NEW	RAW	TEMPORARY
ASC	DEFINITION	IMMEDIATE	NOAUDIT	RENAME	THEN
ASSERT	DELETE	IN	NOCOMPRESS	REPLACE	TO
ASSIGN	DESC	INCREMENT	NOLIST	REPORT	TRIGGER
AUDIT	DISTINCT	INDEX	NOSYSSORT	RESOURCE	UID
BETWEEN	DOES	INDEXED	NOT	REVOKE	UNION
BY	DROP	INDEXPAGES	NOWAIT	ROW	UNIQUE
CHAR	EACH	INITIAL	NULL	ROWID	UPDATE
CHECK	ELSE	INSERT	NUMBER	ROWNUM	USER
CLUSTER	ERASE	INTEGER	OF	ROWS	USING
COLUMN	EVALUATE	INTERSECT	OFFLINE	RUN	VALIDATE
COMMENT	EXCLUSIVE	INTO	OLD	SELECT	VALUES
COMPRESS	EXISTS	IS	ON	SESSION	VARCHAR
CONNECT	FILE	LEVEL	ONLINE	SET	VARGRAPHIC
CONTAIN	FLOAT	LIKE	OPTIMIZE	SHARE	VIEW
CONTAINS	FOR	LINK	OPTION	SIZE	WHENEVER
CRASH	FORMAT	LIST	OR	SMALLINT	WHERE
					WITH

Table 3.2: SQL Commands by Category

COMMAND	DESCRIPTION
SQL Data Definition Language	
ALTER SPACE	Alters a space definition
ALTER TABLE	Adds a column to, or redefines a column in, an existing table
COMMENT	Inserts a comment about a table or column into the data dictionary
CREATE CLUSTER	Creates a cluster which may contain two or more tables
CREATE INDEX	Creates an index for a table
CREATE SPACE	Creates a space definition which then may be used to define the space allocation properties of a table
CREATE SYNONYM	Creates a synonym for a table or view name
CREATE TABLE	Creates a table and defines its columns and other properties
CREATE VIEW	Defines a view of one or more tables or other views
DROP	Deletes a cluster, table, view, or index from the database
RENAME	Changes the name of a table, view, or synonym
SQL Data Manipulation Language	
DELETE	Deletes one or more rows from a table or view
INSERT	Adds new rows to a table or view
SELECT	Performs a query and selects rows and columns from one or more tables or views

Table 3.2: SQL Commands by Category (continued)

COMMAND	DESCRIPTION
SQL Data Manipulation Language (continued)	
UPDATE	Changes the value of fields in a table or view
SQL Data Control Language	
AUDIT	Makes Oracle audit use of a table, view, synonym, or system facility
COMMIT	Makes database transactions irreversible
GRANT	Grants access to objects stored in database
LOCK TABLE	Locks a table and thus permits shared access to the table by multiple users while simultaneously preserving the tables' integrity
REVOKE	Revokes database privileges or table access privileges from users
ROLLBACK	Cancels database transactions

more tables. The UPDATE, INSERT, and DELETE statements alter existing database rows, place new records into a database, or remove one or more records from the database, respectively.

Securing the Database: Data Control Language

Data Control Language statements such as GRANT, REVOKE, COMMIT, and ROLLBACK control access to databases and affirm or revoke database transactions. Used frequently by the database administrator, DCL statements also control who has access to what tables, who can log on to the Oracle system, and what privileges each user has for various database tables. The COMMIT and ROLLBACK commands permit groups of database transactions to be made permanent or to be nullified.

ANATOMY OF A SQL STATEMENT

Starting with one of the SQL command words or phrases, you can create a SQL statement to accomplish almost any database task. After you type a command word or phrase to tell SQL what operation you want to perform, you can add clauses to modify the basic action or to specify data by location or some other characteristic. You'll learn to write a wide variety of SQL statements in this chapter, but a few conditions and rules of syntax will always apply.

As you have seen, SQL commands are typed to the right of the SQL prompt, which appears automatically when you log on to SQL*Plus and reappears after a command is executed. (In this book, the prompt is often printed next to commands that you are instructed to type to emphasize the beginning of a new command.) The line on which the SQL prompt appears is the *command line*. If a command runs over one line, additional lines are automatically numbered on the screen. In SQL, you can run long commands on and let the lines break where they will, or you can end the current line and start a new one at any point by pressing Enter. However, you must never split a word between lines; it is best to end a line after a complete word and punctuation. For clarity, most examples in this book are typed with one clause per line. Occasionally, a short command is typed on only one line.

You cannot abbreviate words in a SQL command. Furthermore, individual words must be separated by at least one space or a tab. Often, our examples use additional spaces to make commands more readable or to line up related clauses on separate lines. You can type SQL commands in upper- or lowercase. This book uses uppercase consistently to set SQL commands off from the text.

SQL syntax includes a few common punctuation marks. Commas separate items in a list (names of table columns, for example). Parentheses set off discrete elements, such as column specifications and subqueries. You can use a period to specify objects precisely by concatenating additional information to the object name. For instance, if two tables contain a PRICE column, you can uniquely identify those columns by referring to them as *table1*.PRICE and *table2*.PRICE.

Single quotation marks (' ') enclose a character string, and a semicolon (;) indicates the end of a SQL command. When you have completed an entire command, pressing the semicolon and Enter ends the command and causes the SQL*Plus interface to interpret and execute it. If you press Enter at the end of a command but forget to type the semicolon, just type it by itself on the new line that appears and press Enter again. When execution is complete, the SQL prompt will reappear and you can begin a new command.

A few additional punctuation marks are reserved for special situations, which we will discuss as the need arises.

In this book (and in the Oracle documentation), you'll encounter three symbols, which are used as conventions but are not typed as part of the commands. They are as follows:

SYMBOL	USE
Square brackets ([])	Enclose optional material
Braces ({})	Enclose sets of alternatives where a choice is required
Vertical bars (|)	Separate alternatives

Entering SQL*Plus Commands

Earlier we mentioned a set of useful SQL*Plus extensions to ANSI standard SQL that are available in SQL*Plus. These extensions include commands for controlling the format of query results, for storing and retrieving SQL commands, and for setting options that affect the SQL*Plus interface. Much of what you learned about SQL commands in the preceding section also applies to the SQL*Plus command set, but there are three important differences in syntax between standard SQL and SQL*Plus commands:

- SQL*Plus commands must be typed continuously; you cannot press Enter to start a new line within a SQL*Plus command.

- Certain abbreviations are acceptable in SQL*Plus commands (see Appendix C).

- You need not terminate SQL*Plus commands with a semicolon, although you may do so. (The single exception is the SAVE command, which you'll encounter later in this chapter.) It is good form to end SQL*Plus commands with the optional semicolon, however, and we will do so consistently in this book.

Some of the most important SQL*Plus commands are introduced later in this chapter, and in Appendix C you'll find a complete alphabetical listing of these extensions to the standard language. However, there is one SQL*Plus command—HELP—that you should become familiar with immediately.

SQL*PLUS ON-LINE HELP

HELP is perhaps the most useful SQL*Plus command for new Oracle users. With this command, you can access on-line help without leaving SQL. To get help with any of a large number of SQL and SQL*Plus commands, type **HELP** followed by the name of a command or feature, like this:

`SQL> HELP SELECT;`

The screen displays information and then control returns to SQL so that you can continue with your work. Figure 3.1 is a sample help display. The help frame shown describes how to use another of the SQL*Plus commands, QUIT. As you proceed through this chapter, explore SQL*Plus help by typing other HELP commands.

```
Q U I T
+----------------------------------------------------------------------------------+
! Syntax !
!--------+
!
!    QUIT;
!
+----------------------------------------------------------------------------------+

TYPE: SQL*Plus command.

DESCRIPTION: Leaves SQL*Plus and returns control to the operating system. Also
commits pending changes to the default database.

QUIT is a synonym for EXIT.

SQL>
```

Figure 3.1: A SQL*Plus on-line help screen

CORRECTING THE CURRENT COMMAND LINE

It is easy to correct mistakes on the command line that you are currently typing. Use ←, Delete, or Backspace to delete the error, and then simply retype the line. However, once you have pressed Enter to end a line, you can no longer use these keys to make changes. This is because pressing Enter commits the line to the SQL *buffer,* a special area of memory that holds the current or most recently executed SQL command. To change a line that is in the buffer, you can invoke the host operating system editor by entering the EDIT command, which is discussed later in this chapter.

SQL*PLUS DATA TYPES

As you know, the data in an Oracle database is stored in tables that contain columns, or fields. Each field is reserved for a particular type of data that is decided upon when the table is created. The more kinds of data, or *data types,* a language allows, the more options you have as you create tables. The Oracle SQL*Plus interface language provides a rich variety of data types, which are listed and described in Table 3.3. You'll learn more about them when you begin to create tables in the following section. A full discussion of data types is reserved for Chapter 4.

Table 3.3: SQL*Plus Data Types

DATA TYPE	DESCRIPTION
CHAR	Character data can consist of characters, digits, and special characters. The maximum field size is 240 characters.
DATE	Date fields can contain valid dates in the range of January 1, 4712 B.C. to December 31, 4711 A.D. Dates are displayed in the form DD-MMM-YY (for example, 17-OCT-88).

Table 3.3: SQL∗Plus Data Types (continued)

DATA TYPE	DESCRIPTION
DECIMAL	Decimal fields can contain digits 0 through 9 and an optional negative sign. No fractional values may be specified (that is, 245 but *not* 245.0).
FLOAT	FLOAT data is the same as NUMBER data.
INTEGER	INTEGER data is the same as NUMBER data, except only whole numbers can be specified.
LONG	LONG data fields can contain character data up to 65,535 characters long. Only one LONG column per table is allowed.
LONG RAW	LONG RAW is raw binary data (such as 2's complement binary). Graphics data can be stored in LONG RAW form.
LONG VARCHAR	LONG VARCHAR data is identical to LONG data.
NUMBER	NUMBER data can contain digits 0 through 9 and an optional negative sign. The number of decimal places and the total number of digits can be specified. This total includes digits before and after the decimal place.
RAW	Raw binary data such as bit graphics can be stored in RAW data columns. Oracle does not attempt to interpret RAW (or LONG RAW) data. The maximum field size is 240 characters.
SMALLINT	SMALLINT data is the same as INTEGER data.
VARCHAR	VARCHAR data is the same as CHAR data.

BASIC SQL OPERATIONS

The SQL operations for querying databases, inserting table rows, updating table rows, deleting table rows, and creating new tables are the primary means of interfacing with relational databases.

To learn these SQL, DML, and DDL commands, you will use a real estate database example. This database contains information that residential real estate appraisers use to help establish the market value of a ''subject'' property being appraised. The properties contained in this database have been sold within the last 12 months, and are called *sales comparables*. Individual properties that most closely match the subject property are selected from the sales comparables database based on characteristics such as number of bathrooms, square footage, zip code, and so on.

Figure 3.2 shows a simplified file that might exist in the sales comparable database. This file consists of information arranged in a table with fields for a property's parcel number (a unique value for each property), sales price, date sold, square footage, number of bedrooms and bathrooms, and address (street number, street name, and zip code). In the next section, you'll learn how to create such a table.

```
PARCEL    PRICE  SALEDATE   SQFT BR   BA STNUM STNAME          ZIP
-------  ------  ---------  ---- --  --- ----- ------          ------
1050601  136500  04-JAN-88  1100  3  2.0  4764 FINSEN AVENUE   92016
1083767  165500  27-JAN-88  1500  3  2.0  4522 ROBBINS STREET  92016
1216019  141000  03-JAN-88  1750  3  2.5 16136 BLAZEWOOD WAY   92016
1248361  211500  05-MAY-88  2789  4  3.0  8053 EASTRIDGE DR    92052
1775591  216500  04-FEB-88  1732  3  2.0  9974 ALTO DRIVE      92052
2198778  209500  25-JAN-88  2236  4  2.5  4194 RAPATEE DRIVE   92052
2823280  128500  04-FEB-88  1247  2  2.0 11476 MEADOWFLOWER    92122
3649828  261500  24-JUL-88  2625  5  3.0   138 BAHAMA BEND     92122
4753652  165500  14-FEB-88  1650  3  2.0  7330 WERNER STREET   92122
6262401  165500  08-DEC-87  1438  3  2.0  4427 ROSCOE DRIVE    92241
6487971  114500  26-MAY-88  1200  4  2.0  2093 DE LACRUZ       92241
6560792  126500  01-NOV-88  1247  2  2.0 16314 RIMSTONE LANE   92241
6842703  102500  22-FEB-88  1300  3  2.0  1665 MONTEREY PARK   92345
7141094  215500  25-MAY-88  2600  4  2.0  4244 MARS WAY        92456
7372020  296500  06-JUL-88  2475  4  3.0   137 CATSPAN         92456
```

Figure 3.2: A table from the sales comparables database

CREATING TABLES

The first step in establishing a database is to create one or more tables to hold your data. Creating a table structure to hold your data is called *defining* a table. Use the DDL statement CREATE TABLE to define tables in SQL.

Let's define a table called PROPERTY that duplicates the sales comparables database table from Figure 3.1. First, type at the SQL prompt the CREATE TABLE statement and the name of the table that you want to create:

```
SQL> CREATE TABLE PROPERTY
```

Now you are ready to specify the names of the columns, or fields, that you want in the PROPERTY table, as well as the type of data and number of characters that each column will contain. For clarity, type each field and its related information on a separate command line. Press Enter to move down one line. Oracle will automatically number the new command line, in this case, line 2.

To enter the first field, PARCEL, on line 2, type

```
(PARCEL  NUMBER(7) NOT NULL,
```

Recall that SQL uses parentheses to set off certain components of a command. The opening parenthesis marks the beginning of the field specification section of this CREATE TABLE command. The first column name, PARCEL, comes next, followed by the data type for that column and the maximum number of digits it can hold.

The PARCEL column will contain a unique, seven-digit ID number for each property in the database. You can add the NOT NULL option to any column specification to indicate that an entry is mandatory for that column. Without a parcel number, the information in the remaining columns of the PROPERTY table could not be uniquely identified; the PARCEL column must be NOT NULL to ensure every parcel is entered with a parcel number. The comma marks the end of the PARCEL column entry. Press Enter to type the next column name, PRICE, and its type definition on line 3.

PRICE is a number field with 8 digits. Enter

```
PRICE    NUMBER(8),
```

and press Enter. Since the SALEDATE column has the data type DATE, which holds a predefined number of characters, you do not need to supply a number in parentheses after this entry. Just type a comma after the data type. The SQFT, BR, and BA columns are all data type NUMBER, and will contain 5, 1, and 2 digits, respectively. The special entry BA NUMBER(2,1) permits a total of 2 digits, one of which is fractional (to allow for homes that have half bathrooms).

Enter these fields on command lines 5 through 7, remembering to separate the information for each field with a comma.

STNUM and STNAME are of data type CHAR. Character data fields can contain any alphabetic or numeric characters, and some special characters.

ZIP is another NUMBER field; it holds 5 digits. Enter the information for the ZIP column on command line 10, but this time do not type a comma at the end. ZIP is the last column in the PROPERTY table. Enter a closing parenthesis to mark the end of the field specification section of the command.

The PROPERTY table is now defined, and this CREATE TABLE command is complete except for the final semicolon. When you type the semicolon and press Enter, SQL*Plus immediately processes the CREATE TABLE command. The message ''Table created.'' is displayed to confirm that the table definition has been successful. The finished command should look similar to this:

```
SQL> CREATE TABLE PROPERTY
  2  (PARCEL    NUMBER(7) NOT NULL
  3   PRICE     NUMBER(8),
  4   SALEDATE  DATE,
  5   SQFT      NUMBER(5),
  6   BR        NUMBER(1),
  7   BA        NUMBER(2,1),
  8   STNUM     CHAR(5),
  9   STNAME    CHAR(20),
 10   ZIP       NUMBER(5));
```

A SQL*Plus command, DESCRIBE, can display the column names and data types for any table. It is *not* an ANSI standard SQL command and it may not be available in other implementations of SQL. The DESCRIBE command displays column names and data types and is an easy way to refresh your memory about the structure of tables. Figure 3.3 shows a sample display produced with the DESCRIBE command for the sales comparables table called PROPERTY that you just created. You'll learn more about the SQL*Plus DESCRIBE command in Chapter 4.

INSERTING DATA INTO TABLES

As soon as you have defined a table, you can enter data into it with the standard SQL statement INSERT. For example, you would

```
SQL> DESCRIBE PROPERTY:
   Name                           Null?      Type
   -------------------------------- --------- ----
   PARCEL                         NOT NULL  NUMBER(7)
   PRICE                                    NUMBER(8)
   SALEDATE                                 DATE
   SQFT                                     NUMBER(5)
   BR                                       NUMBER(1)
   BA                                       NUMBER(2,1)
   STNUMB                                   CHAR(5)
   STNAME                                   CHAR(20)
   ZIP                                      NUMBER(5)

SQL>
```

Figure 3.3: The description of the PROPERTY table

use the following INSERT command to enter a row of data into the PROPERTY table:

```
SQL> INSERT INTO PROPERTY
  2   VALUES (1050601,136500,TO_DATE('04-JAN-88'),1100,
  3          3,2.0,' 4764','FINSEN AVENUE',92016);
```

Notice that the information about each field is not placed on a separate line as it was in the CREATE TABLE command. Remember, either format is acceptable in SQL. You can list as many or as few items as you wish on each command line. The previous INSERT command would function exactly the same if it were entered in this fashion:

```
SQL> INSERT INTO PROPERTY
  2   VALUES
  3   (1050601, 136500,
  4   TO_DATE('04-JAN-88'),
  5   1100, 3, 2.0,
  6   ' 4764', 'FINSEN AVENUE',
  7   92016);
```

The values in this INSERT command correspond, left to right, to the fields defined for the PROPERTY table. The value 1050601 corresponds to the PARCEL column, 136500 corresponds to the PRICE column, and so on. You can use a special SQL∗Plus function called TO_DATE to enter date values. It converts character representations of dates (the most recent sales date, in the example) to an internal date form used by Oracle. (Functions are covered in Chapter 7.)

After you successfully place a row into a database, the message "1 record created." is displayed on the screen. Repeat the INSERT command with the values shown in Figure 3.2 to add the remaining 14 rows to the PROPERTY table.

QUERYING TABLES WITH SELECT

SELECT is probably the most frequently used (standard) SQL command. You use it whenever you want to query a database and produce a listing of selected records. The SELECT command has a basically simple form, but since it can be written as an arbitrarily complex statement it is extremely versatile. What follows is the standard syntax for a simple SELECT statement:

```
SELECT column-names
FROM table-name
WHERE condition;
```

This command could be written on a single line, but the preceding form is easier to read and edit. The following sections demonstrate several simple SELECT commands. Chapter 5 provides a complete description of SELECT.

Using a Simple Query to Display All Columns

A simple use for the SELECT statement is to display all columns in a table. For example, this command displays all columns of the PROPERTY table:

```
SELECT * FROM PROPERTY;
```

When you use the asterisk (*) in place of actual column names, all column names are listed. In other words, the preceding SELECT command is equivalent to the following statement:

```
SELECT PARCEL,PRICE,SALEDATE,SQFT,BR,BA,STNUM,STNAME,ZIP
FROM PROPERTY;
```

Clearly, it is easier to use the * than to use column names when all columns are to be listed.

The output produced by either of the preceding queries is shown in Figure 3.4 (some of the columns have been trimmed so that each row fits on one line).

```
PARCEL   PRICE SALEDATE   SQFT BR   BA STNUM STNAME              ZIP
-------  ------ ---------  ---- --  ---- ----- ----------------   ------
1050601 146055 04-JAN-88  1100  3  2.0  4764 FINSEN AVENUE       92016
1083767 177085 27-JAN-88  1500  3  2.0  4522 ROBBINS STREET      92016
1216019 150870 03-JAN-88  1750  3  2.5 16136 BLAZEWOOD WAY       92016
1248361 226305 05-MAY-88  2789  4  3.0  8053 EASTRIDGE DR        92052
1775591 231655 04-FEB-88  1732  3  2.0  9974 ALTO DRIVE          92052
2198778 224165 25-JAN-88  2236  4  2.5  4194 RAPATEE DRIVE       92052
2823280 128500 04-FEB-88  1247  2  2.0 11476 MEADOWFLOWER        92122
3649828 261500 24-JUL-88  2625  5  3.0   138 BAHAMA BEND         92122
4753652 165500 14-FEB-88  1650  3  2.0  7330 WERNER STREET       92122
6262401 165500 08-DEC-87  1438  3  2.0  4427 ROSCOE DRIVE        92241
6487971 114500 26-MAY-88  1200  4  2.0  2093 DE LACRUZ           92241
6560792 126500 01-NOV-88  1247  2  2.0 16314 RIMSTONE LANE       92241
6842703 102500 22-FEB-88  1300  3  2.0  1665 MONTEREY PARK       92345
7141094 230585 25-MAY-88  2600  4  2.0  4244 MARS WAY            92456
7372020 317255 06-JUL-88  2525  4  3.0   137 CATS PAW            92456
```

Figure 3.4: Output from a simple SELECT statement

Selecting Columns: SQL Projection

You may recall from Chapter 1 that projection is a fundamental relational database operation that produces a new table from selected columns—not all columns—of one or more existing tables. The SELECT statement is often used to perform projections. For example, you can display the subset of columns PARCEL, PRICE, SQFT, and ZIP from the PROPERTY table with this SELECT statement:

```
SELECT PARCEL, PRICE, SQFT, ZIP
FROM PROPERTY;
```

The result of this projection is shown in Figure 3.5.

Selecting Rows: SQL Selection

Selection, another important relational database operation, selects and displays rows of one or more tables that satisfy some criteria. For

```
PARCEL    PRICE    SQFT    ZIP
-------   -------  ------- -------
4753652   165500    1650    92122
6262401   165500    1438    92241
6487971   114500    1200    92241
1050601   136500    1100    92016
1083767   165500    1500    92016
1216019   141000    1750    92016
1248361   211500    2789    92052
1775591   216500    1732    92052
2198778   209500    2236    92052
2823280   128500    1247    92122
3649828   261500    2625    92122
6560792   126500    1247    92241
6842703   102500    1300    92345
7141094   215500    2600    92456
7372020   296500    2475    92456
```

Figure 3.5: Projecting columns

example, if you want to list sales of properties in the zip code 92052 from the PROPERTY table, you can add a WHERE clause to the SELECT statement. The following query selects records only from that zip code:

```
SELECT *
FROM PROPERTY
WHERE ZIP = 92052;
```

The result would be this smaller table whose rows satisfy the zip code criterion that follows the WHERE in the previous query (some fields have been shortened for this display):

```
PARCEL   PRICE SALEDATE   SQFT BR  BA STNUM STNAME              ZIP
-------  ------- ---------  ----- -- ---- ----- ------------------ -----
1248361  211500 05-MAY-88  2789  4  3.0  8053 EASTRIDGE DR        92052
1775591  216500 04-FEB-88  1732  3  2.0  9974 ALTO DRIVE          92052
2198778  209500 25-JAN-88  2236  4  2.5  4194 RAPATEE DRIVE       92052
```

Combining Selection and Projection

You can combine database selection and projection operations to form a SELECT statement that produces specified fields of certain table rows. To project a subset of columns, merely list the desired column names. To restrict the rows that are selected, specify selection criteria with the WHERE clause. Suppose, for example, that you want to list parcel numbers, price, square footage, and zip codes for properties in the price range of $130,000 to $200,000 that have three bedrooms:

```
SELECT PARCEL, PRICE, SQFT, ZIP
FROM PROPERTY
WHERE PRICE BETWEEN 130000 AND 200000
      AND BR = 3;
```

These properties would be listed in response to the previous query:

```
PARCEL    PRICE    SQFT    ZIP
-------   -------  ------- -------
4753652   165500   1650    92122
6262401   165500   1438    92241
1050601   136500   1100    92016
1083767   165500   1500    92016
1216019   141000   1750    92016
```

Using Select to Display Computed Results

You can also use SELECT commands to display computed results based on database columns and combinations thereof. Any of the standard ANSI arithmetic operators (addition, subtraction, multiplication, and division) can be written along with column names, as can the set of Oracle SQL∗Plus arithmetic and string operators, which will be discussed in Chapter 7.

Suppose that an appraiser wants to know the cost per square foot of recently sold homes. (This value is often used to locate good comparable homes that most closely match a subject property being appraised.) You could include the computed value sales price divided by square feet in a column projection by combining the PRICE and SQFT columns from the PROPERTY table with the division operator. This results in a *pseudo column*, a column that is derived from database columns but is not, itself, a field. This SELECT command extracts several columns from the PROPERTY table, including the pseudo column PRICE/SQFT:

```
SQL> SELECT STNUM, STNAME, PRICE, SQFT, PRICE/SQFT
   2   FROM PROPERTY;
```

Ordering the Results

The previous query would be more informative if the rows in the projection were listed in order of increasing cost per square foot. You can place the optional phrase ORDER BY at the end of the previous SELECT command to specify the column on which the listed rows are to be ordered, PRICE/SQFT. However, because that column is a pseudo column it is identified as an arithmetic expression and has no actual name. Instead, you can use a number indicating the column's position in the statement—that is, 5—to order the results. The revised SELECT statement is

```
SQL> SELECT STNUM, STNAME, PRICE, SQFT, PRICE/SQFT
  2   FROM PROPERTY
  3   ORDER BY 5;
```

Figure 3.6 shows the resulting rows displayed in the proper sequence of lowest to highest cost per square foot.

STNUM	STNAME	PRICE	SQFT	PRICE/SQFT
8053	EASTRIDGE DR	211500	2789	75.8336
1665	MONTEREY PARK	102500	1300	78.8462
16136	BLAZEWOOD WAY	141000	1750	80.5714
4244	MARS WAY	215500	2600	82.8846
4194	RAPATEE DRIVE	209500	2236	93.6941
2093	DE LACRUZ	114500	1200	95.4167
138	BAHAMA BEND	261500	2625	99.619
7330	WERNER STREET	165500	1650	100.303
16314	RIMSTONE LANE	126500	1247	101.443
11476	MEADOWFLOWER	128500	1247	103.047
4522	ROBBINS STREET	165500	1500	110.333
4427	ROSCOE DRIVE	165500	1438	115.09
137	CATSPAN	296500	2475	119.798
4764	FINSEN AVENUE	136500	1100	124.091
9974	ALTO DRIVE	216500	1732	125

Figure 3.6: Rows ordered on the PRICE/SQFT column

Formatting Columns with SQL*Plus

The resulting price-per-square-foot column, labeled PRICE/SQFT, is confusing because varying numbers of digits follow the decimal point. You can correct this by adding the SQL*Plus (not standard SQL) statement, COLUMN, to specify the format of displayed columns. Typing a series of COLUMN statements, one per column to be formatted, can greatly enhance the appearance of numeric values. For example, type three SQL*Plus COLUMN statements before typing the previous SELECT statement, as shown here:

```
SQL> COLUMN PRICE FORMAT $999,999;
SQL> COLUMN SQFT FORMAT 9,999;
SQL> COLUMN PRICE/SQFT FORMAT $999.99;
SQL> SELECT STNUM, STNAME, PRICE, SQFT, PRICE/SQFT
  2  FROM PROPERTY
  3  ORDER BY 5;
```

This produces the attractive result displayed in Figure 3.7. Column statements will be used frequently throughout this book to format sample output. They are not required, but without them your results are more difficult to read.

STNUM	STNAME	PRICE	SQFT	PRICE/SQFT
8053	EASTRIDGE DR	$211,500	2,789	$75.83
1665	MONTEREY PARK	$102,500	1,300	$78.85
16136	BLAZEWOOD WAY	$141,000	1,750	$80.57
4244	MARS WAY	$215,500	2,600	$82.88
4194	RAPATEE DRIVE	$209,500	2,236	$93.69
2093	DE LACRUZ	$114,500	1,200	$95.42
138	BAHAMA BEND	$261,500	2,625	$99.62
7330	WERNER STREET	$165,500	1,650	$100.30
16314	RIMSTONE LANE	$126,500	1,247	$101.44
11476	MEADOWFLOWER	$128,500	1,247	$103.05
4522	ROBBINS STREET	$165,500	1,500	$110.33
4427	ROSCOE DRIVE	$165,500	1,438	$115.09
137	CATSPAN	$296,500	2,475	$119.80
4764	FINSEN AVENUE	$136,500	1,100	$124.09
9974	ALTO DRIVE	$216,500	1,732	$125.00

Figure 3.7: Columns formatted with the SQL*Plus COLUMN command

DELETING ROWS FROM TABLES

DELETE, perhaps the simplest of the standard SQL statements, removes one or more rows from a table. (Multiple table delete operations are not allowed in SQL.) The syntax of the DELETE command is

```
DELETE
FROM table
[WHERE condition];
```

This command deletes all rows in the *table* that satisfy the *condition* in the optional WHERE clause. Be careful! Because the WHERE clause is optional, you can easily delete *all* rows from a table by omitting a WHERE clause that limits the scope of the delete operation. For example, executing this command:

```
SQL> DELETE
  2  FROM PROPERTY;
```

removes all rows in the PROPERTY table. If you inadvertently delete rows from a table, all is not lost. You can immediately issue the SQL command ROLLBACK to cancel any database operations since the most recent COMMIT. Like ROLLBACK, COMMIT is a transaction managing command, but it confirms instead of cancels operations. COMMIT and ROLLBACK are described in Chapter 4.

How would you delete selected rows from a table? Suppose you want to delete from the PROPERTY table all rows whose last sale dates are before an arbitrary date (sale dates over one year old, for example). The WHERE clause can contain one or more conditions that candidate rows must satisfy to be deleted. Here is a DELETE command with a WHERE clause that specifies the condition sale dates before February 15, 1988:

```
SQL> DELETE
  2  FROM PROPERTY
  3  WHERE SALEDATE < TO_DATE('15-FEB-88');
```

The TO_DATE function in line 3 converts a character date form to Oracle's internal date form. The function requires that the date be entered as a character string—that is, enclosed in single quotes (see Chapter 7). Were this command executed, eight rows from the fifteen-row sales comparable database would be deleted. To make the deletions irrevocable, you could execute

```
SQL> COMMIT;
```

Or, you could execute a ROLLBACK command to bring back the previously deleted records.

Let's look at a few more examples of the DELETE command. To delete properties whose sale price is empty (not zero, but without any value at all) you would execute

```
DELETE FROM PROPERTY WHERE PRICE IS NULL;
```

The next command would delete properties whose price per square foot is less than $95.00 or greater than $120.00:

```
DELETE FROM PROPERTY
WHERE PRICE/SQFT NOT BETWEEN 95.00 AND 120.00;
```

Finally, to delete *all* rows from the property table, type

```
DELETE FROM PROPERTY;
```

UPDATING ROWS

You can change (update) individual columns of selected rows with the SQL UPDATE command. Here is the command syntax:

```
UPDATE table
SET column = expression[, column = expression] . . .
[WHERE condition];
```

where *expression* can be any combination of characters, formulas, or functions that result in the same data type as the specified column. As with the DELETE and SELECT commands, the WHERE clause is optional. If a WHERE clause is included, it specifies an arbitrarily complex condition that must be met for a row to be updated. If no WHERE clause is included, *all* rows are updated. The SET clause determines which columns are updated and what values are stored in them. Only one table can be updated per UPDATE command.

Suppose that a mistake has been made in the sales prices for homes with zip codes of 92016, 92052, and 92456. The mistake was uniform: all sales prices in the database should be 7 percent higher than they are. Only records satisfying that zip code condition should be updated, and the only field affected is sales price:

```
UPDATE PROPERTY
  SET PRICE = PRICE * 1.07
WHERE ZIP IN (92016, 92052, 92456);
```

This increases the values for PRICE by 1.07 times their current value (a 7 percent increase) for records whose zip code is IN one of the three zip code values listed inside the parentheses. The set operator IN somewhat reduces the complexity of the condition. You'll learn about set operators in Chapter 7. Without the IN set operator, the previous UPDATE command with an equivalent WHERE condition is:

```
UPDATE PROPERTY
  SET PRICE = PRICE * 1.07
WHERE ZIP = 92016 OR ZIP = 92052 OR ZIP = 92456
```

Updating more than one field is equally easy. Any number of column names followed by the equal sign and new values may follow SET. A comma should separate each column name and value pair from its neighbor. The UPDATE command

```
UPDATE PROPERTY
SET SQFT = 2525, STNAME = 'CATS PAW'
WHERE STNUM = '  137' AND STNAME = 'CATSPAN';
```

alters the SQFT field to 2525 and the STNAME (street name) field to ''CATS PAW'' for any row containing the street number and name combination of 137 CATSPAN. Of course, only one record should satisfy that condition.

Again, to make the updates permanent, execute the SQL command COMMIT. If the update is incorrect, you can reverse it and return the affected rows to their original condition by immediately executing the SQL command ROLLBACK. Figure 3.8 shows the PROPERTY table after the preceding two update operations have been completed (no COLUMN commands were used, so the returned rows are not formatted).

ADDING COLUMNS

Just as you can create a new table at any time with the CREATE TABLE command, you can alter an existing table by adding a new column. Currently, ANSI standard SQL does not allow existing table columns to be removed. The standard SQL command ALTER TABLE adds or modifies columns. The syntax for adding columns is

```
ALTER TABLE table-name
  ADD (column-name data-type,column name data-type,...);
```

```
 PARCEL   PRICE SALEDATE   SQFT BR   BA STNUM STNAME                 ZIP
 -------  ----- --------- ----- -- ---- ----- -------------------- ------
 1050601 136500 04-JAN-88  1100  3  2.0  4764 FINSEN AVENUE         92016
 1083767 165500 27-JAN-88  1500  3  2.0  4522 ROBBINS STREET        92016
 1216019 141000 03-JAN-88  1750  3  2.5 16136 BLAZEWOOD WAY         92016
 1248361 211500 05-MAY-88  2789  4  3.0  8053 EASTRIDGE DR          92052
 1775591 216500 04-FEB-88  1732  3  2.0  9974 ALTO DRIVE            92052
 2198778 209500 25-JAN-88  2236  4  2.5  4194 RAPATEE DRIVE         92052
 2823280 128500 04-FEB-88  1247  2  2.0 11476 MEADOWFLOWER          92122
 3649828 261500 24-JUL-88  2625  5  3.0   138 BAHAMA BEND           92122
 4753652 165500 14-FEB-88  1650  3  2.0  7330 WERNER STREET         92122
 6262401 165500 08-DEC-87  1438  3  2.0  4427 ROSCOE DRIVE          92241
 6487971 114500 26-MAY-88  1200  4  2.0  2093 DE LACRUZ             92241
 6560792 126500 01-NOV-88  1247  2  2.0 16314 RIMSTONE LANE         92241
 6842703 102500 22-FEB-88  1300  3  2.0  1665 MONTEREY PARK         92345
 7141094 215500 25-MAY-88  2600  4  2.0  4244 MARS WAY              92456
 7372020 296500 06-JUL-88  2475  4  3.0   137 CATSPAN               92456
```

Figure 3.8: The PROPERTY table after updating rows

and the syntax for modifying an existing column is

```
ALTER TABLE table-name
   MODIFY (column-name data-type,column-name data-type,...);
```

Any of the column name and data type pairs in either the ADD or MODIFY syntax may contain an optional NOT NULL phrase following each column listed. However, you cannot specify NOT NULL if the table you are altering already contains rows—has data. It would be a contradiction to permit a new column to have a NOT NULL attribute when the table already had rows. By definition, newly added columns contain NULL data when you first add them to the table.

Use the following command to add a new column called OWNERID, containing a numeric identification of the property's owner, to the PROPERTY database:

```
ALTER TABLE PROPERTY
   ADD (OWNERID NUMBER(7));
```

This tenth column is initially filled with NULL values.

Once you add the new column, execute the UPDATE command to add owner identification numbers. An identical OWNERID field could also appear in another table that might be called OWNERS.

That table would contain the property owner's identification number and name. By associating OWNERID from the PROPERTY table with OWNERID in the OWNERS table, you could display a complete record of property information that included the present owners' names.

Separating the OWNERS table from the main sales comparables database simplifies database maintenance. Since properties frequently change hands, a good database design should separate the property description from the property ownership information. Furthermore, any piece of property could be jointly owned by several people (a one-to-many association).

Create the new table called OWNERS by typing the SQL command:

```
SQL> CREATE TABLE OWNERS
  2  (OWNERID    NUMBER(7),
  3   OWNERNAME CHAR(20));
```

Figure 3.9 shows the values stored in this database. The rows are displayed in OWNERID order for convenience, but because Oracle is a relational system, the order of rows in a table is of no consequence.

```
OWNERID OWNERNAME
------- --------------------
1245677 FROCKMEISTER
8433258 LATEER
3385761 PERRY
9537481 LADD
2366456 REDFORD
3857263 HOPE
7764530 BURNS
5543212 MCJUNKINS
4375563 BAILEY
6784399 LAZARETTI
8867743 CARROLL
9213783 NEWMAN
5205445 MAHIN
7773359 MONTGOMERY
4909864 LEONARD
```

Figure 3.9: The OWNERS table

You can reference the OWNERID and PROPERTY tables together using the relational database operation, JOIN. Later in this chapter you'll join tables together to create a unified view.

DROPPING TABLES

You can remove tables that are no longer needed by executing the standard SQL command DROP TABLE. Its syntax is

```
DROP TABLE table-name;
```

where *table-name* is the name of the table to be dropped. For example, executing

```
DROP TABLE PROPERTY;
```

removes the PROPERTY table and its contents from the system. Unlike DELETE FROM PROPERTY, the DROP TABLE command removes the entire table definition. Be very careful when you use this command. Once dropped, a table cannot be recovered; it can only be reconstructed.

SECURITY: CREATING VIEWS

CREATE VIEW is a powerful SQL command that permits you to control access to your base tables. Being able to create views of one or more database tables allows you to limit other user's access to your data. This section presents a relatively simple example of view creation. Chapter 6 contains more comprehensive examples of CREATE VIEW.

Our real estate database now contains two tables. Because some people using this information do not need to see all data columns, it is useful to have a special view that combines the PROPERTY and OWNERS tables but omits some columns. This is also an effective means of limiting access to selected columns of the database.

Creating views is similar to creating base tables. The following example creates a view of our two real estate database tables that omits some columns:

```
SQL> CREATE VIEW PROPERTYOWNERS AS
  2    (SELECT PARCEL, SQFT, BR, BA, STNUM, STNAME,
  3     PROPERTY.OWNERID, OWNERS.OWNERNAME
  4  FROM PROPERTY, OWNERS
  5  WHERE PROPERTY.OWNER.ID = OWNERS.OWNERID);
```

Selecting table columns from two or more tables is a join operation. These two tables and their rows are related by a common field called OWNERID. The view just created joins the two tables and displays only selected fields. Note that the period links table names to identically named columns from separate tables, so that it is always clear which column is intended.

You may recall from Chapter 1 that views are called virtual tables. Unlike the base tables from which they are derived, views are "pseudo" tables; only their definitions are stored in the database. To look at the records in the view you just created, type

```
SELECT * FROM PROPERTYOWNERS;
```

The view definition takes over, producing the joined and restricted display of data from both tables. Figure 3.10 shows example results.

```
 PARCEL   SQFT BR  BA STNUM STNAME            OWNERID OWNERNAME
 ------   ---- --  --- ----- ----------------  ------- -------------
 1050601  1100  3  2.0  4764 FINSEN AVENUE     9537481 LADD
 1083767  1500  3  2.0  4522 ROBBINS STREET    9213783 NEWMAN
 1216019  1750  3  2.5 16136 BLAZEWOOD WAY     8867743 CARROLL
 1248361  2789  4  3.0  8053 EASTRIDGE DR      8433258 LATEER
 1775591  1732  3  2.0  9974 ALTO DRIVE        7773359 MONTGOMERY
 2198778  2236  4  2.5  4194 RAPATEE DRIVE     7764530 BURNS
 2823280  1247  2  2.0 11476 MEADOWFLOWER      6784399 LAZARETTI
 3649828  2625  5  3.0   138 BAHAMA BEND       5543212 MCJUNKINS
 4753652  1650  3  2.0  7330 WERNER STREET     5205445 MAHIN
 6262401  1438  3  2.0  4427 ROSCOE DRIVE      4909864 LEONARD
 6487971  1200  4  2.0  2093 DE LACRUZ         4375563 BAILEY
 6560792  1247  2  2.0 16314 RIMSTONE LANE     3857263 HOPE
 6842703  1300  3  2.0  1665 MONTEREY PARK     3385761 PERRY
 7141094  2600  4  2.0  4244 MARS WAY          2366456 REDFORD
 7372020  2525  4  3.0   137 CATS PAW          1245677 FROCKMEISTER
```

Figure 3.10: Using views to restrict information displayed

When a view is no longer needed, you can drop it with a SQL statement similar to the one that drops base tables. For example, you could drop the PROPERTYOWNERS view just created with the statement:

```
DROP VIEW PROPERTYOWNERS;
```

However, there is no SQL statement that permits you to alter a view.

SQL*PLUS EXTENSIONS

As mentioned previously, SQL*Plus provides a rich set of extensions to the ANSI standard SQL commands. Each of these extensions is consistently noted as a SQL*Plus command in the Oracle documentation, the SQL on-line help, and in this book.

You've already encountered two of the most useful commands, HELP and COLUMNS. Here we will focus on a few additional SQL*Plus extensions that can be especially handy. This section is not intended to be exhaustive; you will find a complete list of SQL*Plus commands in Appendix C.

THE PAUSE KEY SEQUENCE

SQL*Plus provides a special key sequence, Ctrl-S, to pause an ongoing operation, such as a display of database rows. To resume the operation, press Ctrl-S again (or any other key).

SAVING AND RETRIEVING SQL COMMANDS

It is often useful to save a frequently used SQL or SQL*Plus command so that you can retrieve and reexecute it later. To save a command, it must be in the current buffer. (SQL*Plus commands are stored in a separate buffer to maintain a clear division between standard and nonstandard commands.) That is, you can only save the current or most recently executed command. To do so, type **SAVE** followed by an operating system file name up to eight characters long. For example, if you type

```
SQL> SAVE PROPERTY
```

and press Enter, SQL*Plus will save the command residing in the current buffer to an operating system file called PROPERTY.SQL. (The file extension .SQL is appended to the file name automatically.)

Notice that you *do not* type a semicolon at the end of the SAVE command line. If you do so, SQL*Plus attempts to save the semicolon as part of the file name. This is not only incorrect, but won't work because the buffer does not store semicolons. They are merely signal characters that tell the SQL*Plus interface when a SQL command is complete.

You can also retrieve stored SQL or SQL*Plus commands. Figure 3.11 displays several saved SQL commands. You retrieve a saved command by typing **GET** followed by the operating system file name. If you specify only the primary file name, omitting the extension, SQL assumes the extension .SQL and fetches the appropriate file. The retrieved SQL command is not executed; it is placed in the SQL buffer where you can either execute it by typing a slash (/) or **RUN** and pressing Enter, or you can edit it with your system editor. Retrieving a stored SQL command called CREATEVU.SQL is as simple as typing

```
SQL> GET CREATEVU;
```

A quick way to retrieve and run a stored SQL command is to type the ''at'' sign (@) followed by the file name. For example, type the following to execute the CREATEVU command (stored as a file named CREATEVU.SQL):

```
SQL> @CREATEVU
```

The @ command is another SQL*Plus command and is not standard SQL.

```
SQL> HOST DIR/W *.SQL

 Volume in drive C is Dr. Perry
 Directory of  C:\ORACLE5\DBS

43ANSI   SQL · 43BIOS   SQL   43DBIOS  SQL   BLUEBIOS SQL   BWANSI   SQL
BWBIOS   SQL   CALCBLD  SQL   CALCDROP SQL   CRT      SQL   DEMOBLD  SQL
DEMODROP SQL   DEMOFMT  SQL   EGAANSI  SQL   EGABIOS  SQL   FORMBLD  SQL
FORMDROP SQL   HELPINDX SQL   HELPTBL  SQL   IADANSI  SQL   IADBIOS  SQL
IADTABLE SQL   LOGIN    SQL   MONOANSI SQL   MONOBIOS SQL   NEWBIOS  SQL
NUBLUBIO SQL   PCANSI   SQL   PCBIOS   SQL   SETUPIAD SQL   VT100    SQL
BOOKLIST SQL   USERLIST SQL
        32 File(s)   1579008 bytes free

SQL> $ DATE

Current date is Sun  6-04-1989
Enter new date (mm-dd-yy):
```

Figure 3.11: Executing host operating system commands

EDITING SQL AND SQL*PLUS COMMANDS

You can edit a command that is currently in the buffer by executing the EDIT command. To do so, type **EDIT** and press Enter, which invokes the host operating system editor. Professional Oracle invokes the editor EDLIN. Once EDLIN is invoked, you can list SQL buffer command lines by typing **LIST** and pressing Enter. Additional EDLIN commands allow you to edit individual lines and delete lines. To exit the editor, press E at the EDLIN asterisk (*) prompt. The edited command will be saved in the buffer. You can then run it by pressing the slash (/) key or by typing **RUN** and pressing Enter. You'll see examples of several editing commands in Chapter 5. Consult your system manual if you need further information about EDLIN.

CAPTURING FILES FOR PRINTING

The SQL*Plus SPOOL command captures information being displayed on your screen and either sends it to your printer or places it in a host system file. Typing **SPOOL LPT1** sends displayed information to the parallel printer. Type **SPOOL** *filename* to capture and save displayed information to a file. Later, you can examine and print the file, which will be stored as *filename*.LST (SQL*Plus attaches the .LST extension).

EXECUTING OPERATING SYSTEM COMMANDS

You can execute host operating system commands from within SQL. The two SQL*Plus commands HOST and $ invoke any of the operating system commands native to your computer platform. A frequently used host operating system command lists stored SQL commands. You can produce such a list by typing either

```
SQL> HOST DIR *.SQL
```

or

```
SQL> $ DIR *.SQL
```

If you wish to execute several operating system commands, type **HOST** and press Enter. This puts you in a DOS shell where you can perform as many DOS commands as you wish. When you are done, type **EXIT** and press Enter to return to SQL*Plus. Figure 3.11 illustrates two operating system commands invoked from SQL: a directory display of stored SQL files and a display of the current system date.

LOGGING ON UNDER A DIFFERENT USER NAME

In single-user microcomputer as well as multiuser operating environments, you can temporarily disconnect from SQL and reconnect under a different username. This is especially useful when groups of database files are ''owned'' by different usernames (the user who creates a file owns that file). All database files associated with the real estate example in this chapter might be owned by username PERRY, while database files associated with accounts payable might be owned (created) by username LATEER. If databases are partitioned according to username, you can switch easily from one SQL username to another with the SQL*Plus commands DISCONNECT and CONNECT.

Typing DISCONNECT at the SQL prompt logs off the current user, but leaves control with SQL. A subsequent CONNECT command followed by username and password information reconnects you to SQL. Figure 3.12 displays examples of the DISCONNECT and CONNECT commands. Notice that it shows two different CONNECT methods. The first requires you to enter the username and password separately (the password is not echoed to the screen).

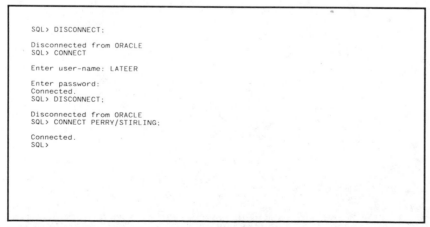

```
SQL> DISCONNECT;

Disconnected from ORACLE
SQL> CONNECT

Enter user-name: LATEER

Enter password:
Connected.
SQL> DISCONNECT;

Disconnected from ORACLE
SQL> CONNECT PERRY/STIRLING;

Connected.
SQL>
```

Figure 3.12: Logging off of and on to SQL*Plus

The second bypasses the username and password prompts by supplying the username and password on the same line as the CONNECT command:

```
SQL> CONNECT PERRY/STIRLING;
```

LEAVING ORACLE GRACEFULLY

When you complete your work, logging off of SQL may require up to three steps. If you merely want to log off of the SQL system, type either **EXIT** or **QUIT** at the SQL prompt and control returns to the host operating system. If you are the DBA and want to remove Oracle and all active users before performing Oracle system maintenance, you can shut down Oracle. The most extreme step you can take is to remove the Oracle Protected Mode Executive from memory altogether. If all three steps are required, they *must* be executed in order or chaos can result. It is vital that you first log off of SQL, then shut down Oracle, and, finally, remove Oracle from memory.

LOGGING OFF OF SQL*PLUS

To log off of SQL*Plus type either

```
SQL> EXIT;
```

or

```
SQL> QUIT;
```

and control returns to the host operating system. After you log off, you can interact directly with the operating system, but you can no longer execute SQL commands. To invoke SQL*Plus again, merely type **SQLPLUS** at the DOS prompt. You'll be prompted for your username and password.

PREVENTING ADDITIONAL
USER LOG ONS: STOPPING ORACLE

You can stop Oracle and prevent new users from logging on by executing a utility program called IOR. Because the IOR program can be dangerous to the database if it is misused, only the DBA should execute it.

Typing

```
IOR SHUT
```

or

```
IOR S
```

at the DOS prompt checks for active database users and shuts down Oracle when all users have logged off the system. Oracle's Protected Mode Executive remains memory-resident, but users cannot log on after Oracle is stopped.

When you shut down Oracle, you'll see these messages:

```
C:\ORACLE5\DBS>IOR S

IOR: Version 5.1.22.1 - Production on Sun Jun 04 22:00:00 1989

Copyright (c) 1987, Oracle Corporation, California, USA.  All rights reserved.

IOR: Connected to ORACLE V5.1.22.6 - Production
IOR: No active transactions found.
IOR: ORACLE shut down complete.

C:\ORACLE5\DBS>
```

If you are using a single-user version of Oracle in a microcomputer environment, you are the DBA and can stop Oracle whenever you like.

REMOVING ORACLE FROM MEMORY

Although the Oracle Protected Mode Executive is memory-resident, you can remove it from memory. Infrequently, the DBA may wish to eradicate Oracle from memory—just before stopping the host computer to perform operating system maintenance, for example. Normally, the Oracle Protected Mode Executive can remain resident even when there are no users logged on to Oracle. Occasionally, however, the DBA may need to go beyond merely stopping Oracle with the IOR program. Typing the command:

```
REMORA ALL
```

removes the Protected Mode Executive from memory, and displays these messages:

```
C:\ORACLE5\DBS>REMORA ALL

REMORA Version 5.1.22.1 - Production on Sun Jun 04 22:05:00 1989

Copyright (c) 1987, Oracle Corporation, California, USA.  All rights reserved.

REMORA: Driver S: removed.

C:\ORACLE5\DBS>
```

Remember that you must log off of SQL and shut down Oracle *before* you issue this command.

SUMMARY

This completes our introductory tour of SQL. Having read this chapter, you should understand how to load Oracle, establish usernames and privileges with the GRANT command, and use other SQL commands to create and manipulate tables. Remember that the commands available in SQL*Plus fall into two categories: ANSI standard SQL commands and SQL*Plus extensions to the standard.

You have gained some experience by using SQL commands to create tables, insert data, and update tables, and you have developed some insight into database security by creating views.

You have used SQL*Plus commands to obtain on-line help, align columns, save and retrieve commands, and edit commands, among other things. Finally, you have learned about the important DBA duties of stopping Oracle and removing Oracle from memory.

The chapters that follow focus on several important SQL commands. Chapter 4 provides details about creating tables and displaying results.

4

DESIGNING
A DATABASE,
CREATING TABLES,
AND ADDING DATA

BY NOW, YOU ARE WELL AWARE THAT TABLES are the primary storage unit in Oracle. After your tour of SQL in Chapter 3, you have some first-hand experience in creating and using tables. In this chapter, you'll get a closer look at several aspects of table definition. First, however, we'll look at tables from the larger perspective of database design. We'll consider how to determine what tables you need for your particular application and how to structure individual tables. Then, we'll discuss in some detail several essential components of table structure as preparation for another look at the CREATE TABLE command and some of the options that you can use with it.

You'll learn a number of ways to document and review your tables, including several that rely on the Oracle data dictionary. We'll review Oracle's many provisions for modifying table structure. We'll also give further consideration to the INSERT command for adding data to a table as well as to an easier method for entering data using SQL*Forms. Finally, we'll review the SQL commands COMMIT, ROLLBACK, and UPDATE.

STRUCTURING A RELATIONAL DATABASE

Because Oracle provides many options for accessing data from a database, you can use techniques for storing data that would not be available with a file manager or a less flexible database manager. For example, you do not have to store data elements together in order to display them together. Oracle has several tools for grouping data from different tables together in output. You can use the SELECT command to join columns from different tables for display based on a common element. You can create a logical view of the data in your database by combining elements from different tables so that they appear to be in the same table. Using the same technique, you can hide parts of a table from other users.

Relational theory is founded on common sense. The information contained in any application will have characteristics and structures in common with data from other applications. This essential fact makes data organization—from file cabinets to relational theory— possible. If you use sound thinking to design your tables, you should have no problem displaying your data later.

DEFINING YOUR DATABASE

First of all, as Joe Friday said in *Dragnet,* get "just the facts" about your application. Start by listing the categories of places, people, and things your application includes. Here are three types of applications and some categories that each might include:

BILLING SYSTEM	RECIPE SYSTEM	THEATRICAL PRODUCTION
Customer	Ingredients	Director
Invoice	Utensils	Producer
Product	Source	Script
Salesperson	Used for	Cast
Sales order		Equipment
Shipment		Audience

BILLING SYSTEM	RECIPE SYSTEM	THEATRICAL PRODUCTION
		Location
		Writers
		Characters
		Performances

Each category will have its own table and all of the data relating to that category will be stored in that table.

A table is displayed as a two-dimensional matrix consisting of columns across the screen or page and rows down the screen or page. Each column should have a name based on the *attribute,* or quality, that describes the data displayed in the column. The CUSTOMER table for the billing application mentioned above might include columns with these attributes:

ID Number

Last Name

First Name

Bill-to Address

Ship-to Address

Type

Credit Limit

Salesperson ID

Finding a Key to Each Table

Each table must have an element that uniquely identifies each row of the table. This element, called the *primary key,* can be stored in one or in a combination of columns. If a single-column key describes each row in a table uniquely, it is called a *prime,* or *primary table;* if several columns must be combined to uniquely describe each row it contains, a table is *nonprime,* or *derived,* and its key is called a *concatenated* key. The key to the CUSTOMER table, a primary table, would be Customer ID.

A key column can be stored in other tables to reference its primary table. When this is done, the column is called a *foreign key* column within the referencing table. In the billing system example, Salesperson ID could be a foreign key linking the CUSTOMER table with the SALESPERSON table.

Normalizing Your Design

In a sound database design, all tables must be reduced to two dimensions. That is, the key column entry alone must suffice to access data from any nonkey column in the same row, and a nonkey entry must not be accessible through any other nonkey entry. A table that meets these specifications is a *flat* table. A database design that has been successfully limited to flat tables is a *normalized* design.

However, adding an Invoice Number attribute to the CUSTOMER table would violate normalized data structure because there could be more than one invoice for each customer ID. Salesperson Name would also be a nonnormal attribute because it could be accessed through the Salesperson ID, which is not a primary key.

A third example would be including multiple Ship-to Addresses for a customer in the CUSTOMER table. In this situation, you could place Ship-to Address in a separate nonprime table that would look like this:

SHIP-TO ADDRESSES

Customer Number	primary key
Ship-to Number	primary key
Ship-to Address	

Note the dual-column primary key. Adding a Customer Name attribute to this table would violate normalized structure because only part of the combined key would be required to access it.

As stated earlier, common sense is an important part of the normalization process. Although your database might not be completely normalized after your initial analysis, you can usually come close by simply trying to fit everything into flat, two-dimensional tables. And fortunately, if you are not entirely successful, it is easy to modify your Oracle structure later to complete the normalization process.

A SAMPLE DATABASE

To demonstrate the process of setting up a database, let's look at an application for tracking medical equipment consigned to various doctor's offices and salespeople. The equipment includes several products, and each piece of equipment has a serial number.

Deciding What Tables You Need

The first step is to identify the categories involved in this application. They are

Products

Serialized Equipment

Warehouses

Doctor's Offices

Salespeople

Movements of Equipment

Each category should describe its own table, and in this case we are only interested in the doctor's offices and salespcople as inventory locations. Because of this, they can be considered as part of one category called Warehouses.

Now that we have established our categories, we can assign table names, as follows:

CATEGORY	TABLE NAME
Products	PROD
Serialized Equipment	SERIAL
Warehouses	WHS
Movements	SERMOVE

Defining Columns and Keys

Figure 4.1 lists the columns, along with their associated attributes, that are required for each table in this application. Notice that an additional table called MOVEITEM has been added. This table is required for normalization, as you'll see in a moment.

Each table must have a key. For the tables in this example, we have identified these keys:

TABLE	TABLE KEY
PROD	Product number
SERIAL	Product number-Serial Number
WHS	Warehouse number
SERMOVE	Packing slip number
MOVEITEM	Packing slip number-Product code-Serial number

The primary key columns and foreign key columns for each table are indicated in Figure 4.1. You can get an idea of the relationships between the tables by examining these designations.

```
PROD                                        WHS
- - - - - - - - - - - - - - - - - - - -     - - - - - - - - - - - - - - - - - - - -
PRODNO(p)      Product number               WHSNO(p)       Warehouse number
DSCRPT         Product description          WHSNAME        Name of warehouse
COST           Product cost                 TERR           Territory
ST             Serial tracking flag         WHSTYPE        Type of warehouse
QIW            Quantity available
                                            SERMOVE
                                            - - - - - - - - - - - - - - - - - - - -
SERIAL                                      MOVENO(p)      Packing slip number
- - - - - - - - - - - - - - - - - - - -     WHSNO(f)       New location
PRODNO(p,f)    Product number               MOVDAT         Date moved
SERNO(p)       Serial number
STATUS         Current status              MOVITEM
WHSNO(f)       Warehouse location          - - - - - - - - - - - - - - - - - - - -
STATDAT        Last date moved             MOVENO(p,f)    Packing slip number
PURDAT         Date purchased              PRODNO(p,f)    Product code
                                            SERNO(p,f)     Serial number
p=primary key   f=foreign key
```

Figure 4.1: Column attributes of the equipment tracking tables

Checking for Normalization

Notice that the new table, MOVEITEM, has a concatenated key of MOVENO-PRODNO-SERNO. Since more than one piece of equipment can be moved with each move ticket, another table was needed to handle the one-to-many relationship between a packing slip and the equipment listed on it. Moving this data to a table with a concatenated primary key reduced it to a one-to-one relationship. Nothing but key attributes will be stored in the MOVEITEM table at this point. Nonetheless, you need the table to allow an unlimited number of items to be moved at one time and to keep operations from being hampered by an arbitrary limit.

The one-to-many problem could have been handled by adding enough columns to the SERMOVE table to accommodate the maximum number of individual items likely to be moved at one time. But, inevitably, the day you added 10 columns to SERMOVE, a transaction for 11 items would appear. Adding columns for individual items is a stopgap; to really solve the problem you need a separate table.

Adjustments like this are a vital part of the database design process. In practice, you will accomplish much of your normalization as you develop the attributes for your tables.

Minimizing Redundancy

Data that is stored in more than one location is termed *redundantly stored* data. In a relational database, only foreign keys can be stored redundantly. In earlier development environments, there was a tendency to enter and store the same data repeatedly. For example, the product name as well as the product number might have been entered into the SERIAL table so that the name could be displayed on serial equipment reports. With the SQL standard, this repetition is no longer necessary. As long as you have a key connecting two tables, it is extremely easy to join separately stored data for output. And by storing only keys redundantly, you no longer have to make revisions in multiple tables when you update data.

Design Flexibility

Because it is so easy to update the table structure with SQL, table definition tends to become table definition, development, and redefinition. It is no more difficult to add and modify columns than it was to create your tables originally—even after data is stored in the tables. As the need arose, you could easily enhance the equipment with tracking application columns for depreciation data and tables for salespeople, doctors, territories, status codes, type codes, and so on. In addition, with a good relational design, your application will integrate more easily into other areas such as billing and general ledger systems.

Before we go on to create the relationally designed tables that we have defined, let's take a more detailed look at some important components of tables.

UNDERSTANDING TABLE COMPONENTS

When you created your first tables in Chapter 3, you covered a lot of territory quickly. Before you use the CREATE TABLE command again, let's look more closely at three components of tables: table names, data types, and display formats.

NAMING A TABLE

There are very few limitations on table names in Oracle. You must observe these rules, however:

1. Begin the name with a letter (A–Z or a–z).

2. Keep it 30 characters or under in length.

3. Do not include spaces.

4. Make it different from other current table names (you are warned if you enter a duplicate).

5. Do not include an Oracle reserved word (see Appendix A).

You can circumvent the first three rules by enclosing the name in quotes in the CREATE TABLE command and anywhere else you use it. Quotes define a literal string that Oracle does not have to interpret. For example, uppercase and lowercase are normally treated the same in SQL. But if you name a table "pROD" you always have to refer to it as "pROD." Table names enclosed in quotes can begin with a character other than a letter (for example, "88OCTSALES") and can include embedded spaces.

Generally, you should choose brief, one-word, alphabetical table names, since you may have to type them frequently. However, you should also make them as descriptive as possible so that you waste less time looking at a document or in the system dictionary to find a table name before accessing it.

ASSIGNING STORAGE DATA TYPES

When you create a table in Oracle, you must define the type of data that each column, or field, will contain. The five data types are character, number, date, long, and raw. These categories were introduced in Chapter 3; here we'll discuss them in detail.

Once a data type is assigned to a column, it becomes the column type, or field type, for that column. Figure 4.2 shows the equipment tracking example defined with column types.

```
PROD                                      WHS
-----------------------------------       ---------------------------------
PRODNO(p)      CHAR(8)                    WHSNO(p)        NUMBER(4)
DSCRPT         CHAR(30)                   WHSNAME         CHAR(30)
COST           NUMBER(8,2)                TERR            NUMBER(3)
ST             CHAR(1)                    WHSTYPE         CHAR(1)
QIW            NUMBER(6)
                                          SERMOVE
                                          ---------------------------------
SERIAL                                    MOVENO(p)       NUMBER(8)
-----------------------------------       WHSNO(f)        NUMBER(4)
PRODNO(p,f)    CHAR(8)                    MOVDAT          DATE
SERNO(p)       CHAR(6)
STATUS         CHAR(2)                    MOVITEM
WHSNO(f)       NUMBER(4)                  ---------------------------------
STATDAT        DATE                       MOVENO(p,f)     NUMBER(8)
PURDAT         DATE                       PRODNO(p,f)     CHAR(8)
                                          SERNO(p,f)      CHAR(6)
p=primary key    f=foreign key
```

Figure 4.2: Column types for the equipment tracking tables

Character Fields

The character column type CHAR(*x*) is used to store alphanumeric characters. The *x* represents a maximum column width, which you must specify. This width cannot exceed 240 characters. Because of the formatting capabilities of SQL*Plus (and SQL*Forms), you are not limited to the value of *x* that you entered for storage when you display a column on output reports or update routines.

Oracle uses only the space actually taken up by characters rather than storing a fixed number of characters per field. A field defined as 30 characters will only take up 20 characters (plus some overhead) of disk space if you enter only 20 characters of text. However, because users tend to fill up field lengths, long field lengths usually do take up more space. It is best to make a careful estimate of expected field length, even though Oracle does allow changes.

VARCHAR(*x*), another way to specify a character type in the CREATE TABLE command, works the same as CHAR(*x*).

Number Fields

Unlike CHAR(*x*), NUMBER does not require you to specify a width, although you may do so. If you do not specify a width, the width defaults to 40 digits. If a number exceeds the display column width, it is converted to scientific notation (such as $6.5E + 10$), so it is best to use another format to define a numeric data type if you already know your requirements.

By specifying the storage width (*x*), which can be up to 105 digits, you can be more precise about the type of number stored. Both decimals and integers can be entered into this field type.

In SQL*Plus, you can alter the default display width for numbers using the SET command. With SET NUMWIDTH, you can override the default of seven digits. Just remember that all numbers will be displayed with the column width you specify.

With the format NUMBER(*size, dec*), you can limit the size of numbers by specifying *size* as the overall width of the field including the decimal point and *dec* as the number of places to the right of the decimal point. More error checking is done on this format than on the previous two. For example, input into a field set up as NUM-BER(8,2) might produce these results:

INPUT	STORED	RESULT
12345.67	12345.67	Stored as is
1234567	error	Maximum width including room for two decimal places exceeded
123	123	Overall length including decimal and two digits less than specified width (8); number accepted and stored as is
123.456	123.46	Number rounded to 2 decimal places

You should use this format to store dollar values.

Although you would expect the DECIMAL data type to require a decimal, it does not. Like NUMBER, it does not allow any options to be set.

The INTEGER data type sets up a number value of 40 digits. Using the INSERT INTO command, which you will learn about later in this chapter, you can even enter a decimal number.

The additional formats and data types NUMBER(*), FLOAT, and SMALLINT all act as synonyms for NUMBER. As with characters, number display formats can differ from number storage formats, but the less exact your storage format, the more definite you have to be at the time of display.

Date Fields

There is only one storage format for dates. To insert a date into a date column by default, use the format *DD-MMM-YY*, where *DD* is a number 01-31, *MMM* is a three-letter designation for a month, and *YY* is a two-digit number representing the year. In Oracle, you can store any date between 12/31/4713(BC) and 1/1/4713(AD)—you can even store the time of day along with it. The DATE format is also used to display time.

Specialty Fields

RAW(*x*) is a specialty format for storing binary data. The field can be up to 240 bytes long. This format is treated as a string and entered in single quotes, but only valid hex numbers are allowed (0–9 and lower- or uppercase A–F).

LONG, LONG VARCHAR, and LONG RAW are long versions of the CHAR and RAW data types. Instead of the 240 character limit, they have a 65,535 character limit. You can only define one LONG column per table. And remember, only the portion of the field in which data is actually stored takes up disk space.

DISPLAY FORMATS

Although data is stored in a few fairly generic formats, you are not limited to these few formats for display. Oracle provides several SQL*Plus commands for displaying data in a variety of *display formats,* or format *models.* You can define storage formats in one way and then use these commands to define output formats in another. (Appendix C contains an alphabetical list and brief description of all the SQL*Plus commands.)

You can globally change the way the SELECT command displays values with the SQL*Plus command SET NUMFORMAT. For example, if a number is stored as a whole number, you can display it as a seven character wide, two-decimal number by typing

```
SQL> SET NUMFORMAT 9999.99;
```

before you enter your SQL commands. However, this SQL*Plus command affects all number columns selected, not just one. To affect just one column, you have to use the SQL*Plus COLUMN command with the following syntax:

```
SQL> COLUMN (column-name) FORMAT (format-model);
```

Table 4.1 lists the numeric formats available with these two commands.

You need few alternatives besides uppercase and lowercase for displaying text characters. For character types, the only thing you can

Table 4.1: Numeric Formats

FORMAT	INPUT	DISPLAY	DESCRIPTION
99999	12345	12345	Width set by number of nines
09999	12	00012	Zero filled
$9999	123	$123	Prefix value with a dollar sign
B9999	0		Display zeroes as blank
999MI	-123	123-	Minus after the number
999PR	-123	<123>	Negative values in brackets < >
9,999	1234	1,234	Comma delimiter where indicated
99.99	12.1	12.10	Fixed decimal (rounded to fit)
999V99	123	12300	Scaled up by a factor of 10 for each 9 after the V
9.99EEEE	123	1.23 + 3	Scientific notation; four E's needed

change using the SQL*Plus format model structure is the column
width. For example, if you enter

```
SQL> COLUMN (column-name) FORMAT A8;
```

the A indicates an alphanumeric format and the 8 sets the column
width to eight characters. If the data within the column is longer than
eight characters, it will either wrap around to the next line or will be
truncated, depending on the SET WRAP and SET TRUNCATE
command settings.

There are numerous options for displaying dates. You can display
dates in numeric and character formats of all types. You can spell out
the day of the week, the month, or the year. You can display time in

12-hour format with an A.M. or P.M. suffix or in a 24-hour format, and you can include minutes and seconds. You can even concatenate the date with a string of your choice, such as "As of date: ". Chapter 7 lists the display formats available for dates and discusses format models in detail.

CREATING A TABLE IN SQL*PLUS

Now you have the essentials for creating tables. As you know, you must log on to SQL*Plus to create a table. If you are using Professional Oracle, type

```
SQLPLUS username/password
```

at the DOS prompt, which should put you at the SQL prompt. You can now enter the CREATE TABLE command. The complete syntax, including all options, looks like this:

```
CREATE TABLE table-name (column spec [NOT NULL], ...)
    [SPACE space definition [PCTFREE n]|
    CLUSTER cluster-name (column,...)]
    [AS query];
```

Everything enclosed in square brackets—that is, everything after *spec*—is optional. (Note that, unlike parentheses, square brackets are *not* part of the SQL command syntax; they merely indicate available options. This convention, which also appears in the Oracle documentation, is followed throughout *Understanding Oracle*.)

The required syntax of the CREATE TABLE command is relatively straightforward, as you'll recall from the previous chapters. Here, we'll briefly review how to create a table before explaining some optional components of the complete CREATE TABLE syntax. To create the PROD table from the equipment tracking example, type

```
SQL> CREATE TABLE PROD
2  (PRODNO   CHAR(8)  NOT NULL,
3   DSCRPT   CHAR(30),
4   COST     NUMBER(8,2),
5   ST       CHAR(1),
6   QIW      NUMBER(6));
```

Remember that SQL*Plus is very forgiving when it comes to spacing. You could have typed this entire command on two lines in this format:

```
SQL> CREATE TABLE PROD (PRODNO CHAR(8) NOT NULL, DSCRPT
2 CHAR(30), COST NUMBER(8,2), ST CHAR(1), QIW NUMBER(6));
```

Once again, you'll recognize the important components of this command from Chapter 3: the table name, the parentheses surrounding the column specifications, the commas between column specs (only 254 columns are allowed), the semicolon at the end, and the NOT NULL option in line 2.

Because NOT NULL requires that a column contain an entry for each row of the table, it ensures that your key column will always have a value. If you try to insert values into a row without including a value for PRODNO, the system will display this message:

```
mandatory (NOT NULL) column is missing or NULL during insert
```

This powerful input editing feature should be used on every key column.

Now let's look briefly at some of the options available with the CREATE TABLE command.

THE SPACE OPTION

You can specify your own space definition if you are not satisfied with the default space location and size that Oracle allocates to a table on disk. (To do so, you need to have created the space definition using the SQL command CREATE SPACE.)

PCTFREE controls the percentage of free disk space left within each block of storage. It is defined along with the CREATE SPACE command, and you can use it to override the initial setting.

THE CLUSTER OPTION

The object of clustering is to store like columns from different tables together for more efficient access. A table can be associated with a cluster when you create it. In a sense, a cluster is a "hardwired" join of two or more tables. A table can also be clustered with itself for performance purposes. Chapter 12 describes clustering in detail.

CREATING TABLES FROM OTHER TABLES

You can create the SERIAL, WHS, and SERMOVE tables from the equipment tracking application the same way you created PROD. However, you can create MOVEITEM with a query of the database. Because MOVEITEM contains columns already defined in SERMOVE and SERIAL, you can take the column descriptions from those two tables by entering the following CREATE TABLE command:

```
SQL> CREATE TABLE MOVEITEM AS
2  SELECT SERMOVE.MOVENO, SERIAL.PRODNO, SERIAL.SERNO
3  FROM SERMOVE, SERIAL;
```

Because the column descriptions are also stored in tables, you can select them as you would any other data element.

CREATING SYNONYMS

If you are the DBA, you can create synonyms for tables. Users can then access a table with its proper name or with the assigned synonym. This is especially helpful in a network structure where you can select tables stored on a remote database, which may have lengthy specifications. The syntax for this command is

```
CREATE [PUBLIC] SYNONYM synonym FOR [username.] table
 [@link];
```

The optional @link refers to the remote network access. PUBLIC is a system-supplied user ID that allows open access to any user.

SQL offers a number of additional commands for structuring the database. Among these are CREATE VIEW, which is the subject of Chapter 6, and CREATE CLUSTER and CREATE INDEX, both covered in Chapter 12.

DOCUMENTING TABLE STRUCTURES

One of the advantages of a dictionary-based database manager is its inherent documentation. All of Oracle's database information is stored in table format in the system dictionary. There are 39 data dictionary tables from which you can obtain information about your application. This section describes some of the ways you can access the information stored in these tables.

DESCRIBING TABLE COLUMNS

The SQL*Plus command, DESCRIBE, allows you to check the structure of your tables. The syntax for the DESCRIBE command is

```
DESC[RIBE] [user.]table;
```

Note the optional abbreviation of DESCRIBE. (Abbreviations are *not* allowed in standard SQL.)

The command for listing the SERIAL table structure is as follows:

```
SQL> DESCRIBE SERIAL;
```

The resultant output would look like this:

```
Name                            Null?     Type
------------------------------- --------  ----
PRODNO                          NOT NULL  CHAR(8)
SERNO                           NOT NULL  CHAR(6)
STATUS                                    CHAR(2)
WHSNO                                     NUMBER(4)
STATDAT                                   DATE
PURDAT                                    DATE
```

This command is similar to the LIST STRUCTURE command in dBASE and to the LIST-DICT command in the PICK operating system.

ADDING A COMMENT

Oracle provides the standard SQL command COMMENT for adding text to describe your tables and columns. To add a comment about the SERIAL table, type

```
SQL> COMMENT ON TABLE SERIAL IS
2  'Serialized Equipment Master Table';
```

To add a comment about a column attribute within SERIAL, type

```
SQL> COMMENT ON COLUMN SERIAL.PRODNO IS
2 'Product Code (primary key along with SERNO)';
```

Notice that the column's table name is used as a prefix.

The larger the system, the more important the effective use of the COMMENT command. The following shows a SELECT statement and projection that you can use to display table comments (note the two SQL*Plus COLUMN commands used to set the column widths):

```
SQL> COLUMN REMARKS FORMAT A40;
SQL> COLUMN TNAME FORMAT A10;
SQL> SELECT TNAME, REMARKS FROM CATALOG;
```

Here is the resulting display:

```
TNAME      REMARKS
---------- ----------------------------------------
MOVEITEM   Move Ticket Line Item Details
PROD       Product Master Table
SERIAL     Serialized Equipment Master Table
SERMOVE    Move Ticket Transactions
WHS        Warehouse Master Table

5 records selected.
```

To display the column comments, you can use the COLUMNS table from the data dictionary as demonstrated here:

```
SQL> SELECT TNAME, CNAME, REMARKS FROM COLUMNS
2 WHERE TNAME='WHS';
```

The following display results:

```
TNAME      CNAME      REMARKS
---------- ---------- -----------------------------------

WHS        WHSNO      Warehouse Number (Primary Key)
WHS        WHSNAME    Warehouse Name
WHS        TERR       Territory Number
WHS        WHSTYPE    Warehouse type, C=Consigned W=WHS

4 records selected.
```

USING DICTIONARY
TABLES TO REVIEW YOUR WORK

You will want to review comments that you have entered about your tables and columns. The dictionary tables TAB and COLUMNS are useful for this purpose.

To get a list of the tables you have created, type

```
SQL>SELECT * FROM TAB;
```

Here is the output you will get (if you are the DBA you'll get a much longer list that includes the system tables):

```
TNAME     TABTYPE CLUSTERID
--------  ------- ---------
MOVEITEM  TABLE
PROD      TABLE
SERIAL    TABLE
SERMOVE   TABLE
WHS       TABLE

5 records selected.
```

TAB is a data dictionary table in which the names of tables, views, and clusters owned by a user are stored. The CATALOG table, also a data dictionary table, stores tables, views, and clusters accessible by a user. A table that you have access to but did not create would appear in the CATALOG table but not in the TAB table.

COLUMNS is a data dictionary table from which you can select information about the individual columns within a table. Figure 4.3 shows one method for listing the column definitions stored in the COLUMNS table.

CHANGING TABLE STRUCTURE

The beauty of Oracle, as of most relation database managers, is its flexibility. Nothing is final with an Oracle database, so it is easy to keep a system relevant. How easily a database structure can be changed is as important or more important than how easily it can be created. Oracle offers a full set of the standard SQL modifying commands as well as a few helpful SQL*Plus enhancements. In this

```
SQL> SELECT TNAME, CNAME, COLNO, COLTYPE, WIDTH FROM COLUMNS;

TNAME      CNAME           COLNO       COLTYP   WIDTH
--------   --------        --------    ------   --------
MOVEITEM   MOVENO              1       NUMBER        8
MOVEITEM   PRODNO              2       CHAR          8
MOVEITEM   SERNO               3       CHAR          6
PROD       PRODNO              1       CHAR          8
PROD       DSCRPT              2       CHAR         30
PROD       COST                3       NUMBER        8
PROD       ST                  4       CHAR          1
PROD       QIW                 5       NUMBER        6
SERIAL     PRODNO              1       CHAR          8
SERIAL     SERNO               2       CHAR          6
SERIAL     STATUS              3       CHAR          2
SERIAL     WHSNO               4       NUMBER        4
SERIAL     STATDAT             5       DATE          7
SERIAL     PURDAT              6       DATE          7
SERMOVE    MOVENO              1       NUMBER        8
SERMOVE    WHSNO               2       NUMBER        4
SERMOVE    MOVDAT              3       DATE          7
WHS        WHSNO               1       NUMBER        4
WHS        WHSNAME             2       CHAR         30
WHS        TERR                3       NUMBER        3
WHS        WHSTYPE             4       CHAR          1
   21 items selected.
```

Figure 4.3: Selecting column definitions from the COLUMNS table

section we'll review this important group of commands, several of which were introduced in Chapter 3.

RENAMING A TABLE

As you would expect, you can easily change the name of a table, view, or synonym by typing

RENAME oldname TO newname;

Oracle edits this command to make sure the new name is truly a new name and advises you if the old name is not found. Your table can have the same name as another user's table, because the system concatenates user IDs with table names (*user.table*) to uniquely identify each table. The same is true of columns; the full description for a column is *user.table.column*. In most situations, you do not need the full description to uniquely identify a column. However, if you prefer you can use this format.

ALTERING A TABLE

Oracle includes the standard SQL command ALTER TABLE. You can use this command to alter the structure of a table by either adding or modifying a column.

Adding a Column

The ALTER TABLE command should look like this when you are adding a column:

```
ALTER TABLE table-name ADD (column spec);
```

Specify the column, as you do with the CREATE TABLE command. You can specify whether the column is NULL or NOT NULL.

Modifying a Column

You can also alter the specifications of an existing column. The syntax for this option is

```
ALTER TABLE table-name MODIFY (column spec);
```

With an empty table, you can modify the fields in any way. Oracle might prevent you from changing a column to NOT NULL. It checks for NULL rows within the column to be changed before executing the ALTER TABLE. If there are null values, Oracle will not allow the change, to avoid potential inconsistencies. To add the NOT NULL option to the key column in the WHS table from the equipment tracking example, type

```
SQL> ALTER TABLE WHS MODIFY (WHSNO NUMBER(4)  NOT NULL);
```

You cannot drop a column from a table. When you cannot make the desired changes to a table structure, use the CREATE TABLE command with the query option to create a new structure into which you can transfer the data from the old table.

DROPPING A TABLE

As with ALTER TABLE, problems can occur if you delete a table after views are based upon it. But you are not prevented from doing so. To delete a table, use this SQL command:

```
DROP TABLE table-name;
```

If you are faint of heart, you might want to delete all the rows from a table instead of dropping the table. The DELETE command can be undone with the ROLLBACK command, whereas the DROP TABLE command cannot. To delete all of the rows of the PROD table, for example, type

```
SQL> DELETE FROM PROD;
```

MANIPULATING THE DATA IN A TABLE

So far this chapter has discussed database design and development. At this point, your structure is in place and it is time to add some data. In SQL terms, we are about to make a transition from Data Definition Language (DDL) to Data Manipulation Language (DML). Again, some of this information will be familiar from the previous chapter.

INSERTING DATA INTO A TABLE

With the SQL INSERT INTO command, you can add data to a table. INSERT INTO, like most SQL commands, is easy to understand and use. However, it is impractical to update a database in an interactive command line. To update the database in an on-line user application, you will probably need to use INSERT INTO in conjunction with other tools such as SQL*Forms and the Pro* precompilers. SQL*Forms is discussed in Chapter 8, and Chapter 13 covers Oracle's programming tools.

The syntax of the INSERT INTO command is:

```
INSERT INTO table [(column-names)]
VALUES [(column-values)] [subquery];
```

You can substitute a subquery which will be used as input to the INSERT command rathern than individually specifying each column value. To experiment with this command, let's enter our first product to be tracked using the equipment tracking database. To add a product, type

```
SQL> INSERT INTO PROD VALUES
2 ('90006005','MUSCLE STIMULATOR',495.00,'Y','');
```

Oracle will respond

```
1 record created.
```

Character fields are enclosed in quotes and numeric fields are not. Oracle will attempt to input the values in the columns that were numbered one through five when the table was created. Notice that the last column value should be for the QIW column, which is numeric, but instead, we have entered a NULL value represented by empty single quotes ('') into the QIW. Null is neither a character or a value—it represents an absence of data and is considered differently than a character or value in sorting orders and mathematical functions. Either single quotes ('') or the word NULL is acceptable.

By specifying into which columns you want to insert the data, you can either reorder the data to be inserted or insert only a portion of a row. For example, if you knew only the product code, description, and whether or not an item was serially tracked, you could enter the second row of PROD like this:

```
SQL> INSERT INTO PROD (PRODNO, DSCRPT, ST)
2 VALUES ('90002005','NEURO STIMULATOR','Y');
```

Again, Oracle responds

```
1 record created.
```

Specify the columns in the same relative order as the values. Because the product code is defined as a NOT NULL column, include PRODNO in the insert command or you'll see this familiar message:

```
mandatory (NOT NULL) column is missing or NULL during insert
```

INSERT INTO uses an easy syntax, which is useful if you can embed the command within a more structured input format like the programming language interfaces discussed in Chapter 13. Oracle also provides SQL*Forms for creating quick default forms or more advanced forms that can be used instead of INSERT. If you are used to the spreadsheet format, Chapter 10 discusses data entry using SQL*Calc.

SQL*FORMS: THE EASY WAY TO INPUT DATA

The standard SQL commands and the enhanced SQL*Plus commands are important for manipulating data. But productions situations require more user-friendly ways to input data. If Oracle never stepped outside the SQL standard, it would be of limited value.

Oracle provides a powerful forms generator called SQL*Forms. The fourth-generation language (4GL) custom form features of SQL*Forms are discussed in-depth in Chapter 8, but you can easily create a default form that can be used as an alternative to the INSERT INTO command. As an example, let's create a default form for the WHS table from the equipment tracking database used throughout this chapter.

To log on to SQL*Forms, you must first exit SQL*Plus and then, from your operating system prompt or login, type

```
SQLFORMS username/password
```

Alternately, you can type

```
SQLFORMS
```

and you will be prompted for your username and password when the SQL*Forms login screen appears. To move on to the next screen, you are instructed to

```
press F10 (Accept) to continue.
```

Because Oracle is available for a variety of systems, it has to be a little vague about which key performs what function. This discussion is based on Professional Oracle for the IBM AT, but the procedure will work on other machines. If you press F1 (Oracle's defined cursor control Help key on the IBM AT), the help screen for function keys, shown in Figure 4.4, will appear.

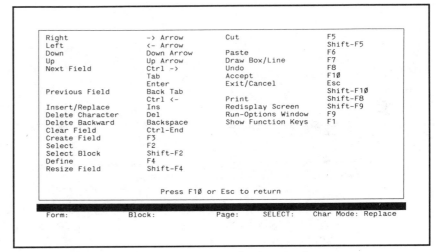

Figure 4.4: The SQL*Forms help screen for function keys

SQL*Forms is a strictly menu-driven program. The most important keys to remember are F2, for selecting a menu item, and F10, for indicating completion of a task.

If you use the username/password screen to identify yourself to the system, press F10 to complete your entry. If you have entered your username and password correctly, you should be at the SQL*Forms CHOOSE FORM menu, shown in Figure 4.5.

THE FORM

Remember, we are creating a default form for entering data from the equipment tracking example into the WHS table, which has the following structure:

```
Name                                Null?    Type
----------------------------------- -------- ----
WHSNO                               NOT NULL NUMBER(4)
WHSNAME                                     CHAR(30)
TERR                                        NUMBER(3)
WHSTYPE                                     CHAR(1)
```

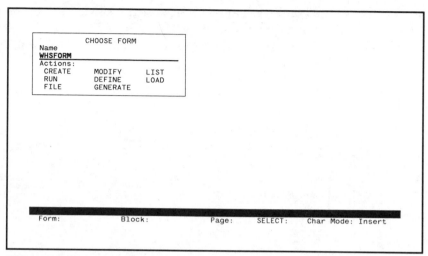

Figure 4.5: The CHOOSE FORM menu

To begin, type the name of the form under Name. This form will be called WHSFORM, as shown in Figure 4.6. Press Enter or Tab to cycle forward through the menu choices, and Shift-Tab to cycle backward through the choices. To create a form, tab to CREATE and press F2 to select that choice. The CHOOSE BLOCK menu will appear overlaying the top menu, as shown in Figure 4.6.

```
                   CHOOSE FORM
        Name
        WHSFORM

            Name     CHOOSE BLOCK
            WHS
            Page Number 1
            Actions:
             CREATE    MODIFY     DROP
             LIST      FIELDS     DEFAULT
             PREVIOUS  NEXT




        Form: WHSFORM    Block:       Page:    SELECT:    Char Mode: Insert
```

Figure 4.6: The CHOOSE BLOCK menu

THE BLOCK

At the CHOOSE BLOCK menu, you must first enter a block name. This block name will appear centered at the top of your form. Because a block corresponds to a table name there is usually one block per table; however, you can have several blocks within a form. WHS is our block name. It could also have been WAREHOUSE, or any other name. You can change the block name later as you become familiar with the functions of SQL*Forms.

The choices in the CHOOSE BLOCK menu are CREATE, MODIFY, DROP, LIST, FIELDS, DEFAULT, PREVIOUS, and NEXT. Even if you want to create a highly customized BLOCK, it is usually faster to create a DEFAULT BLOCK first. You can then return to the menu to add or delete fields.

You can select MODIFY and go into a full-screen editor (also called the screen *painter* in SQL*Forms), in which you can quickly move fields around, add boxes and other text, change the text displayed for a field, and add special edits relating to the block as a whole. For example, you can select one field and have SQL*Forms check the input to make sure that it is not a duplicate record. You can add complex SELECT queries to retrieve information relating to a field. In addition, you can add special display formats and use restrictions and programmed subroutines. But the first and quickest step is to create a default block.

The Default Block

To create a default block, tab to DEFAULT and press F2; the DEFAULT BLOCK menu will appear, as shown in Figure 4.7.

The Table Name entry shown in the figure has to be a valid table. The only element you need to modify on this screen is the Rows Displayed entry. A 1 appears in that field by default, meaning that when you run the form only one record at a time will appear on the screen. Some tables have so many fields that their displays have to be limited to only one row per screen. In this case, however, the total number of characters per row is only 38 and your screen has 79. If you left Rows Displayed set to 1, your input form would look like Figure 4.8.

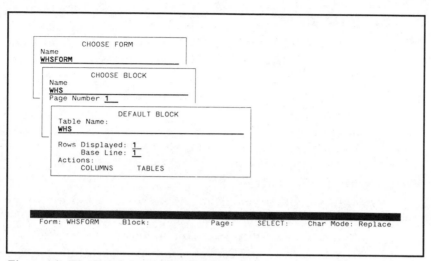

```
              CHOOSE FORM
       Name
       WHSFORM
                    CHOOSE BLOCK
             Name
             WHS
             Page Number 1
                        DEFAULT BLOCK
                  Table Name:
                  WHS

                  Rows Displayed: 1
                      Base Line: 1
                  Actions:
                       COLUMNS      TABLES




   ─────────────────────────────────────────────────

   Form: WHSFORM      Block:        Page:    SELECT:    Char Mode: Replace
```

Figure 4.7: The DEFAULT BLOCK menu

```
                    ======== WHS ========

       WHSNO    _____
     WHSNAME    _____
        TERR    _____                    WHSTYPE _




   ─────────────────────────────────────────────────

        Char Mode:   Replace Page 1              Count: *Ø
```

Figure 4.8: A default form with a single row displayed

To get more rows on the screen, change the Rows Displayed number. If you change it to ten rows displayed, your form will look like Figure 4.9.

The other number, the Base Line, is the line on the screen at which you want your block to be positioned. You do not have to change the

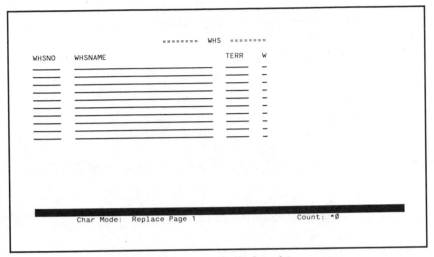

Figure 4.9: A default form with ten rows displayed

Base Line number. If you do, however, you are limited to lines 1 to 14 for a block with only one record displayed or lines 1 to 17 for a multirecord block.

You can change the columns that are automatically included in this form by selecting COLUMNS. You can then move through the columns to flag or unflag each one. But in this case you want all the fields displayed, so this step is not necessary.

Once you have changed Rows Displayed, you are ready to generate the form. Press F10 to indicate that the process is complete. This will move you up to the Block Menu. Press F10 again (or Esc) and the main menu returns. Tab to GENERATE and press F2. You will be prompted for the file name, which is automatically filled in with the form name you have entered. Press F10 and Oracle will accept that name and begin the brief processing. GENERATE creates the compiled input form from your specifications. Professional Oracle generates the input file. If you are using SQL*Forms in real mode (see Chapter 2), after you select GENERATE the message shown in Figure 4.10 appears in the message bar at the bottom of the screen.

Press F10 to complete the process. The FILE menu appears automatically because the raw input form file has not yet been saved. You can either save it or discard it at this point. To save it, select SAVE by pressing Home.

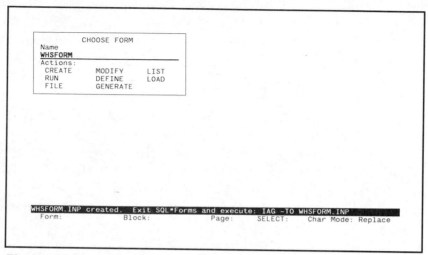

Figure 4.10: Message confirming that a form has been generated

Before you can run your form, it must be converted from a raw input file to a .FRM file. In protected mode on a large system, Oracle makes this conversion automatically within SQL*Forms. If you are using Oracle in protected mode or in a mini or mainframe environment, once you've saved your form you can run it by selecting RUN from the FILE menu.

If you are using Professional Oracle in real mode and you select RUN after saving your form, you'll see the message shown in Figure 4.11. Because of memory limitations, you must exit the system to create the .FRM file in Professional Oracle. To create the .FRM file, run the IAG (Interactive Application Generator) program from the system prompt by typing

IAG formname

Now you can run your form from the system prompt. (In practice, even if you are working on a large system you'll usually run your forms from the system prompt, especially when you are using, rather than designing, forms.) To run your form from the system prompt, type

RUNFORM WHSFORM username/password

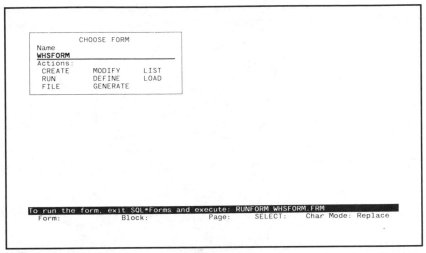

```
                    CHOOSE FORM
     Name
     WHSFORM
     Actions:
       CREATE      MODIFY      LIST
       RUN         DEFINE      LOAD
       FILE        GENERATE
```

```
To run the form, exit SQL*Forms and execute: RUNFORM WHSFORM.FRM
     Form:          Block:          Page:      SELECT:    Char Mode: Replace
```

Figure 4.11: The message that results when you try to run a form in real mode

A blank form similar to the one that you saw in Figure 4.9 will appear. Notice that security is built-in to your form because you have to specify a username/password to run it.

At this point, you can enter new data or query the database for rows. (Remember, because the first field is NOT NULL, you must enter a value to add a row.) SQL*Forms has many built-in editing features that can be customized. Chapter 8 describes these editing alternatives in detail.

Once you've entered your data, press Esc. Oracle will ask if you want to commit your data. Press Y for Yes. Oracle saves the data and exits back to DOS. Then you can press F8 (execute a query) to bring up all records from the table, as shown in Figure 4.12.

SQL*Forms offers an intimidating array of keys for performing special functions such as querying, updating, and cursor positioning. However, once you learn these keys, you will begin to tap the real power of Oracle. And remember, the list of keys is always only a keystroke away (F1). You can print a hardcopy by pressing Shift-PrtSc or you can refer to Figure 4.4.

SQL*Forms is a powerful 4GL tool for creating applications. By customizing your forms, you can check for duplicate records or pull in a corresponding name for a code that is entered. You can have

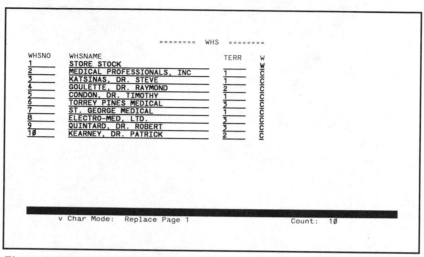

Figure 4.12: A default form after selecting all records

more than one block per form and, by using triggers (discussed in Chapter 8), you can attach special actions to each field. With SQL*Forms, you can go a long way towards eliminating traditional programming altogether.

COMMIT, ROLLBACK, AND AUTOCOMMIT

You may recall from Chapter 3 that Oracle does not commit your data to the database until you COMMIT it yourself. If a process is interrupted or a mistake is made in entry, you can prevent that information from updating the database. To commit your work to the database, type

```
SQL> COMMIT;
```

You will get the resulting message,

```
Commit complete
```

Pressing End (F3) in SQL*Forms produces the same result. To keep your work from updating the database, type

```
SQL> ROLLBACK;
```

This message will result:

```
rollback complete
```

Your database will be preserved as it was before you began. Some commands, such as CREATE or ALTER, automatically execute any open commits before executing.

If you do not trust yourself to remember to commit your data, you can use the SET command in this way:

```
SQL> SET AUTOCOMMIT ON;
```

When AUTOCOMMIT is set on, your changes will be committed automatically when you enter the SQL command.

USING UPDATE TO CHANGE DATA

Recall that within standard SQL you can use the UPDATE command to change data already in a table. Use it to change an individual data item or to update *en masse* the rows of a table. UPDATE is a powerful but simple command. Its syntax has two variations:

```
UPDATE table SET column = expression, column = expression
[WHERE condition=parameters];
```

and

```
UPDATE table SET (column-list) = (subquery)
[WHERE condition=parameters];
```

Figure 4.13 shows a listing of the WHS database as an example of this command's update potential. All of the warehouse names are in uppercase. To change every row of the WHSNAME column to lowercase with initial capital letters, use the UPDATE command and the INITCAP function as shown in Figure 4.14.

```
SQL> SELECT * FROM WHS;

   WHSNO WHSNAME                                 TERR W
------- ----------------------------------- ------- -
       1 STORE STOCK                                 W
       2 MEDICAL PROFESSIONALS, INC            1 C
       3 KATSINAS, DR. STEVE                   1 C
       4 GOULETTE, DR. RAYMOND                 2 C
       5 CONDON, DR. TIMOTHY                   1 C
       6 TORREY PINES MEDICAL                  3 C
       7 ST. GEORGE MEDICAL                    1 C
       8 ELECTRO-MED, LTD.                     3 C
       9 QUINTARD, DR. ROBERT                  3 C
      10 KEARNEY, DR. PATRICK                  2 C

10 records selected.
```

Figure 4.13: A table of WHS values prior to modification

```
SQL> UPDATE WHS SET WHSNAME=INITCAP(WHSNAME);

10 records updated.

SQL> SELECT * FROM WHS;

   WHSNO WHSNAME                                 TERR W
------- ----------------------------------- ------- -
       1 Store Stock                                 W
       2 Medical Professionals, Inc            1 C
       3 Katsinas, Dr. Steve                   1 C
       4 Goulette, Dr. Raymond                 2 C
       5 Condon, Dr. Timothy                   1 C
       6 Torrey Pines Medical                  3 C
       7 St. George Medical                    1 C
       8 Electro-Med, Ltd.                     3 C
       9 Quintard, Dr. Robert                  3 C
      10 Kearney, Dr. Patrick                  2 C

10 records selected.
```

Figure 4.14: Table of WHS values with columns updated to initial cap format

The WHERE option is not required when you update all the rows in a column, as in the example. To update only the doctors, however, you could add the line,

```
WHERE INSTR(WHSNAME,'DR.')>0
```

This uses the SQL*Plus function INSTR to update only rows 3, 4, 5, 9, and 10, which have the substring 'DR.' in the WHSNAME column. The INSTR function returns a value of the character position of the second string within the first for each row. If string 2 ('DR.') does not appear within string 1 (WHSNAME), INSTR evaluates to zero, and the SELECT does not return the row.

SUMMARY

The first part of this chapter dealt with the important topics of database structure and design. You explored several important structural components of Oracle tables, including table names and data types. Next, you reviewed the CREATE TABLE command and learned some of its options. Techniques for documenting and modifying table structures came next, followed by a review of the INSERT command for adding data to tables. You also learned an easier way to enter data using SQL*Forms. Finally, you had a quick review of the important SQL commands COMMIT, ROLLBACK, and UPDATE.

Chapter 5 details how to query a database with the versatile SELECT command.

5

QUERYING
THE DATABASE

ALL OF YOUR EFFORTS TO LEARN ORACLE ARE about to pay off. You have put your data into the database and now it's time to get some information out of it.

Relational databases are designed to ensure that you can access any combination of data elements and display them in a two-dimensional table format. SQL was developed as an English-like structured data access language to be used as an industry standard for querying databases. With SQL, you can specify where to get the data, how to connect multiple tables, which columns you want, what criteria the DBMS should use to give you the rows you want, in which order you want the data displayed, and, to some extent, in what format you want it displayed.

The easiest way to extract information from your Oracle database is to use SELECT, a SQL standard command within SQL*Plus. In this chapter, you will learn how to combine all of the SELECT command options to get just the information you want.

QUERYING A SINGLE TABLE

It is most common to query a single table of data. The simplest form of the SELECT command has the syntax

```
SELECT * FROM table;
```

This SQL statement requests all of the data from one table. Because you want all columns from the table, the asterisk (*), or star, is used in its traditional role as a wild card character in the column selection section. This saves you from having to type each column name individually. Suppose, for example, that you want to display all of the data stored in the PROD table created in Chapter 4. From the SQL*Plus prompt, type

```
SQL> SELECT * FROM PROD;
```

which results in the following listing:

```
PRODNO    DSCRPT                          COST S   QIW
--------  ------------------------------  ------- - -------
90002005  NEURO STIMULATOR-4 CHANNEL       300 Y    200
90006005  MUSCLE STIMULATOR                495 Y     35
90002025  NEURO STIMULATOR-2 CHANNEL       250 Y    450
88904100  ELECTRODES-BANDAID                20 N   1200
88904104  ELECTRODES-CLOTH BACK             30 N    800
88804106  ELECTRODES-SNAP TYPE              40 N    300
75100400  CONDUCTIVE GEL                    15 N    200
72040100  SKIN IRRITATION CREAM             10 N    100

8 records selected.
```

This basic sentence works well if you have a table with only a few rows of information and only a few columns defined. But if your table has either many rows or many columns, this simple form of SELECT will be insufficient because of the limitations of your computer screen or printed output. As you grow more confident with SQL, you will learn to let Oracle sift through data for you. You will learn to use SQL to select a specific answer that you need from your vast database. For years, computers have been able to generate long, detailed, and inflexible reports. In contrast, Oracle is designed to provide selective answers to your requests.

PROJECTION: SELECTING COLUMNS FROM A TABLE

One way to limit the amount of data you select is by using projection to request specific columns from a table. Suppose, for example, that one of the referral sources in the equipment tracking example wants a list of your products, but you do not want them to see the costs of those products. You can request a table consisting of the product number (PRODNO) and the description (DSCRPT) by typing

```
SQL> SELECT PRODNO, DSCRPT FROM PROD;
```

and the following table of values appears:

```
PRODNO    DSCRPT
-------   ----------------------------
90002005  NEURO STIMULATORO-4 CHANNEL
90006005  MUSCLE STIMULATOR
90002025  NEURO STIMULATOR-2 CHANNEL
88904100  ELECTRODES-BANDAID
88904104  ELECTRODES-CLOTH BACK
88804106  ELECTRODES-SNAP TYPE
75100400  CONDUCTIVE GEL
72040100  SKIN IRRITATION CREAM

8 records selected.
```

The output table displays columns from left to right in the order in which you select them. In other words, if you type

```
SELECT DESCRPT, PRODNO
```

the resulting table will be the reverse of the original selection

```
SELECT PRODNO, DESCRPT
```

Printing Your Results

In case you have not yet used the SQL*Plus SPOOL command introduced in Chapter 3, you can begin using it now to print the results of your SELECTs. The syntax of the command is

```
SPOOL [filename|OFF|OUT];
```

The vertical bars represent mutually exclusive options.

As an example, let's print the simple table that resulted from the SELECT in the previous section. First, you need to spool your output to a temporary print file by typing

`SQL> SPOOL TMP;`

Then you can use the SQL*Plus slash (/) command to re-execute the statement "SELECT PRODNO, DSCRPT FROM PROD;", which is still stored in the active buffer. Type

`SQL> /`

The result of the SELECT will appear on the screen and be echoed to the list file TMP.LST on your disk. To print the file, type

`SQL> SPOOL OUT;`

This halts the echo function and prints the report. With Professional Oracle, the report will queue up to print but will not actually print until you exit SQL*Plus. With MS-DOS you can also use Ctrl-PrtSc or Shift-PrtSc to print the output, thus circumventing the SPOOL command.

Specifying Pseudo Columns

The system automatically tracks certain information, such as the current system date, about every database transaction. Although this data is not actually stored in any table, you can include it in a projection by specifying one of the system-level pseudo columns in your SELECT. The pseudo columns are

LEVEL	Level of node that is displayed (see "Connecting with the Tree Relationship" later in this chapter)
NULL	A null value (not useful in SELECT)
ROWID	The complete row descriptor
ROWNUM	The row number of the SELECT
SYSDATE	The system date

UID	The user's description number
USER	The user's logon name

As you'll see in the next section, a pseudo column displays just like a column from an actual table.

Modifying Columns

To modify both columns and pseudo columns, you can select literal strings, columns combined by operators, alternate column headings, functions, and functions that combine columns.

You enter a literal string in quotes, as in this SELECT clause, which inserts an underline for user entry into each row listed:

```
SELECT PRODNO, DSCRPT, "_____"
```

You can combine two or more columns with operators such as the concatenation operator | |, which is used to combine character columns. With numeric columns, you can perform arithmetic using the value operators (+, −, *, and /), as in this example where you multiply the two columns COST and QIW to display their product in a third column:

```
SELECT COST, QIW, COST*QIW
```

If you want to alter a column heading, you can enter a new heading before the next comma. In the previous example, the default heading of the third column is COST*QIW. You might want to give it a more descriptive heading, such as EXTENDED. To do so, enter

```
SELECT COST, QIW, COST*QIW EXTENDED
```

For clarity, especially if you want to use more than one word, you can enclose the new heading in quotes (''EXTENDED'').

Functions, covered along with operators in Chapter 7, are in-line commands that alter the characteristics of values entered as arguments within parentheses after the function. For example, to list the absolute value instead of the raw data of a hypothetical column of values called col1, you can use the absolute value function ABS. Instead of typing

```
SELECT col1
```

in the SELECT clause, you would type

```
SELECT ABS(col1)
```

and each row value for that column would be modified. Depending on the function, arguments can be a variety of combined column values, literals, pseudo columns, and other functions.

Figure 5.1 shows a SELECT statement and the resulting output for a list of products, the date, their description, cost, stored quantity, extended inventory value, and a blank input line for taking a physical count. As you can see, SQL allows a great deal of flexibility. The statement in Figure 5.1 is an example of the minimum required syntax.

```
SQL> SELECT SYSDATE,PRODNO, DSCRPT, COST, QIW, COST*QIW EXTENDED, '_____' COUNT
  1    FROM PROD
  2    ORDER BY PRODNO;

SYSDATE     PRODNO    DSCRPT                          COST    QIW    EXTENDED  COUNT
---------   --------  ------------------------------  ------  -----  --------- -----
15-MAY-89   72040100  SKIN IRRITATION CREAM            10.00    100    1000.00 _____
15-MAY-89   75100400  CONDUCTIVE GEL                   15.00    200    3000.00 _____
15-MAY-89   88804106  ELECTRODES-SNAP TYPE             40.00    300   12000.00 _____
15-MAY-89   88904100  ELECTRODES-BANDAID               20.00   1200   24000.00 _____
15-MAY-89   88904104  ELECTRODES-CLOTH BACK            30.00    800   24000.00 _____
15-MAY-89   90002005  NEURO STIMULATOR-4 CHANNEL      300.00    200   60000.00 _____
15-MAY-89   90002025  NEURO STIMULATOR-2 CHANNEL      250.00    450  112500.00 _____
15-MAY-89   90006005  MUSCLE STIMULATOR               495.00     35   17325.00 _____

8 records selected.
```

Figure 5.1: A SELECT statement and resulting output

SELECTION: SELECTING ROWS FROM A TABLE

Limiting the results of your query to a certain number of rows is called selection, or restriction, in relational theory. To select a subset of rows you can add the standard SQL WHERE option to your query. The basic syntax for this option is

```
SELECT * FROM table WHERE condition;
```

or, if you prefer

```
SELECT *
  FROM table
 WHERE condition;
```

When options make your SELECT statements lengthy, they will begin to wrap around to the next line of your display. At this point, the vertical structure will become more convenient. Because the SQL*Plus command processor ignores blanks, you can position commands anywhere as long as the keywords are correct. Remember, your last SQL statement is automatically preserved in a buffer; the vertical structure makes it easy to go back and edit a long statement. (You'll learn more about editing the contents of the buffer later in this chapter.)

Suppose you want to use selection to determine what products in the PROD table are serially tracked. In English, you might instruct ORACLE to

> Let me see the product number and description for the products that are tracked serially.

To phrase this in SQL, you could type

```
SQL> SELECT PRODNO, DSCRPT, ST
   1   FROM PROD
   2  WHERE ST = 'Y';
```

The result would be a display of three rows:

```
PRODNO    DSCRPT                         S
........  ..............................  .
90002005  NEURO STIMULATOR 4 CHANNEL      Y
90006005  MUSCLE STIMULATOR               Y
90002025  NEURO STIMULATOR-2 CHANNEL      Y
```

There are many ways to state the condition after the WHERE option. In the previous query, ST = 'Y' could also be stated as ST =

'Y', or 'Y' = ST, for example. The command processor is very forgiving; if all the components are there (one or more column names, an operator, and a constant) it will understand your statement. When you misstate something, the erroneous syntax is tagged with an asterisk on the following line and an explanation is provided to help you identify the problem.

Comparison Operators

In the previous statement, we specified a condition of equality using the equal sign (=), but you can choose from many more comparison operators. SQL*Plus provides three other ways to combine an equality with some other logical operator: IN(), LIKE, and IS NULL.

To select rows where a column value is equal to one of several constants, you can insert the OR connective operator into a condition:

```
WHERE PRODNO='90002005' OR PCODE='90002025'
```

However, you can also use the IN(*list*) operator to state it more clearly and concisely:

```
WHERE PRODNO IN('90002005''90002025')
```

You can use the LIKE operator to select multiple values by using the characters % and _, sometimes referred to as wild cards. (These two characters correspond to * and ? in the DOS operating system.) You could state the above condition using LIKE by typing

```
WHERE PRODNO LIKE '900020_5'
```

to replace a single character within the line, or

```
WHERE PRODNO LIKE '900020%'
```

to select all part numbers beginning with '900020', if that is specific enough. Using wild cards can save you a lot of time. You can combine the two wild cards in a variety of ways, such as '%2%', '%20_5', or '9000_0_5'.

When you want to select all records with a blank value (no value stored), you can use the IS NULL operator.

An inequal condition also allows much flexibility in selecting rows. You can use < >, ! = , or ^ = to indicate not equal to. You can also use the industry standard operators,

>   Greater than

> =   Greater than or equal to

<   Less than

< =   Less than or equal to

as well as the timesaving syntax

```
BETWEEN value1 AND value2
```

This syntax replaces the cumbersome phrasing

```
WHERE COST > 100 AND COST < 400
```

with the more English-like

```
WHERE COST BETWEEN 100 AND 400
```

Notice that the values do not require quotes around the constant, only nonvalue functions do.

You can also set up false conditions with the inequal comparison operators. By stating the following list of operators:

BETWEEN *value1* AND *value2*

IN(*list*)

LIKE

IS NULL

with a negative preceding them, like this:

NOT BETWEEN *value1* AND *value2*

NOT IN(*list*)

NOT LIKE

IS NOT NULL

you obtain the opposite result.

Combining Conditions with AND and OR

You can combine conditions within one SQL query. To combine two or more conditions in the WHERE option, use AND to require both conditions to evaluate as true, or OR to require one of several conditions to evaluate as true.

If your logic is complex and contrary to the normal precedence of evaluation (AND logic before OR logic), you might need to surround sections of your sentence with parentheses for grouping and ordering. For example, the condition

```
WHERE ST='N' AND COST > 200 OR QIW > 100
```

would evaluate differently than

```
WHERE ST='N' AND (COST > 200 OR QIW > 100)
```

The first statement would give you serialized products (ST = 'Y') with quantities over 100. If you only want to see nonserialized products, the second statement would be correct.

ORDERING RESULTS: ORDER BY

Up to this point, your table rows have displayed in random order. To control the order in which rows are displayed, you must use the ORDER BY clause. The syntax for the ORDER BY clause is

```
ORDER BY column-name|column-number [ASC|DESC], column-name|column-number [ASC|DESC]
```

Column-number refers to the position that a column occupies within a list of columns. ASC stands for ascending and DESC stands for descending order. The default sorting order is ascending; that is, in the column upon which the sort is based, the row containing the lowest value will list first and the row containing the highest value will list last. If a character column is specified, each row is evaluated from left to right within the value. For numeric values, the sorting order is from lowest to highest value; for dates it is from the oldest to the most recent date. NULL values always appear first within any of these types, whether the order is ascending or descending. The order in which mixed values (alphanumeric, numeric, and special characters) are sorted within a column is somewhat hardware dependent. Because Oracle is implemented on both ASCII and EBCDIC based systems, which each have their own standard sorting orders, the ordering is different for each system. The ORDER BY option has to be the last one specified in your SQL statement.

The most common source of confusion about ordering results is entering numeric values into a character column. If identical values are stored in a numeric column and a character column, their ascending sort will be different:

INPUT ORDER	CHARACTER ORDER	NUMERIC ORDER
1	1	1
15	10	4
4	15	10
20	20	15
10	25	20
25	4	25

You can resolve the problem by entering all of the values of a character column with the same number of digits:

INPUT ORDER	CHARACTER ORDER	NUMERIC ORDER
1	01	1
15	04	4
4	10	10
20	15	15
10	20	20
25	25	25

You can also use the conversion function TO_NUMBER to convert a character column to a numeric column for a SELECT. Likewise, you can use SUBSTR, UPPER, TO_CHAR, TO_DATE, ABS, or any other applicable function within the ORDER BY syntax (see Chapter 7).

You can order a table by one or more columns. If you specify more than one column, the ordering is done from left to right. All rows are arranged based on the first column. Given equal values within that column, they are arranged based on the next column, and so on, until all specified columns are in order. A column does not have to be selected to be stated in the ORDER BY option. Typically, however, if you want a table to be ordered you should display the columns that will be used for the ordering.

You can use ordering to more easily locate a row within the table, or to group similar rows for analysis and subtotaling. If you use ordering for reference purposes, it's easiest to use the primary key of the table. Otherwise, you can use any combination of columns, depending on the situation. In the PROD table, the product number (PRODNO) is the key and should be selected by default as the ORDER BY column. In some circumstances, the description might be used instead, but unless the descriptions are especially well structured, this is a less exact method. Figure 5.2 shows how to order the PROD table by the PRODNO column.

```
SQL> SELECT *
  2    FROM PROD
  3    ORDER BY PRODNO;

PRODNO    DSCRPT                             COST S      QIW
--------  --------------------------------   ------- -  -------
72040100  SKIN IRRITATION CREAM                 10 N      100
75100400  CONDUCTIVE GEL                        15 N      200
88804106  ELECTRODES-SNAP TYPE                  40 N      300
88904100  ELECTRODES-BANDAID                    20 N     1200
88904104  ELECTRODES-CLOTH BACK                 30 N      800
90002005  NEURO STIMULATOR-4 CHANNEL           300 Y      200
90002025  NEURO STIMULATOR-2 CHANNEL           250 Y      450
90006005  MUSCLE STIMULATOR                    495 Y       35

8 records selected.
```

Figure 5.2: Using ORDER BY to order the PROD table by product number

Because neither ASC nor DESC was specified, an ascending sort was done. Because the primary key (a unique identifier) was used, it is unnecessary to specify any additional columns after PRODNO in the ORDER BY clause (nor would doing so change the outcome). However, another column could effect the outcome if entered before PRODNO. In Figure 5.3, all of the serially tracked products are ordered by ascending part number, followed by the supply products in ascending order.

```
SQL> SELECT *
  1  FROM PROD
  2  ORDER BY ST DESC, PRODNO;

PRODNO    DSCRPT                         COST S    QIW
--------  -----------------------------  ------- - -------
90002005  NEURO STIMULATOR-4 CHANNEL       300 Y     200
90002025  NEURO STIMULATOR-2 CHANNEL       250 Y     450
90006005  MUSCLE STIMULATOR                495 Y      35
72040100  SKIN IRRITATION CREAM             10 N     100
75100400  CONDUCTIVE GEL                    15 N     200
88804106  ELECTRODES-SNAP TYPE              40 N     300
88904100  ELECTRODES-BANDAID                20 N    1200
88904104  ELECTRODES-CLOTH BACK             30 N     800

8 records selected.
```

Figure 5.3: ORDER BY with the DESC option

We used DESC in Figure 5.3 because Y is after N in the alphabet and we wanted the serialized products to appear first. When setting up codes in your system, you should consider what effect the coding will have on your SQL queries. You might want a report to list categories of data in a certain order. By creating the right category identifiers in the system, you can produce reports through SQL*Plus that otherwise might require other data extraction tools such as the Pro*C programming interface. For example, suppose your company's sales territory were broken up into four regions: Northeast, Southeast, Midwest, and West, and suppose the marketing department always wanted to see them in that order. A coding scheme such as N, S, M, and W would result in the ascending ordering Midwest, Northeast, Southeast, and West. Numbering your regions from one to four gives you much more flexibility.

The best way to determine the most expensive products in the
PROD table is to order the output by cost in descending order. To
accomplish this, you might produce the statement and results shown
in Figure 5.4.

```
SQL> SELECT *
  1    FROM PROD
  2    ORDER BY COST DESC;

PRODNO    DSCRPT                          COST S    QIW
--------  ------------------------------  ---- -    -------
90006005  MUSCLE STIMULATOR               495  Y        35
90002005  NEURO STIMULATOR-4 CHANNEL      300  Y       200
90002025  NEURO STIMULATOR-2 CHANNEL      250  Y       450
88804106  ELECTRODES-SNAP TYPE             40  N       300
88904104  ELECTRODES-CLOTH BACK            30  N       800
88904100  ELECTRODES-BANDAID               20  N      1200
75100400  CONDUCTIVE GEL                   15  N       200
72040100  SKIN IRRITATION CREAM            10  N       100

8 records selected.
```

Figure 5.4: PROD table in descending cost order

ORDER BY is a simple but powerful SQL SELECT option. You
can order a table based on any column, combination of columns, or
function of columns in either ascending or descending order.

GROUPING THE RESULTS

There are two main tools for summarizing results using standard
SQL and SQL*Plus commands. In SQL, results always come out in
a flat, two-dimensional table format. Consequently, when you ask
for group totals (GROUP BY) or report totals using standard SQL,
only the summary line displaying the group subtotals is displayed—
not the detail and summary lines. To get the row details and summary line, use the SQL*Plus BREAK and COMPUTE commands
together. Let's first look at the standard SQL method.

THE GROUP BY OPTION

With the GROUP BY option, you can total results within a table
based on row groupings. A table containing only summary rows will

result. Since it is used to do this specific task, the GROUP BY option has the most inflexible structure of any of the SELECT options. The syntax for a simple SELECT using GROUP BY is as follows:

```
SELECT group id1, group id2, group function(column(s))
FROM table
GROUP BY group id1, group id2;
```

The selection in the first line of the syntax is more restricted than it is when used without GROUP BY. You can specify only a column or combination of columns that will be the basis for the groupings, a constant, or a group function (AVG, COUNT, MAX, MIN, STDDEV, SUM, VARIANCE). The column you specify in the SELECT list must be included in the GROUP BY clause; however, a column may be included in the GROUP BY clause that is not part of the SELECT clause.

To demonstrate this, let's look at another table in the equipment tracking system. The SERIAL table contains the fields PRODNO, SERNO, STATUS, WHSNO, STATDAT, and PURDAT. To count by product number the number of units in the table, type

```
SQL> SELECT PRODNO, COUNT(*)
  2    FROM SERIAL
  3    GROUP BY PRODNO;
```

The following table results:

```
PRODNO    COUNT(*)
--------  --------
90002005      8
90002025      4
90006005      3
```

COUNT(*) is a group function that counts the number of rows in the table or, as in this query, in each grouping. In this example, since you are only grouping by PRODNO, it is the only column that you can specify in the SELECT clause. The resulting table contains only the summarized values, so it makes no sense to indicate another column in the SELECT list.

Nonetheless, you can base the GROUP BY option on more than one column. For example, to count the number of products in each warehouse, add WHSNO to your SELECT, as shown in Figure 5.5.

```
SQL> SELECT PRODNO, COUNT(*)
  2   FROM SERIAL
  3   GROUP BY WHSNO, PRODNO;

PRODNO   COUNT(*)
-------- --------
90002005        2
90002025        1
90006005        1
90002005        2
90002005        2
90002005        1
90006005        1
90002025        1
90002025        1
90002005        1
90002025        1
90006005        1

12 records selected.
```

Figure 5.5: WHSNO added to GROUP BY clause

As you can see, without adding WHSNO to the SELECT clause the result makes little sense. Figure 5.6 shows the effect of correcting this oversight.

```
SQL> SELECT WHSNO, PRODNO, COUNT(*)
  2   FROM SERIAL
  3   GROUP BY WHSNO, PRODNO;

 WHSNO PRODNO    COUNT(*)
------- -------- --------
      1 90002005        2
      1 90002025        1
      1 90006005        1
      2 90002005        2
      3 90002005        2
      5 90002005        1
      5 90006005        1
      8 90002025        1
      9 90002025        1
     11 90002005        1
     11 90002025        1
     11 90006005        1

12 records selected.
```

Figure 5.6: WHSNO added to GROUP BY and SELECT clauses

The table now shows that no warehouse location has more than two units of any type in stock. Notice that in Figure 5.5 the summarized values are in ascending order. In Figure 5.6, they are in ascending order by WHSNO and by PRODNO within WHSNO. To arrange them differently, you could use the ORDER BY clause.

THE HAVING OPTION

HAVING is a conditional option that is related directly to the GROUP BY option. It is similar to WHERE, but while the input for HAVING processes is the calculated GROUP values, WHERE works on individual rows. Because HAVING does a selection based on the result of the GROUP function, WHERE does not apply. HAVING will always state a condition based on one of the group functions listed in the SELECT clause. It uses the result of the function as input to evaluate whether to omit that group's row from the output table. To demonstrate the difference between WHERE and HAVING, let's first add a WHERE clause to the statement:

```
SQL> SELECT WHSNO, PRODNO, COUNT(*)
   1   FROM SERIAL
   2   WHERE PRODNO = '90002005'
   3   GROUP BY WHSNO, PRODNO;
```

In this example, WHERE is used to select rows equal to one product number. Here is the result:

```
WHSNO PRODNO    COUNT(*)
------ --------- --------
    1 90002005         2
    2 90002005         2
    3 90002005         2
    5 90002005         1
   11 90002005         1
```

(Notice that the number of records selected does not appear in this query. This is because the SET FEEDBACK is set to six, and if the number of records listed is less than six no message will appear).

Now let's add a HAVING option to limit the groups to those with more than one unit:

```
SQL> SELECT WHSNO, PRODNO, COUNT(*)
  1  FROM SERIAL
  2  WHERE PRODNO = '90002005'
  3  GROUP BY WHSNO, PRODNO
  4  HAVING COUNT(*) >1;
```

This is the resulting table:

```
WHSNO PRODNO   COUNT(*)
------- -------- --------
    1 90002005      2
    2 90002005      2
    3 90002005      2
```

Coming up with one total for a report is easy and does not require the GROUP BY or HAVING functions, although it does require a group function. For example, to find out how many serial numbers for product 90002005 are in the SERIAL table, type

```
SQL> SELECT COUNT(*)
  2  FROM SERIAL
  3  WHERE PRODNO='90002005';
```

The result is

```
COUNT(*)
--------
       8
```

As you can see, you can't have it both ways; you either get the individual row detail or you get summary values for groups or for an entire query. Oracle provides some enhanced SQL*Plus commands for reporting in a more traditional style where results appear with subtotals and totals and spaces separate the groups.

THE BREAK COMMAND

The BREAK command is provided with SQL*Plus to enhance the grouping of queries. The syntax of BREAK is

```
BREAK ON(expression|ROW|PAGE|REPORT)...
[SKIPn|[SKIP]PAGE]
[NODUPLICATES|DUPLICATES];
```

Suppose you need to know how many of each product are at each warehouse. Figure 5.7 shows a query that provides this information.

```
SQL> SELECT WHSNO, PRODNO, COUNT(*)
  2  FROM SERIAL
  3  GROUP BY PRODNO, WHSNO;

PRODNO     WHSNO COUNT(*)
--------   ------- --------
90002005      1      2
90002005      2      2
90002005      3      2
90002005      5      1
90002005     11      1
90002025      1      1
90002025      8      1
90002025      9      1
90002025     11      1
90006005      1      1
90006005      5      1
90006005     11      1
```

Figure 5.7: Product grouping

Figure 5.7 looks a little cluttered because the part number is repeated for every row of the table. This is necessary to produce a flat, normalized table. Now look at Figure 5.8 to see the effect of entering the BREAK command (the slash tells SQL*Plus to re-execute the command that is currently stored in the buffer). As you can see, the BREAK command changes the table format so that only new values are displayed in the PRODNO column—that is, a value is displayed only when it differs from the preceding value.

This style of output is called NODUPLICATES, or NODUP, because each group value is shown only once. Although it diverges from the purely relational two-dimensional matrix format, this is the default BREAK output method, because it provides a clear result. You can override the default by specifying

```
SQL> BREAK ON PRODNO DUP;
```

Another option, SKIP, lets you enter one or more blank rows between each group. If you enter

```
SQL> BREAK ON PRODNO SKIP;
```

```
SQL> BREAK ON PRODNO;
SQL> /

PRODNO      WHSNO COUNT(*)
--------  ------- --------
90002005        1        2
                2        2
                3        2
                5        1
               11        1
90002025        1        1
                8        1
                9        1
               11        1
90006005        1        1
                5        1
               11        1

12 records selected.
```

Figure 5.8: Product grouping with BREAK

a blank line will be placed after the end of each group the next time the command is executed. If you enter PAGE instead of SKIP, a page eject will occur at the end of each group, and each group will be preceded by new column heads. This is useful if you are distributing the results of a printed query to various people and want everyone to receive only information that relates to them.

Only one BREAK phrase can be active at a time; each BREAK command you enter replaces the previous one. To check which BREAK is active, type

```
SQL> BREAK
```

and the status will display below it as shown here:

```
break on prodno nodup
```

If you want more than one BREAK to occur, you should enter it as one command:

```
SQL> BREAK ON PRODNO SKIP ON REPORT;
```

It might seem superfluous to break on the full report because the skip factor will not be useful. However, when BREAK is used in conjunction with the COMPUTE command, which we will discuss next, this technique makes sense. You must specify a break each time you want to display a subtotal or total. To get rid of a break, type

```
SQL> CLEAR BREAK;
```

Because BREAK is a SQL*Plus command, and not standard SQL, it is not stored in the SQL default buffer. If you want to store it on file with a SQL statement, you must use the alternate buffer approach discussed at the end of this chapter.

THE COMPUTE COMMAND

COMPUTE is another SQL*Plus command that diverges from the purely relational two-dimensional table approach. When used with BREAK, COMPUTE can display totals as well as details. Its syntax is

```
COMPUTE group function OF column, column ON break-column;
```

For example, to find out how many neuro stimulators (90002005 and 90002025) are in the SERIAL table as well as the warehouse location of each one, you could type the query shown in Figure 5.9.

```
SQL> SELECT PRODNO, WHSNO, COUNT(*)
  2    FROM SERIAL
  3    WHERE PRODNO LIKE '900020%'
  5    GROUP BY PRODNO, WHSNO;

PRODNO    WHSNO COUNT(*)
--------  ----- --------
90002005      1        2
90002005      2        2
90002005      3        2
90002005      5        1
90002005     11        1
90002025      1        1
90002025      8        1
90002025      9        1
90002025     11        1

9 records selected.
```

Figure 5.9: Table grouped by product and warehouse

To include a report total, type the SQL*Plus commands shown in Figure 5.10.

```
SQL> BREAK ON PRODNO ON REPORT
SQL> COMPUTE SUM OF COUNT(*) ON REPORT
SQL> /

PRODNO      WHSNO COUNT(*)
--------    ------- --------
90002005        1        2
                2        2
                3        2
                5        1
               11        1
90002025        1        1
                8        1
                9        1
               11        1
*******            --------
                        12

9 records selected.
```

Figure 5.10: Table using BREAK and COMPUTE

To do subtotals for each product and add a blank line between each group, you can change the BREAK command and add another COMPUTE as shown in Figure 5.11.

Now the output looks like a traditional report. To display the current COMPUTE settings you can type

```
SQL> COMPUTE
```

This display will appear:

```
COMPUTE sum OF COUNT(*) ON REPORT
COMPUTE sum OF COUNT(*) ON PRODNO
```

As you can see, this command is additive. During testing, you might accumulate quite a number of COMPUTE settings. To clear the settings, type

```
SQL> CLEAR COMPUTE
```

Oracle will respond

```
computes cleared
```

```
SQL> BREAK ON PRODNO SKIP ON REPORT
SQL> COMPUTE SUM OF COUNT(*) ON PRODNO
SQL> /

PRODNO    WHSNO COUNT(*)
-------- ------- --------
90002005       1        2
               2        2
               3        2
               5        1
              11        1
********          --------
sum                      8

90002025       1        1
               8        1
               9        1
              11        1
********          --------
sum                      4

                  --------
                        12

9 records selected.
```

Figure 5.11: Table with total and one subtotal

As you become secure in your ability to use SELECT accurately, you'll need to include less detail. However, some circumstances will always require a detailed total structure, especially when more than one person will be using the results.

ACCESSING RELATED DATA FROM SEVERAL TABLES: JOIN

One of the strengths of SQL is its ability to relate data that is stored in separate tables. This allows you to store all the information about products in one table, everything about warehouses in another, and everything about serial numbers in a third. You can then combine the information when necessary.

The syntax for joining is only slightly more complex than a regular single table SELECT. To add the warehouse description from the WHS table to the SERIAL table, for example, you could use the SELECT shown in Figure 5.12.

```
SQL> BREAK ON PRODNO SKIP
SQL> SELECT PRODNO, SERIAL.WHSNO, WHSNAME, COUNT(*)
  2  FROM SERIAL, WHS
  3  WHERE SERIAL.WHSNO=WHS.WHSNO AND PRODNO LIKE '900020%'
  4  GROUP BY PRODNO, SERIAL.WHSNO, WHSNAME;

PRODNO     WHSNO WHSNAME                                 COUNT(*)
--------   ----- ---------------------------------       --------
90002005       1 STORE STOCK                                    2
               2 MEDICAL PROFESSIONALS, INC                     2
               3 KATSINAS, DR. STEVE                            2
               5 CONDON, DR. TIMOTHY                            1
              11 LIND, DR. JEFF                                 1

90002025       1 STORE STOCK                                    1
               8 ELECTRO-MED, LTD.                              1
               9 QUINTARD, DR. ROBERT                           1
              11 LIND, DR. JEFF                                 1

9 records selected.
```

Figure 5.12: Joining two tables

The four elements added to join the SERIAL table and the WHS table were

- Table name prefixes for any columns with the same name in both tables (WHS.WHSNO)

- The added table's name in the FROM clause

- The basis for the join in the WHERE clause (SERIAL-.WHSNO = WHS.WHSNO)

- The addition of the WHSNAME column in the SELECT list and the GROUP BY list

Only columns with the same name require the full *table.column* naming format, but, if you prefer, you can define any column using this more specific format.

There are several types of joins. Because one of the two WHSNO columns (WHS.WHSNO) was not in the SELECT clause, the previous example is a *natural* join. This type of join (WHERE SERIAL.WHSNO = WHS.WHSNO) is also called an *equi-join* because it is based on a condition of equality. Another type of join, a *non-equi-join*, is based on an inequal condition (for instance, WHS.WHSNO < > SERIAL.WHSNO) and is less often used.

USING OUTER-JOINS

Oracle also supports what is called an *outer-join*. This means that a row will appear in the joined table even though there is no matching value in the table to be joined. Suppose you want to know which warehouse locations do not have any serialized equipment on hand (that is, they have no records in the SERIAL table). You can use an outer-join as follows:

```
SQL> SELECT WHS.WHSNO, WHSNAME
  2  FROM WHS, SERIAL
  3  WHERE WHS.WHSNO=SERIAL.WHSNO (+)
  4  AND SERIAL.WHSNO IS NULL;
```

to obtain these results:

```
WHSNO WHSNAME
------- ------------------------------
    4 GOULETTE, DR. RAYMOND
    6 TORREY PINES MEDICAL
    7 ST. GEORGE MEDICAL
   10 KEARNEY, DR. PATRICK
```

The plus sign in parentheses (+) tells Oracle to execute an outer-join. You will learn other methods to obtain the same information in the next section, which discusses subqueries.

You can even join a table to itself by using an *alias* to refer to that table. Use the following syntax:

```
SQL> SELECT X.column, Y.column,
     FROM table X, table Y
     WHERE X.column=Y.column;
```

In this case, *X* and *Y* become aliases for the table so that you can refer to the column as X.*column* and Y.*column* in order to compare it against itself. You can do this for purposes of analysis. For example, to find out which products have more quantity in warehouse than a given product number, type

```
SQL> SELECT X.PRODNO, X.QIW, Y.QIW
  2  FROM PROD X, PROD Y
  3  WHERE X.QIW > Y.QIW
  4  AND Y.PRODNO='88804106';
```

The following display will result:

```
PRODNO      QIW     QIW
........   .......  .......
90002025     450     300
88904100    1200     300
88904104     800     300
```

The QIW on the right, Y.QIW, is the quantity for 88804106, which was compared against the X.QIW for each product in the table. The resulting table lists the three products that have more quantity on hand than 88804106. A non-equi-join such as this is more common when you are joining a table with itself for analysis. In this situation, you are typically interested in comparing a single value against all other values.

USING SUBQUERIES

With SQL, you can use a SELECT query as input to another command in place of a constant value, variable, or function. You can select a table of values to be used in such commands as DELETE, INSERT, UPDATE, and CREATE TABLE. You can also nest a SELECT query inside another SELECT command and chain several queries together with the WHERE clause.

Each SELECT statement can be complex in itself. When SELECTs are nested together, structure becomes particularly important. A subquery must be enclosed in parentheses. For clarity, you should also indent each level of query.

Subqueries are actually fully functional queries. They can return a single value or a list of values. They can return several columns of data from one or more tables, depending on the situation. The operators EXIST, ANY, ALL, and IN are specifically designed for evaluating a subquery.

To demonstrate, lets recall the question from above:

What warehouses do not have any products consigned to them?

In the discussion of joins you solved the question with an outer-join of the WHS and SERIAL tables. The following method:

```
SQL> SELECT WHSNO, WHSNAME
  2  FROM WHS
  3  WHERE NOT EXISTS
  4      (SELECT WHSNO
  5       FROM SERIAL
  6       WHERE WHS.WHSNO=SERIAL.WHSNO);
```

produces the same result:

```
WHSNO WHSNAME
------- ----------------------------
    4 GOULETTE, DR. RAYMOND
    6 TORREY PINES MEDICAL
    7 ST. GEORGE MEDICAL
   10 KEARNEY, DR. PATRICK
```

Because in this case you used two tables, you must equate the two WHSNO columns and refer to them with a table prefix in the nested query. The subquery returns all of the warehouse numbers in the serial table; the primary query requests all warehouse numbers and warehouse names that do not have a matching value in the SERIAL table. (Notice that the subquery is indented and enclosed in parentheses.)

NOT EXISTS, the negative of the operator EXISTS, is used to connect the query and the subquery. EXISTS is true (and so the WHERE clause is true) if at least one row is returned from the subquery. Adding NOT reverses this situation so that the WHERE clause is true only if no rows are returned from the subquery. (Operators are covered in Chapter 7.)

You could not have used a subquery instead of a join if you needed to display columns from both tables in the final main query table. Because you only need the main tables columns, you can use the subquery list for input to the WHERE clause.

Subqueries can be nested within more than one level. In Figure 5.13, the two lower levels are used to select the product with the highest COST by comparing each cost against all of the others. This one-row result is then used to select all of that particular product from the SERIAL table.

```
SQL> SELECT *
  2   FROM SERIAL
  3   WHERE PRODNO =
  4      (SELECT PRODNO
  5      FROM PROD
  6      WHERE COST >= ALL
  7      (SELECT COST
  8       FROM PROD))
  9   AND STATUS='W';


PRODNO    SERNO   ST   WHSNO STATDAT    PURDAT
--------  ------  --   ----- ---------- ---------
90006005 100001  W        1 01-MAY-89 01-MAY-89
```

                                    ─── Main query
                                    ─── First level subquery
                                    ─── Second level subquery

Figure 5.13: A three-level subquery

An additional condition limited the subquery to the most expensive units in the main store's warehouse. If you need to use an ORDER BY clause, place it in line ten, after all of the subqueries and other clauses.

CORRELATED SUBQUERIES

The *correlated subquery* requires Oracle to do more complex processing. To illustrate the difference between a regular subquery and a correlated subquery, let's look at another way to find the answer to the subquery in Figure 5.14. Instead of using > = ALL as this structure states

```
SQL> SELECT *
  1   FROM PROD
  2   WHERE COST >= ALL
  3      (SELECT COST
  4       FROM PROD);
```

change it to

```
SQL> SELECT *
  2   FROM PROD
  3   WHERE COST =
  4      (SELECT MAX(COST)
  5       FROM PROD);
```

to achieve the result

```
PRODNO   DSCRPT                               COST S    QIW
........ ...............................      ....... . ........
90006005 MUSCLE STIMULATOR                    495 Y      35
```

This selects the same product as the most expensive. In this case, the subquery returns one value—the maximum cost in the column table. The processing is then transferred to the main query and each row is compared against the maximum value until the right row is found.

Suppose, however, that you want to find out which product is highest among the serialized products (ST = 'Y') and which product is highest among the nonserialized products (ST = 'N'). The subquery will need a value back from the main query in order to do its calculations. A value is being passed down as well as up the structure. To do this, add the alias X to the main table name and in the subquery add a WHERE clause that equates the main row's ST value with the rows to be included in the MAX(COST) calculation. Figure 5.14 shows this new SELECT statement and its result.

```
SQL> SELECT *
  1    FROM PROD X
  2    WHERE COST =
  3        (SELECT MAX(COST)
  4         FROM PROD
  5         WHERE X.ST=ST)

PRODNO   DSCRPT                               COST S    QIW
........ ...............................      ....... . ........
90006005 MUSCLE STIMULATOR                    495 Y      35
88804106 ELECTRODES-SNAP TYPE                  40 N     300
```

Figure 5.14: A correlated subquery

As you can see, instead of returning only the 90006005 product with the highest cost in the product table, this query returns both the highest costing serialized product and the highest costing nonserialized product. Although this ''conditional subquery'' or correlated subquery interaction is much more complex to process, the difference in logic and syntax is negligible.

CONNECTING QUERIES WITH CONJUNCTION CLAUSES

Oracle provides three conjunction clauses for connecting two queries together. These Query Expression Operators allow you to combine two queries on an equal basis—as opposed to subqueries, where one query result serves as input to the the next query. These conjunctions, INTERSECT, UNION, and MINUS, are probably familiar. When used on a single table, they are like the English language conjunctions and, or, and not. They serve to combine two SQL statements, just as the more familiar conjunctions combine two English sentences.

These three conjunctions can be used instead of WHERE clause conjunctions. Their counterparts in the WHERE syntax are:

QUERY EXPRESSION OPERATOR	LOGICAL OPERATOR
UNION	OR
INTERSECT	AND
MINUS	AND NOT

Let's do a simple query on the serial table, requesting all products that have not changed status in more than 45 days:

```
SQL> SELECT * FROM SERIAL
  2  WHERE TO_DATE('01-AUG-89')-STATDAT > 45;

PRODNO    SERNO  ST  WHSNO STATDAT   PURDAT
--------  ------ --  ------ --------- ---------
90002005  600005 W       1 01-MAY-89 01-JAN-89
90002005  600006 C       3 06-JUN-89 01-JAN-89
90002005  600007 C      11 15-JUN-89 15-JAN-89
90002025  800002 C      11 15-JUN-89 01-MAR-89
90006005  100001 W       1 01-MAY-89 01-MAY-89
90006005  100002 C      11 15-JUN-89 01-MAY-89

6 records selected.
```

If you are just interested in the product 90002005, you could either add another line that says AND PRODNO = '90002005' or do another SELECT and relate the two queries with the INTERSECT operator as follows:

```
SQL> SELECT * FROM SERIAL
  2  WHERE TO_DATE('01-AUG-89')-STATDAT > 45
  3  INTERSECT
  4  SELECT * FROM SERIAL
  5  WHERE PRODNO='90002005';

PRODNO    SERNO  ST   WHSNO STATDAT   PURDAT
--------  ------ --   ------- --------- ---------
90002005 600005 W        1 01-MAY-89 01-JAN-89
90002005 600006 C        3 06-JUN-89 01-JAN-89
90002005 600007 C       11 15-JUN-89 15-JAN-89
```

Only three products meeting both requirements are listed. If you want to see all of the products except for 90002005, change the logic mentioned above to AND PRODNO < > '90002005' or change INTERSECT to MINUS as shown here:

```
SQL> SELECT * FROM SERIAL
  2  WHERE TO_DATE('01-AUG-89')-STATDAT > 45
  3  MINUS
  4  SELECT * FROM SERIAL
  5  WHERE PRODNO='90002005';

PRODNO    SERNO  ST   WHSNO STATDAT   PURDAT
--------  ------ --   ------- --------- ---------
90002025 800002 C       11 15-JUN-89 01-MAR-89
90006005 100001 W        1 01-MAY-89 01-MAY-89
90006005 100002 C       11 15-JUN-89 01-MAY-89
```

Again, three products are listed, but they are the three that were not listed before.

The UNION operator works a little differently. If you change the MINUS to UNION, the resulting table gains rows, as you can see in Figure 5.15. This table includes all of the serial numbers that have not moved in more than 45 days as well as the the other five serial numbers with 90002005 as a product code. Using UNION is equivalent to changing AND PRODNO = '90002005' to OR PROD-NO = '90002005'.

Using the logical operators in the WHERE clause seems to be more practical in Figure 5.15. However, if you are using two identical tables, you will need these conjunction operators. For example, if you are comparing or combining the information from several

```
SQL> SELECT * FROM SERIAL
  2  WHERE TO_DATE('01-AUG-89')-STATDAT > 45
  3  UNION
  4  SELECT * FROM SERIAL
  5  WHERE PRODNO='90002005';

PRODNO    SERNO   ST   WHSNO  STATDAT    PURDAT
--------  ------  --   -----  ---------  ---------
90002005  600001  W        1  01-JUL-89  01-JAN-89
90002005  600002  C        2  03-JUL-89  01-JAN-89
90002005  600003  C        2  03-JUL-89  01-JAN-89
90002005  600004  C        3  05-JUL-89  01-JAN-89
90002005  600005  W        1  01-MAY-89  01-JAN-89
90002005  600006  C        3  06-JUN-89  01-JAN-89
90002005  600007  C       11  15-JUN-89  15-JAN-89
90002005  600008  C        5  12-JUL-89  15-JAN-89
90002025  800002  C       11  15-JUN-89  01-MAR-89
90006005  100001  W        1  01-MAY-89  01-MAY-89
90006005  100002  C       11  15-JUN-89  01-MAY-89

11 records selected.
```

Figure 5.15: Example using UNION

regional or divisional databases for a corporate-wide analysis, the INTERSECT, UNION, and MINUS operators could prove useful.

THE TREE RELATIONSHIP

A special type of SELECT statement uses the clause CONNECT BY along with the clause START WITH. These two options enable you to generate queries on a tree of relationships. Each individual node stores only the next level of reference, but by chain linking up or down the tree, you can get a nested view of the relationship. To envision this more clearly, think of a family tree where each generation is a separate node. If every generation recorded only the names of their own parents and children, you could reconstruct the entire tree by linking the limited information provided by each node.

To see this feature in action, take two tables (the inventory table INV, and the bill of material table BOM) from Stooley's Stool Factory where they make two product lines: a three-legged stool and a four-legged stool. Figure 5.16 shows the data in the two tables.

You can create an indented bill of material listing from just these two tables. A significant amount of logic would go into solving this problem using a traditional programming language. But with the

```
     BOM Table                              INV Table

INVNO  USEDON  USEDQTY          INVNO  DSCR              T       QIW    COST
-----  ------  -------          -----  ----------------  -       -----  ------
90001  60001        1           90001  3-LEG STOOL       A         10      20
90001  60002        1           90011  4-LEG STOOL       A         20      25
60002  60003        9           60001  SEAT-DRILLED      M         20      25
90011  60011        1           60001  SEAT-DRILLED      M         12       5
90011  60012        1           30001  SEAT BLANK        P         30       1
60001  30001        1           60002  LEG ASSY-3        A         15       7
60011  30001        1           60012  LEG ASSY-4        A         12       9
60002  30002        3           30002  LEG-DRILLED       M         18       2
30002  10001        3           30012  LEG-DRILLED4      M         13       2
60012  60003       12           10001  LEG BLANK         P         30       1
30012  10001        4           90000  2 STOOL KIT       T         10      45
60012  30012        4           60003  RUNG              P        200      .5
90000  90001        1
90000  90011        1
```

Figure 5.16: BOM and INV data tables

SQL SELECT...CONNECT BY...START WITH, the SQL*Plus
COLUMN command, the LEVEL pseudo column, the concatenation operator, and the LPAD function (discussed in Chapter 7), you
can complete the query shown in Figure 5.17 in a fraction of the time.

```
SQL>  COLUMN ASSY FORMAT A20
SQL>  SELECT LPAD(' ',3*LEVEL) || USEDON ASSY, LEVEL, USEDQTY
  2   FROM BOM
  3   CONNECT BY BOM.INVNO=PRIOR USEDON
  4   START WITH BOM.INVNO='90000'

ASSY                   LEVEL USEDQTY
-------------------- ------- -------
    90001                  1       1
        60001              2       1
            30001          3       1
        60002              2       1
            60003          3       9
            30002          3       3
                10001      4       3
    90011                  1       1
        60011              2       1
            30001          3       1
        60012              2       1
            60003          3      12
            30012          3       4
                10001      4       4

14 records selected.
```

Figure 5.17: An indented bill of materials

The CONNECT BY feature tells Oracle to equate the Inventory number column in the BOM table with the USED ON number column for each row. Then, an initial value is indicated using the START WITH clause. This clause can state either an equality or an inequality. The LEVEL number is calculated for each row to show how far away from the start of the tree it is. The indentation is then created using the LPAD function and the LEVEL value. The one shortcoming of this solution is that a join cannot be done with a CONNECT BY query.

The COLUMN command will resize your column display and display the column values in a different format. In this case, it defined the derived column ASSY to display within a 20-character-wide format.

USING EDITING COMMANDS AND BUFFERS

Because of the length of some SELECT commands, it can be tedious to retype the entire command each time you change it slightly or misstate the syntax.

Oracle combines several features to simplify altering and reexecuting statements. Oracle stores your standard SQL statements in the SQL buffer to maintain a high level of compatibility with other standard SQL systems that also have SQL buffers. Your SQL statement is stored in the buffer until you issue the SQL*Plus command

```
SQL> CLEAR BUFFER;
```

to empty it, or until you enter another standard SQL statement. This simplifies reexecuting statements because you do not have to retype a command to reexecute it. Instead, you can type

```
SQL> RUN
```

or just press R to redisplay the contents of the SQL buffer and reexecute the command.

If you only want to reexecute the command without redisplaying the buffer contents, you can enter the slash character instead of RUN or R; the table will list without the command.

But you can do more than reexecute commands, you can also edit them. Using the SQL*Plus editing commands listed in Table 5.1, you can alter the contents of the SQL buffer. (The letters in parentheses are acceptable abbreviations.)

Table 5.1: SQL*Plus Editing Commands

COMMAND	DESCRIPTION
APPEND(A)	Append text to the end of the current line
CHANGE(C)	Change the text in the current line
DEL	Delete the current line of the buffer
INPUT(I)	Input lines after the current line
LIST(L)	List one or all of the lines of the buffer
SAVE *filename*	Save the current buffer in a file on disk
GET *filename*	Load a file into the current buffer
EDIT *filename*	Use an optional word processor for editing

To demonstrate, let's recall the first statement you modified in this chapter. You needed to change

✂ **Program insert 5.67: SQL> SELECT PRODNO,DSCRP**

to the more complex statement

```
SQL> SELECT PRODNO,DSCRPT FROM PROD;
  2  FROM PROD
  3  WHERE ST = 'Y';
```

Figure 5.18 shows how you perform the entire transformation with editing commands. Let's examine the individual steps involved.

The first thing to do is list the contents of the buffer by typing **LIST** or pressing L. In this case the buffer contains only one line:

```
1* SELECT PRODNO, DSCRPT FROM PROD;
```

```
SQL> L
  1* SELECT PRODNO, DSCRPT FROM PROD;
SQL> C.FROM PROD.,ST
  1* SELECT PRODNO, DSCRPT ,ST
SQL> I
  2  FROM PROD
  3  WHERE ST = 'Y';
  4
SQL> L
  1  SELECT PRODNO, DSCRPT ,ST
  2  FROM PROD
  3* WHERE ST = 'Y';
SQL> R
  1  SELECT PRODNO, DSCRPT ,ST
  2  FROM PROD
  3* WHERE ST = 'Y';


PRODNO    DSCRPT                              S
-------- ---------------------------------- -
90002005 NEURO STIMULATOR-4 CHANNEL         Y
90006005 MUSCLE STIMULATOR                  Y
90002025 NEURO STIMULATOR-2 CHANNEL         Y
```

Figure 5.18: Using the SQL*Plus editing commands

The SQL buffer is a line editor, which means that only one line is active at a time. The asterisk indicates the current active line (as it does in EDLIN, if you are familiar with that editor).

To change the first line to

```
SELECT PRODNO, DSCRPT, ST
```

you use the CHANGE command, which can be abbreviated as C, as shown here:

```
SQL> C.FROM PROD.,ST
```

The periods enclose the string of characters that you wish to replace with a new string of characters, which you type immediately after the second period. You are changing the string

```
FROM PROD
```

to the string

```
, ST
```

This eliminates the FROM PROD clause (which is going to be on its own line) and adds the ST column to the SELECT clause.

Now that the first line is changed, you need to add two more lines to the buffer. To do so, use the INPUT command or its abbreviation, I. Whatever you type on the next line after I becomes the next line of the buffer. You can add more than one line. To exit the INPUT mode, press Enter at the beginning of a new line. If you want to add text at the end of the current line in the buffer instead of on the next line, you can use APPEND rather than INPUT. If you want to delete the current line from the buffer, type DEL.

The previous step adds lines 2 and 3 (FROM PROD and WHERE ST = 'Y';) to the buffer. In the figure, you execute the new command by typing R for RUN to display the buffer and execute the query.

You can save this edited command to disk with the SAVE command. To do so, decide on a file name and type

`SQL> SAVE `<u>`filename`</u>

The contents of the buffer are saved to disk in a file with the name you specified. Conversely, to retrieve the edited command from disk to the SQL buffer, you type

`SQL> GET `<u>`filename`</u>

and the file is loaded into the buffer.

Another option for editing the buffer is the EDIT command, which you may recall from Chapter 3. It accesses the default editor. In Professional Oracle, the default editor is EDLIN. You can also use GET to retrieve files created with another word processor that creates standard ASCII files.

SAVING SQL*PLUS COMMANDS

Any SQL*Plus commands such as BREAK and COMPUTE in effect in your current session will still work on an edited query if they relate to it. But SQL*Plus commands are not stored in the SQL buffer, so they are not stored on disk when you save the contents of the buffer to a file.

To save the SQL*Plus commands along with your SQL commands, you must use another buffer. To establish this buffer, type

```
SQL> SET BUFFER TO buffername
```

This activates an alternate buffer that accepts SQL*Plus commands. Enter your SQL*Plus commands one after another at the prompt and then enter your SQL statement. Now type

```
SQL> SAVE filename
```

and all the SQL*Plus and SQL commands will be saved to disk in the file you specified.

To run a SQL command that you saved with SQL*Plus commands, type **START**, or an at sign (**@**), like this:

```
SQL> START filename;
```

or

```
SQL> @ filename;
```

Either of these forms will execute the file from disk.

SUMMARY

With SQL, you can move from simple to complex queries with negligible increases in complexity. You can connect tables, join tables, display details, display summaries, and nest your queries within one another. SQL has so many features that several different methods often accomplish the same result. As you become more familiar with the SQL language, you will learn which ways are best for you and your computer.

DEFINING AND
USING VIEWS

ALTHOUGH VIEWS LOOK LIKE ORDINARY DATA-
base tables, they are customized subsets of tables that contain
only selected rows and columns. Views can be thought of as
"windows" into database tables, through which only selected
columns and rows are visible.

A view can be a subset of a base table or can consist of two or
more joined tables. You create views by specifying a SELECT
statement that prescribes what rows, columns, and tables will
be accessed to create the view. A view is not stored as a physical
table; only its definition is saved. For this reason, views are
called *virtual* tables. When you use a view to perform a database
operation, the view definition is retrieved and used to access the
database and invoke the desired action.

The database operations that you can perform on virtual
tables are similar to those for base tables. You can always execute the SELECT statement with a view; it is the SQL statement most often used with views. With some exceptions, you
can also perform the database operations INSERT, UPDATE,
and DELETE with single-table database views.

You can construct a nearly limitless collection of views. In this
chapter, you'll learn how to define and query single-table views
as well as more complex views. You will then experiment with
inserting, updating, and deleting data using views. Finally, you
will learn to drop views from the database.

WHAT VIEWS DO

Views give you a number of options that you don't have with base tables.

By restricting various users to given views of the database, views provide a type of database security known as *discretionary access control*. Different users have different information requirements and different need-to-know levels. A personnel director and a finance manager need different kinds of information, but both may need statistics that apply to the entire company. A project manager may require information about both employees and finances, but only related to a particular project. Using views, you can tailor the information that various employees have access to according to their different information needs, while maintaining only one database.

Alternately, the database administrator could create separate databases based on individual need-to-know criteria; one table for the personnel manager, another table for the financial officer, and so on. The problem with this approach is obvious—it spawns a plethora of tables from what was once a single, consistent, and reliable database.

Views are a better way to provide subsets of database information to users whose needs vary but who want information from one reliable source. Views act like filters, allowing certain information to "pass through" to users but filtering out other information. Numerous views can be created, so that one user group accesses the database through one view while another group sees a different view.

A *column subset* view hides certain columns of the database from some users but makes them accessible to others. A *row subset* view makes certain database rows inaccessible to a user group. For example, a personnel manager may be denied access to his or her supervisor's records, or managers may be denied access to other managers' records. Column and row subset views can be combined to form *row and column* subset views. These views hide certain columns and selected rows of one or more database tables. Figure 6.1 illustrates these three types of base table subset views. The shaded areas represent information that is omitted from each view.

Another advantage of views is *query simplification*. When database queries are complex, you can create a database view to simplify

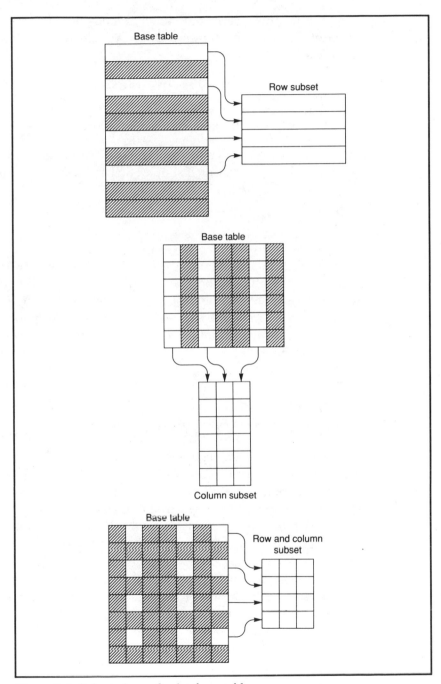

Figure 6.1: Subset views of a database table

them. For example, suppose that a frequently posed query returns a subset of the rows and columns from two joined tables. You could simplify a query such as

```
SELECT AGE, SEX, RACE, HIREDATE, PAYRATE, TABLE1.EMPLOYEEID
FROM   TABLE1, TABLE2
WHERE  TABLE1.EMPLOYEEID = TABLE2.EMPLOYEEID
       AND SEX='FEMALE' AND AGE > 25;
```

by creating a view using the preceding SELECT statement. You could then formulate a much simpler SELECT statement using the view (called EEOTABLE):

```
SELECT * FROM EEOTABLE;
```

Views also provide *logical data independence*. Suppose a table that is queried frequently by many users is subdivided into two or more tables. The old table can be "reconstructed" using a view to join the two new base tables. This insulates you from physical changes to database tables. In effect, a logical view presents the same information (derived from two tables) that you previously viewed from a single-table database.

A PROGRAM MANAGEMENT APPLICATION

The examples in this chapter stress the needs of program managers, project managers, and project team members. *Program managers* oversee and manage several *projects*. Projects and their team members are managed by *project managers* who are responsible for guiding individual projects to successful completion. Project team members are employees who work together to complete a project.

Each project manager must keep track of the number of hours charged against his or her project by the project team members. Project managers periodically produce reports containing information such as total labor hours, total labor costs, and total overhead hours associated with their projects. This information covers a one-, two-, or four-week period and is provided to the program manager. The program manager will occasionally require his or her own reports (usually less detailed) about each project and its manager.

Project team members have the fewest reporting needs. They need to maintain an accurate record of the time they spend on a project. In addition, employees retrieve previously input labor hours and project accounts they are charged against to ensure that the information is accurate.

When time card information for all employees is placed in a single table, views will prevent one employee from retrieving information about another employee. An employee can input and retrieve only the information associated with his employee identification number. Project managers review information and produce reports from the tables and employee time card rows for projects they manage. The program manager's reporting and information needs require unlimited access to all tables. However, he or she may create views to facilitate retrieval of critical information from various tables.

The remaining sections of this chapter use this program management system to describe SQL statements that create views, delete views, report information with views, and grant access to views. Three base tables, shown in Figure 6.2, and several views will be featured. The program manager creates and owns all tables shown in Figure 6.2. Likewise, he or she is responsible for defining the required views of these tables to protect the information they contain.

DEFINING AND QUERYING ONE-TABLE VIEWS

The first view we'll define is based on the "real" table TIMECARD shown in Figure 6.2. That table contains four columns of information: employee identification number (EMPID), project account number (ACCOUNT), reporting period (PERIOD), and number of hours (HOURS). All employees, including managers (whose ID numbers begin with 3), must log hours charged against each project they worked on for the reporting period. We will assume that the reporting period is two weeks, and that there are 26 reporting periods per year. According to the TIMECARD table, during the first reporting period employee number 2101 worked on three projects with account numbers A-2000, B-2500, and C-3000.

PROJECT table

ACCOUNT	MGR
A-2000	3101
B-2500	3102
C-3000	3103
O-0010	4101

RATE table

EMPID	RATEHOUR
2101	21.5
2102	24
2103	18.5
2104	15.5
2105	14
3101	32
3102	36
3103	30
4101	42

TIMECARD table

EMPID	ACCOUNT	PERIOD	HOURS
2101	A-2000	1	20
2101	B-2500	1	40
2101	C-3000	1	20
2102	A-2000	1	30
2102	B-2500	1	50
2103	A-2000	1	48
2103	C-3000	1	32
2104	A-2000	1	80
2105	B-2500	1	24
2105	C-3000	1	56
3101	A-2000	1	20
3101	O-0010	1	60
3102	B-2500	1	40
3102	O-0010	1	40
3103	C-3000	1	40
3103	O-0010	1	40

Figure 6.2: Program management tables

Because the TIMECARD table contains information about the hours, charge accounts, and reporting periods of all employees, it should be protected so that no employee can insert, update, delete, or query information about another employee's work. However, employees must be able to enter, examine, and alter any information about their own hours. In this situation, views are the perfect way to provide restricted access to the TIMECARD table.

DEFINING A VIEW

Several different perspectives can be used to create a view. In addition to row selection views, column projection views, and row and column combination views, which were mentioned earlier, you can also create views containing expressions and functions. In this section, we'll look at examples of all these possibilities, but first, let's examine the syntax of CREATE VIEW, the SQL statement that defines views:

```
CREATE VIEW view-name [ (column-name [,column-name] ...) ]
    AS query
        [ WITH CHECK OPTION ] ;
```

View-name is the name of the view being defined, *column-name* is an optional column name or alias, and *query* is a SELECT statement. You can also include the optional phrase WITH CHECK OPTION, discussed later in this chapter. View definitions may not contain either the UNION or ORDER BY clauses. Otherwise, any table that can be displayed with a SELECT clause can be defined as a view. Let's look at some examples.

Row Selection Views

To implement the TIMECARD restriction described earlier, you can define the following view:

```
CREATE VIEW EMP2101
    AS SELECT EMPID, ACCOUNT, PERIOD, HOURS
        FROM TIMECARD
        WHERE EMPID = 2101
        WITH CHECK OPTION;
```

When the EMP2101 view is executed, the query following the AS is not executed but is saved in the system catalog. The view provides a subset of the base table rows from TIMECARD. This form of view, defined by the query portion of CREATE VIEW, uses the selection operation to filter out rows whose employee identification is not 2101. This row subset view protects any base table rows not returned as a result of the defining query (SELECT ...) in the CREATE VIEW statement. Figure 6.3 illustrates the filtering effect of the view EMP2101. Although it looks like an ordinary table, the view on the left (EMP2101 view) is generated with the following SELECT statement:

```
SELECT * FROM EMP2101;
```

The query portion of the view definition permits all rows whose EMPID equals 2101 to pass through the "wall" created by the view definition. All other rows are blocked.

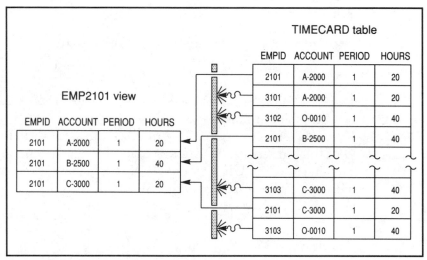

Figure 6.3: View EMP2101 and base table

You can define views for other employees in a similar fashion, as in the statement

```
CREATE VIEW EMP3101 (ID, CHARGENO, REPORTINGPERIOD, HOURS)
    AS SELECT *
       FROM TIMECARD
       WHERE EMPID = 3101
       WITH CHECK OPTION;
```

The column names inside parentheses are aliases for base table names. ID is the alias assigned to the view for the corresponding base table column EMPID, CHARGENO is used instead of ACCOUNT, and so on. Notice that the SELECT query defining view EMP3101 contains an asterisk (*) instead of the list of column names specified before. Generally, it is good practice to list the names of base table columns instead of using the * to include all columns. If you are using DB2 (IBM) and a base table is altered, views defined with a SELECT* on that base table can cause problems. In all other respects, the preceding view is like view EMP2101, except that the selected TIMECARD rows must all have the value 3101 for EMPID in order for them to be accessible.

Column Projection Views

Views in which a subset of the base table columns is available use the projection operation; only certain columns are projected to form the view. For example, the program manager might not be interested in the PERIOD and EMPID columns of the TIMECARD table. Only the ACCOUNT and HOURS columns would be projected by the view defined here:

```
CREATE VIEW PROGRAM_TIMECARD (PROJECT_ACCOUNT, LOGGED_HOURS)
    AS SELECT ACCOUNT, HOURS
       FROM TIMECARD;
```

Notice that the WHERE clause has been omitted; *all* rows are available in the virtual table PROGRAM_TIMECARD. The aliases PROJECT_ACCOUNT and LOGGED_HOURS have been assigned to base table column names ACCOUNT and HOURS, respectively. Only these columns from the base table TIMECARD can be accessed. TIMECARD cannot be updated using this view. (You'll learn why later in this chapter.)

Row and Column Combination Views

A view can contain both a subset of columns *and* a subset of rows— that is, a projection of columns combined with a selection of rows. Suppose, for example, that an employee wanted a view containing only the columns ACCOUNT and HOURS associated with her or his employee ID. Such a view would project those two columns, selecting only rows that correspond to his or her EMPID number. You can create views like this with CREATE VIEW statements such as the following:

```
CREATE VIEW EMP2101_MYHOURS
    AS SELECT ACCOUNT, HOURS
       FROM TIMECARD
       WHERE EMPID = 2101;
```

Alternately, you could write the WHERE clause as WHERE EMPID = USER if Oracle-assigned usernames and employee ID numbers coincide. (USER is an Oracle-defined pseudo column whose value is the current user's username.)

Views Containing Expressions and Functions

Another type of view can display columns that are not found in a base table. These "virtual columns" have values derived from extant database values and functions or expressions using database values. These special columns can lead to views that cannot be updated. These special cases must be handled differently from views composed solely of columns from a table.

As an example, project managers could employ functions and expressions in their view definition to gather summary information from the TIMECARD table. Suppose a project manager wants to know the total hours logged by each employee for the projects he or she manages. You can define a query-simplification view with the aggregate function SUM and the optional clause GROUP BY to provide summary information organized by project account and employee ID. The view can be defined by a statement such as

```
CREATE VIEW PROJECTSUMM (CHARGENO, IDENT, TOTALHOURS)
    AS SELECT ACCOUNT, EMPID, SUM(HOURS)
        FROM TIMECARD
        WHERE ACCOUNT='A-2000'
        GROUP BY ACCOUNT, EMPID;
```

where CHARGENO, IDENT, and TOTALHOURS are the aliases assigned to columns returned by the view. The alias TOTALHOURS is required because its value is computed with the database function SUM. Like other aggregate functions, SUM must reference a column name. Returning the account, employee ID, and total hours per account per employee ID, the view groups the results by account number and employee ID. The expression SUM(HOURS) is one of several functions that compute values from database columns but whose values are not stored in the database. You'll learn more about functions in Chapter 7.

When the previous view is queried with the statement

```
SELECT * FROM PROGMGR.PROJECTSUMM
```

the following rows are displayed:

```
CHARGENO IDENT TOTALHOURS
........ ..... ...........
  A-2000 2102         30
  A-2000 2101         20
```

```
A-2000   2104         80
A-2000   3101         20
A-2000   2103         48
```

where PROGMGR is the assumed username of the program manager—the one who created all views shown in this chapter.

GRANTING VIEW ACCESS TO OTHER USERS

Once the table owner (the program manager in our examples) has created various views, he or she must grant view privileges to users who wish to access data through those views. Only table owners can access views or tables they have created, unless they grant privileges to other users. Furthermore, only the person who creates a view can grant table or view access privileges to her table or views. View access privileges are restricted to SELECT, INSERT, UPDATE, and DELETE.

View privileges are given to others with the SQL statement GRANT, which you used in Chapter 3. Its syntax is

```
GRANT   privileges
ON      object
TO      {user|PUBLIC}
[WITH GRANT OPTION] ;
```

where *privileges* can be one or more of these:

SELECT

INSERT

UPDATE

DELETE

You can also enter ALL to include all four privileges. (Multiple entries must be separated by commas.) *Object* is the name of a table or view. *User* is one or more users who are being given access to the tables or views. Include the WITH GRANT OPTION phrase whenever you want to permit the grantee to pass the stated privileges on to other users. Exercise caution with this option. Once the "cat's out of the bag" it may be difficult to get it back in.

When PUBLIC is listed in place of a username list, all users (present and future) are granted access to the object. If several usernames are listed, they are separated by commas. An example is

```
GRANT SELECT
    ON PROJECTSUMM
    TO EMP3101, PROGMGR;
```

where users EMP3101 and PROGMGR are only allowed to retrieve (SELECT) information from the view PROJECTSUMM. You could grant employees access to their individual, program manager-created views with a series of GRANT commands such as:

```
GRANT SELECT, INSERT, UPDATE, DELETE
    ON EMP2101 TO EMP2101;
```

or

```
GRANT ALL ON EMP2101 TO EMP2101;
```

You will need as many GRANT commands as there are employee views to grant each employee view access to the TIMECARD table. In the previous case, user EMP2101 can perform retrieval (SELECT) operations, insert new records (INSERT), correct information (UPDATE), and remove entire rows (DELETE) through the view EMP2101 (rows whose EMPID field equals 2101). (The other two privileges, ALTER and INDEX, cannot be granted on views—only on base tables.) A GRANT command such as

```
GRANT SELECT ON PROJECT TO PUBLIC;
```

allows any user to retrieve information from the PROJECT table. It may be convenient and acceptable for anyone to be able to see which manager is assigned to which projects. The preceding GRANT will permit such a SELECT-only access.

QUERYING VIEWS

Once you have created views and established access privileges, those views can be queried. Suppose that an employee wants to retrieve information about his hourly rate for a specific project.

Assume that there is a view called RATEEMP2101 which restricts access to SELECT and is only for the given employee's matching ID number. The query

```
SELECT *
FROM PROGMGR.RATEEMP2101;
```

retrieves and displays the single employee ID and hourly rate from the RATE table via the view:

```
EMPID RATEHOUR
..... ........
 2101    21.5
```

A project manager can review selected entries from the TIME-CARD table through the previously illustrated view PROJECT-SUMM and can omit the CHARGE column (a projection of a view) with the statement

```
SELECT IDENT, TOTALHOURS
FROM PROGMGR.PROJECTSUMM;
```

Recall that user PROGMGR created the view, so any reference to PROJECTSUMM must be qualified with the username PROG-MGR. The rows displayed

```
IDENT TOTALHOURS
..... ..........
 2102       30
 2101       20
 2104       80
 3101       20
 2103       48
```

are, as usual, not ordered and show total hours by employee identification for a given manager's project (selected by account number). You can easily produce a more organized display by adding the phrase ORDER BY IDENT. The SELECT statement:

```
SELECT *
FROM PROGMGR.PROJECTSUMM
ORDER BY IDENT;
```

retrieves rows for account A-2000 and orders them by the alias IDENT:

```
CHARGENO IDENT TOTALHOURS
-------- ----- ----------
 A-2000  2101      20
 A-2000  2102      30
 A-2000  2103      48
 A-2000  2104      80
 A-2000  3101      20
```

CREATING SYNONYMS TO SIMPLIFY VIEW REFERENCES

In all preceding SELECT statements, the view name was prefixed with the username to correctly specify the desired view. However, you can create synonyms that eliminate the need to use a fully qualified name like PROGMGR.PROJECTSUMM. With a properly formed synonym, you can simplify the preceding reference to PROJECTS or MYPROJECTS. Creating synonyms is simple. For example, executing

```
CREATE SYNONYM MYSUMMARY FOR PROGMGR.PROJECTSUMM;
```

creates the easy-to-remember synonym MYSUMMARY. Thereafter, you can replace any occurrence of PROGMGR.PROJECTSUMM with MYSUMMARY.

Public synonyms are available to all RDBMS system users. Only a database administrator can create public synonyms. Here is a sample statement that a DBA might use to create a public synonym:

```
CREATE PUBLIC SYNONYM LABORSUMMARY FOR PROGMRG.PROJECTSUMM;
```

Synonyms can be deleted from the system with either

```
DROP SYNONYM synonym-name;
```

or

```
DROP PUBLIC SYNONYM synonym-name;
```

___ *DEFINING AND QUERYING MORE COMPLEX VIEWS* ___

The previous section dealt with single-table views. This section describes more complicated views that can both protect sensitive information and simplify queries. All views in this section are composed of at least two base tables. Some views are defined with the join operator. Others are defined with subqueries involving two and three base tables. The rules for forming views are the same, but multiple table views have restrictions when you use them in conjunction with INSERT, UPDATE, and DELETE statements. These restrictions are discussed later in this chapter.

The program management information illustrated in this chapter has been stored in three tables. Because good database design dictates that each table should have one theme, time card information is restricted to the TIMECARD base table, accounts and their respective managers are found in the PROJECT table, and employee labor rates by employee ID are stored in the RATE table. Were employee labor rates found in the TIMECARD table instead, anomalies would arise. For example, multiple copies of the rate per hour (RATEHOUR in the RATE table) would be stored redundantly in several rows of the TIMECARD table. If and when labor rates were altered, you would have to locate and change multiple copies of them in the TIMECARD table. By segregating rates in a separate table, you can easily change any hourly labor rate by altering one entry (per change) in one table—RATE.

VIEWS DEFINED ON TWO BASE TABLES WITHOUT JOIN

Although the program management information about various projects is distributed across three tables, you can collect and display it as a unified table of information. You can use views to combine information from several sources into one displayed result. Of course, you do not need views to do this, but they provide protection that a simple SELECT statement of base tables cannot. In the first example, information from two base tables, TIMECARD and PROJECT, is merged to provide each of the project managers with summary information about the projects they supervise.

First, a view called MGR1PROG is created that consists of related data from two tables. Once the program manager has created a similar view for each project manager, those views can be queried to retrieve results. Figure 6.4 shows the CREATE VIEW statement, and the SELECT statement used to query the view, along with the resulting table. Remember that the view creator must grant SELECT access to the view for others to be able to use it.

```
CREATE VIEW MGR1PROJ
    AS SELECT EMPID, ACCOUNT, PERIOD, HOURS
        FROM TIMECARD
        WHERE EMPID=3101
            OR
                ACCOUNT IN (SELECT ACCOUNT
                            FROM PROJECT
                            WHERE MGR=3101);


SELECT *
FROM MGR1PROJ
ORDER BY PERIOD, ACCOUNT, EMPID;

EMPID ACCOUNT PERIOD HOURS
----- ------- ------ -----
 2101  A-2000     1     20
 2102  A-2000     1     30
 2103  A-2000     1     48
 2104  A-2000     1     80
 3101  A-2000     1     20
 3101  0-0010     1     60
```

Figure 6.4: Creating and selecting from a view

The view MGR1PROJ is a query-simplification view. That is, it makes it easy for a particular project manager to find out about all projects that he or she manages. This is accomplished by tying together the TIMECARD table and the PROJECT table. In effect, the view selects rows from the TIMECARD table that contain an employee ID equal to the manager's (3101 in this example) or rows from the TIMECARD table containing ACCOUNTS (A-2000) for which the manager is responsible. The view finds these rows by first examining the PROJECT table and looking up the accounts that employee 3101 is responsible for. That information is then used to select rows from TIMECARD that contain those account values.

The SELECT statement (querying the MGR1PROJ view) shown in Figure 6.4 returns all columns of selected rows. It need not. You can use projection with views as well as base tables. That is, a SELECT statement such as

```
SELECT EMPID, ACCOUNT, HOURS
FROM MGR1PROJ
ORDER BY ACCOUNT, EMPID;
```

would yield equally informative results. If you forget the names of the columns of a table or view, you can refresh your memory with the SQL*Plus DESCRIBE command. Type **DESCRIBE** *table* (substituting the view or table name for *table*) to see its structure (column names, whether or not columns are mandatory, and data type). For example, the statement

```
DESCRIBE MGR1PROG;
```

displays this Oracle-generated structure of the view:

Name	Null?	Type
EMPID	NOT NULL	NUMBER
ACCOUNT	NOT NULL	CHAR(6)
PERIOD	NOT NULL	NUMBER
HOURS	NOT NULL	NUMBER

VIEWS DEFINED ON BASE TABLES WITH JOIN

You can define views that combine columns of two or more tables with a join operation. A view containing joined tables can simplify an otherwise complicated query. Views defined with a join operation follow the same rules and restrictions as stand-alone SELECT statements. Typically, you use column name pairs to define the conditions under which a row of one table or view is appended to a row of another table or view. When you use the equal (−) relational operator to relate the two columns, the join operation is termed an *equi-join*. The next example shows how to join two tables into a single view.

Suppose a project manager wishes to display summary information about all projects she or he manages. Further, she or he wants to be able to display the following information: reporting period, employee ID, account number, total hours per employee, employee hourly rate, and total dollars billed per employee per account. Here is one of several possible views that would generate this information:

```
CREATE VIEW MGR2PROJ (PERIOD,ID,ACCT,HRS,HRATE,BILLED)
   AS SELECT PERIOD, T.EMPID, T.ACCOUNT, HOURS,
              RATEHOUR, HOURS*RATEHOUR
      FROM TIMECARD T, RATE R
      WHERE T.ACCOUNT IN
             (SELECT ACCOUNT
              FROM PROJECT
              WHERE MGR=3102)
          AND
              T.EMPID = R.EMPID;
```

Once created, the view can be queried in a variety of ways. Figure 6.5 shows three SELECT statements and their output. Two of the example SELECT statements illustrate the ORDER BY optional clause. One result is in period and employee identification order, while the other is in dollars billed order. Remember, by default output rows are organized in ascending order when you use the optional ORDER BY phrase in a SELECT statement of a table or view. You can organize rows in descending order. Note that you cannot write the ORDER BY phrase as part of the view definition statement.

Look carefully at the previous CREATE VIEW statement. Two tables were joined based on matching EMPID values found in each table: RATE and TIMECARD. The last phrase

```
T.EMPID = R.EMPID
```

ensures that the selected table rows of both tables match on that field. Notice that alias column names, appearing within parentheses, were specified following the name of the view:

```
CREATE VIEW MGR2PROJ (PERIOD,ID,ACCT,HRS,HRATE,BILLED)
```

Aliases were used because one of the values created in the view is a virtual field generated from the mathematically combined values of two other columns. That value is the product of HOURS (from the TIMECARD table) and RATEHOUR (the hourly rate from the RATE table). Views containing virtual values *must* have aliases assigned in order to be referenced by statements invoking the view.

The previous view gathers PERIOD, EMPID, ACCOUNT, and HOURS from the TIMECARD table. The value RATEHOUR is

```
SELECT *
FROM MGR2PROJ
ORDER BY PERIOD, ID;

PERIOD   ID ACCT    HRS HRATE BILLED
------ ---- ------ --- ----- ------
     1 2101 B-2500  40  21.5    860
     1 2102 B-2500  50    24   1200
     1 2105 B-2500  24    14    336
     1 3102 B-2500  40    36   1440



SELECT ID, HRS, BILLED
FROM MGR2PROJ
WHERE ID <> 3102
ORDER BY BILLED;

  ID  HRS  BILLED
---- --- ------
2105   24    336
2101   40    860
2102   50   1200



SELECT ACCT, MIN(BILLED),
       MAX(BILLED),
       SUM(BILLED), COUNT(*)
FROM MGR2PROJ
GROUP BY ACCT;

ACCT   MIN(BILLED) MAX(BILLED) SUM(BILLED) COUNT(*)
------ ----------- ----------- ----------- --------
B-2500         336        1440        3836        4
```

Figure 6.5: Sample SELECT statements for the MGR2PROJ view

found in the RATE table, and the product of HOURS and RATE-HOUR defines the total dollar volume for a given employee. Column name qualifiers (T. and R.) are used in the SELECT and WHERE clauses to shorten the column references and to unambiguously identify column names that appear in two tables (EMPID and ACCOUNT). These substituted table names, or table name aliases, are defined in the FROM clause

FROM TIMECARD T, RATE R

following their respective ''real'' table names.

The SELECT clause defining the MGR2PROJ locates all employees working for the manager by inspecting a third table, PROJECT, to find all accounts for which the manager is responsible. Once located, these account numbers select rows from the TIMECARD table. For example, manager 3102 manages only the project whose account is B-2500 (this information is in the PROJECT table). This account number is then used to locate all rows of the TIMECARD table to extract employee rows containing B-2500 in the ACCOUNT column:

```
WHERE T.ACCOUNT IN
      (SELECT ACCOUNT
       FROM PROJECT
       WHERE MGR=3102)
```

The subquery following the word IN finds matches between account values in the TIMECARD table and account numbers assigned to manager 3102 in the PROJECT table. A given manager may be responsible for several projects, each with a unique account. If you knew that a manager were responsible for only one account, you could use the equal (=) relational operator instead of IN.

Because the TIMECARD table can contain up to twenty-six reporting periods for the year, the project manager may wish to restrict retrieved rows to a particular time period. You should implement this in the query, not in the view. This allows the manager to query more than one period of the view. In fact, you could retrieve an entire year-to-date with the SELECT statement

```
SELECT ID, ACCT, BILLED
FROM MGR2PROJ;
```

or a group of time periods with the SELECT statement

```
SELECT *
FROM MGR2PROJ
WHERE PERIOD BETWEEN 12 AND 15;
```

THREE-TABLE VIEWS

You can combine three base tables in a single view that provides information about all projects for the program manager. A total of eight columns of information are defined in the three tables that make up the program management database. Two columns, EMPID and ACCOUNT, are contained in two distinct base tables so that the three tables can be related through these common columns. A single, comprehensive view that spans the three tables enables the program manager to gather global, project-wide information with relative ease. The statement

```
CREATE VIEW PROGMGR (PERIOD,MGR,ACCT,ID,HRS,HRATE,BILLED)
    AS SELECT PERIOD, MGR, P.ACCOUNT, R.EMPID,
             HOURS, RATEHOUR, HOURS*RATEHOUR
      FROM PROJECT P, RATE R, TIMECARD T
      WHERE (T.EMPID = R.EMPID)
        AND
             (T.ACCOUNT = P.ACCOUNT);
```

joins the three tables PROJECT, RATE, and TIMECARD and pulls together information on the two join columns, ACCOUNT and EMPID. As before, table aliases are assigned (T for TIMECARD, R for RATE, and P for PROJECT) to shorten and simplify the CREATE VIEW statement and to permit unambiguous reference to the two disparate ACCOUNT columns. Column aliases are provided, but only the column alias name BILLED is required. It stands for an underlying virtual column that is the product of rate and hours. The two join conditions T.EMPID = R.EMPID and T.ACCOUNT = P.ACCOUNT are (simultaneously) required to relate the three tables to one another properly. Because the view includes all possible columns from each of the three base tables, users can pose a wide variety of interesting queries. For example, suppose that the program manager wanted to display all information about all projects for the first reporting period (PERIOD = 1), omitting the PERIOD column. The SELECT statement

```
SELECT MGR, ACCT, ID, HRS, HRATE, BILLED
FROM PROGMGR
WHERE PERIOD=1
ORDER BY MGR, ACCT, ID;
```

produces the desired result sorted by MGR, ACCT, and ID, as shown in Figure 6.6.

```
MGR  ACCT       ID   HRS   HRATE   BILLED
----  ------     ----  ---   ------   ------
3101  A-2000    2101   20   21.5      430
3101  A-2000    2102   30    24       720
3101  A-2000    2103   48   18.5      888
3101  A-2000    2104   80   15.5     1240
3101  A-2000    3101   20    32       640
3102  B-2500    2101   40   21.5      860
3102  B-2500    2102   50    24      1200
3102  B-2500    2105   24    14       336
3102  B-2500    3102   40    36      1440
3103  C-3000    2101   20   21.5      430
3103  C-3000    2103   32   18.5      592
3103  C-3000    2105   56    14       784
3103  C-3000    3103   40    30      1200
4101  0-0010    3101   60    32      1920
4101  0-0010    3102   40    36      1440
4101  0-0010    3103   40    30      1200
```

Figure 6.6: Report of all columns from three base tables

You can glean less detailed information from the PROGMGR view by omitting some columns and grouping the results. Place the optional phrase GROUP BY in the SELECT statement to summarize information about unique manager/account column pairs:

```
SELECT MGR, ACCT, SUM(BILLED)
FROM PROGMGR
WHERE PERIOD = 1
GROUP BY MGR, ACCT;
```

The GROUP BY phrase shown in the previous SELECT statement is permitted within a view definition. However, it is best to use it in SELECT statements that access the view rather than locking GROUP BY into the view itself. After all, the manager may not always want the results grouped by manager and account. Note that whenever a SELECT statement contains an expression or function (that is, SUM, AVG, MIN, and so on), the GROUP BY clause is required. The result of the previous query is a good summary of the project activity during the selected reporting period:

```
MGR ACCT    SUM(BILLED)
---- ------  -----------
3101 A-2000      3918
3102 B-2500      3836
3103 C-3000      3006
4101 0-0010      4560
```

USING COLUMN TO FORMAT RESULTS

The SQL*Plus interface language contains a set of easy-to-use SQL formatting commands. Though not ANSI standard SQL, these commands have a number of useful features. You can use the COLUMN command, in particular, to provide more mnemonic column headings and to format dates, numbers, and characters. Oracle maintains a clean separation between SQL commands such as SELECT and DELETE, and SQL*Plus commands. Non-ANSI commands such as COLUMN are kept in a separate memory-buffer so that they are not mingled with standard SQL commands. This section illustrates COLUMN by reformatting the previous example to give the results a more pleasant and easy-to-read look.

Use the SQL*Plus command COLUMN with the HEADING option to provide more mnemonic column labels for your tables. You can issue a series of these commands at the SQL prompt:

```
COLUMN MGR     HEADING 'Manager'
COLUMN ACCT    HEADING 'Account'       FORMAT A7
COLUMN ID      HEADING 'Employee|ID'
COLUMN HRS     HEADING 'Hours|Logged'
COLUMN HRATE   HEADING 'Hourly|Rate'   FORMAT 99.9
COLUMN BILLED  HEADING 'Dollars|Billed' FORMAT $99,999
```

Here the vertical bar is part of the command. It causes a line break, so that you can display long headings in narrow columns. Once established, column headings remain in effect until you either replace them with new definitions or issue the command

```
CLEAR COLUMNS
```

The COLUMN statement, SELECT statement, and their results are shown in Figure 6.7.

You can generate even fancier reports by using the SQL*Plus BREAK and COMPUTE commands. Executing the additional commands

```
BREAK ON MGR SKIP 1
COMPUTE SUM OF BILLED ON MGR
```

before issuing the SELECT statement shown in Figure 6.7 creates a table that "breaks" on a change in the MGR field and subtotals the

```
SQL> COLUMN MGR      HEADING 'Manager'
SQL> COLUMN ACCT     HEADING 'Account'         FORMAT A7
SQL> COLUMN ID       HEADING 'Employee|ID'
SQL> COLUMN HRS      HEADING 'Hours|Logged'
SQL> COLUMN HRATE    HEADING 'Hourly|Rate'     FORMAT 99.9
SQL> COLUMN BILLED HEADING 'Dollars|Billed' FORMAT $99,999
SQL> SELECT MGR, ACCT, ID, HRS, HRATE, BILLED
  2  FROM PROGMGR
  3  WHERE PERIOD=1
  4  ORDER BY MGR, ACCT, ID;


                 Employee  Hours Hourly  Dollars
Manager Account        ID Logged   Rate   Billed
------- -------  -------- ------ ------ --------
   3101 A-2000       2101     20   21.5     $430
   3101 A-2000       2102     30   24.0     $720
   3101 A-2000       2103     48   18.5     $888
   3101 A-2000       2104     80   15.5   $1,240
   3101 A-2000       3101     20   32.0     $640
   3102 B-2500       2101     40   21.5     $860
   3102 B-2500       2102     50   24.0   $1,200
   3102 B-2500       2105     24   14.0     $336
   3102 B-2500       3102     40   36.0   $1,440
   3103 C-3000       2101     20   21.5     $430
   3103 C-3000       2103     32   18.5     $592
   3103 C-3000       2105     56   14.0     $784
   3103 C-3000       3103     40   30.0   $1,200
   4101 0-0010       3101     60   32.0   $1,920
   4101 0-0010       3102     40   36.0   $1,440
   4101 0-0010       3103     40   30.0   $1,200
```

Figure 6.7: Formatting results with the SQL*Plus COLUMN statement

BILLED column. You must BREAK on the column you COMPUTE. Figure 6.8 shows this formatted report.

MAINTAINING A CONSISTENT VIEW OF ALTERED BASE TABLES

Views are a convenient way to maintain a consistent window into base tables that have been altered. For example, suppose that originally the TIMECARD table consisted of the columns

EMPID   ACCOUNT   PERIOD   HOURS   RATEHOUR

containing employee ID, account, reporting period, hours logged, and employee rate/hour. The program manager then realizes that this base table is redundant because, among other things, the column

Manager	Account	Employee ID	Hours Logged	Hourly Rate	Dollars Billed
3101	A-2000	2101	20	21.5	$430
	A-2000	2102	30	24.0	$720
	A-2000	2103	48	18.5	$888
	A-2000	2104	80	15.5	$1,240
	A-2000	3101	20	32.0	$640
*******					--------
sum					$3,918
3102	B-2500	2101	40	21.5	$860
	B-2500	2102	50	24.0	$1,200
	B-2500	2105	24	14.0	$336
	B-2500	3102	40	36.0	$1,440
*******					--------
sum					$3,836
3103	C-3000	2101	20	21.5	$430
	C-3000	2103	32	18.5	$592
	C-3000	2105	56	14.0	$784
	C-3000	3103	40	30.0	$1,200
*******					--------
sum					$3,006
4101	0-0010	3101	60	32.0	$1,920
	0-0010	3102	40	36.0	$1,440
	0-0010	3103	40	30.0	$1,200
*******					--------
sum					$4,560

Figure 6.8: Using the SQL*Plus commands BREAK and SUM

RATEHOUR will be repeated needlessly throughout the table. Each time employees enters hours logged against a particular project, they insert their hourly rate in the RATEHOUR column. Because this can lead to an inconsistency, the program manager decides to vertically cut the TIMECARD table into two constituent tables. One table will then contain only the first four columns: EMPID, ACCOUNT, PERIOD, and HOURS. The second table (RATE) will contain the columns EMPID and RATEHOUR. To make these two tables appear to be unaltered, the program manager can define a view comprising both of the new tables:

```
CREATE VIEW EMP2101 (EMPID,ACCOUNT,PERIOD,HOURS,RATEHOUR)
    AS SELECT T.EMPID,ACCOUNT,PERIOD,HOURS,RATEHOUR
        FROM TIMECARD T, RATE R
        WHERE T.EMPID=R.EMPID
            AND
            T.EMPID=2101;
```

In this view, the two new tables appear as one to those displaying information from them.

If a base table is altered, some single-table views defined on that table may become invalid. In particular, any view defined with the phrase SELECT * will no longer function correctly when you either add or remove one or more columns from the underlying base table. Suppose that you created a simple view called OVERVIEW with the statement

```
CREATE VIEW OVERVIEW
    AS SELECT *
        FROM TIMECARD;
```

You can display the contents of TIMECARD using the OVER-VIEW view by executing

```
SELECT EMPID, ACCOUNT, PERIOD, HOURS
FROM OVERVIEW;
```

Later, you added a new column to the TIMECARD base table with the statement

```
ALTER TABLE TIMECARD
    ADD (MGR NUMBER);
```

Because the structure of the table that the view is based on is part of the view definition, the base table's new structure will no longer correspond to that of the view's stored structure definition. Any operations using the view after the base table is altered will fail.

To avoid this problem, the SELECT clause of the CREATE VIEW statement should always explicitly list the fields included in the view:

```
CREATE VIEW OVERVIEW
    AS SELECT EMPID, ACCOUNT, PERIOD, HOURS
        FROM TIMECARD;
```

INSERTING, UPDATING, AND DELETING DATA THROUGH VIEWS

All views permit you to extract information with SELECT statements. The SQL operations ALTER and INDEX are specifically not supported for views. However, the INSERT, UPDATE, and DELETE commands are supported by some views and not by others. The exact characteristics of views that support these commands have not been determined, so it is not always possible to pinpoint which views qualify. Some cases are clear, but further research remains to be done in this area of relational theory. (For further discussion, see works by C.J. Date listed in the Bibliography.) This section shows examples of views that clearly do support INSERT, UPDATE, and DELETE and examples of views that clearly *do not* support some or all of those operations. Which views are supported and which are not varies from one system to another. Here are some guidelines for the Oracle implementation:

1. You cannot INSERT, UPDATE, or DELETE rows of a view that is made up of more than one table (some of these operations are theoretically possible, but not allowed).

2. You may DELETE rows from a view if the query used to define the view

    - Selects rows from only one table

    - Does not contain a GROUP BY clause, a DISTINCT clause, a group function, or a reference to the pseudo column ROWNUM

3. You can UPDATE rows of a view if the query used to define the view

    - Selects rows from only one table

    - Does not contain a GROUP BY clause, a DISTINCT clause, a group or built-in function, or a reference to the pseudo column ROWNUM

    - Does not define any of the updated columns with an expression

    - Does not contain a nested subquery whose FROM clause refers to the base table on which the view is defined

4. You may INSERT rows into a view if the query used to define the view

    - Selects rows from only one table

- Does not contain a GROUP BY clause, a DISTINCT clause, a group or built-in function, or a reference to the pseudo column ROWNUM
- Does not define any of the columns with an expression
- Does not contain a nested subquery whose FROM clause refers to the base table on which the view is defined
- Includes any NOT NULL columns defined in the underlying base table

ONE-TABLE VIEWS

This section illustrates the INSERT, UPDATE, and DELETE operations for a view based on a single base table, the TIMECARD table. The TIMECARD table is the basis of the several employee views created earlier in this chapter. In particular, this section shows how to use the EMP2101 view to add, update, and delete rows.

Inserting

The view EMP2101 is defined on a single base table. Because this view meets all of Oracle's requirements for using INSERT, UPDATE, and DELETE with views, you can add new rows to it. The only restriction on each of the views of TIMECARD is that employees are permitted to insert information if and only if their employee ID matches the view. That is, view EMP2101 restricts INSERT operations to those whose EMPID value is 2101.

The syntax for inserting rows into views is identical to that for inserting rows into tables. You use the standard SQL statement

```
INSERT INTO table VALUES(value1, value2,...);
```

or

```
INSERT INTO table (column1, column2,...columnn);
VALUES (value1, value2,...,valuen);
```

where *table* is the view name, *valuex* stands for values to be inserted, and *columnx* stands for the column names.

Let's insert some rows that represent hours logged against several project accounts for employee 2101 and time period number two.

Execute these INSERT commands to add hours to three projects:

```
INSERT INTO EMP2101
VALUES (2101,'A-2000',2,30);

INSERT INTO EMP2101
VALUES (2101,'B-2500',2,30);

INSERT INTO EMP2101
VALUES (2101,'C-2500',2,15);
```

Oracle confirms that each record has been inserted with the message

```
1 record created.
```

After executing the three INSERT statements, execute the COM-MIT command to make the insertions permanent. The three INSERT operations are held pending until a COMMIT is executed, or until you disconnect from Oracle. Collectively, the three statements constitute a *transaction*, a group of SQL operations that must occur as a unit. If any one of the operations fails, all operations in the transaction must be nullified to maintain a consistent database. Figure 6.9 shows the display of all rows associated with EMP2101 that results from the preceding transaction.

```
SELECT *
FROM EMP2101
ORDER BY PERIOD, ACCOUNT;


EMPID ACCOUNT PERIOD HOURS
----- ------- ------ -----
 2101 A-2000      1    20
 2101 B-2500      1    40
 2101 C-3000      1    20
 2101 A-2000      2    30
 2101 B-2500      2    30
 2101 C-2500      2    15
```

Figure 6.9: Inserting rows through the EMP2101 view

Recall that when EMP2101 was created, the WITH CHECK OPTION phrase was included in the CREATE VIEW statement. This prevents view users from inadvertently inserting new rows that they cannot retrieve later. If WITH CHECK OPTION were omitted, one employee could insert a row containing another employee's ID. The WITH CHECK OPTION also guarantees that any inserted rows can be displayed. For example, if an employee with EMPID 2101 attempted to insert a record for another employee using this command:

```
INSERT INTO EMP2101
VALUES (3101,'0-0010',2,15);
```

Oracle would detect the error and display the following message:

```
VALUES (3101,'0-010',2,15)
              *
ERROR at line 2: ORA-1402:  view WITH CHECK OPTION where-clause violation
```

If the WITH CHECK OPTION were omitted from the original CREATE VIEW statement, the preceding INSERT would be successful but would not be displayed with the EMP2101 view.

It is a good idea to use COMMIT to make inserted records a permanent part of the database:

```
SQL> COMMIT;
```

Updating

One of the recently added rows in Figure 6.9 has incorrect values for the ACCOUNT and HOURS columns:

```
2101 C-2500     2    15
```

The account entered should have been C-3000, and the number of hours, 50. To correct the mistake, you can delete and then reinsert the record in its corrected form. Or, you can use the UPDATE command to correct the ACCOUNT value.

There are two forms of the UPDATE command. One replaces one or more columns with new values that are given explicitly. The other uses a SELECT statement to retrieve values from other views or tables; these values then replace the current column values. The two forms, respectively, are:

```
UPDATE table [alias]
SET column = expression[, column = expression, ...]
[WHERE condition];
```

and

```
UPDATE table [alias]
SET (column[,column,...,column]) = (subquery)
[WHERE condition];
```

where *table* is the name of a table or view (the alias can be used in subquery); *column* is the name of a column to be updated; *expression* is an expression that generates the replacement value; and *condition* is the logical statement that determines which rows are to be updated. The brackets around the WHERE clause indicate that it is optional. However, most UPDATE operations use a WHERE clause. If you omit the WHERE clause, the indicated changes are made to *every* row of the table or view—an unlikely situation.

Figure 6.10 shows the appropriate UPDATE command and the changed TIMECARD table as viewed through EMP2101. Note the altered record with the corrected values for ACCOUNT and HOURS.

Again, when you have made changes to the database, always execute COMMIT to confirm the changes, additions, or deletions.

Deleting

The DELETE command removes one or more rows from a table. Its syntax is

```
DELETE
FROM table
[WHERE condition];
```

where *table* is a table or view and WHERE is an optional clause that limits the scope of the operation. As with the UPDATE command, if you omit the WHERE clause, *all* rows of the view or table are removed. In other words, be very careful. If you use an incorrect *condition* in the WHERE clause, you may delete rows that you did not intend to.

```
UPDATE EMP2101
SET ACCOUNT='C-3000', HOURS=50
WHERE ACCOUNT='C-2500';



SELECT *
FROM EMP2101
ORDER BY PERIOD, ACCOUNT;


EMPID ACCOUNT PERIOD HOURS
----- ------- ------ -----
 2101 A-2000       1    20
 2101 B-2500       1    40
 2101 C-3000       1    20
 2101 A-2000       2    30
 2101 B-2500       2    30
 2101 C-3000       2    50  ◀────Updated row
```

Figure 6.10: Updating row through the EMP2101 view

Suppose employee 2101 notices an unwanted row associated with his employee ID in the EMP2101 view of the TIMECARD table. The extra record contains account B-2500 for period number two:

```
2101 B-2500      2    30
```

To remove the record, issue the DELETE command

```
DELETE
FROM EMP2101
WHERE EMPID=2101 AND ACCOUNT='B-2500';
```

After executing the preceding DELETE, Oracle responds with the message

```
2 records deleted.
```

Apparently *two* records were removed from the TIMECARD database. The WHERE clause was not restrictive enough. You must fine-tune it to select only one of the two records with an ACCOUNT field equal to B-2500 (there were two in the EMP2101 view).

Because Oracle, like most relational database management systems, is transaction oriented, you can reverse the error. Because transactions are temporary until you execute a COMMIT or

ROLLBACK SQL command, you can make them permanent or reverse them. In this case, reverse the previous DELETE command by executing

```
SQL> ROLLBACK;
```

The Oracle-generated message

```
rollback complete
```

confirms that the rows have been "undeleted."

You can correct the DELETE command by stating *exactly* which row you want to delete. Here is the correct DELETE statement:

```
DELETE
FROM EMP2101
WHERE EMPID=2101
  AND ACCOUNT='B-2500'
  AND PERIOD=2;
```

Figure 6.11 shows the result of this more specific command.

```
SELECT *
FROM EMP2101
ORDER BY PERIOD, ACCOUNT;


EMPID ACCOUNT PERIOD HOURS
----- ------- ------ -----
 2101 A-2000       1    20
 2101 B-2500       1    40
 2101 C-3000       1    20
 2101 A-2000       2    30
 2101 C-3000       2    50
```

Figure 6.11: Result of correctly deleting a row through a view

You can remove all rows of a view of a table by simply executing

```
DELETE FROM table;
```

Be careful! This command removes all rows from the specified table, leaving only the table definition intact.

ONE-TABLE VIEWS THAT CANNOT BE ALTERED

Several kinds of one-table views cannot be altered with INSERT, DELETE, or UPDATE. These include views containing GROUP BY, DISTINCT, or ROWNUM; views with virtual columns (that is, SUM, COUNT, HOURS*RATEHOUR, or other expressions); and views containing nested subqueries referring to the base table that the view is based on. The following CREATE VIEW statements refer to only one base table:

```
CREATE VIEW NODELETE
    AS SELECT DISTINCT EMPID, ACCOUNT, PERIOD, HOURS
        FROM TIMECARD;

CREATE VIEW NOUPDATE
    AS SELECT ACCOUNT, HOURS
        FROM TIMECARD
        GROUP BY ACCOUNT, HOURS;

CREATE VIEW NOINSERT TOTAL_HOURS
    AS SELECT SUM(HOURS)
        FROM TIMECARD;
```

MULTIPLE-TABLE VIEWS

Some multiple-table views could theoretically support the INSERT, UPDATE, and DELETE operations, but Oracle does not actually support those operations. Few relational database management systems, including IBM's DB2, allow INSERT, UPDATE, or DELETE operations on views of more than one base table or multiple views. A complete explanation of why various views are not supported is beyond the scope of this book. This chapter shows some views that are not supported, including the MGR2PROJ view (Figure 6.5), the MGR1PROJ view (Figure 6.4), and the PROGMGR view (Figure 6.7).

Future research will undoubtedly improve our ability to manipulate multiple tables and multiple views. For now, multiple table views are restricted to use with SELECT statements. You can alter views by selecting different components from base tables. By carefully granting various access rights to these base tables, database integrity can coexist with convenient reference capabilities through views.

DROPPING VIEWS

With the ANSI SQL statement DROP VIEW, you can eliminate views that are no longer needed. For example, to remove the views PROGMGR and MGR1PROJ, execute the two statements

```
DROP VIEW PROGMGR;
```

and

```
DROP VIEW MGR1PROJ;
```

The message "View dropped." is displayed after a view has been eliminated. Note that only one view can be dropped at a time; you cannot drop multiple views in one DROP VIEW statement. In addition, only the view creator can drop a view from the data dictionary.

Once a view is dropped, any reference to that view generates an error message. For example, if you execute the statement

```
SQL> SELECT * FROM PROGMGR;
```

after PROGMGR is dropped by the program manager, this error message results:

```
SELECT * FROM PROGMGR
              *
ERROR at line 1: ORA-0942:  table or view does not exist
```

When base tables are dropped, all views defined on those tables are dropped. Executing the statement

```
DROP TIMECARD
```

also drops the views PROGMGR, MGR1PROJ, and MGR2PROJ. Proceed with caution when you drop base tables; be sure that there are no views that reference those tables in their associated CREATE VIEW definitions. You can review view definitions with the command

```
SELECT * FROM VIEWS;
```

This displays the CREATE statement (stored in the data dictionary) originally issued to create the view. VIEWS itself is a system created view containing all views that you have created. Although VIEWS contains all views in the system, you can display only those associated with your username.

SPECIAL SYSTEM VIEWS OF THE DATA DICTIONARY

There are several views stored in the Oracle data dictionary. They describe definitions in the database, other views, synonyms, audit information, and so on. Some of these individual views are restricted to users with the DBA privilege. Others are not. You can display a complete list of the data dictionary views by executing

```
SELECT * FROM DTAB;
```

Appendix B contains a complete list of the data dictionary views displayed by the preceding command. Of particular interest is the view TAB. By executing

```
SELECT * FROM TAB;
```

you can see all tables and views that you have created. Figure 6.12 shows a sample TAB view.

```
SQL> SELECT *
  2    FROM TAB
  3    ORDER BY TABTYPE, TNAME;

TNAME                           TABTYPE CLUSTERID
------------------------------- ------- ---------
PROJECT                         TABLE
RATE                            TABLE
TIMECARD                        TABLE
EMP2101                         VIEW
EMP3101                         VIEW
MGR1PROJ                        VIEW
MGR2PROJ                        VIEW
PROGMGR                         VIEW

8 records selected.
```

Figure 6.12: List of tables and views

SUMMARY

This chapter described how to use views for database security and for simplifying queries. It explained how to define one-table views based on rows, columns, or a combination of rows and columns. You learned how to create views containing expressions and functions, how to query single-table views, and how to grant other users access to your views.

More complex views were also discussed. You saw how to define views on two base tables, with or without the join command. In addition, the chapter showed how to define views for three base tables and how to format results with the SQL*Plus commands COLUMN, BREAK, and SUM.

Next, you learned how to insert, update, and delete your data through both one-table and multiple-table views. Finally, the chapter showed how to drop views and how to access the views in Oracle's data dictionary.

OPERATORS AND
FUNCTIONS

ORACLE OFFERS A FULL COMPLEMENT OF operators and functions to embed within SQL statements. In Oracle, operators are either special words or characters that tell Oracle to execute an operation. These operations can be mathematical calculations, value comparisons, clause connections, or instructions to section, group, or otherwise modify commands, columns, or other values. Functions are a special class of operators that take the form

```
function(argument)
```

where *function* is a function name and *argument* is one or more inputs needed to execute the function. Note that the argument must be enclosed in parentheses. Functions result in a modified value that relates directly to the column, value, constant, or other function included in the argument.

Since operators and functions are inseparable from the commands with which they are used, they appear in examples throughout this book. However, operators and functions are the specific subject of this chapter.

OPERATORS

Because operators have descriptive names, you should recognize and understand most of them immediately. There are logical operators, value operators, syntax operators, query expression operators, and operators that defy any category, which we will call miscellaneous operators.

LOGICAL OPERATORS

The rules of logic have been standardized for many years. Most of the standard logical operators are used in Oracle, along with some advanced ones that combine several logical expressions. Logical operators are primarily used in the WHERE clause of the SELECT command. You can also use them in the HAVING, CONNECT BY, and START WITH clauses and the UPDATE command. You use them to compare one or more columns to one or more expressions. You use the operator to define the relationship between the column and the expressions.

Figure 7.1 is a list of the SERIAL table sample database from Chapter 4 ordered by status date. You will first use logical operators

```
SQL> SELECT * FROM SERIAL ORDER BY STATDAT;

PRODNO    SERNO   ST    WHSNO STATDAT    PURDAT
--------  ------  --   ------- --------   --------
90002005  600005  W        1 01-MAY-89 01-JAN-89
90006005  100001  W        1 01-MAY-89 01-MAY-89
90002005  600006  C        3 06-JUN-89 01-JAN-89
90002005  600007  C       11 15-JUN-89 15-JAN-89
90002025  800002  C       11 15-JUN-89 01-MAR-89
90006005  100002  C       11 15-JUN-89 01-MAY-89
90002005  600001  W        1 01-JUL-89 01-JAN-89
90002005  600002  C        2 03-JUL-89 01-JAN-89
90002005  600003  C        2 03-JUL-89 01-JAN-89
90002005  600004  C        3 05-JUL-89 01-JAN-89
90002025  800003  C        9 06-JUL-89 01-MAR-89
90002025  800004  C        8 06-JUL-89 15-MAR-89
90002005  600008  C        5 12-JUL-89 15-JAN-89
90006005  100003  C        5 12-JUL-89 01-MAY-89
90002025  800001  W        1 12-JUL-89 01-MAR-89

15 records selected.
```

Figure 7.1: The SERIAL table

to select serial numbers from this table based on status date. Notice that there are 15 rows in the sample database; you will be selecting different combinations of these rows.

The Equal Operator

The equal sign (=) is the most common logic operator. You can use it alone, as in this example, which selects the record:

```
SQL> SELECT *
  2   FROM SERIAL
  3   WHERE STATDAT='01-JUL-89';
```

You can also use the equal sign in combination with characters. To request an inequality, use the equal sign with the exclamation point (! =) or caret (^ =). If you add it to the previous example, the query looks like this:

```
SQL> SELECT *
  2   FROM SERIAL
  3   WHERE STATDAT!='01-JUL-89';
```

The resulting table will have fourteen rows instead of one. You can use the "not equal to" operator (< >) instead of ! = or ^ = . As always, Oracle provides more than one way to accomplish the same thing.

The Inequality Operators

The characters < and >, when used independently, mean "less than" and "greater than," respectively. To find out what serial numbers have not moved since the day before July 1st, modify the previous query to say:

```
SQL> SELECT *
  2   FROM SERIAL
  3   WHERE STATDAT<'01-JUL-89';
```

The result will be a table followed by this message:

```
6 records selected.
```

If you are using dates, think of "previous to" rather than than "less than." If you are comparing character strings, the word "before" might make more sense. The same operators work with dates and character strings.

You can add the the equal sign to the inequality operators to form another relationship. Enter:

```
SQL> SELECT *
  2  FROM SERIAL
  3  WHERE STATDAT<='01-JUL-89';
```

This time the message after the table will read

```
7 records selected.
```

You just changed the relationship to "less than or equal" or "previous to or on." In doing so, you added the row with the July 1st status date to the selected table. The equal sign should always come after the less than or greater than sign (< = and > =). Putting the two signs together (< >) is another way to state "not equal to."

Combining Operators with AND and OR

AND and OR are conjunctions with which you combine logic conditions. Use AND to define a condition in which a column must match both parts of the condition to be retrieved. Use OR to make a column match at least one of the two conditions to be retrieved. For example, to narrow the last query down to part number '90006005', enter:

```
SQL> SELECT *
  2  FROM SERIAL
  3  WHERE STATDAT<='01-JUL-89' AND PRODNO='90006005';
```

Adding this AND conjunction reduces the number of records retrieved from seven to two. The first half of the WHERE clause selects seven records. The second part of the WHERE clause narrows that to a two-row subset having a 90006005 product code.

If instead of entering AND you entered OR, like this

```
SQL> SELECT *
  2  FROM SERIAL
  3  WHERE STATDAT<='01-JUL-89' OR PRODNO='90006005';
```

you would see this message following your results:

```
8 records selected.
```

Instead of a subset of the seven rows, you get eight rows. You just added all rows with the 90006005 product code to the rows with a status date on or before July 1. Rows that match both halves of the connected logic are only listed once. They are at what is called the *intersection* of the two sets of rows.

The Between Operator

With one common query you use logic similar to the following:

```
SQL> SELECT *
   2  FROM SERIAL
   3  WHERE STATDAT>='01-JUN-89' AND STATDAT<='30-JUN-89';
```

which selects four records. You might use this same logic to select rows of monthly sales, salary ranges, zip codes, credit limits, or an alphabetic range of customers. However, to make this familiar logic a little less cumbersome, Oracle includes BETWEEN *x* AND *y*. Selecting the following:

```
SQL> SELECT *
   2  FROM SERIAL
   3  WHERE STATDAT BETWEEN '01-JUN-89' AND '30-JUN-89';
```

returns the same records, is less tedious to enter, and reads better.

Remember, the BETWEEN/AND operator includes the values you enter in the range. It is equivalent to ''greater than or equal to x and less than or equal to y'' not ''greater than x and less than y.''

The Like Operator

LIKE is a logical operator that allows you to be less exact in your query because you can use the wild card characters _ and %. LIKE is useful for selecting a range of rows

- that have similar but not identical values

- whose exact values you are unsure of

- that are time-consuming to identify more specifically

With LIKE, you can enter adequate logic when exact logic is unnecessary or not possible. You can substitute the underline character (_) for a single character and the percent sign (%) for several characters. For example, instead of using BETWEEN to select all status dates in June, you can enter

```
SQL> SELECT *
  2  FROM SERIAL
  3  WHERE STATDAT LIKE '%JUN%';
```

which selects four records.

Figure 7.2 is a sample table called CUST that contains a list of customers. If you were unsure of a customer name, you could use LIKE to do a name search in CUST:

```
SQL> SELECT CNAME
  2  FROM CUST
  3  WHERE CNAME LIKE 'S%'
```

CUSTNO	CNAME	CADDR	CCITY	CS	CZIP	CPHONE
308-54-8832	HILL, THEODORE B.	142 CAMINO WEST	SAN DIEGO	CA	92210	4015551212
100001	KELLEHER, BRIAN S.	14 SOUTH 1ST AVENUE	LA GRANGE	IL	61001	3121553567
100002	BOWA, LANDRY	315 OUTPOST ROAD	PHILADELPHIA	PA	31313	2234456757
454864457	SUTTON, TONY	1 CAMEL BACK ROAD	PHOENIX	AZ	84001	6024434323
100003	ORTGIESSEN, JOHN	131 MIRAMAR ROAD	SAN DIEGO	CA	91313	6192244533
545521955	SCHREIBER, CLINT	131 FORDSON LANE	ST. CHARLES	IL	65220	3127757858
100004	CORONADO, MARIO	99 LA BAMBA LANE	SOLANA BEACH	CA	91331	6194548822
100005	VOGELE, MARK	13231 IRVINE RANCH ROAD	IRVINE	CA	91313	7145544040

Figure 7.2: The CUST table

If you wanted to select customers for a range of zip codes, your statement would look something like this:

```
SQL> SELECT CNAME, CZIP
  2  FROM CUST
  3  WHERE CZIP LIKE '91%'
```

All of the following examples are valid:

```
WHERE CZIP LIKE '9___5'
WHERE CZIP LIKE '__5_5'
WHERE CZIP LIKE '9%1'
WHERE CZIP LIKE '9%5%5'
WHERE CNAME LIKE 'A%'
WHERE CNAME LIKE '%B%R'
WHERE CNAME LIKE '_B%R'
```

With ('%B%R'), B has to appear somewhere in the name and R has to be the last letter in the name, but with ('_B%R'), B has to be the second letter of the name and R has to be the last.

It's important to be accurate enough when using LIKE. With a customer table containing 10,000 rows, saying

```
WHERE CNAME LIKE 'A%'
```

will yield an unwieldy amount of data. Using the LIKE operator a bit more specifically will save you lots of time.

SOUNDEX is a related function which is discussed later in this chapter. Whereas LIKE means ''select records that *look* like x,'' SOUNDEX means ''select records that *sound* like x.''

The IN Operator

IN is an operator, that, like BETWEEN *x* AND *y*, simplifies a special type of logic. One form of its syntax looks like this:

```
WHERE column IN ('a','b','c','d')
```

This replaces the equivalent but less economical logic:

```
WHERE column='a' OR column='b' OR column='c' OR column='d'
```

Use this operator in situations where the LIKE operator does not work because of a lack of similar values. *Column* has to be a column name or contain a column name as part of a function. The values inside the parentheses will usually be literal strings (enclosed in single quotes) or values. They can also be column names or column names with functions. Literal strings must use single quotes or they will be

considered column names and an error message will result. A traditional use of the IN operator is

```
SQL> SELECT *
  2  FROM SERIAL
  3  WHERE WHSNO IN (1,5,11);
```

which will list all of the serial numbers located at those three warehouses. But in this situation:

```
SQL> SELECT *
  2  FROM PROD
  3  WHERE COST*2 IN (QIW*3);
```

you are really just substituting the IN operator for an equally effective equal sign.

Subquery Operators

With the second form of the IN operator, you do not have to specify the list of values directly. Instead, you enter a subquery to select a
list which is then used as input to the IN operator. Figure 7.3 demonstrates this form.

```
SQL> SELECT *
  2  FROM WHS
  3  WHERE WHSNO IN (
  4      SELECT WHSNO
  5      FROM SERIAL);

  WHSNO WHSNAME                                   TERR W
------- ------------------------------------- ------- -
      1 STORE STOCK                                   W
      2 MEDICAL PROFESSIONALS, INC                  1 C
      3 KATSINAS, DR. STEVE                         1 C
      5 CONDON, DR. TIMOTHY                         1 C
      8 ELECTRO-MED, LTD.                           3 C
      9 QUINTARD, DR. ROBERT                        3 C
     11 LIND, DR. JEFF                              3 C

7 records selected.
```

Figure 7.3: Using IN with a subquery

In Figure 7.3, the subquery extracts a list of the WHSNO column
from the SERIAL table. SQL*Plus then uses that list to select the
rows from the WHS table. To describe this query, you might say

Show me all of the information in the warehouse table regarding any warehouse that has SERIAL products.

If you prefer, you can rephrase that subquery using the ANY operator. The statement

```
SQL> SELECT *
  2  FROM WHS
  3  WHERE WHSNO =ANY (
  4       SELECT WHSNO
  5       FROM SERIAL);
```

will produce the same table. Without ANY, the subquery is a single-row subquery; that is, the logic is specific enough to return only one row of the table being queried. By adding ANY, you transform it into a multiple-row subquery.

ALL is similar to ANY. However, with ALL, the column in the WHERE clause must match not just one but every value returned in the subquery.

Correlated subqueries (dicussed in Chapter 5) use the operator EXISTS to test whether any rows are returned in the subquery. Figure 7.4 shows how EXISTS is substituted to create the same result shown in Figure 7.3.

```
SQL> SELECT * FROM WHS X
  2  WHERE EXISTS (
  3       SELECT WHSNO FROM SERIAL
  4       WHERE X.WHSNO=WHSNO);

WHSNO WHSNAME                                TERR W
------- ------------------------------------- ------- -
      1 STORE STOCK                                  W
      2 MEDICAL PROFESSIONALS, INC            1 C
      3 KATSINAS, DR. STEVE                   1 C
      5 CONDON, DR. TIMOTHY                   1 C
      8 ELECTRO-MED, LTD.                     3 C
      9 QUINTARD, DR. ROBERT                  3 C
     11 LIND, DR. JEFF                        3 C

7 records selected.
```

Figure 7.4: Using EXISTS

Last But NOT Least

With NOT, you can reverse most of the logical operators discussed above. NOT IN produces a table containing all rows not in the IN list subquery. Saying NOT LIKE returns the complement of the values returned by LIKE. Saying NOT BETWEEN *x* AND *y* returns all of the values outside of the x and y range.

IS NULL is another logical operator often used with NOT. A specific data element containing no value is considered null or blank. Saying IS NOT NULL displays all rows containing values.

Finally, there is an established precedence for combining logical operators. To override the normal precedence, use parentheses, as in arithmetic. The normal descending order of precedence is

1. All logical operators except NOT, AND, and OR are equal

2. NOT

3. AND

4. OR

The clause

```
WHERE PRODNO='90002005' AND WHSNO='11' OR WHSNO='5'
```

is different from

```
WHERE PRODNO='90002005' AND (WHSNO='11' OR WHSNO='5')
```

If you have any doubt about a complex clause, use parentheses to specifically define the logic appropriate to your situation.

VALUE OPERATORS

The four operators for adding, subtracting, multiplying, and dividing column values are +, −, *, and /. You can use them with dates as well as numeric values. If you specify a column not defined as a numeric format, say a character column containing only numbers, Oracle will try to convert those numbers and produce a result before issuing an error message.

For example, in the SERIAL table, PRODNO and SERNO are character columns. You can perform value operations on them because they contain values. If they contained non-numeric characters, however, an error message would appear. You can subtract one date from another, but no other value operator will work with dates.

These four operators use the same rules as their counterparts in math. Multiplication and division are done first and addition and subtraction are done last. You can use parentheses to override the normal order of precedence. Also, you cannot divide a number by 0, and you can use + and − to declare the sign of a value.

Instead of using + to concatenate two character strings, you use the two vertical (linefeed) characters | | . In Figure 7.5, this operator combines three columns from a CUST table: CCITY, CST, and CZIP.

```
SQL> SELECT  CNAME, CCITY||', '||CST||' '||CZIP
  2  FROM CUST;

CNAME                           CCITY||','||CST||''||CZIP
------------------------------  ------------------------------------
HILL, THEODORE B.               SAN DIEGO, CA 92210
KELLEHER, BRIAN S.              LA GRANGE, IL 61001
BOWA, LANDRY                    PHILADELPHIA, PA 31313
SUTTON, TONY                    PHOENIX, AZ  84001
ORTGIESSEN, JOHN                SAN DIEGO, CA 91313
SCHREIBER, CLINT                ST. CHARLES, IL 65220
CORONADO, MARIO                 SOLANA BEACH, CA 91331
VOGELE, MARK                    IRVINE, CA 91313

8 records selected.
```

Figure 7.5: Using concatenation

The values appear by default in trimmed format, but you can change this with the SET TRIM command. You can make the RPAD function display them in a fixed length format (described later in this chapter). Notice that the full description of the column specification shows up in the column heading. To change the column headings, add the desired name right after CZIP in the SELECT clause.

SYNTAX OPERATORS

Syntax operators are special characters that help define your query to Oracle. As you recall, ANSI standard SQL commands can be entered on several lines; however, SQL*Plus extensions to the standard, such as those for report and column formatting, must be entered on one line or with the hyphen (-) character to indicate a line continuation.

In SQL*Plus, parentheses are used to alter precedence, to enclose sections of clauses, and within the syntax of a function. In addition, when you include a subquery in a SELECT command, you must enclose the subquery in parentheses.

The single quote (') and the double quote ('') are not same in Oracle. Single quotes enclose literal strings. With some packages, double quotes surround literals which contain single quotes, like this:

```
"Nancy's House"
```

But because Oracle uses double quotes for another purpose, you have to use two single quotes to depict a single quote within a literal string:

```
'Nancy''s House'
```

Double quotes should enclose a column name or alias that contains a special character such as a blank. For example, to use Full Address as the alias in Figure 7.5, enclose it in double quotes:

```
"Full Address"
```

You also use double quotes to place literal strings in a date format within a function. Figure 7.6 demonstrates how to put the string "of " into the date format of the function TO_CHAR using the SERIAL table. Functions and date formats will be described later in this chapter.

Figure 7.6 also demonstrates the ampersand operator (&). You can create variables that change each time you use an SQL*Plus command in which you have included an ampersand. After you embed the variable in the command and run it, you are prompted to

```
Enter value for n:
```

where n is the nth occurrence of the ampersand in the command. Oracle then displays the old clause containing the variable and the

```
SQL> SELECT WHSNO, PRODNO, SERNO, STATDAT,
  2  TO_CHAR(STATDAT, 'fmMonth DDTH" of" YYYY') DAYCHK
  3  FROM SERIAL
  4  WHERE WHSNO=&&1;
Enter value for 1: 3
old    4: WHERE WHSNO=&&1
new    4: WHERE WHSNO=3

  WHSNO PRODNO    SERNO  STATDAT    DAYCHK
------- -------- ------- --------- --------------------
      3 90002005 600004 05-JUL-89 July 5TH of 1989
      3 90002005 600006 06-JUN-89 June 6TH of 1989
```

Figure 7.6: Using variables

new clause containing the value you enter. Enter the SET command:

```
SQL> SET VERIFY OFF
```

and this old/new display does not echo to the screen. Type **SET VER-IFY ON** to reinstitute the echoing. Appendix C contains a complete listing of SET commands.

Figure 7.6 uses &&1 instead of a constant value in the WHERE clause. If you use two ampersands, you will be prompted with ''Enter value for 1:'' only the first time you execute the SELECT in a session. If you use only one ampersand, you will be prompted each time the SELECT runs. You cannot use the ampersand alone; you must use it with some character to differentiate it because you can have more than one in a command:

```
WHERE WHSNO=&1 OR WHSNO=&2
```

If you embed a variable within a string or value, the variable will be concatenated with the literal string or value:

```
SQL> SELECT *
  2  FROM SERIAL
  3  WHERE WHSNO=1&1;
ENTER value for 1: 3
old    3: WHERE WHSNO=1&1
new    3: WHERE WHSNO=13
```

To concatenate a constant value or string onto the end of the variable, precede it with a period (.) like this:

```
SQL> SELECT *
  2  FROM SERIAL
  3  WHERE WHSNO=&1.1;
ENTER value for 1: 3
old   3: WHERE WHSNO=&1.1
new   3: WHERE WHSNO=31
```

You can use the ampersand with the SAVE and GET commands to save your statement to and retrieve your statement from the disk for repeated use.

If you use the SQL*Plus START command instead of the GET and RUN commands, you can specify the value in the command execution statement. For example, if the previous query were stored in the file WHSINFO as WHERE WHSNO = &1 and you wanted to see what SERIAL numbers were at warehouse three, you could execute the following command:

```
SQL> START WHSINFO 3
```

If you omit the value, you are asked to supply it before the command executes.

The last syntax operator, the at character (@), is used to define tables that are linked from a remote database. You use @ to prefix the name of the remote database.

QUERY EXPRESSION OPERATORS

As you'll recall from Chapter 5, the UNION, INTERSECT, and MINUS operators link two SELECT command queries together. Chapter 5 also covered the plus (+) and PRIOR operators.

FUNCTIONS

Functions are special commands that perform computations or processes on a column, literal string constant, value, or group of values. You can use them anywhere an expression or condition is needed within the full SQL*Plus command set. They are typically used in the SELECT, WHERE, GROUP BY, and ORDER BY clauses.

CHARACTER FUNCTIONS

Character functions are used primarily to modify character columns. Table 7.1 lists the character functions provided in Oracle.

Table 7.1: Character Functions

FUNCTION	DESCRIPTION
LOWER	Converts strings to all lowercase
UPPER	Converts strings to all uppercase
INITCAP	Converts strings to capitalized lowercase
LENGTH	Returns the value of the length of a string
INSTR	Returns the column position value of a substring within a string
SUBSTR	Returns a substring within the string
RPAD	Left-justifies strings and fills in characters or blanks on the right end to round strings to a fixed length
LPAD	Right-justifies strings and fills in characters or blanks on the left end to round strings to a fixed length
RTRIM	Trims off characters on the right end to a fixed length defined by a substring
LTRIM	Trims off characters on the left end to a fixed length defined by a substring
SOUNDEX	Converts strings to their phonetic equivalent
TRANSLATE	Translates characters between two character sets
CHR	Converts ASCII values into characters
ASCII	Converts characters into ASCII values
USERENV	Returns user information

Three of the character functions, UPPER, LOWER, and INIT-CAP, convert character formats. For example, Figure 7.7 shows two alternate ways to display CNAME, which is stored in the CUST table in uppercase format.

```
SQL> SELECT  LOWER(CNAME), INITCAP(CNAME)
  2  FROM CUST;

LOWER(CNAME)                            INITCAP(CNAME)
----------------------------------      ----------------------------------
hill, theodore b.                       Hill, Theodore B.
kelleher, brian s.                      Kelleher, Brian S.
bowa, landry                            Bowa, Landry
sutton, tony                            Sutton, Tony
ortgiessen, john                        Ortgiessen, John
schreiber, clint                        Schreiber, Clint
coronado, mario                         Coronado, Mario
vogele, mark                            Vogele, Mark

8 records selected.
```

Figure 7.7: Using LOWER and INITCAP

LOWER converts all uppercase letters to lowercase. INITCAP converts all letters to lowercase except the first letter of each word in the string. If a string is stored in lowercase or initial capital format, UPPER(*char*) forces all upper letters. If you have any doubt about how a column is stored, you can convert your WHERE clause comparison to uppercase by typing

```
WHERE UPPER(CNAME)='NIELSEN, NORMAN'
```

or if you are using a variable and need to use UPPER on both sides of your comparison, you can type

```
WHERE UPPER(CNAME)=UPPER('&1')
```

This is useful because you cannot guarantee that uppercase will always be entered.

Figure 7.8 demonstrates how, by combining several character functions and operators, you can drastically alter the way your data displays.

```
SQL> COLUMN "First Name" FORMAT A30
SQL> COLUMN ADDRESS FORMAT A30
SQL> SELECT LENGTH(CNAME) LENGTH,
  2   SUBSTR(CNAME,INSTR(CNAME,',')+2)||' '||SUBSTR(CNAME,1,INSTR(CNAME,',')-1)
  3   "First Name",
  4   RPAD(CADDR,30)||
  5   RPAD(CCITY||', '||CST||' '||CZIP,30)
  6   "Address"
  7   FROM CUST;

LENGTH First Name                    Address
------ ---------------------------   ------------------------------
    17 THEODORE B. HILL              142 CAMINO WEST
                                     SAN DIEGO, CA 92210

    18 BRIAN S. KELLEHER            14 SOUTH 1ST AVENUE
                                     LA GRANGE, IL 61001

    12 LANDRY BOWA                   315 OUTPOST ROAD
                                     PHILADELPHIA, PA 31313

    12 TONY SUTTON                   1 CAMEL BACK ROAD
                                     PHOENIX, AZ 84001

    16 JOHN ORTGIESSEN               131 MIRAMAR ROAD
                                     SAN DIEGO, CA 91313

    16 CLINT SCHREIBER               131 FORDSON LANE
                                     ST. CHARLES, IL 65220

    15 MARIO CORONADO                99 LA BAMBA LANE
                                     SOLANA BEACH, CA 91331

    12 MARK VOGELE                   13231 IRVINE RANCH ROAD
                                     IRVINE, CA 91313

8 records selected.
```

Figure 7.8: Character string example

In Figure 7.8, several columns are selected from the CUST table. But the CNAME column is rearranged from *last, first* to *first last* and called "FirstName," and the columns making up the address (CADDR, CCITY, CST, and CZIP) are displayed in one column and called "Address."

The first column displayed uses the LENGTH character function, which calculates and displays the length of the CNAME column.

LENGTH is a simple function with the syntax

```
LENGTH(char)
```

where *char* can be any character string, column name, or character function.

The second column function demonstrates the character functions SUBSTR and INSTR. You can combine these two functions to rearrange the CNAME column from *last,first* to *first last* format. First, break the full name into the last name substring and the first name/ middle initial substring using

```
SUBSTR(CNAME,INSTR(CNAME,',')+2)
```

for the last name, and

```
SUBSTR(CNAME,1,INSTR,(CNAME,',')-1)
```

for the first name and initial. Then recombine the two substrings with a space between them using the concatenation operator, as shown here:

```
||' '||
```

To understand this complex example, you need to know the syntax of the SUBSTR and INSTR functions. The SUBSTR function has the following syntax:

```
SUBSTR(char,m[,n])
```

The first value, m, designates at which character column to begin the substring extraction. The second value, n, designates the length of the substring. If nothing is entered for the second value, the substring will extend to the remainder of the string.

Both of the SUBSTR functions use the INSTR function, which has the following general syntax:

```
INSTR(char1,char2[,n[,m]])
```

Char1 is the full string; *char2* is a substring you want to locate within the string; n is an optional value that identifies the starting position for the substring search; and *m* indicates which substring to use if the string contains more than one. The variable *m* gives the column position of the comma in each row value. That value then locates the starting position of the first name and the length of the last name.

In the CUST table in Figure 7.8, the first row of column CNAME is stored as

```
HILL, THEODORE B.
```

In each row, a comma separates the last name and the first name, so you can use the comma to locate the end of the last name and the beginning of the first name two spaces later. Once you define a substring (the comma), you can use INSTR to find out where it occurs in the name. This is necessary because in each row the name is a different length. If you substitute 'HILL, THEODORE B.' for the column name (CNAME) in the first INSTR function, the following is true:

```
INSTR('HILL, THEODORE B.',',')=7
```

If you substitute the solution to that INSTR into the first name substring from line 2 of the query in Figure 7.8, you get

```
SUBSTR('HILL, THEODORE B.',7+2)='THEODORE B.'
```

This means that you want the substring beginning at column 9 in the string 'HILL, THEODORE B.', which is the beginning of the customer's first name. The +2 is added to eliminate the comma and space preceding the first name from the substring. You can omit the third argument for substring length because you want to extract the rest of the string.

In the second substring in row 2 of the query

```
SUBSTR(CNAME,1,INSTR(CNAME,',')-1)
```

you use the INSTR function to define the length of the substring (the third argument) instead of the starting position. This second SUBSTR function contains three arguments (string, substring starting position, and substring length) instead of the two (string, substring starting position) used to extract the first name.

The starting position for the last name is always 1 because the names are stored with the last name first. To find out how long the last name is, use the comma position between the names. For the first row, the following is still true:

```
INSTR('HILL, THEODORE B.',',')=7
```

When you substitute this into the last-name substring you get

```
SUBSTR('HILL, THEODORE B.',1,7-1)
```

which means that you want the substring that starts at the beginning of 'HILL, THEODORE B.' and extends to the comma in position 6.

Then, if you replace the two SUBSTR functions in line 2 of Figure 7.8 with their result for row 1 of the table you get

```
'THEODORE B.'||' '||'HILL'
```

Here you are recombining the strings using two concatenation operators and a blank space string. The alias "First Name" is added to simplify the column heading for this newly created column. To make the heading display correctly, you must add the command

```
COLUMN "First Name" FORMAT A30
```

so that it fits in a thirty-character format.

This is a complex example, but it demonstrates how you can combine SUBSTR and INSTR to address the common problem of changing the way a name is stored.

In the third column, "Address," you used the RPAD character function to force the columns to fill to the desired width. RPAD takes advantage of the wrap function to force multiple line displays by row; its syntax is:

```
RPAD(char1,n[,char2])
```

where *char1* is the subject string, *n* is the fixed length to fill to, and *char2* is the optional string to use as fill characters. If *char2* is not specified, blanks are used.

The second COLUMN command defined the column as 30. You then concatenated the strings: CADDR, CCITY, ',', CST and

CZIP. CADDR, which by definition is 30 characters wide, will be the first line of the column and has its own RPAD function. You combined the remaining columns on one line using one RPAD command and a comma separator in one position.

If you replace RPAD with LPAD, each address will be right-justified:

```
    142 CAMINO WEST
SAN DIEGO, CA 92210
```

You use the character functions RTRIM and LTRIM to trim down strings. The syntax for LTRIM is

```
LTRIM(char,set)
```

where *char* is the subject string and *set* is a set of characters on which the comparison is based. LTRIM is similar in structure to the IN operator where you have to specify the set of values for comparison. Figure 7.9 demonstrates the LTRIM function on the CCITY column of the CUST table.

```
SQL> SELECT CCITY, LTRIM(CCITY,'SLPI') FROM CUST;

CCITY                   LTRIM(CCITY,'SLPI')
--------------------    --------------------
SAN DIEGO               AN DIEGO
LA GRANGE               A GRANGE
PHILADELPHIA            HILADELPHIA
PHOENIX                 HOENIX
SAN DIEGO               AN DIEGO
ST. CHARLES             T. CHARLES
SOLANA BEACH            OLANA BEACH
IRVINE                  RVINE

8 records selected.
```

Figure 7.9: Using LTRIM

With LTRIM, every character in the set is compared to the beginning character in the string without consideration of the order of the set. RTRIM works on the end of the string.

SOUNDEX is a unique character function that lets you query a database using a sounds-like method. If you cannot locate a record with the normal means, try SOUNDEX. This method works well when there has been a misspelling. Figure 7.10 demonstrates its use.

```
SQL> SELECT SOUNDEX(CNAME)SOUND,CNAME,
   2  SOUNDEX(CCITY), SOUNDEX('SANDY EGO'),CCITY
   3  FROM CUST
   4  WHERE SOUNDEX(CCITY)=SOUNDEX('SANDY EGO');

SOUN CNAME                              SOUN SOUN CCITY
---- ------------------------------    ---- ---- ------------------
H433 HILL, THEODORE B.                 S532 S532 SAN DIEGO
0632 ORTGIESSEN, JOHN                  S532 S532 SAN DIEGO
```

Figure 7.10: Using SOUNDEX

The query in Figure 7.10 also lists the values to which the two columns CNAME and CCITY are converted. The sounds ''Sandy Ego'' and ''San Diego'' are both equal to S532. The beginning letter must be identical but, after that, the SOUNDEX function has a surprising ability to identify a match. Both 'Schneider' and 'Snyder' will match with the value S536, and both 'Sandego' and 'San Dieguito' will match the value S532.

CHR and ASCII are complementary character functions. CHR-(*value*) translates an ASCII character into its decimal equivalent. ASCII(*char*) translates the first character of a specified string (a literal or column) into its ASCII decimal equivalent.

Figure 7.11 demonstrates the use and relationship of ASCII and CHR. The second column displays the ASCII value for the first letter of the CCITY column. The third column shows ''S,'' the ASCII letter equal to the decimal value 83. The last column demonstrates the TRANSLATE character function. This function can translate characters strings between the ASCII representation and the EBCDIC representation. TRANSLATE is also useful in the UPDATE command for loading files from one type to the other.

The character function USERENV displays certain user related values. Only four character strings are valid for this function: ENTRYID, SESSIONID, TERMINAL, and LANGUAGE. Figure 7.12 demonstrates USERENV.

```
SQL> SELECT CCITY, ASCII(CCITY),CHR(83),TRANSLATE(CCITY,'ASCII','EBCDIC')
  2  FROM CUST;

CCITY                   ASCII(CCITY) CH TRANSLATE(CCITY,'ASC
-------------------     ------------ -- --------------------
SAN DIEGO                         83 S  BEN DDEGO
LA GRANGE                         76 S  LE GRENGE
PHILADELPHIA                      80 S  PHDLEDELPHDE
PHOENIX                           80 S  PHOENDX
SAN DIEGO                         83 S  BEN DDEGO
ST. CHARLES                       83 S  BT. CHERLEB
SOLANA BEACH                      83 S  BOLENE BEECH
IRVINE                            73 S  DRVDNE
```

Figure 7.11: Using character functions

```
SQL> SELECT CCITY,
  2  USERENV('ENTRYID')ENTRYID,
  3  USERENV('SESSIONID')SESSIONID,
  4  USERENV('TERMINAL')TERMINAL,
  5  USERENV('LANGUAGE')LANGUAGE
  6  FROM CUST;

CCITY                   ENTRYID SESSIONID TER LANGUAGE
-------------------     ------- --------- --- ----------------
SAN DIEGO                    17         1 con ENGLISH
LA GRANGE                    18         1 con ENGLISH
PHILADELPHIA                 19         1 con ENGLISH
PHOENIX                      20         1 con ENGLISH
SAN DIEGO                    21         1 con ENGLISH
ST. CHARLES                  22         1 con ENGLISH
SOLANA BEACH                 23         1 con ENGLISH
IRVINE                       24         1 con ENGLISH

8 records selected.
```

Figure 7.12: Using USERENV

ARITHMETIC FUNCTIONS

The arithmetic functions will be familiar to you if you have used any spreadsheet. Table 7.2 lists the arithmetic functions provided in Oracle.

These functions are generally straightforward. For example, if you use ABS on a column containing negative values, the positive,

Table 7.2: Arithmetic Functions with Syntax

FUNCTION	DESCRIPTION
ABS(n)	Calculates the absolute value of a number
CEIL(n)	The smallest integer $> = n$
FLOOR(n)	The largest integer $< = n$
MOD(m,n)	The remainder of m/n
POWER(m,n)	The value m raised to the nth power
ROUND($n[,m]$)	The value of n rounded to the mth place
SIGN(n)	-1,0,1 depending on the value of n
SQRT(n)	The square root of n
TRUNC($n,[m]$)	The value n truncated to m places

unsigned equivalents are displayed. The CEIL and FLOOR functions let you quickly round up or down to an integer value. The following inputs and results will occur with each:

INPUT	CEIL RESULT	FLOOR RESULT
1.4	2	1
1.8	2	1
1.0	1	1

TRUNC truncates a number to the specified number of decimal places. If no value is specified, the number is truncated to an integer; if the value specified is negative, the truncation continues to the left of the decimal place. The following examples demonstrate the TRUNC function:

TRUNC FUNCTION	RESULT
TRUNC(41.7374,2)	41.73
TRUNC(41.7374,0)	41
TRUNC(41.7374,-1)	40

ROUND is like TRUNC except that it rounds numbers up or down to the specified number of decimal places (including left of the decimal) or to an integer if nothing is specified. ROUND is illustrated in Figure 7.13 along with ABS and MOD.

```
SQL> SELECT COST, QIW, COST/QIW, MOD(COST,QIW),
  2  COST/QIW-ROUND((COST/QIW)-.5)REMAINDER,
  3  ABS((COST/QIW)-ROUND((COST/QIW)-.5))*QIW "Same as MOD"
  4  FROM PROD;


     COST      QIW COST/QIW MOD(COST,QIW) REMAINDER Same as MOD
 -------- -------- -------- ------------- --------- -----------
      300      200      1.5           100        .5         100
      495       35  14.1429             5   .142857           5
      250      450  .555556           250   .555556         250
       20     1200  .016667            20   .016667          20
       30      800    .0375            30     .0375          30
       40      300  .133333            40   .133333          40
       15      200     .075            15      .075          15
       10      100       .1            10        .1          10
       20       20        1             0         0           0

9 records selected.
```

Figure 7.13: Using arithmetic functions

Line three of the SELECT, which appears in the sixth column of the resulting table, shows what it takes to calculate the remainder without using the MOD function. You could accomplish most of what the arithmetic functions do in some other way, but using a function simplifies your statements and speeds up your queries.

POWER raises a value to a power. SQRT calculates the square root of a value. SIGN returns a -1 if the value being checked is less than zero, a 0 if the value equals 0, and a 1 if it is greater than 0.

DATE AND TIME FUNCTIONS

Between functions and date formats, which are discussed later in this chapter, Oracle allows great flexibility in using dates. Table 7.3 lists all of the DATE functions.

Since you can store the time of day as well as the date within a date field, there are functions that refer to both time and date. These DATE and TIME formats are discussed later in this chapter. If you use the default format 'MM-DD-YY', the time will not be displayed.

Table 7.3: Date and Time Functions

FUNCTION	DESCRIPTION
ADD_MONTHS	Adds months to one date to get another
MONTHS_BETWEEN	Number of months between 2 dates
LAST_DAY	The last day of a date's month
NEXT_DAY	Date of next occurrence of a particular day of the week
NEW_TIME	Conversion between time zones
TRUNC	Date with time eliminated

The date function ADD_MONTHS adds a number to a date to get a date. Its syntax is:

```
ADD_MONTHS(date,value)
```

where the value is added to the date specified and a new, calculated date is displayed. You can also add days to a date by saying:

```
DATE+value
```

Because of leap years, however, this method is not as predictable as the ADD_MONTHS function.

The date function MONTHS_BETWEEN subtracts one date from another to get a value. To use this function, simply enter the two dates into the syntax

```
MONTHS_BETWEEN(date1, date2)
```

and the number of months will be calculated. Figure 7.14 shows ADD_MONTHS and MONTHS_BETWEEN.

The third column shows the number of months between the current status date and the original purchase date. The MONTHS_BETWEEN function helps calculate a unit's depreciated value.

```
SQL> SELECT STATDAT, PURDAT, MONTHS_BETWEEN(STATDAT,PURDAT)"Months Between",
  2  ADD_MONTHS(STATDAT,3),LAST_DAY(STATDAT),NEXT_DAY(STATDAT,'MONDAY')
  3  FROM SERIAL
  4  ORDER BY STATDAT;

STATDAT    PURDAT    Months Between  ADD_MONTH LAST_DAY( NEXT_DAY(
---------  ---------  --------------  --------- --------- ---------
01-MAY-89  01-JAN-89               4  01-AUG-89 31-MAY-89 02-MAY-89
01-MAY-89  01-MAY-89               0  01-AUG-89 31-MAY-89 02-MAY-89
06-JUN-89  01-JAN-89         5.16129  06-SEP-89 30-JUN-89 13-JUN-89
15-JUN-89  15-JAN-89               5  15-SEP-89 30-JUN-89 20-JUN-89
15-JUN-89  01-MAR-89         3.45161  15-SEP-89 30-JUN-89 20-JUN-89
15-JUN-89  01-MAY-89         1.45161  15-SEP-89 30-JUN-89 20-JUN-89
01-JUL-89  01-JAN-89               6  01-OCT-89 31-JUL-89 04-JUL-89
03-JUL-89  01-JAN-89         6.06452  03-OCT-89 31-JUL-89 04-JUL-89
03-JUL-89  01-JAN-89         6.06452  03-OCT-89 31-JUL-89 04-JUL-89
05-JUL-89  01-JAN-89         6.12903  05-OCT-89 31-JUL-89 11-JUL-89
06-JUL-89  01-MAR-89         4.16129  06-OCT-89 31-JUL-89 11-JUL-89
06-JUL-89  15-MAR-89         3.70968  06-OCT-89 31-JUL-89 11-JUL-89
12-JUL-89  15-JAN-89         5.90323  12-OCT-89 31-JUL-89 18-JUL-89
12-JUL-89  01-MAY-89         2.35484  12-OCT-89 31-JUL-89 18-JUL-89
12-JUL-89  01-MAR-89         4.35484  12-OCT-89 31-JUL-89 18-JUL-89

15 records selected.
```

Figure 7.14: Date functions example

However you enter the dates, the resulting value will always be the absolute value of the difference. As you can see, partial months are also counted.

In the figure, you add three months to the status date using the ADD_MONTHS function. If the status date is 01-MAY-89

```
ADD_MONTHS(STATDAT,3)
```

would result in 01-AUG-89. Notice that the day of the month is the same in columns one and four. This makes the ADD_MONTHS function useful for offsetting a date by one or more months. If you used STATDAT + 90 instead of ADD_MONTHS(STATDAT,3), the result would be 30-JUL-89 instead of 01-AUG-89 because the number of days in each month differs.

The other two functions shown in Figure 7.14 are LAST_DAY and NEXT_DAY. LAST_DAY returns the value of the last day of the month specified. NEXT_DAY is more complicated. It returns the next date of the day you entered as an argument. Its syntax is:

```
NEXT_DAY(date1,day of week)
```

Suppose you want to schedule your next visit to a consignee whose area you are always in on Mondays. The function:

```
NEXT_DAY(date1,'MONDAY')
```

returns the date of the Monday following the specified date.

The date functions TRUNC and NEW_TIME have more to do with the time portion of the date. When used with a date column, TRUNC will truncate the date from its full format of date and time, to strictly the date. NEW_TIME allows you to convert your display from one time zone to another. Figure 7.15 shows NEW_TIME converting PST to EST.

```
SQL> SELECT STATDAT, TO_CHAR(STATDAT,'MM-DD-YY HH:MI PM') PST,
  2  TO_CHAR(NEW_TIME(STATDAT,'PST','EST'),'MM-DD-YY HH:MI PM') EST
  3  FROM SERIAL
  4  WHERE STATDAT BETWEEN '01-MAY-89' AND '31-MAY-89'
  5  ORDER BY STATDAT;

STATDAT    PST                      EST
--------   ------------------       ------------------
01-MAY-89  05-01-89 12:00 AM        05-01-89 03:00 AM
01-MAY-89  05-01-89 12:00 AM        05-01-89 03:00 AM
```

Figure 7.15: Using NEW_TIME

STATDAT has a default time of 12:00 A.M. Using the conversion function TO_CHAR and date formats, which will be discussed later in this chapter, we demonstrate the three-hour offset by defining the default (stored) time zone as PST (Pacific Standard Time) and the new time zone as EST (Eastern Standard Time, three hours ahead). Table 7.4 contains a complete list of available time zone abbreviations.

The conversions necessary to display time are cumbersome. But if you need to adjust time between several regions, there is no substitute for the time function's flexibility. In addition, with the tools Oracle provide to access remote databases, time differentials become more important.

Table 7.4: Valid Standard Time Zone Abbreviations for NEW_TIME

ABBREVIATION	DESCRIPTION
GMT	Greenwich Mean Time
AST,ADT	Atlantic Standard, Daylight Time
NST	Newfoundland Standard Time
EST,EDT	Eastern Standard, Daylight Time
CST,CDT	Central Standard, Daylight Time
MST,MDT	Mountain Standard, Daylight Time
PST,PDT	Pacific Standard, Daylight Time
YST,YDT	Yukon Standard, Daylight Time
HST,HDT	Hawaiian/Alaska Standard, Daylight Time
BST,BDT	Bering Standard, Daylight Time

GROUP FUNCTIONS

You can only use group functions within the structure of the GROUP BY clause (discussed in Chapter 5). Generally, each function performs a unique calculation on the groupings created by the GROUP BY clause. Table 7.5 lists the group functions.

You can only use some group functions on numeric columns and arithmetic functions. AVG,STDDEV,VARIANCE, and SUM process all of the values in the column for each group specified in the GROUP BY clause and return their defined result. Others, such as MIN and MAX, can return string phrases as well as values. COUNT will also work on either type of column. Figure 7.16 demonstrates the use of these group functions.

In the example, the serial products in the SERIAL table are grouped by part number. A count of the number of rows in each group is done with the COUNT function. The remaining columns use the MONTHS_BETWEEN function, an aging date of 01-AUG-89, and STATDAT to calculate how long each product has been at its current location. As you can see, 90002025 has been the most active product. It has a lower variance, standard deviation, and maximum value.

Table 7.5: Group Functions

FUNCTION	DESCRIPTION
AVG	Average value of each group of a numeric column
STDDEV	Standard deviation of each group of a column
VARIANCE	Variance of each group of a numeric column
SUM	Sums the values by group of a numeric column
COUNT	Number of non-null column values in a group
MAX	Maximum value in a column expression group
MIN	Minimum value in a column expression group

```
SQL> SELECT PRODNO, COUNT(*),
  2        AVG(MONTHS_BETWEEN('01-AUG-89',STATDAT)) AVG,
  3        MIN(MONTHS_BETWEEN('01-AUG-89',STATDAT)) MIN,
  4        MAX(MONTHS_BETWEEN('01-AUG-89',STATDAT)) MAX,
  5     STDDEV(MONTHS_BETWEEN('01-AUG-89',STATDAT)) STDDEV,
  6   VARIANCE(MONTHS_BETWEEN('01-AUG-89',STATDAT)) VARIANCE,
  7   FROM SERIAL
  8   GROUP BY PRODNO;

PRODNO    COUNT(*)      AVG      MIN      MAX  STDDEV  VARIANCE
--------  --------  -------  -------  -------  -------  --------
90002005         8  1.34677  .645161        3  .773953   .599004
90002005         4  .967742  .645161  1.54839  .397704   .158169
90002005         3  1.73118  .645161        3  1.18801  1.41138
```

Figure 7.16: Using group functions

For each function, you can specify either DISTINCT or ALL. If you specify DISTINCT, no repeated values will be considered in the calculation. If you specify ALL or do not specify anything, each value will be included in the calculation.

When you use the GROUP BY function, only the summary group total row will appear in the table. To get the details of the items, you can use SQL*Plus features described in Chapter 5.

MISCELLANEOUS FUNCTIONS

Table 7.6 lists Oracle's six miscellaneous functions.

Table 7.6: Miscellaneous Functions

FUNCTION	DESCRIPTION
DECODE	Translates column values into other codes
NVL	Displays another value if a null value is found
GREATEST	Displays the highest of a list of expressions
LEAST	Displays the lowest of a list of expressions
VSIZE	Displays the Oracle storage size in bytes
DUMP	Displays areas of Oracle's internal storage

The DECODE function has the syntax:

```
DECODE(char, val1, code1, val2, code2, ...default)
```

It translates a set of values in a column into another set of values for display. You can store a code value in a table and use DECODE to display a more descriptive value. Figure 7.17 demonstrates DECODE on the TERR column of the WHS table.

For each value in the TERR column, an associated value is identified in the DECODE function. The default value HOUSE is used for values in the column that are not itemized or are null.

You can use the DECODE function in many ways to customize tables. You can use it with other functions to create caution flags such as reorder points based on low stock levels. In Figure 7.18, a 47-day offset is set up to start a pickup of equipment that is not moving at a location.

```
SQL> SELECT DECODE(TERR,1,'EAST',2,'MIDWEST',3,'WEST','HOUSE') TERRITORY,
  2  TERR, WHSNO, WHSNAME
  3  FROM WHS
  4  ORDER BY TERR, WHSNO;

TERRITORY              TERR   WHSNO WHSNAME
--------------------  ------- ------- --------------------------------
HOUSE                                1 STORE STOCK
EAST                      1          2 MEDICAL PROFESSIONALS, INC
                          1          3 KATSINAS, DR. STEVE
                          1          5 CONDON, DR. TIMOTHY
                          1          7 ST. GEORGE MEDICAL
MIDWEST                   2          4 GOULETTE, DR. RAYMOND
                          2         10 KEARNEY, DR. PATRICK
WEST                      3          6 TORREY PINES MEDICAL
                          3          8 ELECTRO-MED, LTD.
                          3          9 QUINTARD, DR. ROBERT
                          3         11 LIND, DR. JEFF

11 records selected.
```

Figure 7.17: Using DECODE

```
SQL> SELECT
  2  DECODE(SIGN(TO_DATE('01-AUG-89')-(STATDAT+47)),0,'COMING DUE',1,'PICK UP','OK')
  3  "CHECK",
  4  STATDAT, WHSNO
  5  FROM SERIAL
  6  ORDER BY STATDAT;

CHECK        STATDAT     WHSNO
----------  ----------  -------
PICK UP     01-MAY-89        1
            01-MAY-89        1
            06-JUN-89        3
COMING DUE  15-JUN-89       11
            15-JUN-89       11
            15-JUN-89       11
OK          01-JUL-89        1
            03-JUL-89        2
            03-JUL-89        2
            05-JUL-89        3
            06-JUL-89        9
            06-JUL-89        8
            12-JUL-89        5
            12-JUL-89        5
            12-JUL-89        1

15 records selected.
```

Figure 7.18: Using DECODE for caution flags

The codes PICK UP and COMING DUE are defined if an action is to be taken. TO_DATE, SIGN, and DECODE are combined to create this analysis tool.

GREATEST and LEAST are complementary functions; they both have the syntax:

```
function name(expression1, expression2, expression3,...)
```

Each expression is compared and the greatest or least value for each row is displayed within the column. These two functions are used to compare values between columns.

The function NVL is used to display something other than blanks when a null value is discovered in a row. Its syntax is:

```
NVL(x,expression)
```

where *x* is the subject value and *expression* is what to display if *x* is null. If *x* is not null, it will display.

The VSIZE and DUMP functions are for interacting with the physical structures of Oracle's data. VSIZE returns the size in bytes of an expression, as shown in Figure 7.19.

```
SQL> SELECT CNAME, VSIZE(CNAME)
  2  FROM CUST;

CNAME                             VSIZE(CNAME)
------------------------------    ------------
HILL, THEODORE B.                           17
KELLEHER, BRIAN S.                          18
BOWA, LANDRY                                12
SUTTON, TONY                                12
ORTGIESSEN, JOHN                            16
SCHREIBER, CLINT                            16
CORONADO, MARIO                             15
VOGELE, MARK                                12

8 records selected.
```

Figure 7.19: Using VSIZE

The byte count for each value varies with the number of characters in that value. The full width of the column (including blanks) is not stored on disk in a fixed field length format.

DUMP lists the physical contents of a section of the disk. It has the syntax:

```
DUMP(expr[,radix[,start-position[,bytes]]])
```

Figure 7.20 uses DUMP to show the internal format of the first row of the CUST table.

```
SQL> SELECT CNAME, VSIZE(CNAME),
  2  DUMP(CNAME)
  3  FROM CUST
  4  WHERE ROWNUM=1;


CNAME                                 VSIZE(CNAME)
------------------------------------  ------------
DUMP(CNAME)
------------------------------------------------------------------

HILL, THEODORE B.                              17
Typ=1 Len= 17: 72,73,76,76,44,32,84,72,69,79,68,79,82,69,32,66,46
```

Figure 7.20: Using DUMP

The figure shows the first row's type of value, its length, and the ASCII value for each character in the string.

CONVERSION FUNCTIONS

You use conversion functions to change values from one format to another. This can be necessary where inconsistent data types are not allowed, such as in arithmetic functions. You can also use conversion functions to convert data from generic SQL formats to enhanced SQL*Plus formats. Table 7.7 shows the seven conversion functions.

TO_NUMBER(*char*) converts a character string containing a number into a number. You can then use arithmetic functions and operators with that converted character string. If the string has anything but a number in it, the conversion is not allowed.

TO_CHAR(*expr*[*,fmt*]) converts either a date or a value into a character string. If the format is not specified, a character string long enough to accommodate the significant digits of the number is created if you are converting a number. If you are converting a date, a

Table 7.7: Conversion Functions

FUNCTION	DESCRIPTION
TO_NUMBER	Converts dates and strings to numbers
TO_CHAR	Converts numbers and dates to characters
TO_DATE	Converts characters and numbers to dates
CHARTOROWID	Converts characters to a pseudo column ROWID
ROWIDTOCHAR	Converts a ROWID to a character
HEXTORAW	Converts a hex value to a raw value
RAWTOHEX	Converts a raw value to a hex value

string of the form DD-MMM-YY is created. Formats will be discussed in detail in the next section.

TO_DATE(*expr*[,*fmt*]) converts an expression, either a number or a character string, into a date format. If you enter a character without a format, it must be of the form DD-MMM-YY. You cannot use a number without defining a format, and the number has to make sense for that format. For example, if you specify MM as the format, the number has to be from 1 to 12. Date formats will be discussed in detail in the next section.

Use CHARTOROWID(*char*) and ROWIDTOCHAR(*char*) to convert back and forth between character format and the unique format of the ROWID pseudo column. ROWID is an 18-character long description of the row of a table. To use ROWID in any function, you must convert ROWID to a character string using ROWIDTOCHAR or a datatype mismatch error will occur.

HEXTORAW(*char*) and RAWTOHEX(*char*) are opposing functions for converting between hexidecimal format and the raw storage format used in RAW columns.

FORMAT MODELS

Format models are blueprints for Oracle to use when displaying values, dates, and characters. You can specify format models with the SQL*Plus SET NUMFORMAT, BTITLE, TTITLE, and COLUMN commands, and with the TO_CHAR and TO_DATE functions.

CHARACTER FORMAT MODELS

Although there are detailed format variations for numbers and dates, the only thing that you can vary in a character column is its width. The syntax for doing so is:

```
COLUMN colname FORMAT An
```

where A indicates an alphanumeric format and *n* is the desired column width. If you do not enter a COLUMN command, the column will be as wide as the heading or values require.

NUMERIC FORMAT MODELS

Without a specific format, numbers will display in general format with as many decimal places as necessary. To standardize the display of values, use the SET command

```
SET NUMFORMAT format
```

where *format* is a sample value such as 9999.99. This command applies to all values. If you want a different format for each column, you can use the SQL*Plus COLUMN command. If you use TO_CHAR to convert a value to a character string with a specific format, you will still have to use the COLUMN command to define the width of the character string you have you created.

The fundamental component of a numeric format model is the number nine, which represents one digit of a number. To force numbers to display as integers five digits wide, enter 99999 as the format model. Column widths are based on the number of nines that you define. If a number is larger than the defined format, pound signs (#) appear in place of the value. Decimals are rounded off to fit into the format.

To produce decimals, place a period within the format string where you want the decimal point to appear. The format for a six-digit value to display with two decimal places would be:

999999.99

The column is nine digits wide and values are rounded to two decimal places.

With such large numbers, it's a good idea to add comma separators. To do so, enter

999,999.99

The column will be one character wider because of the comma; it takes a wider column to display a value with commas than one without commas.

You can add three characters to the beginning of the model: the dollar sign ($), the letter B, or the number 0. Inserting an initial zero:

0999,999.99

will zero-fill the column. Adding a B at the beginning:

B999,999.99

makes zero values display as blanks. Adding a dollar sign

$999,999.99

places a dollar sign prefix on each number in the column.

You can add three elements to the end of the digits: MI,PR, and EEEE. Saying

999,999.99MI

gives you a minus sign after the number instead of before it (of course, the value must actually be negative). Adding PR instead of MI, like this

999,999.99PR

makes negative values appear in angled brackets <value>. The last suffix, EEEE, stands for scientific notation and must be entered in the following format:

`9.999EEEE`

The number of decimal places can vary, but there must be four E's.

To scale the numbers up, you can enter a V within the string to indicate the decimal place offset. For example, to display 100 times the stored value, enter

`999999V99`

This would cause the value 300 to appear as 30000. You cannot combine the V character with a decimal point; it requires an integer value.

DATE FORMAT MODELS

Unlike the number and character formats, you cannot define a date format using the COLUMN command. You can only use the TO_CHAR function.

There are hundreds of different date formats. Just about anything is possible. In the TO_CHAR function, a date format is enclosed in single quotes:

`TO_CHAR(STATDAT,'MM-DD-YY')`

In this context, literal strings should be enclosed in double quotes. Special punctuation characters such as dashes, commas, and slashes are an exception to this rule. They can be embedded without quotes and will appear in the result.

Focusing on the Year

The default year format is YY. The following are all of the options for displaying the year:

FORMAT	EXAMPLE
YYYY	1989

YYY	989
YY	89
Y	9
Y,YYY	1,989
YEAR	NINETEEN-EIGHTY-NINE

You can use an S prefix with YYYY and YEAR if you are using dates from the B.C. era. Using SYYYY or SYEAR adds a minus sign to the beginning of the date. You can also include BC, AD, B.C., or A.D. in the year definition.

Make sure you enter spaces where needed. The following two lines demonstrate this:

FORMAT	**EXAMPLE**
YYYYB.C.	1989A.D.
YYYY BC	1989 AD

You can use some of these year formats with the TO_DATE function. The following is a list of right and wrong uses:

EXAMPLE	**VALID?**
TO_DATE(2000,'YYYY')	Yes
TO_DATE(88,'YY')	Yes
TO_DATE(89,'YYYY')	Yes
TO_DATE(1988,'YEAR')	No
TO_DATE(89,'YY BC')	No
TO_DATE(1989,'YYY')	No

Focusing on the Month

The default month format is MMM, a three-letter description of the month. The following are the option formats for entering a month:

FORMAT	**EXAMPLE**	**NOTES**
MMM	AUG	

MM	08	Values from 01 to 12
MONTH	AUGUST	Fixed nine-character width
fmMM	8	fm stands for fill mode

The last format, fmMM, uses the modifier fm (fill mode), which left-justifies the result with no zero fill. Since MONTH is a fixed, nine-character format, it requires fm to eliminate extra spaces. One fm is required each time you switch between fill and non-fill mode.

Focusing on the Day

The default day format is DD, which is a number from 01 to 31. All of the possible day formats are shown below using July 1, 1989 as an example:

FORMAT	EXAMPLE	NOTES
DDD	182	Day of the year from 001 to 365
DD	01	Day of the month from 01 to 31
D	7	Day of the week from 1 to 7
DAY	SATURDAY	Padded to nine characters
DY	SAT	MON, TUE, WED, THU, FRI, SAT, SUN
J	2447709	Julian date from 12/31/4713 BC

You can use the fm prefix with DD and DDD to eliminate the zero fill and with DAY to eliminate the trailing blanks.

Focusing on the Time

Time is not shown unless specified with a format model. Time is broken down into hours, minutes, and seconds. It can be shown in

12- or 24-hour format and can have AM/A.M. and PM/P.M. indicators. The following are sample time formats:

FORMAT	EXAMPLE	NOTES
HH	12	Hour of the day from 1 to 12
HH12	12	Optional method for 12-hour type
HH24	18	24-hour method from 0 to 23
MI	45	Minutes from 00 to 59
SS	45	Seconds from 00 to 59
SSSSS	12433	Seconds from midnight, 0 to 86433

Specialty Dates

You can designate a century, quarter of the year, week of the year, and week of the month. CC designates the century and Q is the quarter. WW is the week of the year (from 1 to 52) and W is the week of the month (from 1 to 5).

You can also use SP to spell out a number from any of the formats and add a TH or ST by using TH. Here are some examples.

FORMAT	EXAMPLE	NOTES
CCTH	20TH	The century indicator
QTH	1ST	The quarter of the year indicator
DDSP	ONE	Day spelled out
DDSPTH	FIRST	The ordinal version of the day

Figure 7.21 shows a fairly comprehensive TO_CHAR conversion using a complex date format model.

Since fm is a toggle, each time you enter it in the format model, the mode is switched. ''Of'' is capitalized because of the INITCAP function. These powerful format model elements support just about everything except roman numerals.

```
SQL> SELECT INITCAP(TO_CHAR(SYSDATE,'fmDDSPthfm "DAY OF "fmMONTH, YEAR'))
  2     TODAY
  3     FROM DUMMY;

TODAY
-------------------------------------------
Fifth Day of June, Nineteen-Eighty-Nine
```

Figure 7.21: Using a date format model

SUMMARY

Operators and functions are the core of the SQL*Plus language. In this chapter, you learned about a wide range of operators, including logical operators, value operators, and query expression operators. You also used a rich variety of functions, including character functions, arithmetic function, date and time functions, group functions, and conversion functions. Finally, you were introduced to format models and learned how to change display formats for characters, numbers, and dates. This chapter also treated dates, explaining how to alter the display format for years, months, days, and times.

Having a thorough understanding of functions and operators will help you to become fluent in other areas of Oracle. And format models are a powerful SQL*Plus feature for query formatting and analysis.

8

UNDERSTANDING SQL*FORMS

SQL*FORMS IS MORE THAN JUST ANOTHER screen generator. To tap its full power, you must open your mind to alternatives in system development. Using nonprocedural methods, you can create highly controlled interfaces with which users can enter, update, and query data in your database. SQL*Forms is a complex application that could easily take up an entire book. This chapter provides an overview of its features and capabilities to help you identify and get started in the areas that will benefit you most directly.

A NEW CONCEPT IN APPLICATIONS DEVELOPMENT

With SQL*Forms, you can create complex structured formats without traditional programming languages. The key programs in most menu-driven systems contain several main data entry form programs, several similar inquiry forms, and some menu-selected reports. To create these form programs with a programming language, you have to open the files, declare variables, load arrays, design and code the screen, define a way to move about the screen, provide some on-line help, update the files after the user completes the form, and then close out the files and move back out to the menu.

SQL*Forms eliminates many steps and uses a more visual approach. With a programming language, the only alternatives the user has are those the programmer creates. With SQL*Forms, the user has complete direct access and flexibility, and your job as the forms designer is to build in limits. The default form for a table allows the user to directly access, query, and update. For tables for your own use, this is probably adequate. For complex, multitable, multipage, general access forms such as invoices, packing slips, or general ledger journal entry forms, you will probably require much more control and structure.

In SQL*Forms, you can break complex forms into blocks. You can only define one primary table in each block, so you usually have at least one block for each primary table your form accesses or updates. For example, if your form is used to enter sales orders you would probably have two blocks: a header block that updates a primary table containing customer information and a line-item block that updates a primary table containing inventory data.

The beauty of SQL*Forms is that it allows you to spend your time on the important components of the form and not on the lower-level tasks of file opening, array definition, and table update. In other words, you can concentrate on what you want, and not on how to get it. With SQL*Forms, you focus on the data elements at the heart of the form and tie your control and logic to those elements.

If you have experience with traditional programming, you will have to readjust your organizational thinking and documentation methods. In SQL*Forms, you attach your logic to an individual data element, a block, or to the form itself within a menu structure rather than storing all of your logic in one source file. For this reason, you must develop new methods for quality assurance, documentation, and debugging. But you can develop a professional looking format that is easy to apply to all of your forms and on all of the platforms that support Oracle.

*WHAT SQL*FORMS CAN DO*

In Chapter 4, you saw the default forms Oracle produces. You can create a form with one record per block or several lines per block. You can also have one record take up more than one line in a multiline environment. You can even have more than one block per screen page.

Through additional customizing efforts, you can access fields from other tables within a block even though only one table is allowed in a block. For example, to create a more user-friendly environment you can easily retrieve a field such as salesman's name when the salesman's number is entered. By simply setting switches, you can force a value to be entered, make a field mandatory, limit the entry to a certain length, or force uppercase. You can quickly check for duplicates in the table, set a range of possible values, set a default value, and display help messages.

You can also link blocks together so that your multiblock forms will update correctly. You can have more than one page of blocks within a form and you can redefine the function keys to move the user through those blocks and pages. With the SQL*Forms macro language, you can create sequences of actions, including conditional actions, using the CASE statement. You can also nest forms within forms and create user exits to other programming languages through which you can pass values for processing and retrieve results to use in the form.

You will find that the default form discussed in Chapter 4 is only the beginning of the development process. In this chapter, we will consider the default form process as the beginning of the development cycle as opposed to the end result. Let's begin the form building process.

*ENTERING SQL*FORMS*

Start by logging on to the main window of this application. SQL*Forms is separate from SQL*Plus, so you will need to call up a different program from the operating system prompt. As you will see later, however, your main database will be updated by your actions in SQL*Forms. The syntax for logging on to SQL*Forms from your system prompt is

```
SQLFORMS (formname) (userid/password)
```

If you do not specify your user ID and password, you will be prompted for them. If you do not enter your form name, you will begin at the CHOOSE FORM window, where you should enter your form name. Otherwise, you will begin at the CHOOSE BLOCK window, which is the next level down in the menu system. To learn the forms process, you will create a complex inventory movement form called MOVE. To begin, type

```
SQLFORMS userid/password
```

substituting your user ID and password. The screen in Figure 8.1 will appear.

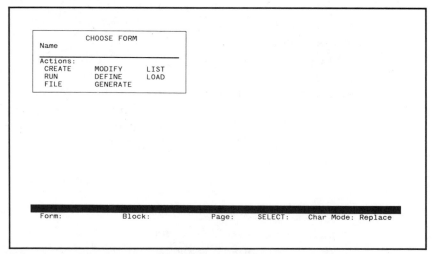

Figure 8.1: The CHOOSE FORM window

In the top half of the screen is the CHOOSE FORM window in which you enter the form name. At the bottom, a bar separates the status line from the rest of the screen. If you had the Char Mode set to Insert instead of Replace in this example, any text you entered would be inserted into the established text instead of writing over it.

Although the rest of the status indicators are blank, they will display key information as you move through the windows. They will describe what Form and Block you are editing and which page of the form you are on. SELECT will tell you whether you have 0, 1, or 2 items or a block (B) selected for some action such as modifying a field or drawing a box.

LEARNING THE FUNCTION KEYS

To use SQL*Forms effectively, you must become thoroughly familiar with its function keys. This may take some time because in SQL*Forms the same key performs different tasks depending on whether you are developing a form, running a form, or using macro commands. To make things easy, concentrate on the developer's function keys listed in Table 8.1 for now. Later in this chapter you'll learn the function keys for macro commands and running forms. By then you'll already be familiar with the developer's function keys. At any time during the forms design process, you can review the developer's function keys on-line by pressing Help (F1 on the AT).

The key that you will use most often is F2, for making selections. A less-used function that will help you immensely at this point is the Print option (in Professional Oracle, this is the Shift-F8 key combination). You can use Print at any point while developing or running a form. Print is especially important if you cannot do a Shift-PrtSc on your terminal to print a screen. When you select Print, Oracle prints the contents of your screen either to a file or directly to the system printer. If you are using Professional Oracle, you may get unpredictable results if you send your screen directly to the printer from SQL*Forms. Instead, print your screen to a file, and then use the DOS PRINT command to print that file after you have exited from SQL*Forms. Try this with the help screen to create a list of the function keys.

THE FORM LEVEL

The CHOOSE FORM window is for taking form level actions. Your choices at this level are:

CREATE	Create a new form
MODIFY	Modify an existing form

Table 8.1: SQL*Forms Developer's Function Keys

SQL*FORMS ACTION	IBM KEY NAME
Accept	F10
Clear Field	Ctrl-End
Create Field	F3
Cut	F5, Shift-F5
Define	F4
Delete Backward	Backspace
Delete Character	Del
Down	↓
Draw Box or Line	F7
Exit or Cancel	Esc or Shift-F10
Help (Show Function Keys)	F1
Insert or Replace	Ins
Left	←
Next Field	Tab, Enter, Crtl-→
Paste	F6
Previous Field	Shift-Tab, Crtl-←
Print	Shift-F8
Redisplay Screen	Shift-F9
Resize Field	Shift-F4
Right	→
Run-Options Window	F9
Select	F2
Select Block	Shift-F2
Undo	F8
Up	↑

LIST	Select a form from a list of your forms
RUN	Run the form
DEFINE	Define form-level triggers and comments
LOAD	Load a new form from your database
FILE	Maintain your form storage activity
GENERATE	Generate the form (similar to compiling)

You must move the cursor to the desired option; you cannot type in a selection.

There are several ways to move the cursor around the window. Oracle is implemented on many different systems with different keyboard configurations. For this reason, there is a generic set of key names, which may be assigned to different keys for each implementation. The generic term for the key used to move through the window is the Next Field key. On the IBM keyboard both Enter and Tab operate as Next Field keys. You can move through the window by pressing Enter as many times as necessary to cycle through the window from top to bottom and back to the top again until you reach the desired choice. Alternately, you can press Tab, Shift-Tab, Ctrl-→, and Ctrl-← to move between the choices, because Tab and Ctrl-→ are defined as Next Field keys and Shift-Tab and Ctrl-← are defined as Previous Field keys. You can also use the arrow keys to move directly to the selection you want, but the cursor must be positioned correctly (one space to the left of the first letter in your selection).

Once you have moved the cursor to your choice, in this case CREATE, you must select it. Since Enter serves used as a Next Field key, you have to use another key to make your selection. With Professional Oracle, use the F2 key for this purpose. The other options do not recognize a new form until it is created. After you create a form, you can move back to the main CHOOSE Form window to DEFINE, GENERATE, and FILE it.

THE BLOCK LEVEL

The second window that appears is the CHOOSE BLOCK window shown in Figure 8.2.

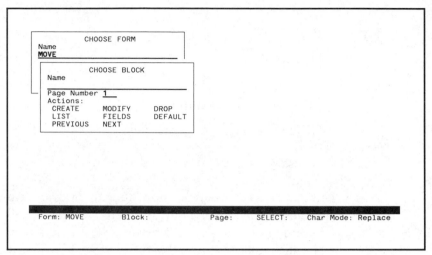

Figure 8.2: The CHOOSE BLOCK window

At this level, your choices are:

CREATE	Create a new block
MODIFY	Modify an existing block
DROP	Drop a specified block
LIST	List the blocks in the form
FIELDS	List the fields in the specified block
DEFAULT	Create a default form
NEXT	Select the next block in the form
PREVIOUS	Select a previous block in the form

The first two choices take you into the full-screen editing feature. LIST, PREVIOUS, and NEXT are ways to select a block to use. FIELDS lists the fields available in the form, but it is a documenting feature from which you cannot select or maintain a field.

To select any choice you must enter a block name. Since you can have only one table per block, you should use a table name as the block name. The only exception is if you create a block that does not specifically refer to a table.

The second option is the Page Number. Because forms can have many pages, you can specify which page this block will appear on. The default page number is 1, but you can enter other page numbers. If you enter page 0, the block will not appear on screen but you can define uses for it.

To create a form, select either DEFAULT or CREATE. It is simplest to start with a default form, even though you will probably modify many of the fields later. This is like laying out all the parts before you assemble something; it sets up your fields for later manipulation and forces you to review each one.

Once you select DEFAULT, the DEFAULT BLOCK window appears, as in Figure 8.3.

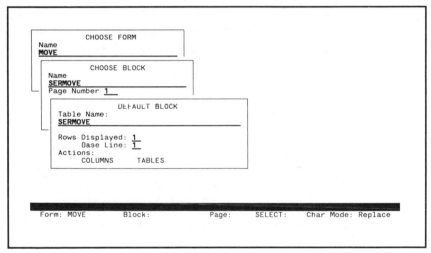

Figure 8.3: The DEFAULT BLOCK window

The block name you entered in the previous window carries forward because Oracle is expecting the block name to be a table name. As discussed in Chapter 4, you can change the number of rows displayed and the row at which the block will begin. With the COLUMNS and TABLES options, you can select which table you want and the columns that you want to include in the default form. Since you want all of the columns included, you can accept the default definition. Press the Accept key (F10 on the AT), which will also take you back to the CHOOSE BLOCK window.

If you want to recreate this default block, you have to DROP the block first. In Oracle, unlike some systems, you cannot change your mind after choosing DROP; the selected block is just eliminated. For this reason, use DROP with caution.

In the equipment tracking example, there will be two main blocks in MOVE: SERMOVE and MOVEITEM. The SERMOVE block is at the top of the form and contains data relating to the overall equipment movement. The MOVEITEM block contains information relating to each piece of equipment moved. This block appears second and has several rows displayed at once.

To create the default form for the MOVEITEM block, enter the new block name in the name line (MOVEITEM) and select DEFAULT to get the default window. You must change the number of rows displayed to six, but can change it later if you want more or fewer rows. Notice that the base line is adjusted to reflect the first default form you have created. The default processor automatically fits the next block in the area on the screen below SERMOVE. Once this is done, press Accept (F10) and return to the CHOOSE BLOCK screen by pressing Esc.

Although you can select the form-related DEFINE function from the CHOOSE FORM window, you cannot select the block-related DEFINE from the CHOOSE BLOCK window. To define block-level processes, you must select MODIFY from the CHOOSE BLOCK window to enter the screen painter, SQL*Forms' full-screen editor. You can then define the block using the DEFINE function by first pressing select BLOCK (Shift-F2) and then DEFINE (F4).

CUSTOMIZING WITH THE FULL-SCREEN EDITOR

You do all of your block level customization in the screen painter. Here you can design the text and manipulate the fields in your form. Before entering the painter, you must select one of the blocks in your form on the name line. Once you are in the painter, you see an entire page of the form but can only modify the fields and the block that you entered on the CHOOSE BLOCK window. However, you can modify any of the text on your form. To modify the first block, enter SERMOVE on the name line in the CHOOSE BLOCK window and select MODIFY. After you create the two default blocks, the screen should look like Figure 8.4, which shows the default positions of all the fields and the block names centered above their related fields.

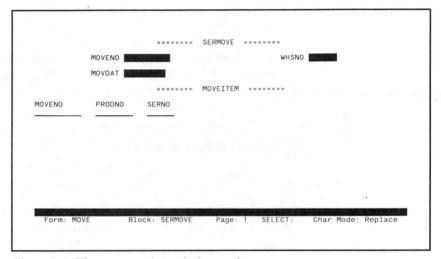

Figure 8.4: The screen painter design environment

DESIGNING A COMPLEX FORM

Before you begin customizing your form, you should do some overall design. In this example, you will use the first block to update the SERMOVE table, which includes all the fields listed in Figure 8.4. The second block is the equipment movement details, which you will link to the SERMOVE table. More than one piece of equipment is allowed for each ticket. This is similar to a variety of header-detail relationships such as those for the sales order, the purchase order, and the invoice.

You will have to update the SERIAL table with the new location of the unit, which will involve a SQL UPDATE statement embedded in the form. Alternately, you could make the SERIAL table the main table of the detail block and update the MOVEITEM table with a SQL statement.

The WHS and PROD tables will also be used in this form to validate the warehouse and product numbers entered and to return and display name verifications to improve user-friendliness.

You can easily modify the actual field and screen layout in the screen editor, so you can do some design work as you develop these forms.

USING THE SCREEN PAINTER

The screen painter is the canvas on which you create your form. It allows you to modify the text, add text boxes, move fields around, create fields, and redefine options. As in the window system, Next Field (Tab, Ctrl-→, or Enter) and Previous Field (Shift-Tab or Ctrl-←) move the cursor between the fields. The screen is fully addressable with the arrow keys. Moving past the right end of the screen makes the cursor appear on the left side in column one. Pressing ← takes you back to the right side of the screen.

Tailoring the Text

To demonstrate Oracle's text tailoring capabilities, we changed some text on the screen. When the default form is created, fields are placed on the screen with field names next to them. If more than one record is displayed, as in the MOVEITEM block, the field names are placed above the fields. The Ins key is most important when changing the text. Figure 8.5 shows the screen after the field descriptors were modified.

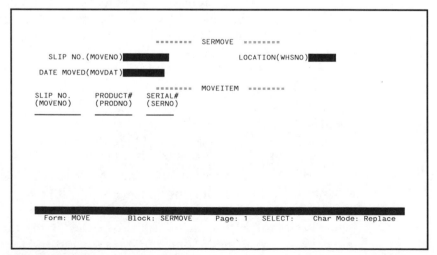

Figure 8.5: Example of text tailoring

The original field names and the inserted block titles were retained in our example, but you can omit them. The text is separate from the fields; if you DROP a block at the CHOOSE BLOCK window, the text from the block remains on the screen.

In Insert mode, text is inserted at the cursor, moving the rest of the characters on the line to the right. In Replace mode, the old text is overwritten by the new. To delete a character, use the Del key. To delete to the left, use the Backspace key.

Selecting Box Frames

With the editor, you can use the Select function key to highlight areas with drawn boxes. To select the area to be enclosed in a box, move the cursor to the upper-left corner of the screen. Then press Select (F2) once. The Select status at the bottom of the screen will change to one item selected (this indicates the upper-left corner of the box). Now move the cursor down to the row below the MOVDAT field. Press ← once to move the cursor to the right side of the screen in the same row. Pressing Select (F1 or Home) again causes the status line to change to two points selected. To draw the box, press the Draw Box/Line function key (F7 on an AT). If the two points you select are aligned horizontally or vertically, you will get a line instead of a box.

If you do not like the box, press the Undo function key (F8) to undo it. Occasionally, while doing something else, you may damage the box. To fix it, you can undo what you did and redraw the box, or you can use the Alt-ASCII value method to make repairs.

In the AT implementation, the complete set of extended ASCII characters is available. Simply press the Alt key and use the numeric pad to enter the value of the character you want. For example, the ASCII equivalents for the box characters are as follows:

KEY COMBINATION	CHARACTER DESCRIPTION	CHARACTER
Alt-218	Upper-left corner	┌
Alt-191	Upper-right corner	┐
Alt-196	Horizontal line	─
Alt-192	Lower-left corner	└

| Alt-217 | Lower-right corner | ⌐ |
| Alt-179 | Vertical line | | |

Cutting and Pasting

Suppose that you want to switch the two fields WHSNO and MOVDAT. You can move MOVDAT to a neutral area, move WHSNO to where MOVDAT was in row 6, and then move MOV-DAT to row 4 where WHSNO was. This rearranging gives you room to display the warehouse name and type to the right of the WHSNO field.

To move MOVDAT to a neutral area, move the cursor to the first letter of DATE MOVED and press Select. This defines the beginning of the area to be moved. Moving the cursor to the right end of the MOVDAT field and pressing Select again defines the entire section. Press the Cut key (F5) to make the section disappear from sight until you are ready to paste it back in. Now move the cursor somewhere out of the way, press the Paste key (F6), and the text and field reappear. Repeat the process for the WHSNO field to move it down to MOVDAT's previous location, and again to move the MOV-DAT section to WHSNO's old location in row 4.

You can also move a multiple-row section of the screen. For example, suppose you want to move the second block down a row and to the right two spaces to make room for a box around it. Because this is a different block, you must leave the screen painter and select the other block. If you try to move the range with the other block's fields in it without leaving the screen painter, you will get the error message shown in Figure 8.6.

To move from the screen painter back to the CHOOSE BLOCK window, press Accept (F10) or Exit/Cancel (Esc). To change the other block, either move down to Next to window select MOVE-ITEM or move up and type it in. Then select MODIFY and return to the screen painter. Although the screen will look similar, the fields from the other block are now highlighted in reverse video and you are manipulating the other block.

To move the block, move the cursor down and select the upper-left corner of the range at row 8, column 1 and the lower-right corner in row 11 and just past the column of the right end of the MOVEITEM title. Press Cut (F5) and the entire block disappears. Move the cursor

Figure 8.6: Cut and paste error message

to the new upper-left corner in column 3 of row 9 and press Paste (F6) to retrieve the block. It is easy to lose your Cut range if you press the wrong combination of keys, so be especially careful while you have a range cut out. Now you can highlight the second block with a box that leaves room for the six rows of values to be entered.

MODIFYING FIELDS

Using function keys, you can move, resize, and redefine a field. You have moved the MOVENO key field. If you also want to shorten it, move the cursor to the left end of the field, press Select, move to the right end, and press Select again. Now the field is selected. By the way, if you press Select in the middle of the field, error IAD-0007 will state that "You can't select partial field. Field is split across selected." To define a new size, move the cursor to the left four spaces to make the field six spaces wide. Then press Resize Field (Shift-F4) once to adjust the displayed field length.

The DEFINE FIELD Window

To create a new field, you first have to select it. For example, to add a field called WHSNAME in the SERMOVE block two spaces to the right of WHSNO, press F10 to go to the CHOOSE BLOCK menu and select PREVIOUS to make SERMOVE the active block. Then select MODIFY to return to the screen pointer. Position the cursor where you want the new field to begin, and press Select (F2). Now move the cursor 30 spaces to the right to define the default width of the new field and press Select again. To create the field, press Create Field (F3). The DEFINE FIELD window will appear on the screen, as shown in Figure 8.7.

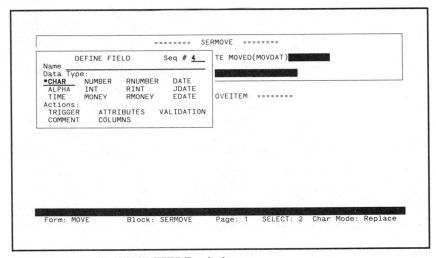

Figure 8.7: The DEFINE FIELD window

Much of the power of SQL*Forms resides in the DEFINE FIELD window. The Seq # in the upper-right corner represents the position of the current field in the block. WHSNAME is the fourth field in the block. By changing this number, you can control the field order. We reversed the two fields MOVDAT and WHSNO. However, if their sequence numbers are not also changed, the operator will still move to WHSNO and then MOVDAT when moving through the block. Enter the new name in the Name line. In this case, it is WHSNAME, a column from the WHS table.

The next section has 12 possible data types from which you can choose. There are six numeric formats, four time and date formats, and two character formats. The value formats RNUMBER, RINT, and RMONEY right-justify the value in the field. You should be careful with these formats. If the displayed size of a field is less than its defined size, the number does not appear to be there until you scroll through the field. Make sure that the lengths associated with the field match, or that users are aware of the storage structures.

The SPECIFY ATTRIBUTES Window

Following the Data Types section is the Actions section. The first action, TRIGGER, taps an elaborate tool that will be discussed in the next section. With COMMENT, you can enter comments about the field. With COLUMNS, you can select the field name from a list of the table-block's columns. Selecting ATTRIBUTES causes the window shown in Figure 8.8 to appear.

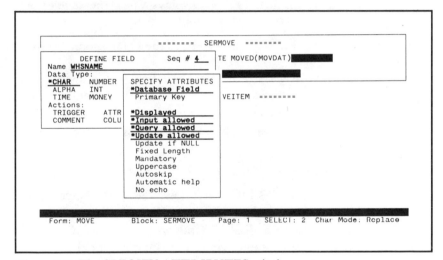

Figure 8.8: The SPECIFY ATTRIBUTES window

In the SPECIFY ATTRIBUTES window, you can select (switch on) and deselect (switch off) attributes of fields that you are creating or modifying. The attributes marked with an asterisk are already selected. The field is assumed to be a database field that you want to display and for which inputs, queries, and updates on queries are allowed. If you switch off Input allowed, Update Allowed is also switched off. If you switch off Displayed, the field value is not shown on the form and you can use the field as an internal processing variable.

In addition, you can define the field as a primary key column in the table and activate or deactivate seven additional characteristics:

ATTRIBUTE	EXPLANATION
Update if NULL	Updates only if query value is null
Fixed length	Forces a fixed length response
Mandatory	Requires a value to be entered
Uppercase	Converts all letters to uppercase
Autoskip	Moves automatically to next field when current field is fully updated
Automatic help	Displays a help message on arrival to the field
No echo	Hides the value (good for password)

WHSNAME is not a database field so it is switched off. It will be displayed on the form, but since only information for validating the number value will be entered, only Displayed need remain selected. Press Accept (F10) to leave this window.

The SPECIFY VALIDATION Window

The VALIDATION window, the next choice on the DEFINE FIELD block, is shown in Figure 8.9. On the screen, it partially covers the DEFINE FIELD window.

In the first blank, you can adjust the field and query lengths. Although its not used for this field, the Copy From option is very helpful. For example, notice that the MOVENO is located in both blocks. To update the MOVENO field in the second block with the value entered into MOVENO in the SERMOVE block, simply enter the block (SERMOVE) and the field (MOVENO) in those two blanks and the value from the first block will update the value in the second block. You can also enter a default value for the field and a low and high range of values.

You can use the List of Values option to allow the user to see a list of possible values from a table. SPECIFY VALIDATION is not a validation mechanism; it is initiated only when you press List Field Values when running the form. Validation is actually done with an

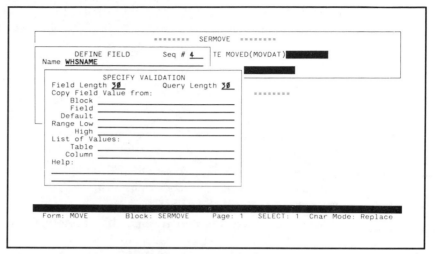

Figure 8.9: The SPECIFY VALIDATION window

SQL statement entered as a Trigger step section, or, with a primary key field, by setting a flag in the Define Block Options window.

You can also enter a help message that will appear to users when they press Help or automatically if the setting is switched on in the SPECIFY ATTRIBUTES window. When you are finished with the DEFINE FIELD section, press Accept (F10) until you return to the main screen painter section.

In SERMOVE, MOVENO has to be set to the primary key value. To do this, switch on Primary Key in the SPECIFY ATTRIBUTES window for MOVENO. In the MOVEITEM block, MOVENO, PRODNO, and SERNO are a concatenated key so switch on Primary Key in the SPECIFY ATTRIBUTES window for each of these fields. Other added fields for this form are:

BLOCK	FIELD	DESCRIPTION
SERMOVE	TYPE	Warehouse type of the warehouse entered
MOVEITEM	STATUS	Prior status of the equipment from the SERIAL table

MOVEITEM	OLD LOC#	Prior location of the equipment
MOVEITEM	LOCATION NAME	Prior location name
MOVEITEM	LAST MOVED	Date moved to the old location

MODIFYING BLOCKS

You can also modify the block definition from the screen painter. In the example, you defined fields as primary keys. To validate the keys that you have defined in each block, select the DEFINE BLOCK window. To do so, make sure nothing is selected and then press the Select Block key (Shift-F2). The select status will indicate B for Block. Then press Define (F4). The window will appear as shown in Figure 8.10.

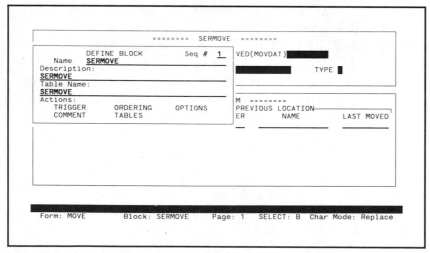

Figure 8.10: The DEFINE BLOCK window

As with fields, you can reorder the sequence of blocks by changing the Seq # value. You can also enter a description and change the table name for this block. Under Actions, you can enter the trigger system to enter a block-level trigger for this block (triggers are covered later in this chapter), alter the ordering of values when a query is done on this block, enter comments pertaining to this block, select the table used in this block by choosing from the tables available, and, finally, specify several block options.

In this case, you want to modify the block options. Selecting this action will bring up the window shown in Figure 8.11.

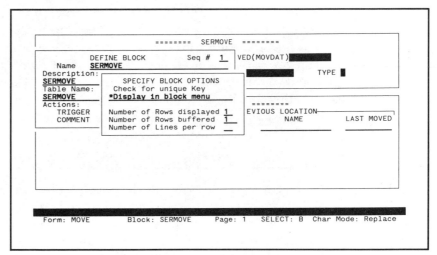

Figure 8.11: The SPECIFY BLOCK OPTIONS window

The first option is the one you want to toggle on. Press Select and this block will check to see if the value entered in a primary key field is already in the table before adding a record to the database. However, this check occurs when users try to insert into or update the table at the end of the form, and not necessarily when they leave the field. To have the check done immediately upon exit from the field, you must create a SQL trigger statement (discussed later in the chapter).

In addition, you can switch off Display in block menu. You can also change the number of rows displayed, the number of rows buffered in memory, and the number of lines taken up by one row of a table.

THE SPECIFY RUN OPTIONS WINDOW

The other window you can access from the screen painter changes the runtime options. To access it, press the Run-Options Window key (F9).

There are several run options. You can make the form run in less memory or more quickly by switching on and off Buffer records with file, Optimize SQL processing, and Optimize transaction processing. Selecting Display window causes a window of the blocks to appear on the first screen when you run a form. You select which block to go to from the window instead of using the block sequence numbers you assigned during the design process.

In addition, you can turn the computer's bell or sound mechanism off by selecting Quiet mode. Runtime statistics will appear at the end of the run program if you select Statistics. And finally, selecting Debug puts you in debug mode. Each step will then display a message indicating that it has executed.

PROGRAMMING WITH TRIGGERS

Triggers are at the heart of SQL*Forms. They give you the strength of a programming language without the effort of learning one. Instead of writing an entire program to create a form, you just have to insert SQL or SQL*Forms commands where they are specifically needed. If some special logic or action is required upon entry to the form, you can create a form-level trigger containing SQL or SQL*Forms commands to handle it. If you need to add some logic as a block of values are committed to the database, you can create a block-level trigger. And when you need field-level logic to verify an entry, to return another value based on an entry, or to conditionally execute another process based on an entry, you can create one or more field-level triggers to handle it.

The languages used in these trigger routines—the SQL data access language and the SQL*Forms macro language—are both high-level languages. The SQL language has data definition, data manipulation, data retrieval, and access control commands specifically tailored to the data management logic required in a form. With the SQL*Forms macro language, which is similar to a spreadsheet macro language, you can conditionally execute macro subroutines, create user exits to other environments, string together function key functions, and manage variables.

TRIGGER TYPES

There are many different kinds of triggers. The TRIGGER option appears throughout this chapter, on the DEFINE FORM window, the DEFINE BLOCK window, and the DEFINE FIELD window. At higher levels, there are more triggers available. At the block level, you can use the triggers available at the field level plus additional block-level triggers. At the form level, you can define all of the triggers available at the field and block level plus two added form-level triggers.

These level-type triggers are what you might call situational or event triggers; a particular situation or event causes them to execute. Some execute as the user enters the form, block, or field. Others execute as the cursor leaves the form, block, or field. Some are triggered by a keystroke such as a pending COMMIT or Query. Since you can enter more than one trigger step for each of these trigger types, you can enter more than one action in a single trigger.

Key Triggers

At all three levels—field, block, and form—you can create a key trigger. A key trigger is a special SQL*Forms macro language trigger for redefining function keys. For example, you can redefine the Previous Block key to perform another process instead, such as Next Block.

Table 8.2 contains a list of all of the macro key commands, the specific key equivalent from the Professional Oracle implementation, a redefine flag (RF), and a description of the function.

Much of your power and control over forms comes from the function keys. You may not want all of this power available to all users. For example, you do not want users to be able to move randomly through the form once a COMMIT is done, and you do not want them to execute a COMMIT until your design will support it. You can disable these function keys by redefining them to the neutral function (NOOP). You must think about controlling as well as creating flexibility.

An asterisk in the RF column in Table 8.2 indicates a key that cannot be redefined. These keys are mostly cursor movement keys and Help keys. Because they cannot be redefined, they do not appear in the key-trigger lists in the CHOOSE TRIGGER window.

Table 8.2: The macro key commands

Macro Key	At-Key	RF	Description
CHRMODE	Ins or Del	*	Insert or replace
CLRBLK	Shift-F5		Clear block
CLRFLD	Ctrl-End	*	Clear field
CLRFRM	Shift-F7		Clear form or rollback
CLRREC	Shift-F4		Clear record
COMMIT	F10		Commit transaction
CQUERY	Shift-F2		Count query hits
CREREC	F6		Create record
DELBACK	Backspace	*	Delete character to the left
DELCHR	Del	*	Delete character
DELREC	Shift-F6		Delete record
DERROR	Shift-F1	*	Display error
DKEYS	F1	*	Show function keys
DOWN	↓		Down a record, same field
DUPFLD	F3		Duplicate field
DUPREC	F4		Duplicate record
ENTER	↵		Next field
ENTQRY	F7		Enter query
EXEQRY	F8		Execute query
EXIT	Shift-F10 or Esc		Exit or cancel form
HELP	F2		Help
LISTVAL	F9		List field values
MENU	F5		Block menu
MOVLEFT	←	*	Cursor left

* Cannot redefine this key

Table 8.2: The macro key commands (continued)

MACRO KEY	AT-KEY	RF	DESCRIPTION
MOVRIGHT	→	*	Cursor right
NXTBLK	PgDn		Next block
NXTFLD	↵ (Enter)		Next field
NXTKEY	Shift-F3		Next primary key field
NXTREC	↓		Next record
NXTSET	Ctrl-PgDn		Next set of records
OTHERS	(None)		All keys except defined key-triggers
PRINT	Shift-F8		Print
PRVBLK	PgUp		Previous block
PRVFLD	Shift-Tab or Ctrl-←		Previous field
PRVREC	↑		Previous record
REDISP	Shift-F9	*	Redisplay the screen
SCRDOWN	Ctrl ↓		Scroll down a set of records
SCRLEFT	Ctrl ←	*	Scroll left a set of records
SCRRIGHT	Ctrl →	*	Scroll right a set of records
SCRUP	Ctrl ↑		Scroll up a set of records
STARTUP	(None)		Auto startup execution
UP	↑		Previous record, same field
UPDREC	(None)		Enable update record (Block mode)

* Cannot redefine this key

Field-Level Triggers

Three types of triggers are available at the field level: pre-field, post-field, and post-change triggers. These triggers have to be attached to each individual field.

A pre-field trigger executes every time the cursor enters the field. Conversely, a post-field trigger executes each time the cursor leaves the field. The post-change trigger executes only after a change is made to the field.

Block-Level Triggers

There are several additional trigger types at the block level: query triggers, commit triggers, record triggers, and pre-block and post-block triggers.

For each of these, you can create a trigger to execute as it begins or concludes the process. The commit triggers are the most elaborate. You can create pre- and post-triggers to execute with a delete, insert, or update process. These triggers execute once for each record modified within the block.

Form-Level Triggers

In addition, there are pre-form and post-form triggers available at the form level. Pre-form triggers execute at the beginning of the form, before the window appears if you have specified that run option.

User-Named Triggers

If you have a generic trigger for several situations, you can name it and then use it in other triggers instead of repeating the logic each time you need it. To call a named trigger, enter

```
#EXEMACRO EXETRG (trigger-name)
```

The processor will search for and execute that trigger.

THE CHOOSE TRIGGER WINDOW

To experiment with the CHOOSE TRIGGER window, you will enter a simple trigger to verify that the slip number is not already in the table. Make sure you are modifying the SERMOVE block in the screen painter area. Move the cursor to the MOVENO field. Press the Define key (F4) and the DEFINE FIELD window will appear. Tab to the TRIGGER action and Select it using F2. Your screen should look like Figure 8.12, which shows the CHOOSE TRIGGER window. First, decide what type of trigger you need. In this case, the trigger should execute each time the field is changed, so you want a post-change trigger. You can either enter this name in the Name space or select it from a list by using the TYPES action from the window. The latter is the preferred method because you will select from a list of valid trigger types for this level and will get the exact spelling. To do this, Tab down and select TYPES. The screen should look like Figure 8.13.

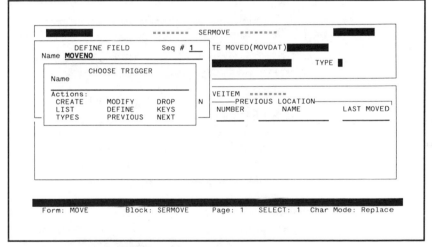

Figure 8.12: The CHOOSE TRIGGER window

As you can see, the three valid trigger types are pre-field, post-field, and post-change. Tab down to post-change and press the Select key (F2). This highlights the selection and places an asterisk to its left. Press Accept (F10); you will return to the CHOOSE TRIGGER window and the trigger type will appear on the Name line.

The two other actions available on this screen are LIST and KEYS. LIST allows you to see and select a trigger you have already created for this field. You would use this when you select a trigger to modify. The KEYS action is similar to the TYPES action. Instead of trigger types, however, it lists all the available key triggers that can be redefined.

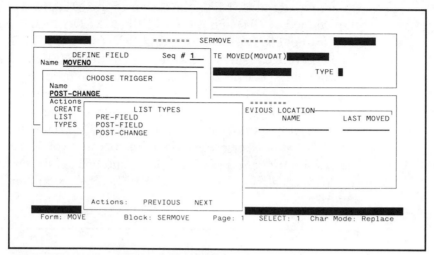

Figure 8.13: The LIST TYPES window

The TRIGGER STEP Window

Steps are individual actions in a multi-action trigger. You use the TRIGGER STEP window to enter your trigger text. To get to this window, select CREATE on the TRIGGER window. The screen will look like Figure 8.14.

```
          ======== SERMOVE ========
       DEFINE FIELD        Seq # 1     TE MOVED(MOVDAT)
 Name MOVENO
                                                          TYPE
       CHOOSE TRIGGER
  Name
  POST-CHANGE

 Seq # 1            TRIGGER STEP          Label _____


 _____
 Message if trigger step fails:
 Actions:
   CREATE        COPY          DROP         ATTRIBUTES    COMMENT
   FORWARD       BACKWARD      PREV STEP    NEXT STEP


 Form: MOVE       Block: SERMOVE     Page: 1   SELECT: 1  Char Mode: Replace
```

Figure 8.14: The TRIGGER STEP window

The first item, Seq #, is 1 in this case. If you have a series of trigger steps, however, you can reorder them by changing their sequence numbers. The second item is the Label, where you must enter a name if you intend to call this trigger step from some other trigger step. Otherwise, you need not enter a label.

Finally, there is the area in which you enter commands. For this example, enter the following SQL command:

```
SELECT 'x'
FROM SERMOVE
WHERE SERMOVE.MOVENO=:SERMOVE.MOVENO
```

Notice first that no semicolon appears at the end of this statement. In SQL*Forms, the semicolon is reserved for use with macro commands and should not be used to end SQL statements. The colon after the equal sign in the WHERE clause is used to prefix a form field ID. Moreover, because no column value result will be used, you use the literal 'x' in the SELECT clause. In English, the statement means

> Look for a row in the SERMOVE table that has a move number equal to the number in this field.

Now move down to the ''Message if trigger step fails'' line and enter

```
Duplicate ticket number
```

This message will be displayed if the trigger fails.

But this statement seems reversed. The SELECT logic will return a row (be true) if there is a row already in the table with this value. However, you want this SELECT statement to fail if there is a row already in the table. To understand this logic, select ATTRIBUTES from the list of actions at the bottom of the window.

The *TRIGGER STEP ATTRIBUTES* Window

The TRIGGER STEP ATTRIBUTES window has four option switches. The first, Abort trigger when step fails, is toggled on by default. If the step fails, the trigger aborts and an error message is displayed. The second one is off by default. However, you can switch it on in order to reverse the logic, in which case a failure will be treated as a success. Figure 8.15 shows this window with the Reverse return code switched on.

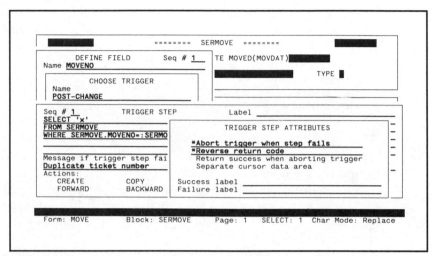

Figure 8.15: The TRIGGER STEP ATTRIBUTES window

In this instance, if a row is found (the SELECT succeeds), it is considered a failure and the trigger causes the message entered on the previous window under ''Message if trigger fails'' to display.

In the bottom two lines, Success label and Failure label, you can enter a label name for another trigger step. By labeling each trigger step, you can conditionally execute other triggers based on the result. In pseudo programming terms, you could say

```
IF succeeds THEN
    GO success label
  ELSE
    GO failure label
END
```

Other Trigger Step Actions

Pressing Accept (F10) moves you back to the TRIGGER STEP window. As you can see, there are several other actions available in this window. Once you are done with the current step, you can choose CREATE and move to the next step window. You can move between steps by selecting PREV STEP and NEXT STEP. You can also enter COMMENTS relating to this step, COPY this step to the next step, and DROP this step.

The FORWARD and BACKWARD actions are used with the trigger step text lines. If your trigger logic takes up more rows than you have available in this window, select FORWARD and more space will be made available. BACKWARD moves you back to the previous lines.

VALID TRIGGER STEP STATEMENTS

There are three types of valid statements you can enter into a trigger step. With certain limitations, you can enter standard SQL commands, SQL*Forms extended macro commands, and user exits.

SQL Standard Statements

In the example, you used a SQL statement checking for a duplicate value. In post-change triggers such as this, you can enter a SELECT clause but not the other SQL commands. You can only use SQL data modification commands (INSERT, UPDATE, and DELETE) in Commit triggers. Moreover, you cannot use SQL-*Plus commands in trigger step statements.

The colon (:) and the INTO clause are two components that you can use with SQL statements only in SQL*Forms. (If you prefer to be compatible with SQL*Plus, you can substitute the ampersand [&] for the colon.) As you saw in the example, the colon indicates to the processor that the value is a block field, which Oracle considers a variable within a SQL statement, as opposed to a table column in the WHERE clause. The INTO clause stores column values into the corresponding fields. In a trigger attached to the SER-MOVE.WHSNO field, you used the following Select statement:

```
SELECT  WHSNAME, WHSTYPE
INTO    SERMOVE.WHSNAME, SERMOVE.WHSSTATUS
FROM    WHS
WHERE   WHS.WHSNO=:SERMOVE.WHSNO
```

In this case, the values are retrieved and displayed to the right of the WHSNO so that you can get visual verification that the correct warehouse number has been entered. Since only variables can be used with INTO, you do not need to differentiate them with the colon prefix.

SQL*Forms Macro Commands

You can also enter SQL*Forms macro commands into the trigger text. These must begin with the command

```
#EXEMACRO macro command;
```

and must end with a semicolon. You can also string several macro commands together within a trigger step, as long as each is terminated with a semicolon.

In the MOVE form, you attached a key name macro KEY-NXTFLD to the WHSNO field in the SERMOVE block. The trigger syntax for this was

```
#EXEMACRO NXTBLK;
```

This is the last field in the SERMOVE block. When you press the Next Field key (Tab, Ctrl-→, or Enter), instead of moving back to the first field in the same block, the Next Field key is redefined to execute the Next Block function (Shift-F2) and the cursor moves to PRODNO in the MOVEITEM block. At the end of each row in the MOVEITEM block, you created a key macro to move the cursor to the next record instead of back to the first field in the same record— you redefined NXTFLD (Tab, Ctrl-→, or Enter) to equal NXTREC (↓). You can use these key macros to gain control over users' movements in the form.

There are other macro commands besides key macros. Several macro commands are used to permanently alter the user's path through the form. They are

COMMAND SYNTAX	DESCRIPTION
GOBLK *blockname*;	Process the named block
GOFLD *fieldname*;	Process the named field
GOSTEP *steplabel*;	Process the named step
NEWFRM *formname*;	Run the named form instead of the current form

Additional macro commands temporarily interrupt the form's flow to do something else and then return to the original spot in the form. They are

COMMAND SYNTAX	DESCRIPTION
CALL *formname*;	Execute another form
CALLQRY *formname*;	Execute another query form
EXETRG *triggername*;	Execute the named trigger
EXEQRY [FOR UPDATE] [ALL];	Execute a query
ENTQRY [FOR UPDATE] [ALL];	Execute a query after it is entered

These macro commands terminate a process:

COMMAND SYNTAX	DESCRIPTION
ENDSTEP [FAIL] MESSAGE *message*];	Ends a trigger step and returns a result code
ENDTRIG [FAIL] [MESSAGE *message*];	Ends a trigger completely and returns a result code
NULL;	Results in no action

Also, there are several macro commands for handling special actions related to interfacing with the user.

COMMAND SYNTAX	DESCRIPTION
SYNCHRONIZE;	Matches the internal system with the screen
BELL;	Rings the system bell
PAUSE;	Pauses processing until the user responds
CALLINPUT;	Pauses processing a function key macro until Exit/Cancel is pressed

MESSAGE *message*; Displays the message entered on the message line

HOST *systemcommand* [NOSCREEN]; Enters an operating system command with or without onscreen feedback

The following macro commands manipulate and define system variables, global variables, field values and constants:

COMMAND SYNTAX	DESCRIPTION
COPY *source* INTO *destination*;	Copies a source value into the destination
DEFAULT *value* INTO *variable*;	Defines a default value for a variable
ERASE *global.variablename*;	Erases a global variable

The final macro command is the CASE command for conditionally executing several alternative commands based on the result of a condition test. The syntax for the CASE macro command is

```
#EXEMACRO CASE
```

With this command you could create a master forms menu for selecting other menus to execute. Or you could create several tailored blocks that execute in response to user input. An example might be a doctor's office in which a special medical coverage input block runs only if the patient has that type of coverage. You could also create conditional on-line help screens. The possibilities are limitless.

Three macro commands—HOST, ERASE, and COPY—can also be entered with the following syntax:

```
#HOST system command [NOSCREEN]
#COPY source [INTO] destination
#ERASE global.variablename
```

When used in this way (notice no semicolon), these commands are referred to as SQL*Forms commands instead of macro commands, but they function essentially the same as their macro counterparts.

The system variables mentioned in this discussion refer to a set of ten values that track key data about a form. They are all referred to with the prefix SYSTEM (for example, SYSTEM.CUR-SOR_BLOCK) and indicate in which form, block, field, and value the cursor is currently positioned. The only other system variable, SYSTEM.MESSAGE_LEVEL, defines which level of error messages appear to the user (from 0, which is the highest, through 5, 10, 15, and 20, to 25, which is the lowest). You can redefine the level with a command like the following:

```
#COPY 10 INTO SYSTEM.MESSAGE_LEVEL
```

This command redefines the level of error messages to 10, limiting error messages to those that occur when the operator makes a procedural error.

User Exits

User exits are programs written in compatible programming languages. There are a variety of compatible program compilers, including ones for C, Cobol, Fortran, PL/I, and Pascal. You need approved compilers that allow use of the SQL precompilers in order to convert SQL statements into the native programming code.

Once you have a user exit debugged and working, you can reference that program in a trigger step using this syntax:

```
#exitname variables/parameters
```

The form will be suspended and this user exit will be executed. The user exit will either succeed, fail, or create a fatal error. Some value must be returned from the exit to indicate whether it was a success or a failure. User exits are discussed in Chapter 13.

GENERATING A FORM

When your form is workable, you should save it, generate it, and try running it. Figure 8.16 shows the MOVE form at a much more advanced stage and ready to be run.

As you can see, several reference fields were added to make the form more friendly, the old status information for each piece of equipment is displayed, and the system date is displayed at the top.

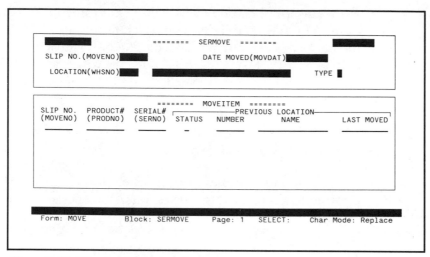

Figure 8.16: The finished example form

Several important triggers tied this form together and updated the tables. The following SQL UPDATE command syntax updates the SERIAL table as each row is inserted into the MOVEITEM table:

```
UPDATE SERIAL
SET    SERIAL.WHSNO=:SERMOVE.WHSNO,
       SERIAL.STATDAT=:SERMOVE.MOVDAT,
       SERIAL.STATUS=:SERMOVE.WHSSTATUS
WHERE  SERIAL.PRODNO||SERIAL.SERNO=
       :MOVEITEM.PRODNO||:MOVEITEM.SERNO
```

To generate this form, move out of the screen painter by pressing Accept (F10) once and then again to move back to the main FORM menu. First, you need to generate the form.

From the FORM window, select GENERATE. This executes the Oracle IAG program. In implementations with memory limitations, you next have to exit SQL*Forms and execute the IAG (Interactive Application Generator) program at the system level by typing

```
IAG formname options
```

If you do not use one of the options, a lengthy dialog will echo on the screen during the generation process. Echoing this to your printer or to a file gives you good documentation of your form. Otherwise, you might want to change the way your form generates by using the -to option to eliminate the echo.

Before you leave SQL*Forms, you have to do something with the form in memory. If you try to leave without saving it or try to load another form, the FILE window appears. Select Save and then exit so that you can generate your form. You can also RENAME your form, DROP it (delete it from storage), DISCARD it (remove it from memory), and save it as another table using SAVE AS.

RUNNING A FORM

Once you have generated your form, you can run it. In some implementations you can run forms from the main CHOOSE FORM window. However, once the design process is completed, you will probably run the form from the operating system prompt.

RUN SYNTAX

The following syntax runs a form from the system level:

```
RUNFORM options formname username/password
```

The form will load into memory and come up on your screen. You can also run a form from within SQL*Plus using the RUNFORM command if your system has enough available memory.

RUN OPTIONS

To see the options for running a form, shown in Figure 8.17, type **RUNFORM ?**; then decide which options you require. Some options complement one another or can be grouped for special purposes. For example, the -e option saves your keystrokes to a special file that you specify. Then, in a later session, the -r option will read those keystrokes in sequence to recreate what you typed previously.

If system efficiency is important, you can use -a, -b, -t, and -s to alter processing characteristics and display statistical reports. The -c, -q, and -m options vary the presentation of the form. The -m option

```
Format is: runform [option]... formname [userid/password].
Options are:
   -a         Don't use array processing.
   -b         Buffer records with temporary file instead of memory.
   -c crt     Use this crt definition.
   -d         Display debugging messages.
   -e file    Echo input keystrokes to file.
   -i file    Write display log file and send to terminal.
   -l         Display screen to specify logon name.
   -m         Display forms menu on startup and clear-form.
   -o         Don't optimize field level SQL statement processing.
   -q         Quiet mode.
   -r file    Read keystrokes from file instead of terminal.
   -s         Print statistics after run.
   -t         Don't optimize transaction mode processing.
   -w file    Write display log file and not terminal.

C:\>
```

Figure 8.17: The RUNFORMS option

tells the RUNFORM processor to display a menu of blocks on the form so that you can move directly to the one you want, as shown in Figure 8.18.

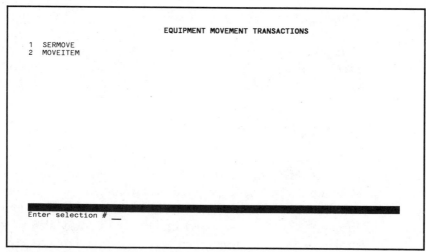

```
                    EQUIPMENT MOVEMENT TRANSACTIONS

      1   SERMOVE
      2   MOVEITEM
```

```
Enter selection # __
```

Figure 8.18: The MENU option in action

You can also access this menu from the form by pressing the Block Menu key (F5).

KEYBOARD FUNCTION

Several powerful key functions are available when you are running forms. Table 8.3 lists the functions available with the keys used in Professional Oracle.

Table 8.3: The RUNFORM environment function key list

FUNCTION	KEYSTROKE(S)
Block Menu	F5
Clear Block	Shift-F5
Clear Field	Ctrl-End
Clear Form/Rollback	Shift-F7
Clear Record	Shift-F4
Commit Transaction	F10
Count Query Hits	Shift-F2
Create Record	F6
Delete Backward	Backspace
Delete Character	Del
Delete Record	Shift-F6
Display Error	Shift-F1
Duplicate Field	F3
Duplicate Record	F4
Enter Query	F7
Execute Query	F8
Exit or Cancel	Shift-F10 or Esc
Help	F2
Insert or Replace	Ins
Left	←
List Field Values	F9
Next Block	PgDn
Next Field	↵ (Enter), Tab, or Ctrl →

Table 8.3: The RUNFORM environment function key list (continued)

FUNCTION	KEYSTROKE(S)
Next Primary Key Fld	Shift-F3
Next Record	↓
Next Set of Records	Ctrl-PgDn
Previous Block	PgUp
Previous Field	Ctrl ← or Shift-Tab
Previous Record	↑
Print	Shift-F8
Redisplay Page	Shift-F9
Right	→
Show Function Keys	F1

The Print key (Shift-F8) pulls up print options. You can print the current page of the form, the entire form, the help screen, or the function keys list to file and to the system printer.

List Field Values (F9) works with the table and column entered in the SPECIFY VALIDATION window under the List of Values section. When you press this key, Oracle looks up the table and column you entered when creating the form, cycles through the column values one at a time, and inserts them into the field on the screen. After each value, you are prompted to

```
Press    Enter to retrieve next value, Shift-F10 to stop
```

For multiple-row blocks, Duplicate Field (F3) and Duplicate Record (F4) come in handy. If you press one of these keys, a value or set of values identical to the last value or values you entered in the previous field or record will be duplicated in the current field or record. Pressing Help (F1) displays either the default help text

```
Enter value for: (fieldname)
```

or custom help text on the block menu bar across the bottom of the screen.

QUERYING

Three keys deal with queries: Enter Query (F7), Execute Query (F8), and Count Query Hits (Shift-F2). If you leave the Query Allowed Attribute on for a field, you can enter a query that will retrieve the values you request. You can use the two wild card characters, % and _, in the SQL LIKE function as a query, and also use variables within it.

You can also use the relational operators = , ! = , >, <, > = , < = , and BETWEEN to retrieve values. To retrieve a value you might enter

`>200`

in the field space. To use these operators on a character string, precede the string with a pound sign (#), like this:

`#BETWEEN'GARCIA'AND'LENNON'`

Figure 8.19 shows a simple query being entered on the WHS form after the Enter Query key was pressed. You can enter a query based on any or all of the fields in the record.

```
                       ========  WHS  ========

   WHSNO    WHSNAME                               TERR    W
   >1       _____             ____    _
   ____     _____             ____    _
   ____     _____             ____    _
   ____     _____             ____    _
   ____     _____             ____    _
   ____     _____             ____    _
   ____     _____             ____    _



   Enter a query.  Press F2 to execute, F3 to cancel.
            Char Mode: Replace   Page 1      ENTER QUERY      Count: *Ø
```

Figure 8.19: A query example

DOCUMENTING A FORM

When you generate the form, first a file with an .INP suffix is generated. The IAG reads this .INP file and creates a .FRM file, which is required to run the application. When a new .FRM file is generated, previous version of the .FRM file on your disk are renamed with a .OLD suffix.

The form data is not stored in these .INP and .FRM files. Like all Oracle data, forms are stored in a series of tables in the database. Forms tables begin with the letters IAP. If you have DBA privileges, you can list these tables by logging on to SQL*Plus and typing

```
SQL> SELECT TNAME
2   FROM TAB
3   WHERE TNAME LIKE 'IAP%'
4   ORDER BY TNAME;
```

Oracle responds by listing the forms storage tables:

```
TNAME
----------------------------
IAPAPP
IAPBLK
IAPCOMMENT
IAPFLD
IAPMAP
IAPSQLTXT
IAPTRG
IAPTRIGGER

8 records selected.
```

Each table stores a different part of your forms definitions. Table 8.4 lists the contents of these tables.

The column definitions for these tables are stored in the SYS-COLUMNS table. With some carefully devised queries, you can create your own customized forms documentation based on the IAP tables.

Table 8.4: The forms storage tables

TABLE	DESCRIPTION
IAPAPP	Overall form descriptions
IAPBLK	Block descriptions
IAPCOMMENT	All levels of comments
IAPFLD	Field descriptions
IAPMAP	The screen text
IAPSQLTXT	The SQL related text
IAPTRG	Trigger step descriptions
IAPTRIGGER	Trigger descriptions

SUMMARY

The application environment SQL*Forms provides is a good alternative to traditional computer programming methods. Using the full-screen painter, the event triggers, which incorporate the SQL data access language, the SQL*Forms macro language, and user exits that interface to other traditional programming languages, you can create complex but user-friendly database access forms.

Much of the time you spend programming forms in traditional languages goes to basic chores like creating cursor movements. With SQL*Forms, cursor movements, commit and rollback functions, powerful querying, and specialty features are available without any added programming on your part.

9

USING
SQL*REPORTWRITER

WITH THE INTRODUCTION OF SQL*REPORT-
Writer, Oracle now offers a complete line of nonprocedural
report tools for their RDBMS. You can use this menu-driven,
easy-to-learn program for many of your report programming
requirements. You use a visually-oriented approach to format
the text on the page, and in many cases, detecting errors during
this design phase will shorten your development cycle and save
you much paper. With SQL*ReportWriter, you can incorporate more than one query into the report. You can mix vertical
and horizontal layouts to combine one or more reports on a
page. And because this report writer uses SQL commands to
define the query, you can use your new knowledge of SQL.

SQL is best used for relating data and for extracting data
from a database in a consistent and dependable manner. It is
not designed to create production reports. With SQL*Plus
Oracle provides several non-ANSI standard commands that
allow you to create some reports. You can use the BTITLE and
TTITLE commands to add page headers and footers. You can
redefine your column headers and formats using the
COLUMN command. You can add subtotals and totals within
groups with the BREAK and COMPUTE commands. And
you can store all of these commands in program files to be run
from the operating system prompt. However, only the simplest
report formats are possible, nor is the interactive style of
SQL*Plus the best for developing these reports.

SQL*ReportWriter gives you the best of both worlds. You
get the SQL language's ability to extract the data for your
report. In addition, you get a fill in-the-blank report layout program for restructuring the data and merging it into the many
different report formats that users require.

TYPES OF REPORTS

SQL*ReportWriter handles many different types of reports, from mailing labels to cross tabulations. To run mailing labels, just enter your selection in one screen, position the text in this manner

```
&NAME
&ADDRESS
&CITY, &ST &ZIP
```

in another screen, and eliminate the field labels in another screen. Also, you can change the print direction to Across/Down or Down/Across to print several labels across the page.

You can do cross-tabulation reports with SQL*ReportWriter. With the crosstab style, you have to enter three groups. One will display horizontally across the top of the page, one will display down the page, and a third will display at the intersection of each of the rows and columns. Time frames are one of the typical horizontal groups. You can match periods in a year to sales by month, purchase dollars by month, daily unit material transfers, and so on.

You can do Master-Detail reports. You can add a summary to that structure for the Master-Detail-Summary format. You can display data in a matrix format, and you can create merged output such as collection or acknowledgment letters.

LOGGING ON TO SQL*REPORTWRITER

As with SQL*Forms and SQL*Calc, you log directly onto the SQL*ReportWriter program to design and run your reports. From the operating system prompt, use the following syntax:

```
SQLREP username/password
```

substituting your own username and password. The screen shown in Figure 9.1 will appear.

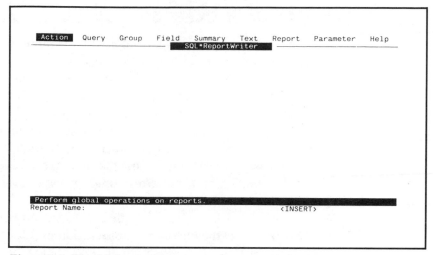

Figure 9.1: The Main menu

You can override the user ID and several other default characteristics when logging on to SQL∗ReportWriter. As with other Oracle programs, you can type

`SQLREP ?`

to see a complete listing of the syntax. PARAMFORM = NO turns off the report parameters screen before the report is run, and DESTYPE, DESNAME, and DESFORMAT specify the output device characteristics. With CMDFILE = filename, you can specify your version of the parameters so that you only have to define them once.

For production applications, you can use the operating system accessible program included with SQL∗ReportWriter instead of the SQL∗ReportWriter menus. RUNREP will run a predefined report directly, bypassing the menu system. GENREP will generate a runfile report for use with RUNREP. DUMPREP and LOADREP can offload and onload report definitions to and from ASCII files for porting to other systems. And finally, you can use PRINTDEF to create a printer definition file.

THE MAIN MENU

Unlike SQL*Forms, the SQL*ReportWriter menus offer only one main layer of choices. The options available across the top of the screen, the Menu Line, remain visible most of the time you are in the program. Below the Menu Line is the Title Line, which indicates what area of the program you are in. The area from the Title Line to the Help Bar at the bottom of the screen is where the input screens appear when you select one of the menu choices. In the Help Bar, an instructive message appears and below that the Status Line provides additional information on keyboard settings and so on.

Oracle has narrowed report development to nine functions. Action, the only choice besides Help that leads to another menu of choices, includes all of the file maintenance activities. Query is where you enter your SQL statements to define the data for the report. In Group, you break down the report fields into logical sections for combining more than one query and report on a page. With Field, you redefine and maintain the fields in the report. You enter calculations and totals in Summary. You manipulate the text for the headers, the footers, and the body of the report in the Text screens. You define overall report parameters such as page length and width using Report, and you define runtime parameters in Parameters. And at any time, you can use the Help program to help you develop reports.

MOVING AROUND THE MENU SYSTEM

SQL*ReportWriter is almost entirely menu-driven. You can even select many of the valid choices on fields from a set of choices. Any time you are at a field that has a predefined set of acceptable answers, the message <LOV> will appear in the Status Line, indicating that you can view the list of answers by pressing the List of Values function key. Other helpful keys are the Zoom key for switching into full-screen editing mode, the Help key for accessing the context sensitive Help system from SQL*ReportWriter, and the Browser key and Window key for previewing a report before printing. These functions are all demonstrated in this chapter.

HELP

Select Help from the main menu or by pressing the Help key from anywhere within SQL*ReportWriter to access a menu-driven help system pertaining to the area of Oracle you are in.

This help system is really an on-line manual with several tools for getting the help you need. Pressing the Help key brings up context sensitive directions relating to the field or screen you are in. You'll also see a menu of choices from which you can select other topics, access an index and table of contents of topics, see a relevant example, or see an error listing. Since the Help system is so extensive, you can use the Bookmark key to mark your current position so that you can quickly return to that spot.

To exit Help, select Quit and you will return to the screen from which you invoked Help.

ACTION

Action is usually the first thing you select from the main menu. This opens the window of options shown in Figure 9.2.

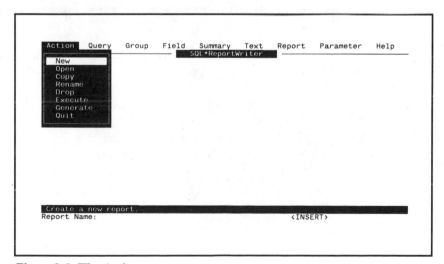

Figure 9.2: The Action menu

You can Open, Copy, Rename, Drop (delete from the database), or Execute (generate and execute if necessary) an existing report. If you make a change to the report but do not want to execute it, you can generate a new .REP file (which stores a compressed copy of the report definition on disk) so that it can be reexecuted. And, last but not least, you use this menu to quit the program.

To create a new report, you should first select New from the Action menu to name the report. A window will appear over the menu prompting you to enter the new report name, as shown in Figure 9.3.

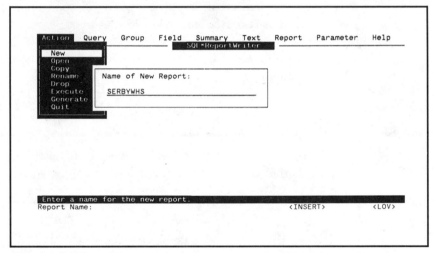

Figure 9.3: The report name prompt

When naming a report, you should use a descriptive name such as SERBYWHS, which has been entered in Figure 9.3. If you have many reports, it is less effective to create descriptive names. You should prepare an easily understood naming structure in which you group your reports by type. The name can be up to 30 characters long, but in MS-DOS you can use only 8 characters for the .REP file stored on your disk. After entering the report name, press Enter to record it.

To learn how to create the SERBYWHS report, you will use the WHS table and SERIAL tables from prior chapters to determine the location of each piece of equipment and how long it has been there. If you did this in SQL*Plus, the result might look like Figure 9.4.

```
Sun Sep 17                                                              page    1
                              Equipment Listing by WHS

    WHSNO WHSNAME                        TERR W PRODNO   SERNO  ST STATDAT      AGE
    ------ -----------------------       ------- - -------- ------ -- --------- ----
        1 STORE STOCK                          W 90006005 100001 W  01-MAY-88   139

        3 KATSINAS, DR. STEVE            1    C 90002005 600006 C  06-JUN-88   103

        4 GOULETTE, DR. RAYMOND          2    C 90002005 600001 C  04-JUL-88    75
                                              90002005 600002 C  04-JUL-88    75
                                              90002005 600003 C  04-JUL-88    75
                                              90002025 800002 C  04-JUL-88    75
                                              90002025 800003 C  04-JUL-88    75

        5 CONDON, DR. TIMOTHY            1    C 90002005 600008 C  12-JUL-88    67
                                              90006005 100003 C  12-JUL-88    67

        8 ELECTRO-MED, LTD.              3    C 90002025 800004 C  06-JUL-88    73

       10 KEARNEY, DR. PATRICK           2    C 90002005 600004 C  26-JUN-88    83
                                              90002005 600005 C  26-JUN-88    83

       11 LIND, DR. JEFF                 3    C 90002005 600007 C  15-JUN-88    94
                                              90002025 800001 C  26-JUN-88    83
                                              90006005 100002 C  15-JUN-88    94


    15 records selected.
```

Figure 9.4: Report created with SQL*Plus

With SQL*ReportWriter, you can easily rearrange these joined tables to create the report shown in Figure 9.5.

This report has two components. On the left side is some data from the WHS table. The right side is a list of serialized equipment at each WHS location.

The data shown in Figure 9.4 is complete. However, you will see how much easier it is to transform the SQL query shown in Figure 9.4 into the production level report shown in Figure 9.5 using the full-screen style of SQL*ReportWriter. To return to the main menu, select Quit.

ENTERING THE QUERY

Now you need to add a SQL SELECT statement that will extract the data you need for the report. To do this, select Query to bring up the Query Settings screen shown in Figure 9.6.

```
      Page: 1                Equipment Listing by WHS           Date: 17-SEP-88


                                      Product# Serial# St Moved Date Age
                                      -------- ------- -- ---------- ---
      Location:     1                 90006005 100001  W  01-MAY-88 139
      Name: STORE STOCK                                               ---
      Territory:                      Avg                            139
      Type: W


      Location:     3                 90002005 600006  C  06-JUN-88 103
      Name: KATSINAS, DR. STEVE       90002005 600001  C  04-JUL-88  75
      Territory:     1                90002005 600002  C  04-JUL-88  75
      Type: C                                                        ---
                                      Avg                             84


      Location:     4                 90002005 600003  C  04-JUL-88  75
      Name: GOULETTE, DR. RAYMOND     90002025 800002  C  04-JUL-88  75
      Territory:     2                90002025 800003  C  04-JUL-88  75
      Type: C                         90002005 600008  C  12-JUL-88  67
                                                                     ---
                                      Avg                             73



      Location:     5                 90006005 100003  C  12-JUL-88  67
      Name: CONDON, DR. TIMOTHY       90002025 800004  C  06-JUL-88  73
      Territory:     1                                                ---
      Type: C                         Avg                             70


      Location:     8                 90002005 600004  C  26-JUN-88  83
      Name: ELECTRO-MED, LTD.                                        ---
      Territory:     3                Avg                             83
      Type: C


      Location:    10                 90002005 600005  C  26-JUN-88  83
      Name: KEARNEY, DR. PATRICK      90002005 600007  C  15-JUN-88  94
      Territory:     2                                                ---
      Type: C                         Avg                            139


      Location:    11                 90002025 800001  C  26-JUN-88  83
      Name: LIND, DR. JEFF            90006005 100002  C  15-JUN-88  94
      Territory:     3                                                ---
      Type: C                         Avg                            139


                                                                     ---
                                      Avg                            139
```

Figure 9.5: Report created with SQL*ReportWriter

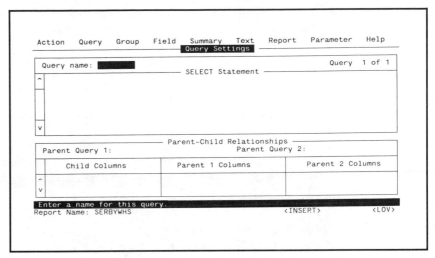

Figure 9.6: The Query Settings screen

You must first enter the name of the Query on this screen. Because you can have up to three queries within a report, you must define a name for each of your queries. The table shown in Figure 9.4 used the following join query:

```
SQL> SELECT WHS.WHSNO, WHSNAME, PRODNO, SERNO, STATUS, STATDAT,
2   SYSDATE-STATDAT AGE
3   FROM SERIAL, WHS
4   WHERE SERIAL.WHSNO=WHS.WHSNO
5   ORDER BY WHS.WHSNO, PRODNO, SERNO;
```

In SQL*ReportWriter, you can easily join two queries and combine more data on the page, so you will enter two separate queries containing a more complete set of columns. For the WHS table (Q _WHS), use

```
SQL> SELECT *
2   FROM WHS
3   WHERE EXISTS
4       (SELECT WHSNO
5        FROM SERIAL
6        WHERE WHS.WHSNO=SERIAL.WHSNO)
7   ORDER BY WHSNO;
```

For the SERIAL table (Q _SERIAL), use

```
SQL> SELECT WHSNO, PRODNO, SERNO, STATUS, STATDAT,
2  SYSDATE-STATDAT AGE
3  FROM SERIAL
4  ORDER BY WHSNO, PRODNO, SERNO;
```

First, enter the WHS query and call it Q _WHS. Type

```
Q_WHS
```

in the Query Name cell and press Next Field to get to the section in which you enter the SELECT statement.

ENTERING THE SELECT STATEMENT

Once in the SELECT statement area, enter the SELECT statement as if you were entering a trigger step in SQL*Forms. Unlike SQL*Plus, you leave off the semicolon because it will be executed later. SELECT is the only SQL command you can enter because this program is strictly for extracting data from the database. You cannot update the database in SQL*ReportWriter.

Although you can only use the SELECT statement, you still have all of Oracle's data extraction power. You can join tables in a query. You can use pseudo columns and all of the format models, functions, and operators described in Chapter 7. Instead of using the SQL*Plus compatible ampersand to define a runtime variable, as discussed in Chapter 5, you use the SQL*Forms compatible colon (:). This is discussed later with the other parameters.

As you have noticed, there is typically more than one way to accomplish the same result with Oracle. With SQL*ReportWriter, you can use a SQL statement or one of SQL*ReportWriter's other features to accomplish the same task. For example, you can join tables using a SELECT statement or by defining a Parent-Child relationship. You can also use a SQL*Plus function or the SQL*ReportWriter formatting features to reformat a column's data. Once you are familiar with the system, you will learn which method works best for you.

You can see nine lines for entering your query, but as the arrows on the left edge of the screen suggest, you can press the ↑ and ↓ keys to scroll up and down through your query statement if you need more room. You can also press the Zoom key to change to a full-screen query editor mode.

The rules for entering a query are the same in SQL*ReportWriter as they are in SQL*Plus. You can enter your query on one or several lines, and you can indent and leave spaces as you please. Remember, you do not need to enter a semicolon at the end of the statement. After you enter your SELECT statement, SQL*ReportWriter checks its syntax and validity. This facilitates debugging because you do not have to wait until you run the report to find out if it is valid.

After you enter the query, if you are in Zoom mode press Next Field to get out of Zoom and to return to the normal Query Settings screen. Zoom is also available in the Text Settings area.

If you have a SELECT statement stored in a file, you can load it in at this point. If this query were stored in a file named PROD.LIS, you could load it by pressing Read File. You will be prompted for the file name to read. In this way, you develop your SQL sentence in SQL*Plus, interactively extracting the data you need. If you then decide to put it into a report format, save it to disk in SQL*Plus by typing

```
SAVE PROD.LIS
```

and you can load it into SQL*ReportWriter.

SQL is a powerful but verbose language: a SQL sentence can quickly turn into something resembling a short story. For this reason, you do not want to reenter a well-defined query once you have it working correctly. Being able to load a query created in SQL*Plus directly into SQL*ReportWriter provides a working link and combines the strengths of the two applications. While creating a report, you might begin by interactively refining the SELECT statement required to get to the data. This is more easily done in SQL*Plus. You can then determine how to best present the data in a report format. This is more easily done in SQL*ReportWriter.

To enter the next query, press Insert Record Below. The counter on the screen increments by 1 (Query 2 of 2). For this query name enter

`Q_SERIAL`

and enter the SELECT statement shown in Figure 9.7.

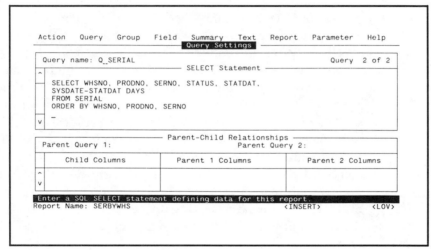

Figure 9.7: Entering the second query

Through the Query Settings screen, you are generating several necessary components for your report. SQL*ReportWriter uses the columns and other SELECT expressions in the query to create fields with the same data type and width (the column name is a default field label). One group for positioning and subtotaling is generated for each query you enter. Default column headings are created as in SQL*Plus, and default group body text is created for positioning the fields on the report.

Because other items are created from the query, deleting a query can affect other areas. If you press Delete Record to delete a query, a window offering these three choices will appear:

- Abort the delete operation
- Delete only this object
- Cascade to related objects

If you select the second choice, your summaries, fields, groups, and other queries change to a status of *Undefined*. Choosing the third choice deletes all related components of this query from your report. Now move on to Parent-Child Relationships by pressing Next Field.

PARENT-CHILD RELATIONSHIPS

If you want something other than the flat table format of SQL-*Plus, it is easier to enter two queries instead of one joined query. Then you can join them using a SQL*ReportWriter Parent-Child Relationship. Each column from your query is defined as a report field. All of the fields from a query are logically related by default into one group for format purposes. As you shall see later in the chapter, you can manipulate, redefine, and regroup these fields in the Field Settings screen and you can reposition your groups on the report page in the Group Settings screen. By entering two queries, you create two groups of columns and take better advantage of the default field and group settings. Otherwise, you will have to make more modifications later in the Field and Group screens.

To use the SQL*ReportWriter Parent-Child linking mechanism, you must create a parent-child relationship between Q _WHS and Q _SERIAL. A parent-child relationship is a one-to-many relationship. In this example, there is only one warehouse location for each piece of equipment, but each location can have many pieces of equipment. The one-to-many/master-detail relationship is shown in Figure 9.8. As you can see, the warehouse number takes on the parent role and the serial numbers take on the child role.

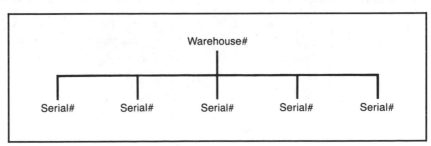

Figure 9.8: The parent-child relationship

In the Parent-Child Relationships screen, enter

```
Q_WHS
```

in the Parent Query 1 field. Then, define the fields in each table on which to base the link, just like the WHERE clause in a joined SELECT statement. Because the key to a table might be two columns combined (a concatenated key), you can select more than one field in the Child Columns section and the Parent 1 Columns section. In this case, however, the key column (field) for both tables is WHSNO, which you can select from the list of available columns in each field.

Although you do not need it for this example, you need the Parent Query 2 field to link this query to both of your other queries. For example, you could create a cross tabulation with a count of serialized equipment by product and warehouse with totals in each direction.

The first query, Q _WHS, included a subquery to select only the warehouses with equipment. Because the parent-child relationship works differently than a join, if you omitted that subquery a row would print out for each record in the warehouse whether or not it had any records in the SERIAL table.

This example requires only one link. After you enter PARTNO into each section, press Accept to go back to the main menu. You only need the query to run the report, since there are defaults for all of the other required report components.

FORMATTING YOUR REPORT

At this point, you have named the report and entered the queries. Next you need to tailor the report output to make it more presentable. You can style the report format by adding report and page headers and footers; changing the column headings, widths, and formats; and modifying the relative positioning of the two groups on the page. This process takes only a little more time and should make the output much more legible.

MODIFYING FIELD SETTINGS

To make the column headings more descriptive, select Field from the main menu. The screen in Figure 9.9 will appear.

```
  Action   Query   Group   Field   Summary   Text   Report   Parameter   Help
                                  Field Settings                          1 of 3

    Field Name          Source Column        Group          Label

  ^ WHSNO               Q_WHS.WHSNO          Q_WHS          WHSNO
    WHSNAME             WHSNAME              Q_WHS          WHSNAME
    TERR                TERR                 Q_WHS          TERR
    WHSTYPE             WHSTYPE              Q_WHS          W
    WHSNO               Q_SERIAL.WHSNO       Q_SERIAL       WHSNO
    PRODNO              PRODNO               Q_SERIAL       PRODNO
    STATUS              STATUS               Q_SERIAL       ST
    STATDAT             STATDAT              Q_SERIAL       STATDAT
    AGE                 AGE                  Q_SERIAL       AGE

  v

   Enter a name for this field.
   Report Name: SERBYWHS                              <INSERT>        <LOV>
```

Figure 9.9: The first Field Settings screen

As you can see in the upper-right corner of the screen, this is only one of three Field Settings screens. You use your cursor control keys to scroll right and left through these three screens of columns. The Field Name column remains on screen, but the rest of the columns will scroll on and off screen. The following is a list of all of the field columns:

COLUMN	DESCRIPTION
Field Name	Name of the field
Source Column	Column from the query
Group	Group in which it is included
Label	Text column label to be used to describe it
Data Type	Column type (NUM, DATE, CHAR) cannot be changed
Field Width	Display width of the field

COLUMN	DESCRIPTION
Display Format	Mask for number or date columns
Relative Position	Position relative to rest of fields in its group
Lines Before	Number of lines preceding the field
Spaces Before	Number of spaces preceding the field
Align	Alignment (left, center, right)
Skip	An x suppresses its display on the report
Repeat	An x causes the field to repeat as a label for each text panel
Function	One of 12 functions that can be performed on a computed value
Reset Group	The group that will reset the calculation to zero

Each column or SELECT expression in your queries automatically appears in this screen. The field names and labels are both defined by default as the column name or alias from the query. A default group name is also defined. Notice in Figure 9.9 that all of the fields in the first query, Q _WHS, are in the group G_WHS by default. The same is true for the second query, Q _SERIAL. These fields are logically grouped together for positioning and summarizing on the report.

When you scroll to the right to Field Settings screen 2 of 3, the screen will look like Figure 9.10.

In this screen, the data type is displayed but you cannot change it. Besides the field width, you can change the display format (similar to the format models discussed in Chapter 4), relative position of the field compared to the previous field, and lines and spaces before the field as it will be displayed on the report. These last three are left blank unless you want to override the default values. With the final three columns, you have to consider the general print direction of the group. For example, Lines Before only makes sense with groups printing Across or Across/Down. The default is zero, meaning that

```
   Action   Query   Group   Field   Summary   Text   Report   Parameter   Help
                                   Field Settings                            2 of 3

         ┌──────────────────┬──────┬──────┬─────────┬────────┬───────┬────────┐
         │                  │Data  │Field │Display  │Relative│Lines  │Spaces  │
         │  Field Name      │Type  │Width │Format   │Position│Before │Before  │
       ^ │ WHSNO            │NUM   │  7   │         │        │       │        │
         │ WHSNAME          │CHAR  │ 3Ø   │         │        │       │        │
         │ TERR             │NUM   │  7   │         │   .    │       │        │
         │ WHSTYPE          │CHAR  │  1   │         │        │       │        │
         │ WHSNO            │NUM   │  7   │         │        │       │        │
         │ PRODNO           │CHAR  │  8   │         │        │       │        │
         │ STATUS           │CHAR  │  1   │         │        │       │        │
         │ STATDAT          │DATE  │  9   │         │        │       │        │
         │ AGE              │NUM   │  3   │         │        │       │        │
         │                  │      │      │         │        │       │        │
       v │                  │      │      │         │        │       │        │
         └──────────────────┴──────┴──────┴─────────┴────────┴───────┴────────┘
   ▓Enter the width of this field in spaces.▓
   Report Name: SERBYWHS                               < INSERT >
```

Figure 9.10: The second Field Settings screen

this field will print on the line immediately below the previous field in the group. If you enter a 1, you will have double spacing. On the other hand, Spaces Before relates only to Down or Down/Across groups. A Down group is like a traditional table, with the columns laid out across the page. Entering a value in it affects how far apart the columns appear across the page.

Scroll to the right to get to the third screen, shown in Figure 9.11.

```
   Action   Query   Group   Field   Summary   Text   Report   Parameter   Help
                                   Field Settings                            3 of 3

         ┌──────────────────┬──────┬──────┬─────────┬─────────────────────────┐
         │                  │      │      │         │    Computed Value        │
         │  Field Name      │Align │Skip  │Repeat   │Function      Reset Group │
       ^ │ WHSNO            │      │      │         │                          │
         │ WHSNAME          │      │      │         │                          │
         │ TERR             │      │      │         │                          │
         │ WHSTYPE          │      │      │         │                          │
         │ WHSNO            │      │      │         │                          │
         │ PRODNO           │      │      │         │                          │
         │ STATUS           │      │      │         │                          │
         │ STATDAT          │      │      │         │                          │
         │ AGE              │      │      │         │                          │
         │                  │      │      │         │                          │
       v │                  │      │      │         │                          │
         └──────────────────┴──────┴──────┴─────────┴─────────────────────────┘
   ▓Choose the justification for this field.▓
   Report Name: SERBYWHS                               < INSERT >          < LOV >
```

Figure 9.11: The third Field Settings screen

You can realign the data in the column to the left, center, or right. If you enter an x in the Skip column in line with a field, that field will not appear on the report. WHSNO occurs twice because it is the link column between the two queries. However, since it only needs to be shown once (in this case with the warehouse information), the WHSNO column in the G_SERIAL group gets an x. In the third field settings column, you can make the field repeat as a label column for each text panel by entering an x in the Repeat column. You need more than one text panel only if your report is more than one page width in size.

CALCULATED FIELDS

You can also add a new field that you did not create in the SELECT statement. If you want this field to be a calculated field, enter the function on which to base the calculation in the Function column. You can add a calculation function such as % Total in this screen instead of adding it in the SELECT statement. If you press List of Values when you are at the Function column, you will see the following list of available functions:

FUNCTION	DESCRIPTION
Sum	Summarizes the column values
Min	Calculates the minimum value from the column
Max	Calculates the maximum value from the column
Count	Counts the number of values included
Avg	Calculates the average value of the list
% Total	Calculates each row as a percent to total
R_Sum	The running sum of values up to that row
R_Min	The running minimum value up to that row
R_Max	The running maximum value up to that row
R_Count	The running count of values up to the row (rank)
R_Avg	The running average of values up to that row
R_% Total	The running percent to total up to that row

The first six functions are called periodic functions. Given a field displaying down in a column of values, a computed field defined with % Total will display what percent the current value is of the total of the values in the column. The percentage column here is an example:

DAILY SALES DOLLARS	CALCULATED PERCENTAGE	CALCULATED SUM
120,000	28%	420,000
100,000	24%	420,000
95,000	23%	420,000
105,000	25%	420,000

In comparison, the rest of the periodic functions work like the calculated sum column from above. Sum causes the total amount of all the values in the column to appear next to each row value.

The remaining six functions, prefixed with R_ for running, produce different results. Where % Total and Sum created the calculated columns values in the above example, R_% Total and R_SUM create this result:

DAILY SALES DOLLARS	CALCULATED PERCENTAGE	CALCULATED SUM
120,000	29%	120,000
100,000	52%	220,000
95,000	75%	315,000
105,000	100%	420,000

These running functions create a running total. As you can see, all of them require SQL*ReportWriter to know the eventual balance of the group when calculating each row value. This forward referencing is one of the most powerful features of this report writer.

In the last column, you enter the Reset Group. Entering a group name in this column makes the calculation reset when it encounters the end of this group. Generally, you should enter a group or designation that is one summary level higher in the parent-child order. By default this is true. If you required a calculated field in G_WHS, the default reset group is Report, which means it will not be reset for the entire report. For a calculated field in G_SERIAL, the default is G_WHS, which is the parent of that group.

Suppose you want to replace the default labels shown in Figure 9.9 with more descriptive ones. To do so, scroll left to the first screen of columns and replace the default labels with the ones shown in the Label column in Figure 9.12.

```
 Action   Query   Group   Field   Summary   Text   Report   Parameter   Help
 ─────────────────────────── Field Settings ──────────────────── 1 of 3

 ┌────────────────┬─────────────────────┬──────────────┬──────────────────────┐
 │  Field Name    │  Source Column      │  Group       │  Label               │
^│                │                     │              │                      │
 │ WHSNO          │ Q_WHS.WHSNO         │ Q_WHS        │ Location:            │
 │ WHSNAME        │ WHSNAME             │ Q_WHS        │ Name:                │
 │ TERR           │ TERR                │ Q_WHS        │ Territory:           │
 │ WHSTYPE        │ WHSTYPE             │ Q_WHS        │ Type:                │
 │ WHSNO          │ Q_SERIAL.WHSNO      │ Q_SERIAL     │ WHSNO                │
 │ PRODNO         │ PRODNO              │ Q_SERIAL     │ Product#             │
 │ STATUS         │ STATUS              │ Q_SERIAL     │ St                   │
 │ STATDAT        │ STATDAT             │ Q_SERIAL     │ Move Date            │
 │ AGE            │ AGE                 │ Q_SERIAL     │ Age                  │
v│                │                     │              │                      │
 └────────────────┴─────────────────────┴──────────────┴──────────────────────┘

 Enter a name for this field.
 Report Name: SERBYWHS                              <INSERT>           <LOV>
```

Figure 9.12: Adding descriptive labels

Notice that because WHSNO from G_SERIAL will not appear on the report, you need not change the label.

When you are satisfied with the new settings, press Accept to exit the screen, clear the screen, and return to the main menu. If you press Menu instead of Accept, you return to the main menu but the Field Settings screen remains visible.

REVIEWING THE GROUP SETTINGS

Next you need to make any necessary adjustments to the Group Setting screen. As mentioned, each query is assigned a unique group by default. Because the data from a query will typically appear in the same area of the printed page, many manipulations will affect the query as a whole. Groups are defined so you can manipulate queries at this level, creating summaries and adjusting placement.

To go into Group Settings, select GROUP from the main menu and the screen shown in Figure 9.13 will appear.

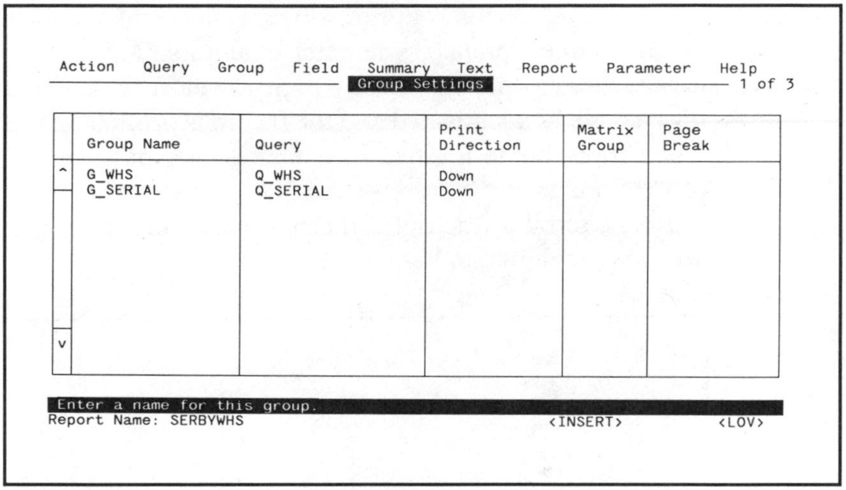

```
 Action    Query    Group    Field    Summary    Text    Report    Parameter    Help
 ─────────────────────────────────┤ Group Settings ├─────────────────────────── 1 of 3

 ┌─────────────────────────────────────────────────────────────────────────────────────┐
 │                                             Print        Matrix    Page               │
 │       Group Name        Query               Direction    Group     Break              │
 │^                                                                                      │
 │       G_WHS             Q_WHS               Down                                       │
 │       G_SERIAL          Q_SERIAL            Down                                       │
 │                                                                                       │
 │                                                                                       │
 │                                                                                       │
 │                                                                                       │
 │v                                                                                      │
 └─────────────────────────────────────────────────────────────────────────────────────┘
  Enter a name for this group.
 Report Name: SERBYWHS                                      <INSERT>           <LOV>
```

Figure 9.13: The first Group Settings screen

There are two group entries shown in this screen, G_WHS and G_SERIAL, which are defined in the first column. The query names are entered in the next column. Move to the Print Direction column, which follows Query. Both of the groups in this example have a default print direction of Down. Although this is correct, you can press List of Values to see the five different possibilities for displaying groups: Across, Across/Down, Down, Down/Across, and Crosstab. Down and Across are straightforward, printing records either down the page or across the page, respectively. Down/Across and Across/ Down also print either down or across, but multiple sets of records will print per page instead of just one set. When the bottom or right end of the page is encountered, the list continues on the same page to the right (Down/Across) or below (Across/Down) the last set of records for that group if there is adequate space on the same page. These display types are useful for doing mailing labels with several columns of labels across the page.

The last direction type, Crosstab, is when you have three groups to be printed in a matrix format. The first group goes across the page as column labels, the second group goes down the page as row labels, and the third group displays at each row/column intersection in the Crosstab format. For a Crosstab format, each group must have an x in the column entitled Matrix Group or it is left blank.

In the Page Break column, you can enter one of two choices if the default is inadequate. If you enter Conditional, SQL*ReportWriter makes sure a complete record can print before the end of the page. If not, a page break is issued and the record is printed on the next page. The other choice is Always, which does a page break after each record in a group.

If you scroll to the right, the second screen of the group settings appears, as shown in Figure 9.14.

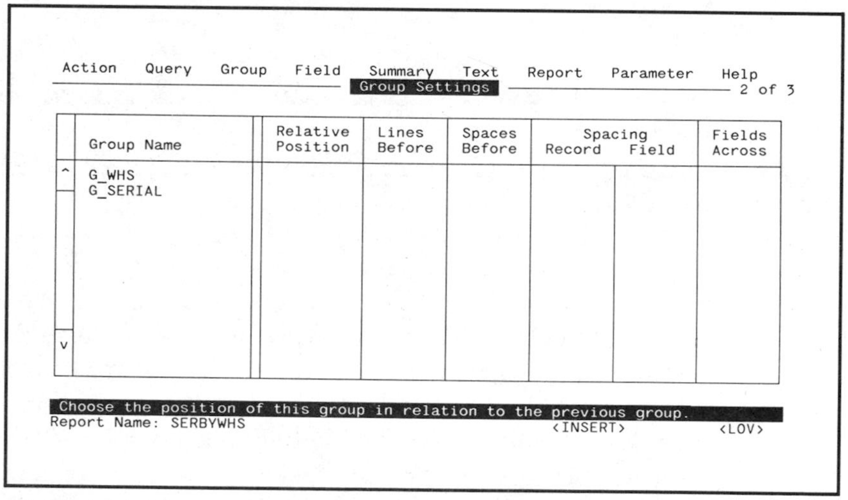

```
 ┌──────────────────────────────────────────────────────────────────────────┐
 │   Action   Query   Group   Field   Summary   Text   Report  Parameter  Help │
 │                               ▐Group Settings▌                    ─ 2 of 3  │
 │  ┌───┬────────────┬──────────┬────────┬────────┬───────────────┬─────────┐ │
 │  │   │            │ Relative │ Lines  │ Spaces │   Spacing     │ Fields  │ │
 │  │   │ Group Name │ Position │ Before │ Before │ Record  Field │ Across  │ │
 │  │ ^ │ G_WHS      │          │        │        │               │         │ │
 │  │   │ G_SERIAL   │          │        │        │               │         │ │
 │  │   │            │          │        │        │               │         │ │
 │  │   │            │          │        │        │               │         │ │
 │  │   │            │          │        │        │               │         │ │
 │  │   │            │          │        │        │               │         │ │
 │  │ v │            │          │        │        │               │         │ │
 │  └───┴────────────┴──────────┴────────┴────────┴───────────────┴─────────┘ │
 │ ▐Choose the position of this group in relation to the previous group.▌     │
 │ Report Name: SERBYWHS                        <INSERT>           <LOV>       │
 └──────────────────────────────────────────────────────────────────────────┘
```

Figure 9.14: The second Group Settings screen

This screen is similar to screen 2 of the Field Settings. In the Relative Position, Lines Before, and Spaces Before columns, you adjust the position of the group on the page as you adjust the field in the Field Settings screen. In the example, since you want one line before each G_WHS group, enter a 1 across from G_WHS in the Lines Before column. The Spacing columns for Record and Field allow you to adjust the field spacings on this screen instead of the Field Settings screen.

The last column, Fields Across, limits the number of times Down/ Across or Across/Down defined groups repeat on the page. For example, if you want several columns of labels to print on the page, you can make the group print Across/Down and enter 4 in the Fields Across column to limit the number columns of labels to 4 across.

Scroll to the right again to reach Screen 3 of 3 on the Group Settings screen, shown in Figure 9.15.

```
  Action    Query    Group    Field    Summary   Text   Report   Parameter   Help
                                      Group Settings                          3 of 3
  _____

     |                        | Multi- | Label    |          Highlight
     |      Group Name        | Panel  | Position |   Field             Label
   ^ |  G_WHS                 |        |          |
     |  G_SERIAL              |        |          |
     |                        |        |          |
     |                        |        |          |
     |                        |        |          |
     |                        |        |          |
     |                        |        |          |
   v |                        |        |          |
  _____
   Keep all fields in a record on the same panel.
   Report Name: SERBYWHS                              <INSERT>            <LOV>
```

Figure 9.15: The third Group Settings screen

On this screen, mark the Multi-Panel column if you want the records in a group to overflow to another panel on another page if the current page is full.

In the second column, also blank by default, you alter the location of the labels in relation to the print direction of the records. If the print direction is Down or Down/Across, the labels will appear as column headers above the records. On the other hand, if the print direction is Across/Down, the labels will appear to the left of the records. If you select Left for the two down print directions or Above for the two across print directions, the labels will be embedded within the body of the group, repeating for each field in the group instead of being positioned along the edge of the report.

In this example, both of the groups, G_WHS and G_SERIAL, have print direction Down. The column titles will appear across the top of the report as column headings like this:

Location

&WHSNO

You want to change the label direction to Left for G_WHS, which will make all of the labels appear in the body of the group like this:

Location: &WHSNO

With the Highlight column, you can use the following highlighting methods to set off all of the fields and/or labels in a group:

Blank

Underline

Reverse

Bold

All

Whether these settings actually have an effect depends on your printer.

In the example, you want both of the groups to print down the page with G_WHS on the left and G_SERIAL on the right. Because of the parent-child link between them, all of the G_SERIAL records for a given G_WHS record will print before the next G_WHS record prints.

ADDING SUMMARIES

You can add subtotals and totals to your reports as well as perform other summary calculations. To do so, select Summary from the main menu, which takes you to the first of two Summary Settings screens. Figure 9.16 shows this screen.

There is only one additional screen of summary attributes. The two summary screens have the following list of attributes:

COLUMN	DESCRIPTION
Summary Name	Name for the summary
Field	Field/column to base the summary on

COLUMN	DESCRIPTION
Function	Name of one of the 12 functions that can be processed
Data Type	Data type of the summarized field
Width	Width of the summarized field
Display Format	Format model for the summary
Print Group	Group to include summary in
Reset Group	Group level at which summary is reset to 0

The settings you need to create a summary are similar to the settings you need to define a calculated field. However, a summary will print and calculate once per group and a calculated field will print and calculate once per record within a group.

To add a summary for a field, press the Insert Record Above or Insert Record Below key. Then enter the name of the summary in the first column and the name of the field you are summarizing in the next column. To calculate the average days for the warehouse as a whole based on the age in days of each unit to the bottom of Age field, enter a unique summary name (OVERALL_AVERAGE) in the first column. In the second column, enter the field name (AGE).

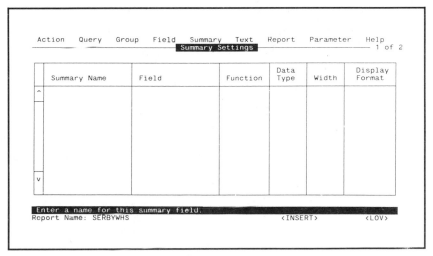

Figure 9.16: The first Summary Settings screen

In the third column, enter the function you want to perform. Typically, you want to sum up a column of values. You can also find the minimum or maximum value in the column, count the number of items in the column, calculate the percent to total for this field, or, as in this example, calculate the average. For each function, you can select the running version (R_AVG), which includes all records up to that point in the report, or the periodic version (AVG), which includes only the records within the print group that you specify. In this case, select AVG to average the values.

You can enter more than one summary for a field. For example, you can show the minimum, maximum, and average values of a field by basing three summary records on the same field. In another case, you might want to have both the running and periodic versions of the function. To create a report that breaks down sales by month for a year, you could create one summary to show the current month's total sales and another to show the year-to-date amount.

Regardless of the function, the Data Type and Width fields are created by default when you select a field on which to base the summary. The default values for each are brought over from the specified field's data type and width. You can alter the width of the value but cannot alter the field type. The Display Format is also defined by default by the field but does not display automatically. As with width, you can enter a format model in the Display Format column to override the field values.

Scroll to the screen on the right and it prompts you for the Print Group and Reset Group for the summary. If you enter Report as the print group, the summary will only print once for the report. In this example, you would get the total average days based on all of the units age. If you enter a group other than Report, it must be the parent group of the group that contains the field being summarized. That is, you cannot say that G_SERIAL is the print group in this example because Age is a field in the G_SERIAL group. This is because the summary will print out once for each record in the print group. If you could enter the same group as the defined field, the result would be like a calculated field, which prints on each detail record. By defining it as the parent of the query, it will print out once for each record, but it will be the record (WHS) from the parent group instead of the record from the source group.

The Reset group defines when to reset the function register to zero. If the Reset Group is the same as the print group, as it often is, the printed value includes only amounts from the group just printed. In the example, the average printing for each G_IWHS group will contain the average for the G_SERIAL records relating to that G_IWHS record. If you instead say Report for the Reset Group, the average for the entire report will be calculated but it will print along with each G_IWHS record. This combination requires SQL*ReportWriter to reference forward to the report average and insert it within the report.

When you create a summary record, a default method for displaying it is also created in the Text objects, which are described in the next section. For this report, which is a Down format, text would be added in the group subfooter record of G_SERIAL, the group containing the field Days. The default descriptor would be the name of the function being processed.

MODIFYING TEXT SETTINGS

To produce the results shown in Figure 9.5, you have to modify the Text Settings for your report. In the Text Settings screens, you can add or modify text objects for report headers and footers, page formats, and text that is tied in with each Group of data. This feature affords you much design flexibility. You can manipulate the report text to create form letters. You can also reposition the fields and text to get the layout you need.

To alter the Text Settings, select Text on the main menu to bring up the screen in Figure 9.17.

The first field on the screen is the Object. Here is a list of the text objects and types within objects possible for your report:

OBJECT	TYPE	DESCRIPTION
Report	Title Page	Prints on a separate page before the report
Report	Report Header	Prints on top of the first page of the report
Page	Page Header	Prints on top of each page

OBJECT	TYPE	DESCRIPTION
Group	Group Header	Prints once above a group
Group	Column Heading	Prints once for each column
Group	Body	Defines the structure of each record in the report
Group	Subfooters	Prints after the columns or rows of a crosstab report
Group	Group Footer	Prints once after a group
Page	Page Footer	Prints on the bottom of each page
Report	Report Footer	Prints out once at the end of the report
Report	Trailer Page	Prints out on a separate page after the report

The objects described above fall into three classes: Report Objects, Page Objects, and Group Objects. Report Objects occur once per report, whether on a separate page (title page or trailer page), or at the beginning (report header) or end (report footer). Page Objects

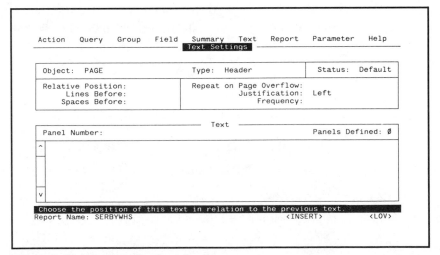

Figure 9.17: The Text Settings screen

include traditional headers and footers and are repeated for each page of the report. These are like the headers and footers you place in your word processing documents or spreadsheet printouts, which might include the page number, date, and report name. With Group Objects, you can directly edit the position of the text within the group and the position of the group upon the page.

Some of your text objects are created by default based on the settings you chose in other areas. For example, in this Inventory report, the column headings and the body objects for both of the groups are generated by default. As mentioned earlier, default text for the summary is also generated.

You can review all of the objects and types for a report by pressing Next Field for each object. Although several text objects are created by default, some of them are created with no text. For each Text object, you will see the Object name (Report, Page, Group name) and type.

All text objects begin with the status Default. Once you edit and alter the text, the status will change to Edited. If the object has Edited status, default values will not be generated for it if you change one of the report settings in another area. If you add a summary setting or a column, for example, the default text for that column or summary will not appear if the object that normally contains it has been previously Edited. In other words, make sure your report is at an advanced stage before editing the text objects. If you later want to recreate the default texts, just delete the Edited objects and SQL*ReportWriter will automatically recreate the default objects.

For each object type, you can change the relative position, the number of lines and spaces before, whether it repeats when the page overflows to the next page, the text justification (Left, Center, Right), and how frequently it occurs (Report or Group name).

You might occasionally have a report wider than your printer can handle. Instead of squeezing it onto one page, you can create up to ten panels to print your wide report on more than one page.

The first text object in the text area is the page header. Suppose you want to add some page headings to the equipment report. Move to the justification field on the screen and change it from Left to Center. Now move down to the text entry section and enter the text shown in Figure 9.18.

```
    Action   Query   Group   Field   Summary   Text   Report   Parameter   Help
                                     Text Settings

    Object:  PAGE                    Type:  Header          Status:   Edited

    Relative Position:          Repeat on Page Overflow:
          Lines Before:                     Justification:  Center
         Spaces Before:                         Frequency:


    ────────────────────────────── Text ──────────────────────────────
    Panel Number: 1                                     Panels Defined: 1
    ^  Page: &PAGE         Equipment Listing by WHS          Date: &DATE_

    v

    Edit the text.
    Report Name: SERBYWHS                           <INSERT>
```

Figure 9.18: Page header text

This title will appear at the top of each page of the report. Notice the &DATE and &PAGE in the header. These are system variables. &DATE substitutes the system date when the report is run and &PAGE inserts the correct page number for each page of the report. You can also say

```
Page &PAGE of &NUM_PAGES
```

because &NUM_PAGES is a system variable for calculating the total number of pages for the report.

The Group Object for the body of G_IWHS in the example report contains the text of the fields. The field names are each preceded by an ampersand (&). Remember to change the label for this group to Left so that the labels are in line with the fields. Then change the labels to display below each other by placing the cursor after each field name and pressing Enter. This will make the labels display below each other on the report while the other group of values display across. Figure 9.19 shows this group after it has been edited to display down the page.

Once you change the data in this object, the status automatically changes from Default to Edited. Once a text object has Edited status, no changes that you make in the field section will update it. To return

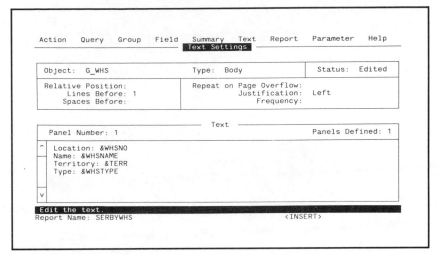

Figure 9.19: The edited group

it to default, you have to delete this object by pressing Delete Record. A default record that reflects your most recent changes in the field and group settings will be substituted for it.

Notice that the entire report format is not visible, just the part relating to G_IWHS. You can only edit one group's text at a time, so only the text relating to the group you are editing will appear. This makes it easier to identify the group level text.

Once you are done editing the Text Objects, press Accept to commit the changes and return to the main menu.

REPORT MENU

If you select Report from the main menu, the screen shown in Figure 9.20 appears. In the Report screen, you can define three Print Options, Type, Name, and Format, which are carried over to the Parameter screen for running reports. Type, meaning type of output, is assigned to Screen by default, but you can change it to File or Printer instead. When you enter SQL*ReportWriter, you can change this setting with the DESTYPE = Printer option. Name will

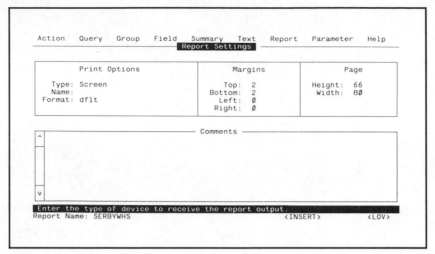

Figure 9.20: The Report Settings screen

be the printer name if you have Printer selected for the output type, the file name if you have File selected for the type, and blank if you left the output type as Screen. If the type is Printer, you can define a printer-specific format file for communicating control codes to the printer.

You can also change the page characteristics for all four margins, the number of lines per page (Height), and the number of character columns per line (Width).

PARAMETER SETTINGS

In the Parameter Settings screen, you can define parameters for output. If you put a parameter in your query, you will have to enter a new value for it whenever you run the report. This will save you from changing your report parameter each time you run the report.

To call up the Parameter Settings screen, select Parameter from the main menu to bring up the screen shown in Figure 9.21.

This screen should contain a list of any variables you entered as parameters in your queries. In this example, if you had entered

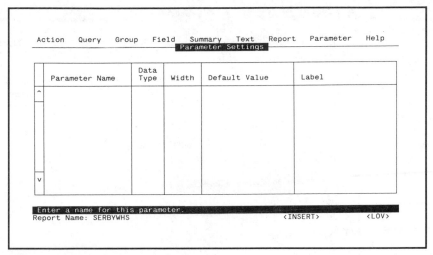

Figure 9.21: The Parameter Settings screen

:AGEDATE as a parameter in the Q _SERIAL query instead of the system date (SYSDATE) you would have to add it in this screen. To add a parameter, press Insert Record Above. For :AGEDATE you would have entered a Date Data Type, which would automatically fill in a 9 for the Width. You could then enter DATE for the Default Value to have the system date used if you did not enter a value when you ran the report.

PREVIEWING A REPORT

At this point, you probably want to see the result of your efforts. SQL*ReportWriter makes this easy. To run the report, select Action from the main menu and then select Execute. The report will display on screen.

With the Browser, you can preview wide and long reports through your screen window in the WYSIWYG ("what you see is what you get") mode, including all forward references to the end of the report. To invoke the Browser, press the Browser key. A section of the report shown in Figure 9.5 will appear on screen. If your report is larger than one screen, select Window from the Browser mode to move through it.

RUNNING A REPORT

You run the report using Execute from the Action menu or the RUNREP command from the operating system prompt. You will be prompted by the runtime parameters screen shown in Figure 9.22.

Figure 9.22: The Parameter Values screen

In this screen, you can change the settings you defined in the Report screen. Any parameters defined for your report are also listed on this screen and you can enter a value for each of them. If you had used :AGEDATE, it would appear on this screen and you would have to enter a date to use for the aging.

You can specify which special printer driver you want used when this report is run. To create a new printer device driver, use the printer definer, a separate utility that you run from the operating system prompt. To invoke the printer definer, type

```
PRINTDEF PRINTER=printer OUTFILE=outfile PDFILE=pdfile.dat
```

The three variables in the command string are for naming the printer, the location of the new printer definition, and the printer definition text file. The default definition file is named PRINTDEF.DAT.

If you change the number of copies from the default of 1, the report will print the number of copies you specify each time it runs.

SETTING PARAMETERS IN THE COMMAND LINE

When you run the report from the command line using RUNREP, you can specify the parameters as arguments in the command. As usual, you specify the report name and your username/password combination to avoid the login screen. But you can also choose whether to display the runtime parameters form (PARAMFORM =), define specific parameters in line (PARTNO = '90002005'), or set up a complicated parameter string in a previously defined command file with CMDFILE = . In addition, you can change your terminal characteristics, performance specifications, output assignments, and copies values all through the command line parameters.

For example, if you wanted to run 2 copies of SERBYWHS and had used the :AGEDATE parameter, you could type

```
RUNREP SERBYWHS user/password copies=2 AGEDATE='01-SEP-88'
```

to run the report two times based on that age date. If you leave out the :AGEDATE parameter, you will be prompted for it later. If you say PARAMFORM = NO, the system will use any default value you have specified or it assumes. If you did not enter a default value for variable parameters, NULL is used.

THE DATABASE DEFINITION TABLES

All of your report definitions are stored in several tables in your database. The following list includes the table name and a description of the table definition stored in each table.

TABLE NAME	TABLE DESCRIPTIONS
FR_FIELD	Field Settings
FR_FKEY	Key definition in Parent-Child relationships
FR_GROUP	Group Settings
FR_MAXIMA	ID of newest object in report

TABLE NAME	TABLE DESCRIPTIONS
FR_PARAM	Parameter definitions
FR_QUERY	Query data including the SELECT
FR_REPORT	Overall report settings
FR_STE	Object ID and cross-reference
FR_SUMMARY	Summary Settings
FR_TEXT	Text Settings
FR_TEXT_LONG	Text of Text Objects
FR_TEXT_COUNT	Text object panel statistics
FR_LIMITS	Maximum pages defined

SUMMARY

SQL*ReportWriter offers great reporting flexibility in a user-friendly, easily traceable, error-checking format. This chapter used a Master-Detail style report as an example. However, there are many more formats available to you, including crosstabs and Master-Detail-Summary reports. You can assign values to parameters at runtime and can set up reports in batches for production use.

SQL*ReportWriter is the perfect complement to SQL*Plus. With SQL*ReportWriter, you can apply your understanding of SQL to the process of writing reports.

10

USING SQL*MENU

SQL*MENU IS AN ORACLE MANAGEMENT TOOL for linking all of the components of your application. Actually, SQL*Menu is more like a toolbox than a tool. You can use it to combine the individual applications you have created into one overall application. The database serves as the central repository of your data; SQL*Menu is the central repository of your applications. Once you have combined all of your individual applications into a SQL*Menu application, you can log on to SQL*Menu and access the applications through a set of options presented in a traditional menu style.

Like other Oracle tools, SQL*Menu is specifically designed to work within the Oracle environment. You use the same usernames and passwords that you do in SQL*Plus and the other Oracle tools. Many of the function keys are similar to SQL*Forms and, in fact, most of the SQL*Menu entry screens use forms created in SQL*Forms. The application information is stored in tables in the database. This similarity to SQL*Forms means that the look and feel of the application will not change between the menus and the entry forms.

There are several advantages to using menus. With menus, you can restrict a user to a limited set of functions. When users choose from a menu, you can be more sure that the correct parameters are passed to the application. Selecting from a menu of choices also requires less effort and expertise. With menus, users require less training and need not memorize complex command syntax.

With SQL*Menu, Oracle has defined the common components of a menu application. You can fit your specific application—including menu options, navigation keys, on-line help, and option-sensitive security—into Oracle's generalized menu skeleton. In fact, Oracle has reduced the application development process to a simple, fill-in-the-blank exercise. Creating menus will take only a fraction of the time it takes to design them.

Map out your entire menu system before you begin. Make sure to place logically related components together (for example, all reports should be within one menu path) and to use standard text for each choice. Make your menu structure as shallow as possible so users don't have to go through many menus to find their choice. Also, decide whether to use just the standard menu navigation keys of SQL*Menu or to add menu choices for navigation as well.

*UNDERSTANDING SQL*MENU*

Before you begin learning the SQL*Menu development system, look at these key SQL*Menu terms.

- A *menu* is a set of command actions. It consists of a text description and a reference designator that you can select by pointing to the action with navigational keys or by keying the reference designator.

- An *application* is a set of menus and form, report, and program choices within menus. Together these make up all of the actions against a related set of tables in a database.

- A *library* is a file stored on disk containing all of the data relating to an application.

- A *work-class* is a method of grouping users with similar access requirements so that you can define menu option security for a work-class of users rather than individual users.

- A *language* is a way to refer to an entire set of SQL*Menu messages. You can copy the default set (language) of messages to another language skeleton where you can reword each message.

In SQL*Menu, you must name your application and name each menu within it. You must define one or more work-classes in your application and associate each user with a work-class before they can use the application.

ACCESSING SQL*MENU

The syntax for logging on to SQL*Menu is

```
SQLMENU [appl] [username/password] [-tcrt] [-llang] [-q] [-r] [-w] [-e]
```

Several of these options are the same in other Oracle tools. The -e option echoes all of your keystrokes to a file, -w writes output to a file instead of the terminal, and -r reads the input from a file instead of the terminal. The -q (quiet) option suppresses the terminal bell. If you have defined another message language, you can access it with the -l and the two-character language designator. You can specify an alternative CRT with the -t option. If you enter your username and password as a command line argument, no authorization screen appears. If you specify the application name as a command line argument, the first menu that appears will be the top menu of your application instead of the main SQL*Menu Application menu.

Your menu selections will vary depending on which username you specify and which authorization level that username has in SQL*Menu and in your application. In order to explore all possible options, log on initially with the following command sequence:

```
SQLMENU SYSTEM/systempassword
```

where *systempassword* is MANAGER if you did not redefine the system password. When you first install SQL*Menu, SYSTEM is the only authorized user. You have to add users when you first log on to SQL*Menu.

The first screen to appear is the Application menu, as shown in Figure 10.1.

```
            A P P L I C A T I O N   M E N U
        SELECT AN APPLICATION FROM THE LIST BELOW


    -->   1   SQL*Menu Development of Dynamic Menus
          2   Exit






            Make your choice:   1


    v   Mon Sep 26 23:05:43 1988              Replace      ($apl$ )
```

Figure 10.1: The Application menu

As you develop applications in SQL*Menu, they will automatically be added to the list of applications that appear on this menu. Now, there is only one application shown on this screen, the SQL*Menu Development of Dynamic Menus. In SQL*Menu, even the system-level maintenance programs and database administration programs use the same SQL*Menu structure and function that your applications use.

Each menu that you define will have the same components as the Application menu. At the top of the menu is the Title line. In this case, it says

```
A P P L I C A T I O N    M E N U
```

For your applications, however, you can enter any title you want. The same is true for the Subtitle line, which in this case says

```
SELECT AN APPLICATION FROM THE LIST BELOW
```

A third title line, called the Bottom Title, is located below the line that reads "Make your choice:" near the bottom of the screen. In this case, nothing is shown in the Bottom Title, but this line is used in other SQL*Menu menus.

The arrow pointer (– >) points to the option displayed after the Make your choice option. If you press ↓, the pointer will move through the menu choices and the number at the bottom will change. At the lower-left corner of the screen are arrows that indicate the directions in which you can move the arrow pointer. In the same line are the day, date, time, and year, the Insert/Replace indicator, and the menu name, apl, in parentheses. Other features will become apparent as you move through this procedure.

Besides the arrow keys, there are several important keys with which you can execute special functions. Press F2 to see the function keys available for this or any menu. Figure 10.2 shows the Application menu function keys.

```
    FUNCTION                     Keystroke(s)    FUNCTION               Keystroke(s)
    ---------------------        ------------    --------------------   ------------
    Next field                   Enter           Move cursor down       Down Cursor
                                 Ctrl ->         Delete character       Del
                                 Tab                                    <- Back Space
    Previous field               Ctrl <-         exit                   Esc
                                 Back Tab                               F10
    Clear field                  Ctrl End
    Enter menu parameters        F5
    Enter application parm.      F6
    Previous menu                Pg Up
                                 PgUp
    Goto main menu               F3
    Goto application menu        F9
    Help                         F1
    Where-display                F4
    Change char. mode            Ins
    Display function key's       F2
    Redefine user-id             Ctrl-U
    Redisplay screen             Ctrl-R
    Terminate input on form      Ctrl-T
    Move cursor left             <- Left Cursor
    Move cursor right            -> Right Cursor
    Move cursor up               Up Cursor
                                 Type any key to continue.....
```

Figure 10.2: Application menu function keys

The functions displayed on this screen depend on what class of user you are and what menu or application you are in. For example, when you are running a SQL*Form, the SQL*Forms function keys appear. If your user ID has been assigned special functions, the corresponding function keys will be displayed on your function key help screen.

MAIN SQL*MENU DEVELOPMENT MENU

If you press Enter to select option 1, the Dynamic Menu Utility Main menu will appear. Figure 10.3 shows the three choices available at this level.

```
        S Q L * M e n u   D y n a m i c   M e n u   U t i l i t y
                        SQL*Menu Main menu


        -->  1  Create and Maintain SQL*Menu Applications
             2  Generation of SQL*Menu Documentation
             3  SQL*Menu System Maintenance
             4  Previous Menu




                Make your choice:  1

   v   Mon Sep 26 23:06:22 1988     BGM OSC DBG      Replace    DMU (DMU )
```

Figure 10.3: The Dynamic Menu Utility Main menu

Notice that the bottom line of the menu has changed slightly. Before the menu name (DMU) is the application name (also DMU in this case). In the middle of the bottom line are the terms:

BGM OSC DBG

BGM stands for Background menu, OSC stands for Operating System commands, and DBG stands for Debug mode, which makes it easier to trace SQL*Menu program steps. Because the user SYSTEM has all three of these capabilities, the following function keys are interspersed into the function key list, which you can see by pressing F2:

KEYSTROKE(S)	FUNCTION
F8	Enter >1 OS-command
Ctrl-D	Change debug mode
F7	Enter 1 OS-command
PgDn	Show Background menu

KEYSTROKE(S)	FUNCTION
Shift-F1	Background menu option 1
Shift-F2	Background menu option 2
Shift-F3	Background menu option 3

The Background menu is a set of common actions that you can link to all of your applications so that these actions are always waiting in the background and readily accessible. If your user ID is authorized to do so, you can select two different methods of executing operating system commands from a SQL*Menu.

The three choices available on the Dynamic Menu Utility Main menu constitute the major functions of the SQL*Menu system. You do most application development through the first choice, from which you create application, work-class, user, menu, and parameter information. With the second choice, you create detailed or summary application documentation. The third choice is for doing a variety of administrative tasks, including granting a new user access to SQL*Menu and creating and maintaining a new "language" for SQL*Menu messages.

MANAGING MENU SECURITY

Much of what you do with SQL*Menu will involve managing and defining system security levels. First, you will enroll a new user for access to SQL*Menu so you will not need the SYSTEM user. To do this, select 3, SQL*Menu System Maintenance, on the SQL*Menu Main menu. This brings up the menu shown in Figure 10.4.

From this menu, select 4, Granting of a New User of SQL*Menu. Figure 10.5 shows the Parameter screen that will result.

This Option Parameter form is a generic form for entering parameters to pass through to a process. You can easily create a parameter form and associate it with the menu choice that you create for your applications. In this case, you need two parameters for the Grant program: the Grantee and the Grant option. In the Grantee field, enter a username. Leave the Grant option blank if this user will only access SQL*Menu to use your applications. If you want this user to design and create applications, enter -a. To give the user full access to the DBA capabilities of SQL*Menu, enter -w in the Grant option field.

```
            S Q L * M e n u   D y n a m i c   M e n u   U t i l i t y

                       Database Administrator Menu


            --> 1  Creation of a New SQL*Menu System Library
                2  Maintenance of Message Database
                3  Creation of a New Language Definition
                4  Granting of a New User of SQL*Menu
                5  Compressing the SQL*Menu System Library
                6  Compressing Application Library
                7  Creating a Skeleton for a New Language
                8  Previous Menu




                   Make your choice:  1

        Options on this menu are for tailoring general appearance of SQL*Menu
    v    Mon Sep 26 23:07:22 1988     BGM OSC DBG      Replace    DMU (DMUDBA )
```

Figure 10.4: The Database Administrator menu

```
               O P T I O N   P A R A M E T E R   F O R M


                         Grantee
                    Grant option







       Mon Sep 26 23:07:39 1988                  Replace      page 1 : 1
```

Figure 10.5: The Option Parameter form

You will enter a user called CHAP10 with a design level (-a) clearance. After the program completes, the menu in Figure 10.4 will return.

To finish this grant process, add the username (CHAP10) to a work-class in the SQL*Menu application. To do this, select Previous Menu to move up from menu DMUDBA to DMU, and select 1,

Create and Maintain SQL*Menu Applications. Figure 10.6 shows the Menu Information Maintenance menu.

```
            S Q L * M e n u    D y n a m i c    M e n u    U t i l i t y

                          Menu Information Maintenance


              -->   1   Update Application Information
                    2   Update Work-class and User Information
                    3   Update Menu Information
                    4   Update Substitution Parameter Information
                    5   Generate One Menu
                    6   Generate All Menus for One Application
                    7   Manage Libraries and Applications
               .    8   Previous Menu




                          Make your choice:   1

         NOTE: The meaning of function keys can change when running SQL*Forms
      v    Mon Sep 26 23:22:37 1988     BGM OSC DBG        Replace    DMU (DMUMNU )
```

Figure 10.6: The Menu Information Maintenance menu

This menu (DMUMNU) is where you will do all of your application development and maintenance. In this case, select Update the Work-class and User Information to change the SQL*Menu application itself. To do this, select 2 to run a SQL*Form program called DMUWCU.FRM. Figure 10.7 shows the screen for this application after you enter the information necessary for CHAP10 to be added as a work-class of 10.

To get to this screen, enter DMU in the first field. The lowest work-class of 5, Simple SQL*Menu User, will appear on the screen. Press Enter to move to the Work_class field and press ↓ to get to the next record containing Work_class 10, Advanced SQL*Menu User. Then press PgDn to get to the first line of the next block where the user information is entered.

In SQL*Menu, the work-classes have been set up as follows:

CLASS	DESCRIPTION
5	Simple SQL*Menu user
10	Advanced SQL*Menu user
15	SQL*Menu DBA

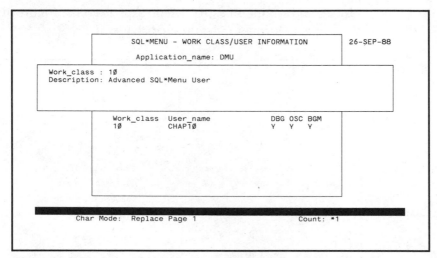

Figure 10.7: Updating the work-class and user information

You can set up from 1 to 9999 work-classes. 9999 is automatic open access to all menus of an application. You need to define a work-class for each application that a user want to access. Users can be a different work-class in each application, but they must be set up for each one. Only SQL*Menu requires the Granting of a New User of SQL*Menu step, but the Update Work-class and User Information step is always required.

As you will see in later sections, you can tailor individual options within menus to be available for a range of work-classes. For this reason, you should create a work-class scheme which incorporates increasing use and authority as the work-class values increase from 1 to 9999. As in the SQL*Menu DMU application, typically only a few work-classes are needed for an application.

The last three columns, DBG, OSC, BGM, are where you indicate the user's right to the special Debug, Operating System Command, and Background menu application. The Debug feature executes the option command when you select an option to display the bottom row of the screen, below the time and date. For example, when you select the Previous Menu choice, the macro command PRVMENU shows up on that line, indicating that it is being executed. This can help you fix errors. The OSC option lets you exit to a screen and execute an operating system command. Entering Y in the BGM option lets the user access the special Background menu that you can create for your application. The Background menu is accessible by a keystroke from any menu in your application if your username has a Y in the BGM field.

After committing the user, the process is complete for this user.

CREATING A MENU

Now that you have learned how to add a user to the SQL*Menu system, you are ready to build a new application. As mentioned, the first step in creating an application is to create an overall design. Figure 10.8 is a diagram of a simple equipment tracking menu system that incorporates some of the forms and reports created in other sections of this book.

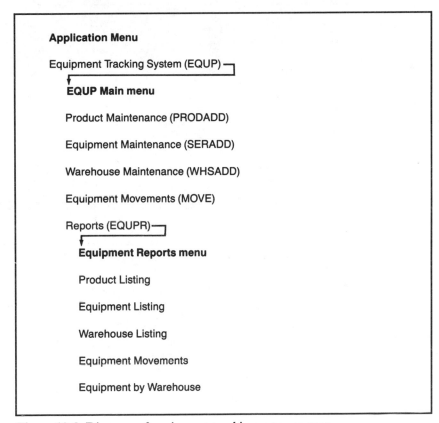

Figure 10.8: Diagram of equipment tracking menu system

As the figure suggests, this menu application, called EQUP, is only two menus deep. The top menu contains the table maintenance options and the second menu contains the report options. To create this application, go through options 1, 2, 3, and 4 on the Menu Information Maintenance menu to put the pieces in place. Then select option 6 to generate the application.

UPDATING THE APPLICATION INFORMATION

To enter the application information, select 1, the Update Application Information form, from the Menu Information Maintenance menu. Figure 10.9 shows the screen after you have entered the data for that form.

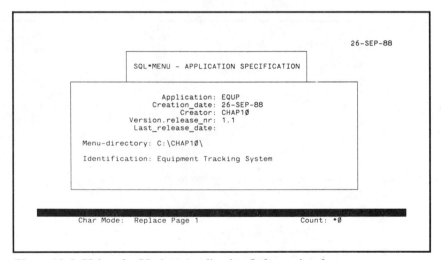

Figure 10.9: Using the Update Application Information form

Two of the fields, the Creation_date and Version.release_nr, are filled in by default when you enter the screen. You can change the version number if you like. The field Last_release_date is optional. In the Menu-directory field, make sure that you follow your subdirectory with a backslash in DOS. SQL*Menu will require that final slash to identify it as a subdirectory. Pressing F10 will commit the record to the database.

CREATING THE TOP MENU

Update the work-class and user information with the methods and work-classes mentioned for the SQL*Menu update. Then update the menu information. To do this, select 3 from the Menu Information Maintenance menu (DMUMNU). Figure 10.10 shows the first screen after you have entered the first menu name.

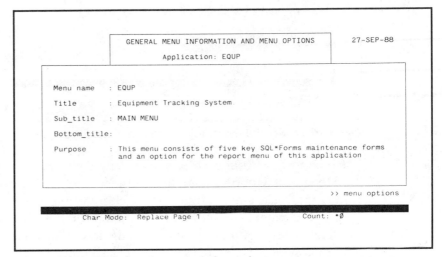

```
          GENERAL MENU INFORMATION AND MENU OPTIONS         27-SEP-88
                     Application: EQUP


   Menu name    : EQUP

   Title        : Equipment Tracking System

   Sub_title    : MAIN MENU

   Bottom_title:

   Purpose      : This menu consists of five key SQL*Forms maintenance forms
                  and an option for the report menu of this application



                                                        >> menu options

         Char Mode:  Replace Page 1                  Count: *Ø
```

Figure 10.10: Updating the menu information

This first menu must have the same name as the application. The text you insert in the five fields will appear on the screen when you access EQUP. The last field is for documentation purposes only. If you want to include a Background menu in your application, you must use the three-letter designator BGM in the menu name field of this screen. Otherwise, creating a Background menu is just like creating the other menus in your system.

The arrows in the lower-right corner of the screen indicate that the menu options are on the next page of the form. Press Commit (F10) to commit this block to the database and press Next Block (PgDn) to get to screen two of this menu development form.

Figure 10.11 shows the second screen of this form. The first four options of the EQUP menu have been filled out.

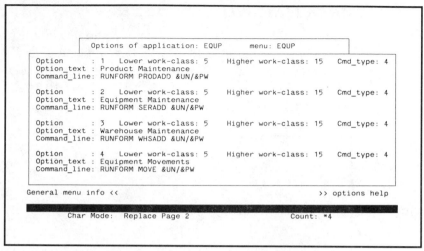

Figure 10.11: Second screen for updating menu information

In the first fields of each option, specify the number that will be used to select the option from the menu. You use the next two fields, Lower work-class and Higher work-class, to limit access to that option. For example, to limit the first option, Product Maintenance, to a higher level of authorization, set the lower work-class to a 15. This option would then not appear on class 5 and 10 users' menus. You could also set up a functional work-class structure where inventory control users are one range and accounting people are another.

In the last field in the first row of each option, Cmd_type, enter the type of command that will be executed from this menu. Six command types are allowed:

TYPE	DESCRIPTION
1	Invoke submenu
2	Execute operating system command
3	Execute operating system command and pause
4	Invoke SQL*Forms (Run*Form)
5	Invoke SQL*Plus
6	Execute a menu macro command

The first command type is necessary because you can have nested menus. If you enter a 1 in the field, SQL*Menu will interpret the command line entered two rows below as a SQL*Menu menu name. You use the second and third command types if you want to execute an operating system command. Type 3 pauses before returning to the menu and type 2 does not.

You can run a SQL*Form form or a SQL*Plus script using the operating system command types. However, if you select 4 or 5, the transfer into the other Oracle tools will execute more quickly because a separate logon is not required. This is only true if you installed SQL*Menu on your system correctly with a link to either of the other tools. Even if you classify form options with type 4 and SQL*Plus scripts with type 5 and the link does not exist, the command will be processed as a regular operating system command. The advantage of a type 4 linked connection is that it leaves global variables defined in a form active for use in other forms. Otherwise, use of these variables is limited to the form in which they are defined.

Command type 6 indicates that you will enter a SQL*Menu macro command in the command line. You use macro commands, like their SQL*Forms macro key counterparts, to execute a function key process. The Previous Menu option in the SQL*Menu menu system is an example of a macro command. The command line for the Previous Menu option is PRVMENU, which works like PgUp.

The next line of each option contains the Option_text. This is the text that shows up next to the option number on the menu. This text should be consistent, brief, and descriptive.

The Command-line is where you actually enter the command to be executed.

USING PARAMETERS

Notice that the command lines contain values preceded by ampersands (&). This should look familiar if you have used the other Oracle tools. Values after ampersands are option parameters. The parameters in this example are system parameters or variables. The five system-defined parameter values are:

PARAMETER	DESCRIPTION
UN	Username
PW	Password
SO	Make your field choice (that is, 1-4)
TT	Terminal type
LN	Language

Although these system parameters already have values that will be passed automatically to the command processor, you can create your own two-character parameters. When you use a parameter that you create in a command line, users are presented with an Option Parameter screen when they select the menu option containing the parameter. They are expected to fill in this parameter, which is then passed to the command processor. A classic example of this is dates for use with reports. You can define starting and ending dates or an aging date. You can also define a warehouse location, a serial number, a product code, and so on.

USING MACRO COMMANDS

You can use macro commands to incorporate function key processes into selectable menu choices. You enter macros into the command line followed by a semicolon, as follows:

```
PRVMENU;
```

SQL*Menu will now move to the previous menu. You can combine more than one macro on a command line, terminating each with a semicolon. In some cases, you enter command line arguments like this

```
OSCMD1 DIR;
```

This will process an exit to the operating system and display a list of the disk directory.

Table 10.1 lists the macro commands.

Table 10.1: Macro Commands

MACRO	KEY EQUIVALENT	DESCRIPTION
APLMEN	F9	Go to application menu
MAINMENU	F3	Go to the main application menu
APLPARM	F6	Run the Application Parameter form
MENUPARM	F5	Run the Menu Parameter form
ASSIGN	*	Assign a value to a substitution parameter
BGMv	Shift-Fv	Run background option v where v is from 1 to 10
CHRMODE	Ins	Insert/replace toggle
CLRFLD	Ctrl-End	Erase contents from the current field
DELCHR	Backspace	Backspace and erase
DISP	*	Echo macro output to the screen
NODISP	*	Do not echo macro output to the screen
REDISP	Ctrl-R	Redisplay the screen
DOWN	↓	Move menu selector down one row
UP	↑	Return to previous menu choice
LEFT	←	Cursor left
RIGHT	→	Cursor right
NEXTFLD	Enter/Tab	Advance to the next field
PRVFLD	Shift-Tab	Return to the previous field

* No key equivalent

Table 10.1: Macro Commands (continued)

MACRO	KEY EQUIVALENT	DESCRIPTION
PRVMENU	PgUp	Return to the previous menu
EXIT	Esc/F10	Leave SQL*Menu
TRMNATE	Ctrl-T	Terminate the input
NEWAPL	Ctrl-U	Begin a new application
NEWUSER	Ctrl-U	Reset username and password
HELP	F1	Display the help information
SHOWBGM	PgDn	Run background menu
SHOWKEYS	F2	Display the function keys
SUSPEND	*	Termporarily halt macro
WHERE	F4	Show the user location in the menus
OSCMD	F8	Process operating system commands
OSCMD1	F7	Process one operating command

* No key equivalent

As the asterisks indicate, four macros handle special processes that do not translate to any function key. These macros are: DISP, NODISP, SUSPEND, and ASSIGN. You use NODISP and DISP to turn screen output echo off and on during SQL*Menu command processing. You can interrupt the flow of the menu with the SUSPEND command. To restart processing, press Terminate Input (Ctrl-T) or Previous Menu (PgUp). Finally, you can assign a value to a parameter using the ASSIGN command.

There are six defined *states* within SQL*Menu. They are AMENU, FORM, LFORM, MENU, MFORM, and OFORM. LFORM is the Logon menu form state. AMENU is the Application menu state. The function keys shown in Figure 10.2 are the valid function keys for this state. MENU is the generate state for any menu of an application. FORM, MFORM, and OFORM are the states of the Application Parameter Form, Menu Parameter Form, and Option Parameter Form states. Be sure to execute a macro command for a function key that is valid in the state of SQL*Menu in which it will be executed.

HELP TEXT MENU

After you complete the command options, press Next Block (PgDn) to get to the third screen of the form, which is for entering Help text for each option. This screen is shown in Figure 10.12.

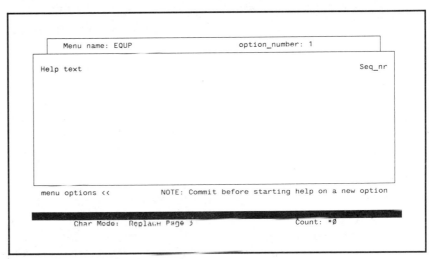

Figure 10.12: Third screen for updating menu information

The first two fields of the block are filled in automatically and the cursor is placed at the first line of the Help text area. You can resequence the lines you have entered by altering the default values in the Seq_nr column. When you are done, press Commit (F10) to add the text to the database and press Exit (Shift-F10) to return to the Menu Information Maintenance menu.

SUBSTITUTION PARAMETERS MENU

If you want to add any parameters to an option, you can do so through the substitution Parameter Information form (selection 4 from the Menu Information Maintenance menu). When you select 4, the screen in Figure 10.13 appears.

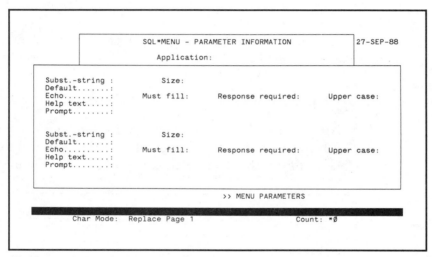

Figure 10.13: The Substitution Parameter Information form

In the first field, enter the application name (EQUP). In this case, you want to create a function called AD for Aging Date. It is nine characters long and has no default value. Enter Y for Must Fill to indicate that the function must be nine characters wide; a response is required; and the month date can be converted to uppercase. The system will not automatically check the validity of this date through SQL*Menu. You can enter help text for the parameter and define a prompt to display to the left of it on the Option Parameter form. Once you complete the entry, you can press Next Block (PgDn) to go to the second page of this form, shown in Figure 10.14.

In this screen, you can cross-reference the parameters you entered on the first screen and the menu you want the parameters to be used in. If you do this, the parameter is considered a menu parameter instead of an option parameter. As the column headings suggest, you enter the parameter subst.-string in the first column and a valid menu name from the application in the second column. Once you

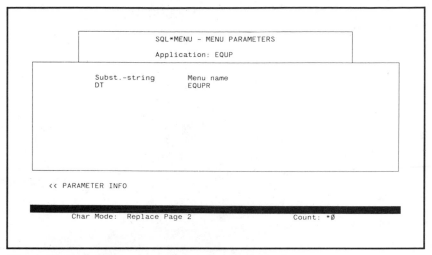

Figure 10.14: Second screen of parameter information

have done this, press Commit (F10) to complete the process and Shift-F10 to exit the form.

GENERATING THE MENUS

Once you update the first four options of the Menu Information Maintenance menu, choose 6 to generate all menus for one application. Doing this creates a library in which to store the application information. This library is a necessary component; you will not be able to access your application unless you generate it first. Once you create a library, your new application will appear on the main Application menu when you next enter SQL∗Menu. If you later change a menu in your application, you can select 5, Generate One Menu, to update your application library with the latest version of your menu.

MANAGING LIBRARIES AND APPLICATIONS

You use selection 7 on the Menu Information Maintenance menu to update and maintain your applications and libraries. Figure 10.15 shows that menu.

```
              S Q L * M e n u   D y n a m i c   M e n u   U t i l i t y

                       Manage Libraries and Applications


           -->   1   Rename a Menu
                 2   Rename an Application
                 3   Delete a Menu
                 4   Delete an Application
                 5   Back-up an Application
                 6   Create a Library Listing of Application Library
                 7   Create a New Menu Library
                 8   Previous Menu




                       Make your choice:   1


       v   Tue Sep 27 00:21:34 1988     BGM OSC DBG      Replace     DMU (DMULIB )
```

Figure 10.15: The Manage Libraries and Applications menu

This menu contains options for doing basic maintenance on your
application. You can rename or delete a menu or application. You can
select 5 to export an application to another Oracle installation or to back
it up onto another medium. SQL*Menu will create a SQL*Plus script
for adding the data for this application to the SQL*Plus database tables,
which you can then easily transfer onto another Oracle database.

Selecting Create a New Menu Library is an initial step for generating all menus for an application. Finally, you can create a list of all of
the menu in your application library by selecting 6.

The only other maintenance action you might want to perform is
on the Database Administrator menu. Any time you generate or
alter any part of your application, you should compress the library to
eliminate any wasted space or date in it. You can do this by selecting
6 on the Database Administration menu.

DOCUMENTING YOUR MENUS

The Menu Documentation menu includes two options for generating and displaying documentation for your entire application. You
can access this menu, shown in Figure 10.16, from the SQL*Menu
Main menu.

```
            S Q L * M e n u   D y n a m i c   M e n u   U t i l i t y

                           Menu Documentation


     -->   1   Generate SQL*Menu Application Information
           2   Show SQL*Menu Application Documentation on the Screen
           3   Print SQL*Menu Application Documentation
           4   Generate SQL*Menu Summary Information
           5   Show SQL*Menu Summary Documentation on the Screen
           6   Print SQL*Menu Summary Documentation
           7   Previous Menu







                         Make your choice:  1

                    Filenames: 'aplnum'/SUM/APL/.DOC
     v   Tue Sep 27 00:23:06 1988    BGM OSC DBG        Replace      DMU (DMUDOC )
```

Figure 10.16: The Menu Documentation menu

This menu includes six options. The first three have to do with the detailed SQL*Menu documentation and the last three have to do with the summary SQL*Menu documentation. With the detailed documentation, you are provided a well-formatted display or printout of the application information, each set of menu options, each work-class, and the option and menu parameters for your application.

Option 4, the summary version of this documentation, is very similar to the other options. However, the help text for each menu option is left off and the parameters are not printed.

SUMMARY

SQL*Menu is a powerful and flexible menu design and development system. Using the menu and fill-in-the-form interface of SQL*Menu, you can quickly develop a secure, user-friendly format for presenting the forms, reports, and queries you created with Oracle. With selection 1 through 4 on the Menu Information Maintenance menu, you can create applications that are closely tied to Oracle's other tools.

11

MAINTAINING
DATABASE
SECURITY

SECURITY PROTECTS DATA IN DATABASES FROM unauthorized disclosure, modification (including removal), and delivery delay. Over the last decade, several research articles and government publications have collectively established different levels of security assurance. One of these documents, provided for the benefit of the defense industry, is a military standard—*Trusted Computer Systems Evaluation Criteria* (the "orange book") produced by staff members of the National Computer Security Center (see bibliography). Although no database system meets the most stringent requirements set forth by the security community, the Oracle RDBMS provides sufficient security to be accepted as the heart of one of the largest government software procurements in history. This chapter describes the security features Oracle provides to implement discretionary access control and user authentication. No attempt is made to establish (or refute) a case for so-called *mandatory access control* mechanisms wherein objects (users, tables, and so on) are kept separate from one another by security (clearance and classification) levels.

AN EMPLOYEE DATABASE APPLICATION

The database that illustrates Oracle security mechanisms comprises three base tables, shown in Figure 11.1, and two views. The employee database paradigm, similar to the one in the Oracle manuals, is used to demonstrate system-, table-, and field-level protection.

PROTECTION PROVIDED

Oracle includes two independent mechanisms for database security. The authentication subsystem requires you to supply a username and password. The authorization subsystem assigns system- and object-level rights and specifies the activities that various users may engage in. Oracle's powerful view mechanism is part of its authorization subsystem. The authentication mechanisms permit you to log on to the Oracle system, while the authorization mechanisms permit you to share database objects (tables, views, and so on) and allow the DBA to assign system-wide privileges.

AUTHENTICATING USERS

The authentication subsystem is your first line of defense. You must have a valid username and correct associated password to log on to Oracle, as well as to access Oracle via SQL*Plus, SQL*Forms, SQL*ReportWriter, SQL*Calc, SQL*Menu, or Oracle for 1-2-3. The authentication procedure checks usernames and passwords before permitting you to retrieve or alter any database tables, views, or other objects in any way. Entering Oracle through SQL*Plus, for example, requires you to supply a username/password combination either from the system prompt or after you have invoked SQL*Plus but before the appearance of the SQL> prompt. SQL*Calc permits you to build spreadsheets; however, you cannot create or retrieve tables until you have logged on to Oracle. Once a user has been successfully authenticated, authorization provides continuous database object protection and partitions system-wide privileges.

```
EMPLOYEES Table:

EMPID DEPTNO SALARY HIREDATE  DEPENDENTS
----- ------ ------ --------- ----------
10004    318 $1,326 15-MAY-74      4
10008    720 $1,900 17-SEP-75      1
10012    181 $1,962 10-NOV-77      1
10025    631 $1,454 20-MAY-79      3
10122    100 $1,895 06-MAY-79      2
10147    318 $1,910 01-JAN-80      2
11221    631 $1,264 19-FEB-81      1
11344    100 $1,457 01-NOV-81      1
11678    318 $1,651 15-MAY-82      3
11788    318 $1,166 15-MAY-82      4
12223    366 $1,351 15-DEC-82      1
12679    720 $1,800 14-JUN-83      3
13006    181 $1,742 14-MAR-84      0
13114    366 $1,617 15-APR-85      1
14007    181 $1,210 23-JAN-86      1
14204    100 $1,971 07-JUL-87      4
40001    100 $4,500 01-APR-76      4
40002    181 $2,500 01-JAN-82      4
40003    318 $2,700 15-JAN-76      2
40004    366 $3,400 15-JUN-81      0
40005    631 $3,700 07-DEC-81      2
40006    720 $3,250 21-SEP-84      2

SECURITY Table:                    MANAGERS Table:

EMPID CLEARANCE SEX DOB            DEPTNO EMPID MGRNAME
----- --------- --- ---------      ------ ----- -------
10004 C         M   16-JUN-26         100 40001 PERRY
10008 U         F   06-JUN-66         181 40002 LATEER
10012 S         F   07-JUN-60         318 40003 CORDELL
10025 U         F   10-JUN-49         366 40004 ZAKS
10122 TS        M   12-JUN-43         631 40005 KING
10147 TS        M   10-JUN-49         720 40006 SIMPSON
11221 U         F   12-JUN-42
11344 TS        M   09-JUN-55
11678 U         F   14-JUN-34
11788 TS        M   05-JUN-70
12223 S         F   15-JUN-29
12679 TS        M   15-JUN-28
13006 TS        M   09-JUN-54
13114 U         F   14-JUN-35
14007 TS        M   10-JUN-49
14204 C         M   05-JUN-68
40001 TS        M   10-JUN-50
40002 S         F   05-JUN-68
40003 U         F   11-JUN-47
40004 S         F   10-JUN-49
40005 TS        M   15-JUN-29
40006 TS        M   14-JUN-34
```

Figure 11.1: Employee database tables

SYSTEM- AND OBJECT-LEVEL PRIVILEGES

The authorization subsystem allows DBA users to grant and revoke privileges to other users with the SQL statements GRANT and REVOKE. The decisions about which users are granted what privileges are company policy decisions that are merely enforced by Oracle. The decisions are yours alone as the DBA of Professional Oracle for microcomputers. Oracle ensures that accesses to the RDBMS are always checked against all the authorization constraints it stores and maintains.

Oracle maintains two levels or groups of privileges: system privileges and object privileges. *System privileges* refer to the CONNECT, RESOURCE, and DBA privileges granted to users by the DBA. The privilege classes determine whether you can log on to Oracle, whether or not you can create objects, and whether or not you can authorize other users to log on to Oracle.

Object privileges provide detailed control over database objects (tables, views, and so forth) once you are logged on to the Oracle system. Enforced with object privileges, views allow you to control table access down to the level of selected columns of selected rows of a particular table. Object privileges determine what you may do at that level—whether you may merely ''see'' a value, alter a value, or create a new value and insert it into a table. The sections that follow describe the security that Oracle provides at the system and object levels. Although views have been described fully in Chapter 6, they are reviewed here as a means of restricting privileges to subsets of tables. We also discuss Oracle's ability to audit system access. Throughout this chapter we assume that the Oracle authentication system checking stored usernames and encrypted passwords functions correctly. Thus, it is not described explicitly—only mentioned peripherally.

ESTABLISHING USER SYSTEM-LEVEL PRIVILEGES: ENROLLING USERS

Every Oracle user must have access to the host operating system. On minicomputers and mainframes, you are assigned a user identification and associated password. You log on to the host system by supplying both. Microcomputer systems do not generally require either a username or password to execute MS-DOS functions and utility programs. However, you need an Oracle username and password to log on to Oracle regardless of the host platform that runs it. The Oracle DBA assigns usernames and passwords, which is also known as enrolling users. Once enrolled, you are restricted to one of the three system-level privileges.

CHANGING THE "SUPERUSER" PASSWORDS

As you recall, the three classes of system-level access are CON-NECT, RESOURCE, and DBA. CONNECT carries the lowest while DBA carries the highest level of privilege. As shipped to you, Professional Oracle already contains two superuser passwords with DBA privileges. When you first enter Oracle to establish other usernames and passwords, log on with one of these usernames, SYS-TEM. Initially, the username SYSTEM has the the default password MANAGER. You should change this password to protect the integrity of your system. Do so by loading Oracle (type **ORACLE** at the DOS prompt—see Chapter 3) and typing the following at the DOS prompt:

```
SQLPLUS SYSTEM/MANAGER
```

and pressing Enter. Once the SQL> prompt appears, change the password using the GRANT command. The following statement changes SYSTEM's password to SHERLOCK:

```
SQL> GRANT CONNECT TO SYSTEM IDENTIFIED BY SHERLOCK;
```

Remember to terminate all SQL statements with a semicolon. Once the statement is executed, Oracle responds with the message "Grant succeeded."

GRANT has two forms: one to grant system-level privileges and one to grant object-level privileges. The syntax for granting system-level privileges is

```
GRANT {CONNECT [,RESOURCE] [,DBA]} TO username
      IDENTIFIED BY password;
```

Braces indicate that one or more options (for example, privileges such as CONNECT, RESOURCE, or DBA) are required. Brackets indicate optional entries. Professional Oracle requires the IDENTIFIED BY phrase. You can substitute any acceptable words for *username* and *password*.

You can change the other "superuser" password (SYS) by executing the SQL statement

```
SQL> GRANT CONNECT TO SYS IDENTIFIED BY newpassword;
```

where you substitute any password up to 30 characters in length for *newpassword*. The two preceding SQL statements show how passwords are changed for existing users. Adding new usernames and passwords is a similar process.

CREATING A NEW DATABASE ADMINISTRATOR USERNAME

At least one username must have DBA privileges in order to enroll additional usernames with varying levels of system privileges. Because the two superuser usernames SYS and SYSTEM are so essential, you should *never* use them to access Oracle after you have changed their passwords. Instead, establish your own username and password with DBA privileges, and use it sparingly. You may wish to establish one or more usernames that have less privilege.

You can establish your own special username with the DBA privilege by logging on to Oracle with the username SYSTEM and its recently-changed password:

```
C>SQLPLUS SYSTEM/SHERLOCK
```

Then, establish the new username with DBA privilege using the GRANT command:

```
SQL> GRANT CONNECT, RESOURCE, DBA TO mydbaname
  2  IDENTIFIED BY mypassword;
```

where *mydbaname* is any username (up to 30 characters) and *mypassword* is any password (up to 30 characters). Notice that all three of the system-level privileges have been granted in one statement. This permits user mydbaname to create new usernames and to create tables and other database objects. If you grant the DBA privilege without specifying CONNECT or RESOURCE, the CONNECT privilege is granted automatically but the RESOURCE privilege is not.

After creating your own DBA username, you can log off and then immediately log back on with the newly-created DBA username. Now you can enroll additional username/password pairs with lower system-level privileges.

ESTABLISHING NON-DBA USERNAMES AND PASSWORDS

You may wish to limit the number of DBA-class users, because anyone with DBA privileges can enroll new users or grant any system-level privileges to existing users. (Most installations have only one user with DBA privileges.) For example, the DBA can enroll a new user with the username CORDELL and password SPIFFY and only allow her to access tables that other users have created.

```
GRANT CONNECT TO CORDELL IDENTIFIED BY SPIFFY;
```

CORDELL can then log on to Oracle by executing

```
SQLPLUS CORDELL/SPIFFY
```

or by merely typing **SQLPLUS**, pressing Enter, and typing the username and a password when prompted to do so. This second method does not echo the password on the screen.

ENROLLING USERS WITH THE RESOURCE PRIVILEGE

If you need to create database objects such as tables, clusters, and indexes, you must have the system privilege RESOURCE. Once you have RESOURCE privilege, you can create and drop tables, clusters, or indexes (see Chapter 12). At this level of privilege, you can drop only tables and views that you have created.

Log on to Oracle with the DBA username and execute

```
GRANT CONNECT, RESOURCE TO newuser IDENTIFIED BY newpassword;
```

to establish user *newuser* with password *newpassword* and RESOURCE privileges. Notice that both CONNECT and RESOURCE have been listed. Giving a new user RESOURCE privileges does not give them CONNECT privileges. If you omit CONNECT in the preceding GRANT command, Oracle generates the error message

```
ERROR at line 1: ORA-0933:  SQL command not properly ended
```

You need to list both CONNECT and RESOURCE when creating a new username with the RESOURCE privilege, but the order in which you list them is unimportant.

You can assign several usernames and passwords with one GRANT command. For example, you can assign users USER1, USER2, and USER3 CONNECT and RESOURCE privileges and passwords with the single GRANT statement

```
GRANT CONNECT, RESOURCE TO USER1, USER2, USER3
IDENTIFIED BY CURLY, MOE, LARRY;
```

where USER1 is assigned password CURLY, USER2 is assigned password MOE, and USER3 is assigned password LARRY.

LISTING PRIVILEGES

Anyone with the CONNECT privilege can display username information. Oracle maintains username and privilege information in a special data dictionary view called SYSUSERLIST. Executing

```
SQL> SELECT * FROM SYSUSERLIST;
```

lists the USERID, USERNAME, and TIMESTAMP columns of SYSUSERLIST along with the system privileges of each username. Figure 11.2 shows a typical listing.

```
USERID USERNAME                              TIMESTAMP C D R
. . . . . . .  . . . . . . . . . . . . . . . . . . . . . . .  . . . . . . . . . .  .  .  .
    31                                       12-JUL-87
     0 SYS                                   24-MAR-89 Y Y Y
     1 PUBLIC                                12-JUL-87
     2 SYSTEM                                24-MAR-89 Y Y Y
     4 ORACLEUSER                            26-APR-89 Y
    13 DATABASEADM                           26-APR-89 Y Y Y
    15 ACCOUNTINGVP                          03-JUN-88 Y
    16 SPECIALPROJECTS                       18-MAY-89 Y Y
    20 RESEARCH                              31-MAY-89 Y
    23 ZAKS                                  31-MAY-89 Y Y
```

Figure 11.2: Oracle user information obtained from SYSUSERLIST

Because SYSUSERLIST is like any table, you can display a subset of its columns or rows with a SELECT statement such as

```
SELECT USERNAME, USERID
FROM SYSUSERLIST
WHERE CONNECTAUTH IS NOT NULL
ORDER BY USERNAME;
```

to obtain a username and userid list in username order. Or, you might want to display only those users having DBA privileges with the statement

```
SELECT * FROM SYSUSERLIST
WHERE DBAAUTH = 'Y'
ORDER BY TIMESTAMP;
```

Clearly, you can issue a great variety of SQL SELECT statements for the SYSUSERLIST view. Though not displayed fully in Figure 11.2, the structure of SYSUSERLIST reveals the full column names as well as types. You can list the structure of any table or view with the SQL*Plus command DESCRIBE. For example,

```
SQL> DESCRIBE SYSUSERLIST;
```

returns the following description:

```
Name                    Null?     Type
--------------------    -------   -------
USERID                  NOT NULL  NUMBER
USERNAME                          CHAR(30)
TIMESTAMP               NOT NULL  DATE
CONNECTAUTH                       CHAR(1)
DBAAUTH                           CHAR(1)
RESOURCEAUTH                      CHAR(1)
```

The first number in the USERID column (see Figure 11.2) indicates the number of new users enrolled since Oracle was last initialized. The TIMESTAMP column contains the date of the last change to the associated username; this includes adding a username, changing a user password, or altering a user's system privileges.

Users with CONNECT privilege can

- Log on to Oracle
- Create views and synonyms
- Retrieve data from other users' tables and views to which they have been granted access
- Perform INSERT, DELETE, and UPDATE operations on other users' tables and views to which they have been granted the appropriate access

However, such users cannot create tables, indexes, or clusters of their own.

Users with CONNECT and RESOURCE privileges inherit all the previous abilities and can also do the following:

- Use the AUDIT command to control auditing of object access for objects they own
- Create database tables, indexes, and clusters
- Grant and revoke object privileges on objects they own

Users with the DBA privilege, in addition to the preceding abilities, can

- Perform full database export and import operations

- Access and perform any SQL statement on any other users' data
- Grant and revoke users' system level privileges
- Create public synonyms
- Create and alter partitions
- Control auditing and table-level auditing defaults on the entire Oracle system

REMOVING SYSTEM-LEVEL PRIVILEGES: REVOKE

System-level user privileges can be selectively removed for one or more usernames with a REVOKE statement. REVOKE has one form for removing system privileges and another for removing object privileges. The syntax for revoking system privileges is:

```
REVOKE ([CONNECT] [,RESOURCE] [,DBA]
   FROM (user1,user2,...) ;
```

where *user1,* and so on are usernames. Revoking object-level privileges is described later in this chapter.

To remove the RESOURCE privilege from username NAGY, simply execute the SQL statement

```
REVOKE RESOURCE FROM NAGY;
```

You can revoke multiple users' privileges with a statement like

```
REVOKE RESOURCE FROM USER1, USER2, USER3;
```

When REVOKE is successful completed, Oracle issues the message "Revoke succeeded."

When your CONNECT privilege is revoked, you are removed from the system and can no longer log on to Oracle. However, your database objects are not removed from the system. The DBA and other users who have been given access to them can continue to access those tables or views. If your CONNECT privileges are reinstated, your tables are again available to you. Usernames with

RESOURCE or DBA privileges can be removed with the statement

```
REVOKE CONNECT FROM CARROLL;
```

Be careful *never* to revoke the privileges of either SYS or SYSTEM—chaos will result if you do.

ESTABLISHING USER OBJECT-LEVEL PRIVILEGES

Once users have CONNECT, RESOURCE or DBA privileges, they can be granted object-access privileges so that they can insert, update, delete, or retrieve data that they have not created. Of course, users have all privileges on any tables or views they create (subject to their system-level privileges granted by the DBA). Object creators must grant object-level privileges whenever they want to share an object with other users.

You can rescind object privileges with the REVOKE statement. Any object-level access privileges thus removed are also rescinded for any users that inherited those rights from other users. If object privileges are revoked from the PUBLIC user, all users instantly lose privileges to objects they had acquired through the PUBLIC user. Details of revoking privileges from both individual users and the PUBLIC user are presented later in this chapter.

GRANTING OBJECT PRIVILEGES

Object-level privileges protect each database table and view maintained by Oracle. There are seven object-level privileges: ALL, SELECT, INSERT, UPDATE, DELETE, ALTER, and INDEX. Any of the preceding privileges can be granted on one table for use by one or more users or by PUBLIC. The privileges that can be granted on views are SELECT, INSERT, UPDATE, and DELETE. If several privileges are granted at once, they must be separated by commas. The syntax of the object-level GRANT command is:

```
GRANT (privilege, privilege,...|ALL) ON table
   TO (username1 [,username2]...|PUBLIC)
   [WITH GRANT OPTION] ;
```

where *privilege* is one of the seven allowed for tables or one of the four allowed for views.

Among the object-level privileges, UPDATE offers the finest degree of control because you can restrict access to particular columns. To do so, simply list the column names in parentheses after the word UPDATE in the GRANT command, as shown here:

```
GRANT SELECT, UPDATE(EMPID, DEPTNO)
ON EMPLOYEES TO LATEER;
```

In this case, user LATEER will be able to update only the columns EMPID and DEPTNO of the EMPLOYEES table.

Granting Privileges on One Table to Another User

You can receive privileges on a single table from its owner even if you have only the CONNECT system privilege. You do not need to have RESOURCE privilege to do useful database work. As long as you have, for example, INSERT privilege on a table, you can add data to it. Furthermore, if you are granted the appropriate SELECT, UPDATE, DELETE, or ALL privileges, you can retrieve, change, or delete information from others' tables.

Suppose that the owner of all tables shown in Figure 11.1 is the username PERRY. That is, PERRY created the EMPLOYEES, SECURITY, and MANAGERS tables. Suppose that the other five managers should be able to retrieve and alter all entries in the EMPLOYEES table. However, they should not be able to delete entries from nor insert new information into the EMPLOYEES table. The following GRANT statement provides the appropriate privileges to the five managers:

```
GRANT SELECT, UPDATE
ON EMPLOYEES TO LATEER, CORDELL, ZAKS, KING, SIMPSON;
```

Oracle displays the message "Grant succeeded." to indicate successful completion of the GRANT command.

Once user PERRY issues the preceding statement (only he can grant those privileges to EMPLOYEES), then CORDELL, for example, could retrieve information by executing the statement

```
SELECT * FROM EMPLOYEES;
```

But this message would result:

```
ERROR at line 1: ORA-0942:  table or view does not exist
```

The query was ill-formed. When you issue SQL statements against another's table, that table (or view) name must be fully qualified. Because PERRY owns the EMPLOYEES table, a reference to it by anyone except PERRY must be preceded by "PERRY." The corrected query is:

```
SELECT * FROM PERRY.EMPLOYEES;
```

The resulting table is identical to the EMPLOYEES table shown in Figure 11.1.

What if you attempt to use privileges that you do not possess on another's table or view? Oracle security mechanisms check your access privileges every time a SQL statement is executed. Suppose user CORDELL attempted to delete an entry from the EMPLOYEES table. The DELETE statement is

```
DELETE FROM PERRY.EMPLOYEES
  WHERE EMPID=40005;
```

The Oracle error message generated is

```
DELETE FROM PERRY.EMPLOYEES
            *
ERROR at line 1: ORA-1031:  insufficient privileges
```

Oracle correctly determined that CORDELL had "insufficient privileges" to delete information from EMPLOYEE.

If CORDELL has only the CONNECT privilege, PERRY can tightly control the EMPLOYEES table. However, if CORDELL has has both CONNECT and RESOURCE system privileges, she can take and keep her own copy of the entire table. This may or may not be a security problem. CORDELL can "steal" a copy of the EMPLOYEES table with only SELECT access to it but with the RESOURCE system privilege using the following statement:

```
CREATE TABLE MYCOPYOFEMPLOYEES AS
  SELECT * FROM PERRY.EMPLOYEES;
```

Be aware of this potential security breach when granting other users access to your tables.

Granting Privileges on One Table to All Users

You can grant all users access to one or more of your tables. However, keep in mind that as the enrolled user population changes, so do the names of users who have access to your tables. A special username, PUBLIC, allows the entire database user population access to your tables (every Oracle system automatically enrolls the PUBLIC user). PUBLIC comprises all usernames with the CONNECT system privilege. As members of PUBLIC, database users can be granted access to all data dictionary tables and any tables that PUBLIC has been granted access to by table owners. The object privileges that you grant to PUBLIC restrict the table and view activities of all users on that table.

Suppose that the MANAGERS table containing department numbers, manager identification numbers, and manager names is public information within the company. As owner of the MANAGERS table, you do not want any employee altering the table. You can grant read-only access to all users with the following GRANT command:

```
GRANT SELECT
   ON EMPLOYEES TO PUBLIC;
```

Any database user can then inspect the EMPLOYEES table by executing

```
SELECT * FROM PERRY.MANAGERS;
```

to retrieve the six-line MANAGERS table.

Creating Public Synonyms

Often-used table references can be simplified if the DBA creates a public synonym such as COMPANY_MANAGERS. Any user can then use the more easily remembered synonym in place of the more awkward table reference. Only a DBA can create public synonyms, which can be created for tables, views, or other synonyms. The statement

```
CREATE PUBLIC SYNONYM COMPANY_MANAGERS FOR PERRY.MANAGERS;
```

creates the public synonym COMPANY_MANAGERS. For example, if PERRY has granted CORDELL the SELECT privilege on table MANAGER, CORDELL could execute the SELECT statement

```
SELECT * FROM COMPANY_MANAGERS;
```

to retrieve manager's names from the table PERRY.MANAGER. You can display the list of current public synonyms by executing the SELECT statement

```
SELECT * FROM PUBLICSYN;
```

Figure 11.3 shows part of a typical display produced by the previous statement. Only the SNAME (synonym name) and CREATOR (the user who created the synonym) are displayed.

Users without DBA privilege can create their own *private* synonyms with the CREATE SYNONYM statement. With the following statement, user LATEER can create a synonym MYMANAGERS for the table PERRY.MANAGERS:

```
CREATE SYNONYM MYMANAGERS FOR PERRY.MANAGERS;
```

Private synonyms can be accessed only by their creator.

Granting Update Privileges to Other Users

Like the SELECT privilege, the UPDATE object privilege may be granted to one or more users on one or more tables. With update privilege on a table, you can use the UPDATE command to alter one or more entries in any number of table rows. A table creator can also permit *limited* UPDATE capabilities to other users. By granting UPDATE to a limited number of columns of a particular table, you can restrict update activity.

```
SNAME              CREATOR
----------------   -------
AUDIT_ACCESS       SYSTEM
AUDIT_ACTIONS      SYSTEM
AUDIT_CONNECT      SYSTEM
AUDIT_DBA          SYSTEM
AUDIT_EXISTS       SYSTEM
AUDIT_TRAIL        SYSTEM
CATALOG            SYSTEM
CLUSTERCOLUMNS     SYSTEM
CLUSTERS           SYSTEM
COL                SYSTEM
COLUMNS            SYSTEM
DBLINKS            SYSTEM
DEFAULT_AUDIT      SYSTEM
DTAB               SYSTEM
DUAL               SYSTEM
...                ...
SYSPROGS           SYSTEM
SYSSTORAGE         SYSTEM
SYSTABALLOC        SYSTEM
SYSTABAUTH         SYSTEM
SYSTEM_AUDIT       SYSTEM
SYSUSERAUTH        SYSTEM
SYSUSERLIST        SYSTEM
SYSVIEWS           SYSTEM
TAB                SYSTEM
TABALLOC           SYSTEM
TABLE_AUDIT        SYSTEM
TABQUOTAS          SYSTEM
VIEWS              SYSTEM
```

Figure 11.3: Typical display of public synonyms

UPDATE may be followed by a list of columns enclosed in parentheses to restrict the columns that other users can update. For example, the GRANT statement:

```
GRANT SELECT, UPDATE(EMPID, DEPTNO)
ON EMPLOYEES TO LATEER;
```

allows username LATEER to retrieve all rows of the EMPLOYEES table, but allows him to alter only values in columns EMPID and DEPTNO. A typical UPDATE statement that LATEER might execute is

```
UPDATE PERRY.EMPLOYEES
SET DEPTNO=631 WHERE DEPTNO=720;
```

in which department 720 has been eliminated. All employees in department 720 are transferred to department 631.

In similar ways, object access privileges DELETE, INSERT, ALTER, and INDEX may be granted to other users. You should exercise care when granting other users any access privileges on tables you create. If ALL is the only privilege listed following the word GRANT, as in this command:

```
GRANT ALL ON EMPLOYEES TO LATEER;
```

all object privileges are given to the listed users on the specified table or view.

Passing Privilege Granting Rights to Other Users

You can grant other users the right to pass their granted access privileges on to other users. Other users inherit this privilege granting capability when you add the optional phrase WITH GRANT OPTION to a GRANT statement. For example, suppose that the owner of the SECURITY table, PERRY, issued the the following GRANT statement:

```
GRANT SELECT, UPDATE
ON SECURITY TO LATEER
WITH GRANT OPTION;
```

User LATEER, having gained the rights to retrieve and update data in the SECURITY table, could pass those two rights on to *anyone*. For example, he could subsequently issue the statement

```
GRANT SELECT, UPDATE
ON PERRY.SECURITY TO CORDELL, KING;
```

by which users CORDELL and KING receive the same privileges on the SECURITY table that LATEER received from PERRY. However, LATEER could not grant additional SECURITY table privileges such as DELETE to CORDELL or KING. Here is an example GRANT command issued by username LATEER:

```
GRANT DELETE ON PERRY.SECURITY
TO CORDELL, KING;
```

which results in the Oracle-issued error message

```
GRANT DELETE ON PERRY.SECURITY
        *
ERROR at line 1: ORA-1712:  you cannot grant a privilege which you do not have
```

Generally, users cannot pass on rights to other's tables that they did not explicitly receive themselves. (Again, notice that a username must precede the table name for tables not created by the grantor).

Listing Object Access Privileges

After you have granted or received object access privileges, they may be difficult to remember. Fortunately, one of the data dictionary views, SYSTABAUTH, contains all object-level grant information about all objects protected by Oracle. Any Oracle user can display the contents of this view.

The SYSTABAUTH view contains eleven columns of information for each object for which privileges have been granted. Three columns note who granted the privilege (the GRANTOR), who received the privilege (the GRANTEE), and the object on which the privilege was granted (TNAME). The remaining columns contain details about the six object-level privileges: SELECT, UPDATE, INSERT, DELETE, ALTER, and INDEX. Figure 11.4 shows a SELECT statement that displays the privileges user PERRY has either granted or received (two columns have been omitted). Because you are probably not interested in all object privileges held by all users in the system, the SELECT statement shown extracts only the rows of SYSTABAUTH related to the currently logged user (PERRY, in the figure). Figure 11.4 also includes the SQL*Plus COLUMN statements that format the extracted information into an easy-to-read table.

Each row in Figure 11.4 corresponds to the privileges that the currently logged username (PERRY) has for the table shown in the Table Name column. The second column contains the username receiving the privilege. The privileges granted and received are contained in the last six columns (their order is unimportant). A "G" indicator means that the privilege was received via the WITH GRANT OPTION phrase and may be granted to other users. When a "Y" appears, the grantee holds the corresponding privilege to the

```
COLUMN GRANTOR  HEADING "Granted |By" FORMAT A10
COLUMN GRANTEE  HEADING "Granted |To" FORMAT A10
COLUMN TNAME    HEADING "Table |Name" FORMAT A12
COLUMN ALT      HEADING "Alter"       FORMAT A5
COLUMN DEL      HEADING "Delete"      FORMAT A6
COLUMN NDX      HEADING "Index"       FORMAT A5
COLUMN INS      HEADING "Insert"      FORMAT A6
COLUMN SEL      HEADING "Select"      FORMAT A6
COLUMN UPD      HEADING "Update"      FORMAT A6
SELECT GRANTOR,GRANTEE,TNAME,SEL,UPD,INS,DEL,ALT,NDX
FROM SYSTABAUTH
WHERE GRANTEE=USER
   OR GRANTOR=USER
ORDER BY GRANTOR, GRANTEE;


Granted    Granted    Table
By         To         Name      Select Update Insert Delete Alter Index
---------- ---------- --------- ------ ------ ------ ------ ----- -----
PERRY      PERRY      FINANCIAL    G      G      G      G      G     G
PERRY      PERRY      EMPLOYEES    G      G      G      G      G     G
PERRY      PERRY      SECURITY     G      G      G      G      G     G
PERRY      PERRY      MANAGERS     G      G      G      G      G     G
PERRY      PERRY      HRM          G      G      G      G      G     G
PERRY      CORDELL    EMPLOYEES    Y
PERRY      CORDELL    MANAGERS                          Y
PERRY      LATEER     EMPLOYEES   .Y      *
PERRY      LATEER     SECURITY     G
PERRY      PUBLIC     EMPLOYEES    Y
VPRES      PERRY      PROGRESS     Y      Y      Y

11 records selected.
```

Figure 11.4: Object access privileges granted or received

table/view in that row. The asterisk (*) can appear only in the UPDATE column and indicates that the grantor has limited update capability. In this case, the grantor limited the table columns that could be updated by the grantee. If privileges are null (appear blank), the grantee does not have that privilege for the table or view.

Notice, for example, that username PERRY has granted username CORDELL the SELECT privilege on the EMPLOYEES table. In addition, PERRY has granted the SELECT privilege on the table SECURITY to LATEER with the WITH GRANT OPTION phrase. All rows in which PERRY is both the grantor and the grantee contain ''G,'' because PERRY created those objects and thus has full privileges, all of which he can grant to other users.

The last row in Figure 11.4 reveals that username VPRES has granted SELECT, UPDATE, and INSERT privileges to PERRY. Because all privilege indicators in that row are "Y," PERRY cannot grant other users access to the PROGRESS table.

You can modify the SELECT statement in Figure 11.4 slightly to scc all privileges received and granted by all usernames. Merely drop the entire WHERE clause to obtain a listing of all privileges recorded in the SYSTABAUTH view. Likewise, you can revise the ORDER BY phrase to sort your result in a different manner (perhaps by GRANTEE and then SELECT order).

REVOKING OBJECT PRIVILEGES

Object privileges can be removed from one or more users similar to the way they were granted. The syntax for object privilege revocation is:

```
REVOKE (privilege list|ALL} ON table
   FROM (user1 [,user2]...|PUBLIC} ;
```

where *user1* and *user2* are usernames and *privilege list* is one or more of the six privileges. *Table* is a table, view, or synonym. If all privileges are to be revoked, ALL follows the word REVOKE.

If you have been granted access to a table or view by more than one user, you can access that table until your privileges have been revoked by *all* users who granted them. For example, the SELECT and UPDATE privileges to table SECURITY granted to LATEER earlier in this chapter can be revoked by executing:

```
REVOKE SELECT, UPDATE
   ON SECURITY FROM LATEER;
```

or

```
REVOKE ALL
   ON SECURITY FROM LATEER;
```

When one of these commands is executed by the original grantor (PERRY), LATEER can no longer access the SECURITY table. In the second example, he loses all privileges to that table, whereas he loses only SELECT and UPDATE in the first. If LATEER held a DELETE option, for example, the first form still permits him to delete records from the SECURITY table. If your object privileges are revoked, so are any rights you may have had to grant those privileges to others.

Similarly, privileges previously granted to the entire enrolled group of users through the PUBLIC facility can be revoked:

```
REVOKE ALL ON EMPLOYEES FROM PUBLIC;
```

Now no user can access the EMPLOYEES table unless explicitly given access. For example, a particular user may still have SELECT privilege to EMPLOYEES if he or she were granted them by an earlier GRANT statement such as:

```
GRANT SELECT ON EMPLOYEES TO LATEER;
```

Revoking object privileges can have a "ripple" effect whenever rights were granted with the WITH GRANT OPTION. Suppose the EMPLOYEES table owner PERRY granted SELECT access to LATEER with the statement

```
GRANT SELECT ON EMPLOYEES TO LATEER
   WITH GRANT OPTION;
```

And suppose LATEER issued the GRANT command

```
GRANT SELECT ON PERRY.EMPLOYEES
   TO CORDELL, KING, ZAKS;
```

Now CORDELL, KING, and ZAKS could all retrieve data from the EMPLOYEES table, having inherited the SELECT right from LATEER. But, when PERRY revokes the SELECT privilege from LATEER, all other usernames with access to EMPLOYEES granted by LATEER also lose that privilege. You can control object access even if the WITH GRANT OPTION is used, since revoking the original recipient's privileges revokes the same rights from all subsequent recipients.

GRANT and REVOKE control only what activities can occur with respect to a table and who can invoke those activities. Alone, they cannot restrict access to a subset of a table. That is, you can grant SELECT to a particular user on a particular table, but that user can then retrieve the entire table. Views fill this gap by providing a way to grant various privileges to subsets of table columns and/or rows. Together, GRANT, REVOKE, and the view mechanism provide tight security for a relational database management system.

ENFORCING PRIVILEGES ON TABLE SUBSETS: VIEWS

In Chapter 6, you used views to enforce data hiding by using the SELECT phrase as part of the CREATE VIEW statement to define subsets of rows, columns, or rows and columns. Here, views are explored further using the three base tables EMPLOYEES, MANAGERS, and SECURITY. Once you create views, you grant users access to them with the GRANT statement as with base tables. Access to views is limited to the four object privileges SELECT, INSERT, UPDATE, and DELETE. You can remove view access with the REVOKE statement.

The GRANT and REVOKE statements adequately control access to tables. With views, you can grant users access to something less than an entire table. In effect, views permit you to fabricate images of partial tables that can consist of selected rows, selected columns, or a combination of selected rows and selected columns. These *virtual tables,* coupled with the access privileges granted to them, provide table access control down to the field level.

RESTRICTING ACCESS TO SELECTED COLUMNS

You can define a view that provides only a subset of the table's columns. This protects a base table on a column-by-column basis from unwanted disclosure and alteration. Suppose a company's financial officer needs access to the three EMPLOYEES table columns EMPID, SALARY, and HIREDATE, but should be prevented from inspecting or altering the DEPTNO and DEPEN-DENTS columns. The view definition:

```
CREATE VIEW FINANCIAL AS
SELECT EMPID, SALARY, HIREDATE
FROM EMPLOYEES
WITH CHECK OPTION;
```

will provide data hiding while permitting access to the three required columns. You could construct a more elaborate CREATE VIEW to ensure that any rows updated through this view conform to a set of data integrity rules.

Once the view is defined by the EMPLOYEES table owner, access is then granted to that view, not to the EMPLOYEES table. In particular, to grant username KING (the financial officer requiring limited access) INSERT, UPDATE, DELETE, and SELECT privileges on the view, you would execute the following GRANT statement:

```
GRANT INSERT, UPDATE, DELETE, SELECT
ON FINANCIAL TO KING;
```

KING can log on to Oracle and retrieve, insert, remove, or update any record in the view and thus in the EMPLOYEES table (for the allowed columns). For example, KING could issue the statement

```
SELECT * FROM PERRY.FINANCIAL
ORDER BY EMPID;
```

to retrieve rows in ascending employee identification number order. Figure 11.5 shows the result of the preceding query.

Another example of a column subset is the view defined on the EMPLOYEES table as follows:

```
CREATE VIEW ALLEMPLOYEES (DEPT, IDENT) AS
SELECT DEPTNO, EMPID
FROM EMPLOYEES
GROUP BY DEPTNO, EMPID;
```

```
EMPID SALARY HIREDATE
----- ------ --------
10004   1326 15-MAY-74
10008   1900 17-SEP-75
10012   1962 10-NOV-77
10025   1454 20-MAY-79
10122   1895 06-MAY-79
10147   1910 01-JAN-80
11221   1264 19-FEB-81
11344   1457 01-NOV-81
11678   1651 15-MAY-82
11788   1166 15-MAY-82
12223   1351 15-DEC-82
12679   1800 14-JUN-83
13006   1742 14-MAR-84
13114   1617 15-APR-85
14007   1210 23-JAN-86
14204   1971 07-JUL-87
40001   4500 01-APR-76
40002   2500 01-JAN-82
40003   2700 15-JAN-76
40004   3400 15-JUN-81
40005   3700 07-DEC-81
40006   3250 21-SEP-84
```

Figure 11.5: Retrieving selected columns through a view

Only the department number (renamed DEPT in the view) and the employee identification number (renamed IDENT) are visible through this view. The returned results are in ascending order by DEPTNO and by EMPID within departments.

RESTRICTING ACCESS TO SELECTED ROWS

Defining views that return only selected rows of one or more base tables prevents user access to entire rows of information. For this reason, these views are often called row subset views. Suppose that the EMPLOYEES table owner wants all department managers to be able to extract, alter, or remove information from the EMPLOYEES table. Suppose, however, that the owner wants to restrict those activities to managers, and wants managers to be able to manipulate rows only for employees that they manage. A view definition that accomplishes this follows:

```
CREATE VIEW MANAGERSDEPT AS
SELECT EMPID, DEPTNO, SALARY, HIREDATE, DEPENDENTS
FROM EMPLOYEES
WHERE DEPTNO IN (SELECT DEPTNO
                  FROM MANAGERS
                  WHERE MGRNAME=USER)
  AND EMPID NOT IN (SELECT EMPID
                    FROM MANAGERS
                    WHERE MGRNAME=USER)
WITH CHECK OPTION;
```

The first part of the WHERE clause ensures that only employees managed by a manager who is currently logged on are retrieved. The part of the WHERE clause following AND prevents managers from altering their own rows (from increasing their own salaries, for example). No other employee rows are returned. The WITH CHECK OPTION assures that managers can only insert employees who are in the department they manage.

After creating the view, access privileges must be granted to it, as with a base table. EMPLOYEES's owner (and the user that created the preceding view) can execute a simple GRANT instruction:

```
GRANT SELECT, INSERT, UPDATE, DELETE
ON MANAGERSDEPT TO PUBLIC;
```

The easiest way to grant access to several selected users is to grant those rights to the special user PUBLIC. The view definition contains the appropriate username restriction (WHERE MGRNAME = USER) limiting access to the subset of managers. Notice that this view accesses the MANAGERS table to verify that the requesting username is that of a manager, and then accesses the EMPLOYEES table to actually retrieve selected rows. The results of retrieval requests by two managers are shown in Figure 11.6.

CREATING VIEWS OF MULTIPLE BASE TABLES

You create views to simplify data retrieval as well as to hide data. Views often include derived data, columns whose values are

```
SELECT * FROM PERRY.MANAGERSDEPT;

EMPID DEPTNO SALARY HIREDATE   DEPENDENTS
----- ------ ------ --------- ----------
10004   318   1326  15-MAY-74      4
11678   318   1651  15-MAY-82      3
11788   318   1166  15-MAY-82      4
10147   318   1910  01-JAN-80      2


SELECT * FROM PERRY.MANAGERSDEPT;

EMPID DEPTNO SALARY HIREDATE   DEPENDENTS
----- ------ ------ --------- ----------
10012   181   1962  10-NOV-77      1
14007   181   1210  23-JAN-86      1
13006   181   1742  14-MAR-84      0
```

Figure 11.6: Retrieving selected rows using two base tables

computed by expressions that can include database column names, Oracle functions, and Oracle operators (see Chapter 7). For example, here is a query-simplifying view containing a derived value:

```
CREATE VIEW HRM (EMPID, AGE, SEX, HIREDATE) AS
SELECT SECURITY.EMPID, FLOOR(MONTHS_BETWEEN(SYSDATE,DOB)/12),
       SEX, HIREDATE
FROM EMPLOYEES, SECURITY
WHERE EMPLOYEES.EMPID=SECURITY.EMPID;
```

The second field in the SELECT statement computes an employee's age using two functions (FLOOR and MONTHS_BETWEEN), an Oracle generated pseudo column (SYSDATE), and the date of birth (DOB) database field. When you include a derived field in a view, you must provide an alias column name for the column list that follows the view name. In the previous example the derived column is called AGE.

The preceding view not only simplifies queries but protects the base tables from which it is derived. In particular, the SECURITY table contains sensitive information that should not be fully available to all database users. Access to the HRM view and to the underlying base table SECURITY should be granted sparingly. Figure 11.7 contains a list of rows retrieved using the preceding view definition. The SELECT statement is also shown.

```
SELECT * FROM PERRY.HRM
   ORDER BY EMPID;

EMPID AGE SEX HIREDATE
----- --- --- ---------
10004  61 M    15-MAY-74
10008  22 F    17-SEP-75
10012  28 F    10-NOV-77
10025  38 F    20-MAY-79
10122  44 M    06-MAY-79
10147  38 M    01-JAN-80
11221  45 F    19-FEB-81
11344  32 M    01-NOV-81
11678  53 F    15-MAY-82
11788  18 M    15-MAY-82
12223  58 F    15-DEC-82
12679  59 M    14-JUN-83
13006  33 M    14-MAR-84
13114  52 F    15-APR-85
14007  38 M    23-JAN-86
14204  20 M    07-JUL-87
40001  37 M    01-APR-76
40002  20 F    01-JAN-82
40003  40 F    15-JAN-76
40004  38 F    15-JUN-81
40005  58 M    07-DEC-81
40006  53 M    21-SEP-84
```

Figure 11.7: Retrieving rows that contain derived columns

LISTING VIEW DEFINITIONS

Because views that you define are not actual tables, only their definition is saved by Oracle in the data dictionary. Whenever you access a view, the view definition is retrieved from the data dictionary and executed. For this reason, views are called virtual tables; their lifetime is only as long as it takes to execute a SQL statement using a view. Each time you invoke a view, its definition is obtained and used to retrieve, alter, or delete the specified data again.

You can retrieve view definitions from a special Oracle view called VIEWS, which is accessible to all database users with the CONNECT privilege. A simple SQL statement retrieves the view definitions you have created. By using SQL*Plus extensions to the standard language, you can render the retrieved definitions more understandable. Figure 11.8 contains the SQL and SQL*Plus statements for retrieving and formatting view definitions and a sample display of several view definitions. Among others, the view definitions created in this chapter appear there.

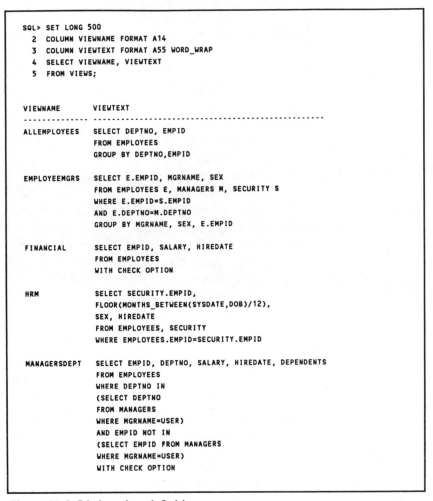

```
SQL> SET LONG 500
  2  COLUMN VIEWNAME FORMAT A14
  3  COLUMN VIEWTEXT FORMAT A55 WORD_WRAP
  4  SELECT VIEWNAME, VIEWTEXT
  5  FROM VIEWS;


VIEWNAME        VIEWTEXT
.............   ................................................
ALLEMPLOYEES    SELECT DEPTNO, EMPID
                FROM EMPLOYEES
                GROUP BY DEPTNO,EMPID

EMPLOYEEMGRS    SELECT E.EMPID, MGRNAME, SEX
                FROM EMPLOYEES E, MANAGERS M, SECURITY S
                WHERE E.EMPID=S.EMPID
                AND E.DEPTNO=M.DEPTNO
                GROUP BY MGRNAME, SEX, E.EMPID

FINANCIAL       SELECT EMPID, SALARY, HIREDATE
                FROM EMPLOYEES
                WITH CHECK OPTION

HRM             SELECT SECURITY.EMPID,
                FLOOR(MONTHS_BETWEEN(SYSDATE,DOB)/12),
                SEX, HIREDATE
                FROM EMPLOYEES, SECURITY
                WHERE EMPLOYEES.EMPID=SECURITY.EMPID

MANAGERSDEPT    SELECT EMPID, DEPTNO, SALARY, HIREDATE, DEPENDENTS
                FROM EMPLOYEES
                WHERE DEPTNO IN
                (SELECT DEPTNO
                FROM MANAGERS
                WHERE MGRNAME=USER)
                AND EMPID NOT IN
                (SELECT EMPID FROM MANAGERS
                WHERE MGRNAME=USER)
                WITH CHECK OPTION
```

Figure 11.8: Listing view definitions

AUDITING

Auditing allows you to record security-relevant events. These events are controlled by, maintained by, and stored in several data dictionary tables and views. Although you may be using a single-user

Oracle system in which only one person at a time can use the database, several people may have access to the database. With auditing, you can monitor and record significant events that occur to any number of tables or views or on the system as a whole. Many government systems that require discretionary access control and mandatory access control also require auditing. (For specific information on government auditing requirements, see *Trusted Computer Systems Evaluation Criteria,* the ''orange book'' mentioned earlier in this chapter and listed in the bibliography.)

Oracle provides a rich set of auditing commands and associated tables and views in which to store audit information. It satisfies many of the audit requirements set forth by the government, although mandatory access control (verified separation by security levels and clearances) is not inherent in Oracle. Audit information is collected and maintained by several tables and views that are part of the Oracle data dictionary. Any user can list the names of the audit tables and views with the SQL command

```
SELECT * FROM DTAB WHERE TNAME LIKE '%AUDIT%';
```

DTAB describes the tables that make up the data dictionary. Selecting only those tables whose names (TNAME) contain the characters AUDIT (capitalized), lists only audit-relevant data dictionary table or view names. Table 11.1 contains the retrieved list of names and brief comments about the function of each table.

ENABLING AUDITING

Before you can collect any audit data, the entire auditing mechanism must be enabled. You do this by adding the following line to the file called INIT.ORA

```
AUDIT_TRAIL 1
```

where the integer value following AUDIT_TRAIL is a value greater than zero. If you use a value of zero, auditing is disabled. Similarly, auditing is disabled if you omit the statement from the INIT.ORA file. When you change the AUDIT_TRAIL parameter, you must shut down Oracle (IOR S) and then warm start it (IOR W) with the

Table 11.1: Audit-Relevant Data Dictionary Tables

TNAME	REMARKS
AUDIT_ACCESS	Audit entries for accesses to users' tables/views (DBA sees all)
AUDIT_ACTIONS	Maps auditing action numbers to action names
AUDIT_CONNECT	Audit trail entries for user logon/logoff (DBA sees all)
AUDIT_DBA	Audit trail entries for DBA activities—for DBA use only
AUDIT_EXISTS	Audit trail entries for objects which do NOT EXIST—for DBA use only
AUDIT_TRAIL	Audit trail entries relevant to the user (DBA sees all)
DEFAULT_AUDIT	Default table auditing options
SYSAUDIT_TRAIL	Synonym for SYS.AUDIT_TRAIL—for DBA use only
SYSTEM_AUDIT	System auditing options—for DBA use only
TABLE_AUDIT	Auditing options of user's tables and views (DBA sees all)

edited INIT.ORA parameters to enable security. You can then collect security-relevant events by issuing SQL statements specifying what types of data are to be collected. There are two major classes of auditing information: system audit and object audit.

AUDITING SYSTEM ACCESS

Even if auditing is enabled, no auditing occurs automatically. Users or the DBA must use the SQL AUDIT statement to indicate which actions should be audited. Only the DBA can initiate system access audit and collect system access audit information. In addition, he or she can choose to audit any other users' tables or views. The SQL AUDIT statement syntax has one form that only the DBA can issue and another that any user with CONNECT privilege can issue. The DBA-only form is

```
AUDIT {[CONNECT] | [,RESOURCE] | [,DBA]
      [,NOT EXISTS] | [ALL]}
[WHENEVER [NOT] SUCCESSFUL] ;
```

As usual, braces indicate that at least one item enclosed must be chosen, and brackets indicate optional choices.

The main difference between table audits and system audits is the actions that they monitor and record. System CONNECT auditing records Oracle logon and logoff actions. System RESOURCE auditing collects data whenever CREATE/DROP TABLE, VIEW, SPACE, SYNONYM, or CREATE, ALTER, DROP CLUSTER statements are executed. System DBA auditing collects information whenever system-wide GRANT, REVOKE, AUDIT, or NOAUDIT statements are issued. DBA auditing information is also recorded whenever partitions are created or altered or public synonyms are created or dropped. Additionally, system auditing records all references to objects that result in the Oracle message "...does not exist."

Table auditing is controlled and initiated by object owners—as well as users with DBA authority. Users can record all accesses to objects they own. A great deal of audit information is placed in the AUDIT_TRAIL view described briefly in this section.

Initiating System Audit Information Collection

The DBA can use the AUDIT command to record both successful and unsuccessful attempts to log on to Oracle. For example, the following statement

```
AUDIT CONNECT WHENEVER SUCCESSFUL;
```

records every successful logon to Oracle. Likewise, the statement

```
AUDIT CONNECT WHENEVER UNSUCCESSFUL;
```

records all unsuccessful attempts to log on to Oracle. If you omit the optional clause WHENEVER, all logons are recorded. Whenever a SQL AUDIT statement is executed successfully, you'll see the Oracle message

```
Audit succeeded.
```

When a DBA executes any system AUDIT command, the SYSTEM_AUDIT table is updated to reflect the current system-level auditing options in effect. A one-row table, SYSTEM_AUDIT contains four columns that correspond to the four system-level audit options. A sample SYSTEM_AUDIT is shown in Table 11.2, along with corresponding AUDIT statements that altered the table.

Table 11.2: SYSTEM_AUDIT Table for Various System Audit Options

SYSTEM_AUDIT TABLE CONTENTS	CORRESPONDING AUDIT STATEMENT:

`CON DBA NOT RES`
`... ... ... ...`
`-/- -/- -/- -/-`
	`(system auditing inactive)`

`CON DBA NOT RES`
`... ... ... ...`
`S/- -/- -/- -/-`
	`AUDIT CONNECT`
	`    WHENEVER SUCCESSFUL;`

`CON DBA NOT RES`
`... ... ... ...`
`-/S -/- -/- -/-`
	`AUDIT CONNECT`
	`    WHENEVER NOT SUCCESSFUL;`

`CON DBA NOT RES`
`... ... ... ...`
`S/S -/- -/- -/-`
	`AUDIT CONNECT;`

`CON DBA NOT RES`
`... ... ... ...`
`S/- S/- -/- -/-`
	`AUDIT CONNECT, DBA`
	`    WHENEVER SUCCESSFUL;`

Displaying AUDIT_TRAIL Rows

If you issue the statement AUDIT CONNECT; the SYSTEM-_AUDIT table is updated (the value ''S/S'' is placed in the CON column) to reflect the current classes of system information being audited. From that point on, any logon attempts are recorded in the AUDIT_TRAIL view. This view is owned by the special system username, SYS.

Users or the DBA can execute a simple SELECT statement to list the view's contents. Figure 11.9 shows SQL and SQL*Plus statements to display the AUDIT_TRAIL vew along with a small sample of audit records. AUDIT_TRAIL contains over 20 columns, so only a subset of the audit information is shown. The complete structure of AUDIT_TRAIL is displayed in Figure 11.10.

```
SQL> COLUMN USERID      FORMAT A8
   2 COLUMN ACTION_NAME FORMAT A15
   3 SELECT SESSIONID,USERID,TIMESTAMP,ACTION,ACTION_NAME
   4 FROM AUDIT_TRAIL;


SESSIONID USERID   TIMESTAMP ACTION ACTION_NAME
......... ........ ......... ...... ...............
        2 LATEER   17-OCT-89     61 LOGOFF
        3 INTRUDER 17-OCT-89     60 LOGON
        4 PERRY    17-OCT-89     61 LOGOFF
        5 CORDELL  17-OCT-89     61 LOGOFF
        6 SYSTEM   17-OCT-89     61 LOGOFF
        7 LATEER   17-OCT-89     61 LOGOFF
        8 PERRY    17-OCT-89     60 LOGON
```

Figure 11.9: Listing selected AUDIT_TRAIL rows

Notice in Figure 11.9 that only logoff actions appear to be recorded. In fact, logon actions are also recorded. But when a given user successfully logs on and off, only the logoff action is recorded. Username INTRUDER attempted to log on to Oracle, but was unsuccessful. Username PERRY is currently logged on, although that is not evident.

Terminating System Audit Information Collection

You can disable any system audit action with the NOAUDIT statement. Its syntax is similar to that of AUDIT. Any user with

```
Name              Null?      Type
---------------   --------   --------
USERID                       CHAR(30)
USERHOST                     CHAR(240)
TERMINAL                     CHAR(240)
TIMESTAMP         NOT NULL   DATE
OBJ$CREATOR                  CHAR(30)
OBJ$NAME                     CHAR(30)
ACTION            NOT NULL   NUMBER
ACTION_NAME       NOT NULL   CHAR(27)
NEW$NAME                     CHAR(30)
AUTH$PRIVILEGES              CHAR(6)
AUTH$GRANTEE                 CHAR(30)
SES$ACTIONS                  CHAR(11)
LOGOFF$TIME                  DATE
LOGOFF$LREAD                 NUMBER
LOGOFF$PREAD                 NUMBER
LOGOFF$LWRITE                NUMBER
LOGOFF$DEAD                  NUMBER
COMMENT$TEXT                 CHAR(240)
SESSIONID         NOT NULL   NUMBER
ENTRYID           NOT NULL   NUMBER
STATEMENT         NOT NULL   NUMBER
RETURNCODE        NOT NULL   NUMBER
```

Figure 11.10: The structure of AUDIT_TRAIL

DBA authority can halt recording of selected system events by issuing a statement such as

```
NOAUDIT CONNECT
```

or

```
NOAUDIT CONNECT, RESOURCE
```

Oracle issues the message

```
Noaudit succeeded.
```

when any NOAUDIT command is executed. If you execute the first example statement, audit information about logon attempts will not be recorded. If you execute the second, both logon and resource creation and deletion audit information will no longer be collected.

AUDITING TABLES AND VIEWS

Any user with CONNECT privileges can AUDIT his or her own tables, views and synonyms. Users cannot, of course, audit others' tables, views, or synonyms, although the DBA can do so.

Initiating Object Auditing

Object auditing is initiated by using the non-DBA form of the AUDIT statement. The syntax for users with lower privilege levels is

```
AUDIT <option [,option]... | ALL>
ON <tname | DEFAULT>
[BY <ACCESS | SESSION>]
[WHENEVER [NOT] SUCCESSFUL] ;
```

where *option* can be any of the following: ALTER, AUDIT, COMMENT, DELETE, GRANT, INDEX, INSERT, LOCK, RENAME, SELECT, or UPDATE, and *tname* can be the name of a table, view, or synonym. For base tables, you can audit all listed actions. For views, the auditable actions are: AUDIT, COMMENT, DELETE, GRANT, INSERT, LOCK, RENAME, SELECT, and UPDATE. For example, the statement

```
AUDIT INSERT, SELECT, UPDATE ON PERRY.EMPLOYEES
    WHENEVER UNSUCCESSFUL;
```

writes an audit record whenever any user (including PERRY) unsuccessfully attempts to execute INSERT, SELECT, or UPDATE on the table or view PERRY.EMPLOYEES. The optional BY clause in the AUDIT syntax determines when rows are written to AUDIT_TRAIL. The BY clause also determines how frequently rows are inserted into the AUDIT_TRAIL. Choosing the BY SESSION option causes specified SQL operations to be updated in a user's session record. The BY ACCESS option causes auditing information to be inserted in one or more rows of the AUDIT_TRAIL for each operation on a user's database object. Since a large number of rows can accumulate in the AUDIT_TRAIL, the DBA should monitor and periodically purge it. As with system audit statements, you can choose to audit successful and/or unsuccessful accesses to your objects.

Listing Your Audit Options

The data dictionary table TABLE_AUDIT contains one row for each Oracle table or view, and a column for each of the auditable actions. To see the audit settings that you have stipulated for your tables and views, you can select the rows from TABLE_AUDIT that pertain to your username. Figure 11.11 shows a sample listing of the TABLE_AUDIT table for username PERRY and includes the SQL statement that produced the display. Each column contains "-/-" if no actions are being audited, "S/-" if only successful actions are being audited, "-/S" if unsuccessful actions are being audited, and "S/S" if both successful and unsuccessful actions are being audited.

```
SQL> COLUMN CREATOR FORMAT A7
  2  COLUMN TNAME    FORMAT A13
  3  SELECT *
  4  FROM TABLE_AUDIT
  5  WHERE CREATOR = USER
  6  ORDER BY TNAME, TABLETYPE;


CREATOR TNAME         TABLETYPE ALT AUD COM DEL GRA IND INS LOC REN SEL UPD
------- ------------- --------- --- --- --- --- --- --- --- --- --- --- ---
PERRY   ALLEMPLOYEES  VIEW      -/- -/- -/- -/- -/- -/- -/- -/- -/- -/- -/-
PERRY   EMPLOYEEMGRS  VIEW      -/- -/- -/- -/- -/- -/- -/- -/- -/- -/- -/-
PERRY   EMPLOYEES     TABLE     -/- -/- -/- -/- -/- -/- -/- -/- -/- -/- -/-
PERRY   FINANCIAL     VIEW      -/S -/S -/S -/S -/S -/S -/S -/S -/S -/S -/S
PERRY   HRM           VIEW      -/- -/- -/- -/- -/- -/- -/- -/- -/- -/- -/-
PERRY   MANAGERS      TABLE     S/- S/- S/- S/- S/- S/- S/- S/- S/- S/- S/-
PERRY   MANAGERSDEPT  VIEW      S/S S/S S/S S/S S/S S/S S/S S/S S/S S/S S/S
PERRY   SECURITY      TABLE     -/- -/- -/- -/- -/- -/- S/S -/- -/- S/S S/S
```

Figure 11.11: Object audit options stored in AUDIT_TABLE

SUMMARY

This chapter covered all aspects of database security provided by Oracle. It described the authentication subsystem, which requires all users to supply a username and password in order to log on to Oracle. More importantly, it detailed the authorization subsystem, which allows you to grant and revoke both system- and object-level privileges within Oracle. Various users can be granted varying levels of system privilege—from the limited CONNECT privilege to the more flexible RESOURCE privilege to the most powerful DBA privilege. Users can also be granted different object privileges from the seven possible: ALL, SELECT, INSERT, UPDATE, DELETE, ALTER, and INDEX.

Next, the chapter explained how to use views in tandem with granted privileges to further secure a database by restricting access to specified columns or rows of particular tables. Finally, the chapter discussed Oracle's new auditing capabilities, which allow you to record security-relevant events.

12

OPTIMIZING
SYSTEM
PERFORMANCE:
INDEXING AND
CLUSTERING

THIS CHAPTER PRESENTS TWO SQL COMMANDS that can optimize database performance—INDEX and CLUSTER. Although not required for efficient database management, these commands provide faster service. Indexing and clustering reduce processing time under many circumstances. If you use indexes or clusters improperly, however, processing times can actually increase. You should produce performance timing statistics on smaller, representative database tables before using these techniques on full tables. The Oracle-supplied manuals *Installation and User's Guide* and *Database Administrator's Guide* will help to guide you in your system tuning and performance enhancement decisions.

Of course, the most important consideration for optimal database performance is careful table design. Poorly designed tables and databases not only lead to less efficient processing but can also produce unexpected and unwanted side effects. As you'll recall from Chapter 4, database design involves table layout, multi versus single table design decisions, normalization, and minimizing redundancy. No tool can give you instant mastery of these vital skills, but reading and experience will help. C. J. Date provides lucid and complete examples in his chapters devoted to database design and normalization (see Bibliography). Before you produce applications that rely on the Oracle Database engine, you would do well to familiarize yourself with his work.

INDEXING

Indexes are small tables used to organize other database tables. They can contain any logical arrangement of row numbers that you specify. Oracle automatically maintains indexes and determines when they will speed access to your data. Once you have created an index, it does its work without further attention from you.

Indexes optimize system performance in two ways. First, they can minimize database access time by significantly reducing the number of disk input and output operations. Frequently, you can issue queries to examine adroitly-chosen index columns rather than the database itself. Second, indexes enforce (when desired) primary key uniqueness. Using an index based on one or more table columns ensures that table rows are uniquely identifiable by the column upon which the index is based. It is extremely important to guarantee key uniqueness by indexing, since truly relational database systems must have uniquely identifiable rows. Oracle maintains its own indexes on all tables, using a "hidden" column present in all tables to guarantee its own "internal" row uniqueness for all tables.

USING INDEXES SELECTIVELY

Usually, using indexes with database tables enhances overall performance. However, in several circumstances indexes can actually slow down database processing. Index files require additional disk space to store index values and associated pointers to rows of tables. However, the speed advantages that indexes provide are well worth the small amount of disk space they occupy.

Using indexes can also potentially increase database access time. Whether or not you incur increased database access time depends on how and when you use indexes. For example, issuing UPDATE, INSERT, and DELETE commands for an indexed database will certainly be slower (perhaps insignificantly) than performing the same operations on a table with no indexes. This is because the separate index files associated with indexed tables must be updated whenever data is inserted, updated, or deleted from base tables.

INDEXES THAT MOST DRAMATICALLY AFFECT PERFORMANCE

In several situations, indexes can dramatically improve database performance. In his article "Selecting the Right Index" (see Bibliography), Mr. Paul Bass discusses five such situations. This section highlights two of the five: primary keys and foreign keys in joined tables.

Primary Key

Perhaps the most important index is on the table's primary key. Because tables should have identified, unique primary keys, each row of any given table can be identified uniquely. Thus, indexing the primary key (using the UNIQUE option) guarantees that the key is unique within a table. An example of a primary key in the PROPERTY database, illustrated in several chapters of this text, is the key PARCEL. PARCEL is the property's identifier and is unique for each row of the table. Other columns, such as PRICE, SQFT, and ZIPCODE, are not unique and cannot be used to select a single property. Collectively, they could form a composite key that is unique.

Foreign Keys in Joined Tables

Performance can also be improved by indexing the join columns of tables. For example, the real estate database used in this book can comprise three tables: PROPERTY, AGENCY, and AGENT-SALES. PROPERTY contains basic sales and property description information; AGENTSALES contains the columns PARCEL and SALESID associating a sales agent with a property sold; and AGENCY contains columns SALESID and AGENCY associating a sales agent with his home office (broker). Properly linked, these three tables contain all the fundamental information about recently sold properties. PROPERTY and SALESAGENT are joined on the common column (primary key/foreign key) PARCEL. SALES-AGENT and AGENCY are joined on the common column (primary key/foreign key) SALESID. Pairs of these tables are frequently joined by SELECT statements such as

```
SELECT P.PARCEL, PRICE, SQFT, BR, BA, ZIPCODE,
       SALEDATE, MKTTIME,
       SALESID
FROM   PROPERTY P, SALESAGENT S
WHERE  P.PARCEL = S.PARCEL;
```

in which PARCEL is the primary key in the PROPERTY table and the foreign key to locate associated rows in the SALESAGENT table. Indexing the SALESAGENT table on the PARCEL column will speed the join operation.

CREATING INDEXES

Any user can create indexes on his or her own tables. You need not have the system privilege RESOURCE to create indexes. Only the CONNECT privilege is required to create indexes. In addition, you can create indexes on any tables for which you have been granted INDEX access by the table's owner. INDEX access is granted to other users with the GRANT statement. For example,

```
GRANT INDEX ON table-name TO anotheruser;
```

permits username *anotheruser* to create one or more indexes on a specified table. You use CREATE INDEX standard SQL statement to create indexes. Its syntax is

```
CREATE [UNIQUE] INDEX name
   ON table (column [ASC|DESC], column [ASC|DESC], ...)
   [COMPRESS|NOCOMPRESS]
   [SYSSORT|NOSYSSORT]
   [ROWS = n]
   [PCTFREE = {20|n}];
```

where *name* is the name of the index and *table* is the name of the table. As usual, brackets indicate optional entries and braces indicate required entries. The columns used to create the index are indicated by *column*. You can index columns in ascending (ASC) or descending (DESC) order. You can create any number of indexes for a table, as long as no two indexes have identical column names (in identical order) following the table name.

Creating Single-Column Indexes

You can execute the following CREATE INDEX statement to create an index in ascending order on the PARCEL column of the PROPERTY table:

```
CREATE INDEX IPARCEL
ON PROPERTY (PARCEL);
```

The CREATE INDEX statement orders each row in the index. The sort is done on the specified column and the hidden, Oracle-maintained (unique) ROWID column of a table. Indexes are automatically maintained and used by Oracle. In addition, indexes are transparent; you need not specify an index once it is created. For example, selecting rows from the PROPERTY table is the same whether one or more columns are indexed or not.

Creating Indexes of Concatenated Table Columns

When more than one column is enclosed in parentheses following the table name, the index is called a *concatenated* index. You may include up to 16 columns in the concatenated index, and the order of the columns in the CREATE INDEX bears no relation to the ordering of the table columns. For example,

```
CREATE INDEX THE_FARM ON PROPERTY (SQFT, ZIPCODE);
```

is logically equivalent to

```
CREATE INDEX THE_FARM ON PROPERTY (ZIPCODE, SQFT);
```

However, the former index will, in general, be better whenever queries frequently include WHERE clauses referencing SQFT but not always ZIPCODE. Correspondingly, the latter index is better if queries to the PROPERTY table frequently contain WHERE clauses like

```
WHERE ZIPCODE < 92055 AND ZIPCODE > 92010;
```

That is, you can speed up queries by placing the most frequently referenced column first in the CREATE INDEX column list enclosed in parentheses.

Creating Unique Indexes with Concatenated Table Columns

Whenever a table contains multiple occurrences of a particular column value, you need to include more than one column in the CREATE INDEX statement in order to generate a unique index value. For example, assume that the SQFT and PRICE columns are not individually unique for all records. Together, however, they specify a particular property. That is, given square footage and sales price, only one row would be chosen. To create a unique index, include both SQFT and PRICE to produce a concatenated index:

```
CREATE UNIQUE INDEX ISQFTPRICE
ON PROPERTY (SQFT DESC, PRICE DESC);
```

The preceding creates a (guaranteed) unique index based on table columns SQFT and PRICE. As long as there is not more than one row with the same combination of SQFT and PRICE, the index named ISQFTPRICE will uniquely identify each row in PROPERTY. If there is such a row, however, as in this case

```
SQL> CREATE UNIQUE INDEX ISQFTPRICE
  2  ON PROPERTY (SQFT DESC, PRICE DESC);
```

Oracle will generate an error message when you attempt to produce a unique index:

```
ERROR at line 2: ORA-1452:  cannot CREATE UNIQUE INDEX;
                            duplicate keys found
```

To guarantee that values in a particular column are unique, first create an index on that column and then insert data into the table. Processing data insert operations will be slow for large tables because the index must be updated each time a row is inserted into the table. If you attempt to insert a record containing data that would create a duplicate value on the index column, you'll see this message:

```
ERROR at line 1: ORA-0001:  duplicate value in index
```

Ensuring that Index Names are Unique

Every index (for example, ISQFTPRICE or IPARCEL) created by a given username must be unique. However, different users can use identical index names. For example, each user in the system could create an index named IPRIMARY for one of his or her tables. But only one index named IPRIMARY could exist for each user. The UNIQUE option is independent of this index name requirement. UNIQUE guarantees row uniqueness, not index name uniqueness. Only one index can exist for a given column.

Compressing Indexes

The COMPRESS option specifies that indexes be compressed when stored. Indexes are stored in compressed form by default. When you specify NOCOMPRESS, indexes are stored in ''clear,'' uncompressed form. When they are compressed, indexes occupy less disk space. Oracle is prevented from retrieving the value of an index field from the index alone. It must access a table to locate a desired column value. For example, suppose you created an index on the SALESAGENT table:

```
CREATE INDEX ISALESID
ON SALESAGENT (SALESID ASC) NOCOMPRESS;
```

Stored in ascending order, the SALESID field could be retrieved efficiently from the index (not the table) if you issued the SELECT statement

```
SELECT SALESID
FROM SALESAGENT
WHERE SALESID > 0;
```

However, if the index were stored in compressed form when created:

```
CREATE INDEX ISALESID
ON SALESAGENT (SALESID ASC);
```

the previous SELECT statement would cause Oracle to search the SALESAGENT table to locate and display the SALESID column. Generally, it is better not to compress indexes so that Oracle can retrieve values (when appropriate) from the index file using more efficient binary search techniques. Otherwise, Oracle must search the base table using sequential search methods (searching an average of half of the file).

LISTING INDEXES

Once you have created several indexes, you can list the names of indexes and other index data by displaying selected rows of the data dictionary view called INDEXES. Figure 12.1 shows a SQL

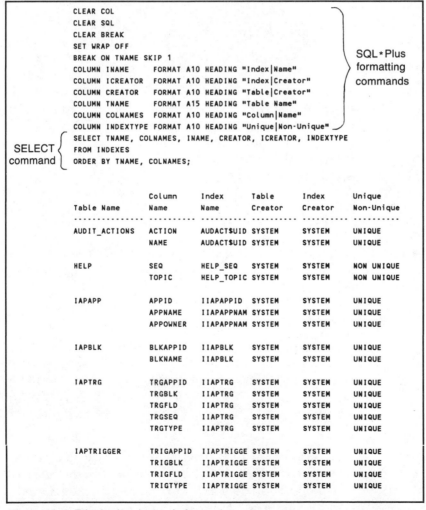

Figure 12.1: Displaying index information

SELECT statement used to select columns from the INDEX view and the resulting display. SQL*Plus formatting commands have been used to make the displayed results more readable. Several less interesting columns from the INDEXES view have been omitted, and some rows have been omitted in the interest of brevity.

The INDEXTYPE column, called "unique non-unique" in Figure 12.1, indicates whether or not the UNIQUE option was used when the index was created. The listing shows tables owned by the special user SYSTEM. Figure 12.2 shows the structure of the data dictionary view INDEXES.

```
Name          Null?      Type
-----------   --------   --------
INAME         NOT NULL   CHAR(30)
ICREATOR                 CHAR(30)
TNAME         NOT NULL   CHAR(30)
CREATOR                  CHAR(30)
COLNAMES      NOT NULL   CHAR(30)
INDEXTYPE     NOT NULL   CHAR(10)
IORDER        NOT NULL   CHAR(4)
COMPRESSION   NOT NULL   CHAR(10)
SEQ           NOT NULL   NUMBER
CONCATID                 NUMBER
```

Figure 12.2: Structure of the data dictionary view INDEXES

WRITING SQL SELECT STATEMENTS THAT USE INDEXES

Oracle automatically determines whether or not to use existing indexes to boost performance. The way you write SELECT clauses can affect that determination. Indexes are used to process a SELECT statement if a WHERE clause is present and at least the first predicate (for example, ZIPCODE > 92041 or PRICE = 125000) references an indexed column. Oracle would use an index to process the query

```
SELECT PARCEL, PRICE, SQFT MKTTIME
FROM PROPERTY
WHERE ZIPCODE > 92011;
```

if an index (by any name) exists for the ZIPCODE column of PROP-ERTY. On the other hand, Oracle would not use the performance-enhancing index for the ZIPCODE column if you issued the following SELECT statement:

```
SELECT PARCEL, PRICE, SQFT, MKTTIME
FROM PROPERTY;
```

Indexes are chosen only when a WHERE clause is part of the SELECT statement and only if the predicates reference one or more indexed columns. Concatenated indexes are also used to search a table when the leading index columns of the CREATE INDEX statement correspond to one or more (left to right) predicates in a SELECT clause.

Oracle will not use an index if any of these three conditions are true:

- The SQL statement contains no WHERE clause
- The WHERE clause, though present, alters the displayed value of the index column in some way (with an Oracle function or other mathematical expression, for example)
- The WHERE clause contains NULL or NOT NULL for values in the indexed column (for example, if the predicate WHERE PRICE IS NULL were included in a SELECT statement, Oracle would not use an index created on the PRICE column)

Often, you can rephrase a query so that Oracle will use (or not use) an existing index.

VALIDATING INDEXES

The VALIDATE INDEX command checks a specified index to determine whether or not it is accurate and consistent. This command, though used infrequently, can validate indexes you have created as well as indexes created by other users. Its syntax is as follows:

```
VALIDATE INDEX index-name [ON table-name] [WITH LIST];
```

where *index-name* is the name of the index and *table-name* is the table on which the index was created. The WITH LIST option normally should not be included. It produces a trace that is used only by Oracle personnel.

If the index is valid, the message "Index validated." is displayed. To validate the index ISALESID created on the table SALES-AGENT, type

```
SQL> VALIDATE INDEX ISALESID;
```

If you receive any message other than "Index validated," the index is corrupt and should be discarded. Drop the index and recreate it.

DROPPING AN INDEX

Like unwanted tables, you can remove indexes from the system. There are two ways to remove indexes. The first, and customary, way is to issue the DROP INDEX statement. The second way is to drop a table. When you drop a table (with the command DROP TABLE *table-name*), *all* indexes created on that table by you or other users are automatically dropped.

The syntax for DROP INDEX is

```
DROP INDEX index-name [ON table-name];
```

where *index-name* is the index to be dropped. The optional phrase ON specifies a table name. If you have two indexes by the same name— one on a table you own and one on a table owned by someone else, you must use the ON phrase to uniquely identify the index. To drop an index named IMYINDEX on your table AGENCY, type

```
DROP INDEX IMYINDEX;
```

Correspondingly, to drop an identically named index on another person's table SALESDATA, type

```
DROP INDEX IMYINDEX ON CORDELL.SALESDATA;
```

Note, however, that Professional Oracle for microcomputers does not support duplicate index names. It requires that all index names for a given username are unique.

MEASURING PERFORMANCE: TIMING

You can gather your own performance data with the SQL*Plus TIMING statement. By doing selective timing operations on indexed and un-indexed tables, you can decide whether or not indexing makes sense for your applications. The syntax of the TIMING command is

```
TIMING [START text] | STOP | SHOW];
```

where *text* is the name of a timing area (an identifier). Issuing TIMING START initiates a timing operation. Because all times are elapsed seconds, you may want to create a SQL*Plus command file that starts the timing operation, executes the SQL statement to be timed, and halts the timing operation. Otherwise, you will get false times because timing is displayed only after you issue TIMING SHOW or TIMING STOP. The time between the end of the timed SQL command and when you type either of the preceding TIMING commands will be included in the reported time.

The optional phrase START creates a named *timing area* and makes *text* the timing area's title. You can thus refer by title to various timing areas. Several timing areas can coexist. The most recently created timing area is the current timing area. Whenever SQL*Plus runs a command, it adds the execution time of that command to the stored time in the current timing area.

SHOW displays the current timing area's title and accumulated time but does not halt timing. STOP displays the current timing area's title and accumulated time and halts further timing for that area. If any other timing areas exist, the next most recent timing area becomes the current timing area. Accumulated times are not merely CPU time and/or input and output time; they are the elapsed time between the start of the timing operation and the point at which it was displayed or halted. The SQL*Plus command CLEAR TIMING deletes all timing areas created by the TIMING command.

Suppose you want to measure the time it takes to execute a SELECT statement for a join operation on all of the real estate tables associated with recent sales of single-family properties. The TIMING statements and the SQL SELECT statement to be timed are shown in Figure 12.3, along with a small subset of returned rows from the three tables. Note that SQL*Plus COLUMN commands are used to format the table and SQL*Plus REM commands are used to add internal comment lines.

```
COLUMN PRICE    FORMAT $999,999
COLUMN SQFT     FORMAT 9,999
COLUMN BR       FORMAT 99
COLUMN BA       FORMAT 9.9
COLUMN ZIPCODE FORMAT 99999
COLUMN MKTTIME FORMAT 999
COLUMN SALESID FORMAT 9999
REM   Begin Timing Operation:
TIMING START
REM   Execute SQL Statement To Be Timed:
  SELECT P.PARCEL, PRICE, SQFT, BR, BA,
         ZIPCODE, SALEDATE, MKTTIME, A.SALESID, AGENCY
  FROM PROPERTY P, SALESAGENT S, AGENCY A
  WHERE P.PARCEL=S.PARCEL
    AND S.SALESID = A.SALESID
  ORDER BY P.PARCEL;
REM   Halt Timing Operation and Display Elapsed Time:
TIMING STOP


PARCEL     PRICE    SQFT  BR   BA ZIPCODE SALEDATE  MKTTIME SALESID  AGENCY
-------  --------- ------ --- --- ------- --------- ------- -------  ------
8712831  $223,500  2,100   3 2.0   92060 02-DEC-87     265    1014      45
8715512  $166,000  1,815   4 1.7   92060 04-DEC-87     280    1002      16
8719187  $106,500  1,100   3 1.5   92020 22-NOV-87     216    1002      16
8719249  $240,500  2,530   4 2.5   92015 08-JAN-88     266    1001      25
8719784  $116,500  1,500   3 1.5   92050 28-NOV-87     215    1012      25
8722523  $221,500  2,570   3 2.7   92020 30-NOV-87     198    1012      25
8722794  $155,500  1,050   2 1.0   92050 05-JAN-88     171    1008      72
8723601  $526,500  4,200   5 3.0   92050 08-FEB-88     283    1002      16
8723735  $211,500  1,650   3 2.0   92015 29-JAN-88     191    1002      16
8723900  $146,500  1,550   3 2.5   92015 13-JAN-88     131    1012      25

...        ...      ...   ...  ...   ...   ...          ...    ...      ...

8868030  $216,500  1,638   2 1.7   92020 11-AUG-88       7    1007      16
8868344  $109,500    900   2 1.0   92050 30-AUG-88       5    1005      18
8868613  $146,500  1,200   2 1.0   92050 06-SEP-88       8    1012      25
8869331  $215,500  2,600   4 2.0   92020 22-SEP-88      22    1008      72
8869786  $144,000  1,050   3 1.7   92050 11-NOV-88      13    1010      16
8870883  $153,500    900   2 1.0   92055 23-SEP-88      18    1004       9
8871401  $219,500  3,350   4 3.0   92020 12-SEP-88      27    1010      16
8871573  $296,500  2,375   4 3.0   92055 03-NOV-88      30    1012      25

250 records selected.

elapsed seconds: 56
```

Figure 12.3: Timing a SELECT statement

CLUSTERING

The purpose of *clustering* is to store related tables that are *used together* in the same disk area. Clustering can reduce disk storage by keeping only one copy of identical data for groups of related tables and rows. Additionally, you can reduce database access time by clustering tables. Clustering two or more tables that are joined in SELECT statements can reduce storage requirements *and* access times.

Single tables can benefit from clustering also. Peripheral storage requirements can be greatly reduced for single tables containing one or more columns with many rows of the same values. Columns with a large number of repeating values are candidate *cluster columns*.

For example, there is a county tax assessor's database that contains *all* of the parcels of land for a large metropolitan area such as Los Angeles County (approximately 2.2 million parcels). The table contains over 70 columns. Many of these columns contain large numbers of repeating values. One column, for example, contains each parcel's use code (distinct from zoning code) which describes whether the parcel is a single-family condominium, duplex, or motel, for example. Since there are fewer than 100 use codes, each use code value repeats (on the average) 22,000 times! Similarly, a column called exemption type has fewer than ten possible values and therefore many values are repeated.

For each of the preceding example columns, clustering would yield significantly smaller database storage requirements. However, in certain situations database storage requirements actually could increase when you use clustering. These situations are considered later.

When you access clustered tables, the fact that they are in clusters is transparent. You can manipulate tables in a cluster in the same ways you would access unclustered tables. Clustering affects the way tables are physically stored on disk, but has no apparent effect on how tables appear logically when they are queried or updated.

Clustering tables is a two-step procedure. First, you create a cluster. Then, you place one or more tables into the defined cluster.

CREATING A CLUSTER

If several tables are to be clustered, each must share at least one common column with identical types, lengths and meanings. However, the cluster columns need not have the same name. Clustering a group of tables has three effects:

- Each distinct value that appears in the cluster columns is stored in the database only once.
- The rows from tables having the same value in their cluster columns are stored in the same disk area (sometimes called a *disk page*).
- SQL*Plus creates an index, called a *cluster index,* on the cluster columns. Oracle uses the index to improve access times for queries searching the cluster column.

To create clustered tables, first create a cluster. Then create the tables and specify that they are members of the cluster. You use the SQL command CREATE CLUSTER to create a cluster. Its syntax is

```
CLUSTER cluster-name
       ( cluster-col-1 data-type, cluster-col-2 data-type,...)
       [ SIZE logical-block-size ]
       [ SPACE space-name ]
       [ COMPRESS | NOCOMPRESS ];
```

where *cluster-name* is the name of the cluster and *cluster-col-n* is the cluster column name by which each column is known in the cluster. Although this cluster column need not have the same name as the table to be loaded into the cluster, it often does. The optional entry *logical-block-size* is the size, in bytes, of a logical block. Specifying a small block size can reduce the amount of disk space needed to store a cluster; however, this may also increase the access time. The optional *space-name* parameter defines the cluster's initial disk space allocation and related factors. The COMPRESS/NOCOMPRESS option determines if the cluster column index is compressed or not. Uncompressed cluster indexes occupy larger index disk space but frequently reduce access time when access is by cluster columns.

Writing Cluster Column Specifications

Perhaps most important in the CREATE CLUSTER command is correctly specifying the parenthesized list of cluster columns. The *data-type* portion of the specification is like the form used in the

CREATE TABLE command. It specifies the type of data in the cluster column and whether or not NULL values are permitted. There are four important rules to remember when you specify cluster columns:

- No more than sixteen columns are allowed in a single cluster.
- A cluster column may consist of multiple cluster table columns.
- At least one of the cluster columns of each table in the cluster must be NOT NULL.
- The data type and size of a cluster column (for example, NUMBER(5), CHAR(30)) must match those specified in the CREATE TABLE statement.

Creating a One-Column Cluster Definition

Suppose that a table contains a large number of repeated values for a particular column. For example, one of the real estate sales data tables called PROPERTY contains a ZIPCODE field with only seven distinct zip codes that occur many times. You can create a one-column cluster by executing

```
SQL> CREATE CLUSTER PROPERTYZIP (ZIPCODE NUMBER(5));
```

After successfully storing the cluster definition, SQL*Plus responds ''Cluster created.'' You'll learn how to load a table into such a cluster later in this chapter.

Creating a Multiple-Column Cluster Definition

You can define more than one cluster column by simply inserting additional cluster column names and corresponding data type pairs in the column list enclosed in parentheses. Cluster columns in the list are separated by commas. Here is a two-column cluster definition in which the PROPERTY data rows are grouped by ZIPCODE and BR (number of bedrooms):

```
SQL> CREATE CLUSTER PROPERTYZIPBR
  2    (ZIPCODE NUMBER(5), BR NUMBER(1));
```

Oracle will respond with the message:

```
Cluster created.
```

Creating a Cluster Definition for Joined Tables

Suppose that a large number of real estate sales information queries involve joining the two tables PROPERTY and SALESAGENT on the join column PARCEL (see Figure 12.4 for a description of these two tables).

```
PROPERTY Table:

Name           Null?    Type
------------   -------  ----------
PARCEL         NOT NULL NUMBER(7)
PRICE                   NUMBER(6)
SQFT                    NUMBER(4)
BR                      NUMBER(1)
BA                      NUMBER(2,1)
ZIPCODE                 NUMBER(5)
SALEDATE                DATE
MKTTIME                 NUMBER(3)


SALESAGENT Table:

Name           Null?    Type
------------   -------  ----------
PARCEL         NOT NULL NUMBER(7)
SALESID        NOT NULL NUMBER
```

Figure 12.4: Columns of two real estate sales information tables

You could define a cluster to save time whenever these two tables are joined on their respective PARCEL columns. The cluster defining statement is:

```
SQL> CREATE CLUSTER PROPERTYPARCEL (PARCEL NUMBER(7));
```

The cluster is named PROPERTYPARCEL and the cluster column name is PARCEL. Later, you will load two cluster tables, PROPERTY and AGENTSALES, into this cluster.

Obtaining Help

Remember, on-line help is available for many SQL and SQL-*Plus topics. To obtain help on clustering, type **HELP CREATE CLUSTER**. Figure 12.5 shows part of the help display.

```
C R E A T E    C L U S T E R
+-------------------------------------------------------------------+
| Syntax |                                                          |
|--------+                                                          |
|                                                                   |
|   CREATE CLUSTER cluster                                          |
|           ( column spec [NOT NULL], column spec [NOT NULL],... )  |
|           [SIZE n]                                                |
|           [SPACE space]                                           |
|           [COMPRESS|NOCOMPRESS];                                  |
|                                                                   |
+-------------------------------------------------------------------+


TYPE: SQL command.


DESCRIPTION: Creates a cluster which may contain two or more tables. Tables
are added to the cluster with CREATE TABLE's CLUSTER clause.

Also commits pending changes to the default database.
```

Figure 12.5: CREATE CLUSTER on-line help

CREATING CLUSTERED TABLES

After defining a cluster with the CREATE CLUSTER statement, you specify which tables it will contain. There are two methods. You can create the table and place its definition into the cluster, or you can create the table and load it into the cluster from an existing table. In either case, use the CREATE TABLE command discussed in Chapters 3 and 4. The CREATE TABLE syntax used for clustering is shown in Figure 12.6. Use form 1 if you are creating a table for the first time. Use form 2 to load an existing table into a cluster. Both forms must contain the phrase CLUSTER in order to place a table in a cluster.

```
Form 1:

        CREATE TABLE table-name ( column-spec [ NULL | NOT NULL],... )
                [ SPACE space-definition [ PCTFREE n ] |
                  CLUSTER cluster-name ( column-name,... ) ];


Form 2:

        CREATE TABLE table-name [ ( column-name [ NOT NULL ],... ) ]
                [ SPACE space-definition [ PCTFREE n ] |
                  CLUSTER cluster-name ( column-name,... ) ]
                [ AS query ];
```

Figure 12.6: CREATE TABLE syntax for clustering tables

Creating a Clustered Table from Scratch

To create a clustered table PROPERTIES and place it in the previously defined cluster PROPERTYZIP, execute the following statement:

```
CREATE TABLE PROPERTIES
    (PARCEL   NUMBER(7) NOT NULL,
     PRICE    NUMBER(6),
     SQFT     NUMBER(4),
     BR       NUMBER(1),
     BA       NUMBER(2,1),
     ZIPCODE  NUMBER(5) NOT NULL,
     SALEDATE DATE,
     MKTTIME  NUMBER(3))
CLUSTER      PROPERTYZIP(ZIPCODE);
```

Oracle affirms that the preceding statement was correctly executed with the familiar "Table created" message. PROPERTIES behaves like any other, nonclustered table. The fact that it is in a cluster is transparent. The only task that remains now is to insert data rows into the table.

Creating and Loading a Clustered Table in One Step

Another way to create a clustered table and place data into it is to *load* a clustered table. Form 2 in Figure 12.6 creates a clustered table and also loads data from an available database table. In the next example, you will modify the preceding CREATE TABLE command by adding the optional AS clause followed by a query. The query will automatically insert selected row values into the clustered table immediately after the table is created. The results are identical to those of the previous example, except that the clustered table is filled with data.

```
CREATE TABLE PROPERTIES
CLUSTER       PROPERTYZIP(ZIPCODE)
AS SELECT * FROM PROPERTY;
```

For the preceding statement to work, the ZIPCODE column of PROPERTY (not PROPERTIES) must have NOT NULL in its definition. Otherwise, Oracle will display the error message

```
ERROR at line 3: ORA-1761:  at least one cluster column in
table must be mandatory (NOT NULL)
```

Creating a Clustered Table for Improved Join Operations

The best candidate cluster columns for the real estate sales information (see Figure 12.4) are their common join column PARCEL. You can store rows from both tables with identical values for PARCEL in the same disk pages. Queries that join the two tables on that column will probably execute more quickly because related rows are stored together. Remember that clustering the two tables does not affect the way the individual tables appear or behave. It only affects query performance.

To create (and load) two clustered tables into the previously created cluster PROPERTYPARCEL, execute the statements shown in Figure 12.7.

```
SQL> CREATE TABLE PROPERTY_CL
  2  CLUSTER       PROPERTYPARCEL(PARCEL)
  3  AS SELECT * FROM PROPERTY;


SQL> CREATE TABLE SALESAGENT_CL
  2  CLUSTER       PROPERTYPARCEL(PARCEL)
  3  AS SELECT * FROM SALESAGENT;
```

Figure 12.7: Two statements that create and load related tables into a cluster

If you create clustered tables from existing tables, you may wish to remove the unclustered (clone) tables once they have been loaded into a cluster. Simply execute DROP TABLE for each unclustered table that you want to remove. In the example shown in Figure 12.7, you could safely drop the PROPERTY and SALESAGENT tables after you loaded them into the PROPERTYPARCEL cluster. Again, the clustered tables "look and feel" like their predecessors. They are simply stored in a more efficient form.

Queries that join PROPERTY_CL and SALESAGENT_CL on their PARCEL join columns would be particularly efficient due to the proximity of related rows. For example, the SELECT statement

```
SELECT *
FROM PROPERTY_CL P, SALESAGENT_CL S
WHERE P.PARCEL = S.PARCEL;
```

takes full advantage of the way these two tables are clustered and produces results more quickly than if the tables were unclustered.

Listing Cluster Information

You can list information about what tables are in a cluster, what the cluster columns are, and so on, using the data dictionary views CLUSTERS and CLUSTERCOLUMNS. Because of the definitions for these views, you can only list your own clusters and associated tables. The structures of these two views are shown in Figure 12.8. A SQL SELECT command to list the joined views is shown in Figure 12.9, along with SQL*Plus formatting commands and sample output. Note that the column widths have been reduced to reduce the width of the displayed results. This query might take several minutes to execute.

CLUSTERS view:			CLUSTERCOLUMNS view:		
Name	Null?	Type	Name	Null?	Type
CLCREATOR		CHAR(30)	CLCREATOR		CHAR(30)
CLNAME	NOT NULL	CHAR(30)	CLNAME	NOT NULL	CHAR(30)
LOGBLK		NUMBER	CLCOL	NOT NULL	CHAR(30)
TCREATOR		CHAR(30)	TCREATOR		CHAR(30)
TNAME	NOT NULL	CHAR(30)	TNAME	NOT NULL	CHAR(30)
TCLUSTERID		NUMBER	TCOL	NOT NULL	CHAR(30)

Figure 12.8: Structure of data dictionary views CLUSTERS and CLUSTER-COLUMNS

```
SQL> BREAK ON CLNAME SKIP 1
  2  COLUMN CLCREATOR  FORMAT A10  HEADING "Cluster|Creator"
  3  COLUMN CLNAME     FORMAT A15  HEADING "Cluster|Name"
  4  COLUMN CLCOL      FORMAT A10  HEADING "Cluster|Col. Name"
  5  COLUMN TCREATOR   FORMAT A10  HEADING "Table|Creator"
  6  COLUMN TNAME      FORMAT A15  HEADING "Table|Name"
  7  COLUMN TCOL       FORMAT A10  HEADING "Table|Clus. Col."
  8  SELECT A.CLCREATOR, A.CLNAME, B.CLCOL,
  9         A.TCREATOR,  A.TNAME,  B.TCOL
 10  FROM CLUSTERS A, CLUSTERCOLUMNS B
 11  WHERE A.CLCREATOR = B.CLCREATOR
 12    AND A.CLNAME    = B.CLNAME
 13    AND A.TNAME     = B.TNAME;
```

Cluster Creator	Cluster Name	Cluster Col. Name	Table Creator	Table Name	Table Clus. Col.
PERRY	PROPERTYPARCEL	PARCEL	PERRY	PROPERTY_CL	PARCEL
PERRY		PARCEL	PERRY	SALESAGENT_CL	PARCEL
PERRY	PROPERTYZIP	ZIPCODE	PERRY	PROPERTIES	ZIPCODE

Figure 12.9: Listing cluster information with a SELECT statement

DROPPING CLUSTERS

Before you drop a cluster, you must remove all tables from it. If you forget to do so, Oracle issues the message

```
ERROR at line 1: ORA-0951:  cluster not empty
```

If you forget which tables are members of a cluster, execute a SELECT command like the one in Figure 12.9, or use a simpler command that just lists the cluster and table names:

```
SELECT CLNAME, TNAME
FROM CLUSTERS;
```

It is easy to drop a table from a cluster. However, before dropping its clustered version you may wish to extract each table in order to preserve it for later use.

Extracting a Table from a Cluster

No single SQL command removes and saves a clustered table. However, you only need a few SQL commands to extract (save) a clustered table as an unclustered table. First, create a new table outside the cluster with exactly the same column definitions as the clustered table. Next, copy the clustered table's rows into the new table. Then, drop the clustered table. You may wish to also rename the new table.

Use the following statement to extract the table PROPERTY_CL from the PROPERTYPARCEL cluster, create a new table (for example, PROPERTY_NEW), and load it with rows from the clustered table in one step:

```
CREATE TABLE PROPERTY_NEW AS
   (SELECT * FROM PROPERTY_CL);
```

When the table creation/loading operation shown above is complete, you can drop the clustered table PROPERTY_CL.

Dropping a Clustered Table

Tables located in clusters are dropped as are ordinary tables: with the DROP TABLE command. Execute

```
DROP TABLE PROPERTY_CL;
```

to drop the clustered property table from the PROPERTYPARCEL cluster. You may wish to rename the unclustered table with the RENAME statement. For example,

```
RENAME PROPERTY_NEW TO PROPERTY;
```

After you have dropped all tables from a cluster, you can remove the cluster itself. Before you drop the PROPERTYPARCEL cluster, you must drop the other clustered table it contains, SALES-AGENT_CL:

```
DROP TABLE SALESAGENT_CL;
```

Dropping the Cluster Definition

When you have dropped all tables from a given cluster, you can drop the cluster (that is, the cluster definition) with the command DROP CLUSTER. For example,

```
DROP CLUSTER PROPERTYPARCEL;
```

Oracle confirms that a cluster has been removed with the message "Cluster dropped."

SUMMARY

This chapter described indexing and clustering, two techniques for optimizing the performance of your database system. Indexes can not only enforce primary key uniqueness but can minimize database access time. The chapter described how to create indexes, ensure that index names are unique, and compress indexes in order to save disk space. Next, you learned how to list indexes and incorporate them into SQL statements. You also learned how to validate and drop indexes as well as how to measure index performance with the SQL*Plus TIMING statement.

This chapter then explained how to cluster tables to reduce the amount of disk storage space they occupy. You learned how to define a cluster and create the tables to be contained in the cluster. You saw how to list information about clusters, and, finally, experimented with dropping clusters.

13

PROGRAMMING
WITH ORACLE:
USING PRO*C

THIS BOOK INTRODUCES MANY WAYS TO UPDATE and access the Oracle database. SQL*Plus is the most direct and interactive method. If you are more comfortable with the right-angle bar of a spreadsheet interface, you can use SQL*Calc or Oracle for 1-2-3. Or, if you need a more structured interface for general use by others, you can use Oracle's 4GL tool, SQL*Forms. And if you just want printed data, you can use the report generator, SQL*ReportWriter. But all these options use the same, powerful SQL data access language.

With the Oracle Pro series, you can use SQL in familiar programming languages. You can embed SQL commands directly into program source code, feed this code (stored in a file with a .pc suffix) into one end of the "black box," and retrieve out of the other compilable programs that access the Oracle database (stored in files with the traditional .c suffix).

Oracle did not invent the idea of "host language coupling." The concept originated in 1976, when an IBM research group headed by D.D. Chamberlin defined the specs for the data access language SEQUEL 2. They defined it as a stand-alone language for interactive use and "a data sublanguage embedded in a host programming language." Although implementation seldom lives up to conceptualization, Oracle offers several flexible packages for embedding logical database calls into a variety of traditional languages.

NEW AND IMPROVED: PRECOMPILER INTERFACE

Oracle now offers the Pro series for embedding SQL commands into program source code. After you insert SQL statements prefaced with the words EXEC SQL into program source code, an Oracle precompiler program converts these statements into an output file containing only code native to your compiler. Then you compile your program with your normal language compiler.

These statements define variables, log on to Oracle, handle security, accessing and update the database, commit or roll back modifications, handle errors, and log off of Oracle. Some of the commands are specifically for use with the precompiler, but most of them are familiar SQL commands.

There are actually two methods of embedding SQL commands. Oracle still supports its old method of embedding SQL, called Pro*SQL. Pro*SQL uses a set of called subroutines to handle the same tasks you now enter with the EXEC SQL syntax. This chapter focuses on the new method (the PCC precompilation) because it is more powerful and more easily conceptualized.

LANGUAGE ALTERNATIVES

Oracle provides many familiar language alternatives. Since it incorporates its Pro* language into well-known, third-party compilers, it offers a broader range of alternatives. At last count, you could select Fortran, C, Cobol, Ada, PL/1, or Pascal. This impressive list varies somewhat between implementations because of the compilers available on different machines. But since Oracle constantly upgrades and modifies its language offerings, it is more flexible than other RDBMS offerings.

Oracle docs not support all compilers. Because of the industry's lack of standardization, Oracle Corporation has to verify each implementation and provide a unique library to handle each brand of compiler. In Professional Oracle, which runs on MS-DOS compatible machines, Oracle supports Microsoft C version 4 or later, Lattice C versions 3.0H or later only in conjunction with the Phoenix Linker Plink86plus, and Realia Cobol version 2.0 and later. Because these are name brand compilers, you will get full programming functionality while Oracle concentrates on its specialty—database access.

This chapter uses the Microsoft C compatible Pro*C package running on Professional Oracle. It focuses on the embedded commands rather than the language, so you should be able to extrapolate this chapter into your own combination of operating system, hardware, and compiler. The old Oracle Call Interface method (OCI) required unique syntax for each language. In contrast, the syntax for the Pro series is very similar for the various languages since this common EXEC SQL language is precompiled into the native language calls by the precompiler instead of by you.

WHERE TO USE PRO*C PROGRAMS

As mentioned, you can use these embedded SQL commands to access the Oracle database from a stand-alone executable program. In addition, you can use the same process to create user-exits out of SQL*Forms.

In user-exits, you create the program, precompile it, and then link it in with the SQL*Forms RUNFORM program to create a modified runform program. There are certain limitations to this approach, however. You have to use the Lattice C compiler and you have to have an IBM or Microsoft Assembler program to set up the user-exit creation system. Once you do this, you can call that user-exit in from a SQL*Forms trigger step with the following syntax:

```
#user-exit name parameters
```

You can also pass values back and forth between the form and the exit. But since user-exits are not easily implemented, this chapter concentrates on their stand-alone counterparts.

COMPONENTS

Just as SQL*Forms processes require a few added SQL clauses and features, so does Pro*C. The syntax for these added Pro*C features may remind you of the SQL*Forms trigger environment.

C FUNDAMENTALS

Before we move too far into the discussion, let's review a C program. Figure 13.1 is a short C program called NAME.C.

```
/*      name.c      */
#include <stdio.h>
main()
{
    /*      define the variables            */
        char lname[20];
        char fname[20];

    /*    scan for the user's full name     */
        printf("Enter your last name: ");
        scanf("%s",lname);
        printf("\nEnter your first name: ");
        scanf("%s",fname);

    /*    print the result                  */
        printf("\n\nYour name is %s %s\n",fname,lname);
}
```

Figure 13.1: A C language program listing

This program prompts you to enter your last and first names on the screen and then embeds them in a string and redisplays them two lines below. Comments are enclosed with a slash and asterisk, like this:

```
/* this is an example of a C comment area */
```

as you embed comments in SQL*Plus statements.

The first command, #include <stdio.h>, includes a predefined set of global constants and general purpose functions stored in a header file called STDIO.H. This saves you from having to repeat the definitions in each program you create with the #define command. The STDIO.H file stores screen characteristic values.

The variable *fname* is defined as a 20 character wide string. All variables must be defined before you use them.

Main(), printf(), and scanf() are functions (like subroutines in other languages). Every C program must have a main() function to indicate where the program execution begins and ends. The other two functions are stored in a library of pre-programmed functions on disk. These functions are like the SQL*Plus functions described in Chapter 7. Although main() does not have any arguments, printf() and scanf() do have arguments, which are placed between the parentheses. These arguments can be mixtures of literal strings enclosed in quotes, cursor controls (such as \n for carriage return), and combinations of string conversion characters and variables such as

```
("%s",lname);
```

The printf() function prints an argument on the standard output (your computer screen); scanf() scans for input into the program from the standard input.

The main body of the program is enclosed in braces ({}) and, as in SQL, the way you position the text is generally not an issue. Also as in SQL, each command must end with a semicolon. In C, whether a variable or function is in uppercase or lowercase makes a difference. Main() and MAIN() are not the same as main().

Figure 13.2 shows the result of executing the program shown in Figure 13.1.

```
C:MSC>NAME
Enter your last name: O'FERNICHR
Enter your first name: PATTY

Your name is PATTY O'FERNICHR

C:\MSC>
```

Figure 13.2: Output from NAME.EXE

Although this program leaves out many of the powerful features of C, it is a simple example that will help you understand this chapter.

A PRO*C PROGRAM EXAMPLE

Figure 13.3 is a Pro*C source code listing for a program called PRODADD based on a structure like the one shown in Figure 13.1.

```
/* prodadd.pc                    pre-pre-compiler source code */
#include <stdio.h>

EXEC SQL BEGIN DECLARE SECTION;
VARCHAR userid[20];                 /* username            */
VARCHAR password[20];               /* password            */
VARCHAR prodno[10];                 /* product number      */
VARCHAR dscrpt[30];                 /* description         */
float   cost;                       /* cost                */
VARCHAR st[1];                      /* serially tracked    */
int     qiw;                        /* quantity in warehouse */

EXEC SQL END DECLARE SECTION;
EXEC SQL INCLUDE SQLCA;
main()
{
    printf("Enter your user-name: ");    /* get the userid and password.*/
    scanf("%s",userid.arr);
    userid.len=strlen(userid.arr);

    printf("\nEnter password: ",password.arr);
    scanf("%s",password.arr);
    password.len=strlen(password.arr);

    printf("\n\nYour i.d. is %s/%s\n",userid.arr,password.arr);

    EXEC SQL WHENEVER SQLERROR GOTO errexit;
    EXEC SQL CONNECT :userid IDENTIFIED BY :password;  /* log to Oracle */

    printf("You are now logged into Oracle as user: %s \n",userid.arr);

    strcpy(prodno.arr,"70050001");
    prodno.len=strlen(prodno.arr);
    strcpy(dscrpt.arr,"ELECTRO-BIORYTHM MONITOR");
    dscrpt.len=strlen(dscrpt.arr);
    cost=91.25;
    strcpy(st.arr,"Y");
    st.len=strlen(st.arr);

    EXEC SQL WHENEVER SQLERROR GOTO errexit;
    EXEC SQL INSERT INTO PROD(PRODNO,DSCRPT,COST,ST)
            VALUES (:prodno,:dscrpt,:cost,:st);

    printf("\n\n %s added to the product table\n", prodno.arr);

    EXEC SQL COMMIT WORK RELEASE;        /* commit and log off from ORACLE */
    printf("\nYou have logged off and the update is complete.\n");
    exit();                              /* exit to the operating system   */
errexit:
    errmsg();
    EXEC SQL WHENEVER SQLERROR CONTINUE;
    EXEC SQL ROLLBACK WORK RELEASE;
    return;
```

Figure 13.3: A SQL INSERT statement embedded in a Pro*C program

```
  }
  errmsg()              /* errmsg() prints the ORACLE error msg and number. */
    (
    printf("%.70s \n", sqlca.sqlerrm.sqlerrmc);
    return(0);
    }
```

Figure 13.3: A SQL INSERT statement embedded in a Pro∗C program (continued)

When you enter your username password, this program accesses Oracle and inserts a new product record into the PROD database table. Figure 13.4 shows what your screen will look like when you execute this Pro∗C program.

```
C:\MSC>PRODADD
Enter your user-name: CHAP

Enter password: JGL


Your i.d. is CHAP/JGL
You are now logged into Oracle as user: CHAP


 70050001 added to the product table

You have logged off and the update is complete.

C:\MSC>
```

Figure 13.4: Output from the Pro∗C-based program PRODADD.PC

All of the commands that begin with

```
EXEC SQL
```

are Pro∗C commands that will be converted to C source code when you run the precompiler. As you can see, you enter the commands in a high-level SQL style format and the C code is all generated for you. The precompiler makes the job easy by acting as a code generator. The code from Figure 13.4 will be over four times longer after precompiling.

There are two groups of Pro∗C commands: declarative statements and executing statements. Declarative statements handle the special circumstances of Pro*C. They include the following commands:

BEGIN DECLARE SECTION

END DECLARE SECTION

DECLARE CURSOR

WHENEVER

INCLUDE

The executing statements, which translate into calls (subroutines), are mostly SQL standard DML, DDL, and DCL commands that you will recognize from SQL*Plus. These commands, such as ROLLBACK and COMMIT, are called executing statements because they are converted to called functions (sqlrol() and sqlcom()). Besides these familiar commands, the following commands and clauses are executing statements:

INTO

EXECUTE IMMEDIATE

WHERE CURRENT OF CURSOR

PREPARE FROM

EXECUTE USING

DECLARE CURSOR

OPEN

FETCH INTO

CLOSE

These commands all relate to executing a SQL statement and handling the resulting values. All but the first one have to do with the concept of cursors, or work areas, which you will explore in an upcoming section.

This example uses only SQL standard commands beginning with EXEC SQL. However, to execute Oracle-specific, non-SQL standard functions, you can use EXEC ORACLE OPTION to indicate runtime options. In addition, if you are designing a user-exit you can use EXEC IAF to indicate a form-related command.

DECLARING VARIABLES

In order to access Oracle, you need to pass data between it and the program. This involves defining variables and arrays, integrating those variables into the SQL commands, converting data between the host language and the RDBMS, controlling input and output screen activities and actions, and controlling and processing errors.

In C, you must declare all variables before using them. In Figure 13.1, this was done within the main() function. In Figure 13.3, all of the variable definitions are placed before main() in an area called the DECLARE section. This section is framed by the commands

```
EXEC SQL BEGIN DECLARE;
     variable declarations
EXEC SQL END DECLARE;
```

Any variable that you insert into a SQL statement in the program has to be declared in this opening section and is called a *host* variable. When you use a host variable in a SQL statement, you must precede it with a colon (:), as in the following statement from the program in Figure 13.3:

```
EXEC SQL CONNECT :userid IDENTIFIED BY :password;
```

When you use a host variable in a C statement, it should not be preceded by a colon, for example:

```
cost=95.07;
```

Host variables cannot be SQL reserved words and if you declare them in lowercase you must also use them in lowercase.

Another class of variables is called *indicator* variables. These variables are paired with a host variable in the DECLARE section to indicate a null value return code. They must be defined as a short variable type, which can store a signed number. Short variables will be discussed in more detail in error handling.

Pointer variables are a special class of C variables that you can also define in the DECLARE section. C identifies these by the asterisk preceding them in the declaration. However, if you use them in a SQL statement, use a colon instead of an asterisk.

Data Types

The most common C data types are int (integer) and char (character string). There are these additional data types:

NAME	DESCRIPTION
float	single precision floating point (32 bits/6 dgts)
double	double precision (64 bits/14 + dgts)
short int	signed integer
unsigned int	unsigned integer
long int	double the length of an integer
long float	double the length of a float

The example uses a datatype called VARCHAR in the precompiler, which you might recognize as an Oracle datatype from SQL-*Plus. The statement

```
VARCHAR userid[20];
```

defines a 20 character array to which it attaches an unsigned short integer indicator variable. After precompilation, this declaration is translated into a C structure:

```
struct {
  unsigned short len;
  unsigned char arr[20];
  } userid;
```

A *structure* is a way to define and associate two or more logically related variables. For each VARCHAR definition, there are two variables:

```
variable-name.arr
variable-name.len
```

The first variable is the string and the second is the length of the string. The example in Figure 3.3 uses the variables userid.arr, password.arr, prodno.arr, descrpt.arr, and st.arr with the .arr suffix in the C statements but without the suffix in the SQL statements. Oracle uses both parts (.arr and .len) to insert and evaluate trimmed values in the database because Oracle and C handle varying length strings differently.

Make sure that you enter a VARCHAR length greater than the size of the column you are retrieving or updating. When a value fills up the array (eight characters long in an eight character array), unpredictable output results.

INCLUDING ORACLE FUNCTIONS

Between the DECLARE section and main() is another part of the Pro∗C Application Prologue. In this section, you include the Oracle header files for use with the precompiler. They are SQLCA.H, ORACA.H, and SQLDA.H (SQLDA is an acronym for SQL Data Area). The most common of these is SQLCA.H, which contains all of the standard SQL communication area functions. The command for including this file is

```
EXEC SQL INCLUDE SQLCA;
```

SQLCA takes care of passing values between Oracle and the program and handling errors. SQLCA is discussed in detail later in this chapter in the section "Handling Errors and Status Changes."

CONNECTING TO THE DATABASE

The commands for logging on to the database are considered part of the Pro∗C Application Prologue area even though they appear within the main() function, which means they are part of the main C program body. The command for connecting to the database is

```
EXEC SQL CONNECT :userid IDENTIFIED BY :password;
```

:userid and :password are two host variables. The C code from the beginning of the main() function to this Pro∗C statement is prompting for input of our userid/password combination. In both of the three-line code groups, the function printf() prompts you for your input, scanf() scans for your string (%s) input, and the final line defines the length of the string for the second part of each of the VARCHAR structures.

The line just before the CONNECT section in Figure 13.3 shows you how to insert those variables (without colons) back into a print string that tells you what you have entered. You can see where this shows up during execution in Figure 13.4. This first section of code is just like the structure in Figure 13.1 but with variable types and purposes changed to work with the CONNECT.

The EXEC SQL CONNECT command must be the first executable Pro*C command encountered by the processor. The command preceding it, EXEC SQL WHENEVER, is a declarative statement for error handling so it does not count as the first command (it will be discussed later under error handling).

The EXEC SQL CONNECT command begins your logical unit of work in the program, which is completed only when you do a COMMIT or a ROLLBACK.

EXECUTING STATEMENTS

You can enter all SQL commands through the Pro*C interface. However, because you are using a more structured environment, their use is subject to some limitations and additional requirements. Comparing the Pro*C program interface with the SQL*Plus interactive interface is like comparing a horse and a car. To make a horse's "engine" function, you enter all of its resources in one place—its mouth. To make a car's engine function, you enter the coolant in one spout, the gas in another, and the oil in a third. As long as you structure and categorize your inputs into Pro*C, it, like the car, can outperform its SQL*Plus counterpart.

You can use four types of SQL commands with Pro*C. First are the INSERT, UPDATE, and DELETE commands. These commands transfer structured data from the program into Oracle; all you need in return are simple responses indicating success or failure. Programming languages are well suited for this type of operation and require less Pro*C code to perform it. The example in Figure 13.3 demonstrates this type of process with the SQL statement

```
INSERT INTO PROD(PRODNO,DSCRPT,COST,ST)
      VALUES(:prodno,:dscrpt,:cost,:st);
```

The second type of SQL statement is a SELECT query that returns a complete single row for processing. This requires more complex data to be passed back to the program, but because it is predictable—you get back either one row or no rows—it is still easy for the program to handle. A SELECT statement that fits into this category is:

```
SELECT PRODNO, DSCRPT
FROM PROD
WHERE PRODNO=:prodno;
```

A third type of SQL command is a SELECT query that returns a variable number of rows. This type of command requires additional declaration statements to define a cursor—a work area, that is—in common between the program and Oracle. With this type of statement, you must program in flexibility—a more difficult task. An example is:

```
SELECT PRODNO, DSCRPT
FROM PROD
WHERE PRODNO >= :prodno;
```

The final type of SQL command requires the most flexibility because you must create receiving resources called cursors to handle dynamic SQL statements in which the statements themselves vary upon each execution. Instead of demonstrating this type with a SQL statement, imagine the complexity of supporting the following simplified C prompt:

```
printf("Enter your query:  SELECT ")
scanf("%s",select)
```

Inserting, Updating, and Deleting

Our first example, from Figure 13.3, is an executing command. As with all executing commands, you must enter this command within the main body of the Pro*C program, after the CONNECT and before the COMMIT or ROLLBACK. The statement after the EXEC SQL CONNECT statement in the program in Figure 13.3 is another C printf() function, which will verify that you successfully logged on to the database.

For this demonstration you update the variables :prodno, :dscrpt, :cost, and :st with constant values for insertion into the columns PROD-NO, DSCRPT, COST, and ST in the example table PROD. In reality, you would probably get this data from a user's input, as you would their user ID and password, and it would vary from execution to execution. Either way, the host variables now contain data for the EXEC SQL INSERT command.

To illustrate what the precompiler does, Figure 13.5 shows an excerpt of PRODADD.C that replaces the EXEC SQL INSERT command with a series of variables, arrays, and function calls. All of the functions listed in this example (that is, ssqlsch(), sqlbs2(), and sqosq()) are resident in a library of functions provided by Oracle for the Microsoft C compiler called SQLMSC.LIB.

```
/* SQL stmt #6
    EXEC SQL WHENEVER SQLERROR GOTO errexit;
    EXEC SQL INSERT INTO PROD(PRODNO,DSCRPT,COST,ST)
            VALUES (:prodno,:dscrpt,:cost,:st);
*/
sqlsca(&sqlca);
if ( !sqlusi[0] )
  { /* OPEN SCOPE */
sq002.sq002T[0] = (unsigned short)10;
SQLTM[0] = (int)4;
sqlbs2(&sq002.sq002N, sq002.sq002V,
   sq002.sq002L, sq002.sq002T, sq002.sq002I,
   &SQLTM[0], &sqlusi[0]);
   } /* CLOSE SCOPE */
sqlsch(&sqlusi[0]);
sqlscc(&sqlcun[0]);
sqltfl(&SQLTM[0], &SQLBT0);
if ( !SQLTM[0] )
  { /* OPEN SCOPE */
SQLTM[0] = (int)16384;
sqlopn(&SQLTM[0], &SQLBT3, &sqlvsn);
SQLTM[0] = (int)62;
sqlosq(sq003, &SQLTM[0]);
   } /* CLOSE SCOPE */
sq004.sq004V[0] = (unsigned char *)&prodno.len;
sq004.sq004L[0] = (unsigned long)12;
sq004.sq004T[0] = (unsigned short)9;
sq004.sq004I[0] = (unsigned short *)0;
sq004.sq004V[1] = (unsigned char *)&dscrpt.len;
sq004.sq004L[1] = (unsigned long)32;
sq004.sq004T[1] = (unsigned short)9;
sq004.sq004I[1] = (unsigned short *)0;
```

Figure 13.5: A code excerpt from PROADD.C

```
sq004.sq004V[2] = (unsigned char *)&cost;
sq004.sq004L[2] = (unsigned long)4;
sq004.sq004T[2] = (unsigned short)4;
sq004.sq004I[2] = (unsigned short *)0;
sq004.sq004V[3] = (unsigned char *)&st.len;
sq004.sq004L[3] = (unsigned long)3;
sq004.sq004T[3] = (unsigned short)9;
sq004.sq004I[3] = (unsigned short *)0;
sqlab2(&sq004.sq004N, sq004.sq004V,
  sq004.sq004L, sq004.sq004T, sq004.sq004I);
SQLTM[0] = (int)1;
sqlexe(&SQLTM[0]);
if (sqlca.sqlcode < 0)  goto errexit;

    printf("\n\n %s added to the product table\n", prodno.arr);


/* SQL stmt #8
    EXEC SQL COMMIT WORK RELEASE;        /o commit and log off from ORACLE o/
*/
```

Figure 13.5: A code excerpt from PROADD.C (continued)

Single Row Queries

PRODINQ.PC, a Pro∗C source listing shown in Figure 13.6, demonstrates a single row query.

```
/* prodinq.pc                    pre-pre-compiler source code */
#include <stdio.h>
#include <ctype.h>

EXEC SQL BEGIN DECLARE SECTION;
VARCHAR userid[20];                 /* username           */
VARCHAR password[20];               /* password           */
VARCHAR prodno[12];                 /* product number     */
VARCHAR dscrpt[35];                 /* description        */
float   cost;                       /* cost               */
VARCHAR st[1];                      /* serially tracked   */
int     qiw;                        /* quantity in warehouse */

EXEC SQL END DECLARE SECTION;
EXEC SQL INCLUDE SQLCA;
main()
{
    printf("Enter your user-name: ");  /* get the userid and password. */
    scanf("%s",userid.arr);
    userid.len=strlen(userid.arr);
    printf("\nEnter password: ");
```

Figure 13.6: A Pro∗C single row query program listing

```
    scanf("%s",password.arr);
    password.len=strlen(password.arr);
    printf("\n\nYour i.d. is %s/%s\n",userid.arr,password.arr);

    EXEC SQL WHENEVER SQLERROR GOTO errexit;
    EXEC SQL CONNECT :userid IDENTIFIED BY :password; /* connect to Oracle */

    printf("You are now logged into Oracle as user: %s \n",userid.arr);

    printf("\nEnter product number: ");
    scanf("%s",prodno.arr);
    prodno.len=strlen(prodno.arr);

    EXEC SQL WHENEVER SQLERROR GOTO errexit;
    EXEC SQL WHENEVER NOT FOUND GOTO errexit;
    EXEC SQL SELECT DSCRPT,COST,ST
            INTO :dscrpt,:cost,:st
            FROM PROD
            WHERE PRODNO = :prodno;

    printf("PRODUCT NO.          DESCRIPTION                 COST    ST\n");
    printf("------------ ------------------------------ ---------- --\n");
    printf("%-12s %-30s %10.2f %1s\n",prodno.arr,dscrpt.arr,cost,st.arr);


    EXEC SQL COMMIT WORK RELEASE;        /* Commit and log off from ORACLE */
    printf("\nYou have logged off of Oracle.\n");
    exit();
 errexit:                                /* handles all error exits  */
    errmsg();
    EXEC SQL WHENEVER SQLERROR CONTINUE;
    EXEC SQL ROLLBACK WORK RELEASE;

    return(1);
 }
 errmsg()               /* errmsg() prints the ORACLE error msg and number */
    (
    printf("%.70s \n", sqlca.sqlerrm.sqlerrmc);
    return(1);
    }
```

Figure 13.6: A Pro*C single row query program listing (continued)

This is very similar to the PRODADD.PC program in Figure 13.3. However, instead of defining a product record with literals and inserting it into the PROD table with EXEC SQL INSERT, you prompt for the product number and use EXEC SQL SELECT to retrieve it for use by the program.

This example introduces *input host variables* and *output host variables*, which can pass data both ways between the program and Oracle.

The SELECT statement in Figure 13.6 contains the clause

`INTO :dscrpt,:cost,:st`

which takes the three column values retrieved in the SELECT clause and stores them in the output variables :dscrpt, :cost, and :st. These are values which are output from the SQL command. On the other hand, the variable :prodno in the phrase,

`WHERE PRODNO = :prodno`

is an input variable because it is input into the SQL statement from the program.

Although you have to define the length of the input variable array prodno, you do not have to do so for the output variables, even though they are defined as VARCHAR types. Oracle defines the length of the string for you.

This program includes one additional error handling statement:

`EXEC SQL WHENEVER NOT FOUND GOTO errexit;`

If the product code you enter is not found in the table, the program will exit the Oracle database, go to the errexit label in the program, and execute the errmsg() function, which prints the message.

Figure 13.7 shows the row of values retrieved and displayed on the screen.

```
C:\MSC>PRODINQ
Enter your user-name: CHAP

Enter password: JGL


Your i.d. is CHAP/JGL
You are now logged into Oracle as user: CHAP

Enter product number: 72040100
PRODUCT NO.       DESCRIPTION                  COST    ST
.............  ..............................  .........  ..
72040100      SKIN IRRITATION CREAM            10.00 N

You have logged off of Oracle.

C:\MSC>
```

Figure 13.7: Output from the Pro∗C-based program PRODINQ.EXE

Variable Row Queries

The previous example is simple because it outputs a finite set of values (1) from the SELECT statement. To retrieve several rows in the SELECT statement, you have to create a working area, as does the Pro*C program in Figure 13.8.

```
/* prodall.pc                  pre-pre-compiler source code */
#include <stdio.h>
#include <ctype.h>

EXEC SQL BEGIN DECLARE SECTION;
VARCHAR userid[20];               /* username               */
VARCHAR password[20];             /* password               */
VARCHAR prodno[12];               /* product number         */
VARCHAR dscrpt[35];               /* description            */
float   cost;                     /* cost                   */
VARCHAR st[1];                    /* serially tracked       */
int     qiw;                      /* quantity in warehouse  */

EXEC SQL END DECLARE SECTION;
EXEC SQL INCLUDE SQLCA;
main()
{
    printf("Enter your user-name: ");   /* get the userid and password.*/
    scanf("%s",userid.arr);
    userid.len=strlen(userid.arr);
    printf("\nEnter password: ");
    scanf("%s",password.arr);
    password.len=strlen(password.arr);
    printf("\n\nYour i.d. is %s/%s\n",userid.arr,password.arr);

    EXEC SQL WHENEVER SQLERROR GOTO errexit;
    EXEC SQL CONNECT :userid IDENTIFIED BY :password;  /* log to Oracle */

    printf("You are now logged into Oracle as user: %s \n",userid.arr);

    EXEC SQL DECLARE PRODUCTS CURSOR FOR
             SELECT PRODNO,DSCRPT,COST,ST
             FROM PROD;
    EXEC SQL OPEN PRODUCTS;

    printf("PRODUCT NO.       DESCRIPTION                    COST    ST\n");
    printf("-----------  ----------------------------- ---------- --\n");

    EXEC SQL WHENEVER SQLERROR GOTO errexit;
    EXEC SQL WHENEVER NOT FOUND GOTO done;

    for ( ; ; )
    {
        EXEC SQL FETCH PRODUCTS INTO :prodno,:dscrpt,:cost,:st;
```

Figure 13.8: A Pro*C variable row query program listing

```
            dscrpt.arr[dscrpt.len] = '\0';
            printf("%-12s %-30s %10.2f %1s\n",prodno.arr,dscrpt.arr,cost,st.arr);
    }
done:
/* close the cursors and log off from ORACLE */
    EXEC SQL CLOSE PRODUCTS;
    EXEC SQL COMMIT WORK RELEASE;
    printf("\nYou have logged off of Oracle.\n");
    exit();

errexit:                                        /* handles all error exits */
    errmsg();
    EXEC SQL WHENEVER SQLERROR CONTINUE;
    EXEC SQL ROLLBACK WORK RELEASE;
    exit();
}
errmsg()  /* errmsg() prints the ORACLE error msg and number. */
    (
    printf("%.70s \n", sqlca.sqlerrm.sqlerrmc);
    return(0);
    }
```

Figure 13.8: A Pro*C variable row query program listing (continued)

Again, this work area is called a *cursor*. It consists of several sections that store data relating to the query. Some of the information and status codes stored in the cursor include

- Return code (value defining result of the query)
- Function type (value defining the SQL command)
- Function code (value defining the OCI function)
- Rows processed count
- Null fetch, column truncated, and end of fetch codes
- The internal rowid of the row CURRENT OF CURSOR
- An operating system dependent Oracle error code

A cursor, or working area, is always required between a program and Oracle. For the first three examples the cursor was implicit. You did not have to actually define it; it was defined automatically. Now, however, the cursor is explicit. You have to use the commands DECLARE CURSOR, OPEN CURSOR, FETCH, and CLOSE CURSOR to define the cursor, open it for use, retrieve the current row values into the variables, and close the cursor.

In the code in Figure 13.7, the product number prompt is eliminated in order to display all of the products and the SELECT statement is moved within the DECLARE CURSOR statement so that it looks like this:

```
EXEC SQL DECLARE PRODUCTS CURSOR FOR
        SELECT PRODNO,DSCRPT,COST,ST
        FROM PROD;
```

You need to choose the name PRODUCTS for the cursor or working area. You also need to add PRODNO to the SELECT clause because it is not being input by the user, and eliminate the WHERE clause so that you select all of the records. Also, move the INTO clause to the FETCH statement.

The next statement is the OPEN statement which opens the PRODUCTS cursor area:

```
EXEC SQL OPEN PRODUCTS;
```

When this is executed, the cursor is activated and positioned just before the first row of the set defined by the SELECT statement.

You then print the column headers prior to the FOR statement repeating logic so that the column headers only print once. The for (; ;) statement is a C looping function. It continues to loop until the WHENEVER NOT FOUND (end of file) is true and then execution shifts to the done label, where everything is closed out and you are logged off of Oracle. You can also use the WHILE statement instead of FOR to iterate.

The first line in the loop is the FETCH statement:

```
EXEC SQL FETCH PRODUCTS INTO :prodno,:dscrpt,:cost,:st;
```

Use this statement to insert the values of the current row of the SELECT statement into the variables bound into the SQL statement (:prodno, :dscrpt, :cost and :st). That is why the INTO clause is used in the FETCH statement and not the SELECT statement, as in the last example. The SELECT statement only defines the set of rows to use and the FETCH statement retrieves the rows from the SELECT one at a time for use in the program. The *current row* is the row that is currently fetched. For each time through the loop, the cursor moves to the next row until it reaches the end of the SELECT set. You can only fetch a row in the order in which it was selected. Once you have fetched another row, there is no going back to a previous row; the cursor only moves one direction through the active set. To fetch a previous row, you have to close and reopen the cursor.

After the row values are fetched into the host variables, the C command

```
dscrpt.arr[dscrpt.len] = '\0';
```

is executed. This creates a null-terminated C string the current width of the column value by adding a null value at the end of the string. If you do not add this statement, the product list will look like Figure 13.9.

```
C:\MSC>PRODALL
Enter your user-name: CHAP

Enter password: JGL


Your i.d. is CHAP/JGL
You are now logged into Oracle as user: CHAP
PRODUCT NO.       DESCRIPTION              COST    ST
. . . . . . . . . . . .   . . . . . . . . . . . . . . . . . . . . . . . . .   . . . . . . . . . .   . .
90002005       NEURO STIMULATOR 4 CHANNEL    300.00 Y
90006005       MUSCLE STIMULATOR4 CHANNEL    495.00 Y
90002025       NEURO STIMULATOR 2 CHANNEL    250.00 Y
88904100       ELECTRODES-BANDAID CHANNEL     20.00 N
88904104       ELECTRODES-CLOTH BACKANNEL     30.00 N
88804106       ELECTRODES-SNAP TYPEKANNEL     40.00 N
75100400       CONDUCTIVE GELP TYPEKANNEL     15.00 N
72040100       SKIN IRRITATION CREAMANNEL     10.00 N
65403500       WIRE SETITATION CREAMANNEL     20.00 N
70050001       ELECTRO-BIORYTHM MONITOREL     91.25 Y


C:\MSC>
```

Figure 13.9: An unexpected result from PRODALL.EXE

This is caused by characters that remain from previously fetched lines.

After the last record, close the cursor with

```
EXEC SQL CLOSE PRODUCTS;
```

and log off of Oracle. Figure 13.10 shows the screen output from the entire sequence.

```
C:\MSC>PRODALL
Enter your user-name: CHAP

Enter password: JGL


Your i.d. is CHAP/JGL
You are now logged into Oracle as user: CHAP
PRODUCT NO.        DESCRIPTION                 COST    ST
------------ ------------------------------- ---------- --
90002005      NEURO STIMULATOR 4 CHANNEL      300.00 Y
90006005      MUSCLE STIMULATOR               495.00 Y
90002025      NEURO STIMULATOR 2 CHANNEL      250.00 Y
88904100      ELECTRODES-BANDAID               20.00 N
88904104      ELECTRODES-CLOTH BACK            30.00 N
88804106      ELECTRODES-SNAP TYPE             40.00 N
75100400      CONDUCTIVE GEL                   15.00 N
72040100      SKIN IRRITATION CREAM            10.00 N
65403500      WIRE SET                         20.00 N
70050001      ELECTRO-BIORYTHM MONITOR         91.25 Y

You have logged off of Oracle.

C:\MSC>
```

Figure 13.10: PRODALL.EXE output after trimming DSCRPT.ARR

Dynamic Queries

Dynamic queries are especially complex because you cannot assume anything about the query before executing the program. You have to use the DESCRIBE command coupled with the SQLDA structure (SQLDA.H file) to attach detailed descriptors to each step of the query. You do not know ahead of time the number of columns, host variables, or rows involved. For this reason, you have to break down each statement with the PREPARE command, define a cursor for the statement, use SQLDA type structures to store information about the host variables involved and the columns involved, and then execute the FETCH statement. A discussion of these queries is beyond the scope of this introductory book. If you need further information, see the Pro*C user's guide.

HANDLING ERRORS AND STATUS CHANGES

Each time you embed a SQL statement into your code, an error may occur or a status may change. The statement will either succeed or fail and you need to include a method for handling both results. Result codes are updated in the SQL communication area; you can act on the result by preceding each SQL statement with a WHEN-EVER statement.

The WHENEVER Statement

All of the examples have the EXEC SQL WHENEVER command embedded for processing return codes and checking for errors before each embedded SQL statement. The syntax for the WHEN-EVER statement is as follows:

```
EXEC SQL WHENEVER status-flag conditional-execution
```

In the first part of the statement (*status flag*) you can check for one of three statuses: SQLERROR, SQLWARNING, or NOT FOUND. When any of these evaluates as true, you can do one of three things: STOP, CONTINUE, or GOTO another labeled statement.

An example of SQLERROR from the program listings is

```
EXEC SQL WHENEVER SQLERROR GOTO errexit;
```

Whenever the statement following the WHENEVER statement executes and an Oracle error occurs, the program will transfer execution to the C code following the label errexit:. If no error is returned, WHENEVER does not alter anything. Similarly, you might want to GOTO errexit: if a SQLWARNING is encountered.

You should embed a NOT FOUND statement prior to all executing statements that retrieve rows from Oracle. Here is one from the examples:

```
EXEC SQL WHENEVER NOT FOUND GOTO done;
```

Whenever no rows are returned in response to the SQL statement, the program should branch to done:. In some situations, this is not an error. When used with EXEC SQL FETCH, it is a way to loop until their are no rows left in the active set and then continue on with the program. Saying:

```
EXEC SQL WHENEVER SQLWARNING CONTINUE
```

indicates that you want the program to continue instead of stopping. On the other hand, if you use STOP, the program terminates and the logical unit of work is rolled back. Use this option with caution because it displays no further messages and can cause unpredictable results when you are logging off of Oracle.

Indicator Variables

You can monitor the result of an action affecting a host variable by declaring an indicator variable along with it in the DECLARE section. An indicator variable is a C short int type variable. Each time a host variable is used, a result code is stored in the indicator variable. If the result code is 0, the response is not null and no truncation is required to fit the response into the host variable. If the result code is -1, no response was entered and the host variable is not changed. If the value is greater than 0, truncation occurred and the value equals the length of the input prior to the truncation.

Indicator variables have to be defined in the same case as their associate host variable and follow the same guidelines as their host counterparts. To use an indicator variable in a SQL statement, you must insert the following, where *hv* stands for host variable, *iv* stands for indicator variable, and *cv* stands for column value:

```
INSERT INTO table-name(cv1,cv2,cv3,cv4)
       VALUES(:hv1:iv1,hv2:iv2,hv3:iv3,hv4:iv4);
```

As a result, you can check to see if any of the values are null by checking the *iv* values for each.

Sqlca

The statement

```
EXEC SQL INCLUDE SQLCA;
```

causes a structure called sqlca to be added to the C program. The structure looks like this:

```
struct   sqlca
         {
               char      sqlcaid[8];
               long      sqlabc;
               long      sqlcode;
               struct
               {
                     unsigned short sqlerrml;
                     char           sqlerrmc[70];
               } sqlerrm;
               char      sqlerrp[8];
               long      sqlerrd[6];
               char      sqlwarn[8];
               char      sqlext[8];
         };
```

As you recall, in C a structure is a way to group variables into logical entities. In this case, the logical entity is a communications area for exchanges between your program and Oracle. It is designed to be SQL standard for compatibility with other SQL standard systems. There is actually a structure within a structure because sqlerrm is a Pro*C VARCHAR character type. Here is a list of each variable's meaning:

VARIABLE	DESCRIPTION
sqlcaid[8]	The communication area ID
sqlcabc	Integer length of the sqlca structure
sqlcode	A value defining the result of a SQL statement
	sqlcode $= 0$ = success
	sqlcode > 0 = success with a status code
	sqlcode < 0 = error or failure
sqlerrm	VARCHAR array containing the text of the sqlcode status code
sqlcrrp	unused
sqlerrd	Number of rows processed by a DML statement

VARIABLE	DESCRIPTION
sqlwarn	Eight precompiler and inconsistency warning flags
sqlext	unused

You can use these variables to handle the errors in the examples. When an error occurs, the error routine is called. The first step in errexit: is to print the error message on the standard output device. This is done through the errmsg() function, which consists of the the following code:

```
errmsg() /* errmsg() prints the ORACLE error and number.*/
{
    printf("%.70s \n", sqlca.sqlerrm.sqlerrmc);
    return(0);
}
```

It prints the value of sqlca.sqlerrm.sqlerrmc in a 70-character string. This is the full-length definition of sqlerrm because it is part of the sqlca structure and is a two-part VARCHAR structure as well. Sqlerrmc is the character array component of the sqlerrm structure.

An example error exit is if you execute PRODADD.EXE and have not loaded Oracle into memory. The following message will appear:

```
Oracle error 003120 osd error 0000000000
```

Without the sqlca communication area, such a message is difficult to retrieve.

Oraca

In addition to sqlca, which is standard SQL communication flags, Oracle now provides oraca for handling Oracle-specific communication. To include it in your program, add these two statements:

```
EXEC ORACLE OPTION (ORACA=YES);
EXEC SQL INCLUDE ORACA;
```

Oraca contains values for monitoring cursor statistics, text and values relating to the current SQL statement, and system statistics and options settings.

However, you must decide whether you want to develop SQL standard programs. Only Oracle will be able to call oraca, so accessing it narrows the applicability of your code.

COMMITTING, ROLLING BACK, AND EXITING

Depending on how the program went, you might want to complete the processing by either rolling back your work or committing it to the database. Either way, if you are finished with the program you should also officially log off the database by adding the RELEASE option to the statement, as in

```
EXEC SQL COMMIT WORK RELEASE;
```

or

```
EXEC SQL ROLLBACK WORK RELEASE;
```

It is a good idea to include both statements in your programs. You usually insert COMMIT in line in the program logic and include ROLLBACK after a named-label that you can only reach through a WHENEVER statement.

THE COMPILING PROCESS

To demonstrate the compiling process, this section shows you how the first Pro∗C program, PRODADD.PC, was compiled using Professional Oracle and Microsoft C on an IBM-AT. Some of the specifics might vary with your installation, but most of the steps will be identical. To create a stand-alone executable program using the Pro∗C method, you must:

1. Create a Pro∗C program in a text file with a .pc suffix
2. Run the Pro∗C precompiler program

3. Compile the resulting .C code with a C compiler

4. Link the resulting .OBJ file into an executable .EXE file

Once the Pro*C commands are added, the program code looks like Figure 13.3.

PRECOMPILING THE C CODE

When you install Pro*C on an AT, the PCC.EXE precompiler program is copied over to the \ORACLE5\BIN directory and the PCC.MSG file is copied over to the \ORACLE5\DBS directory. The rest of the files, including the C header files (*.h) and the Microsoft C compatible function library (SQLMSC.LIB) are copied to \ORACLE5\PRO. Move to the directory that contains your Pro*C program. In this case, it is on the Pro*C subdirectory of Oracle called C:\ORACLE5\PRO.

PCC.EXE is the program used to precompile Pro*C programs in Professional Oracle. If you execute PCC.EXE from your operating system without any options (type **PCC** and press Enter), a list of the precompiler options will appear on your terminal (see Figure 13.11).

The first column shows the option name and syntax, the second column shows the default values, and the third column explains the option. Although there are many options, you will typically only need to use a few of them. Use INAME to enter the name of your edited file (PRODADD.PC) and INCLUDE to define the directory path to the Pro*C header files and libraries if you are not on the Pro*C subdirectory. To precompile PRODADD.PC using the minimum syntax, type

```
PCC INAME=PRODADD.PC
```

Because the .pc suffix is included, the compiler knows that the host language is C. Alternately, you can use the HOST command to define the language:

```
PCC INAME=PRODADD HOST=C
```

If you are not in the Pro*C subdirectory, you can add the option

```
PCC INAME=PRODADD.PC INCLUDE=C:\ORACLE5\PRO
```

```
Developer copy only.  Production use prohibited by license agreement.


Pro*ORACLE: Version 1.1.9.4DX - Development on Mon Aug  1 22:01:19 1988

Copyright (c) 1986, Oracle Corporation, California, USA.  All rights reserved.


Command line options:

areasize=<integer>         16     *Size of Context Area (in K)
asacc=yes/no               no      If yes, use ASA carriage control
beglabel=<integer>         90000  Beginning Fortran label to generate
define=<symbol>                   Define a symbol for use in IFDEF
endlabel=<integer>         99999  End Fortran label to generate
errors=yes/no              yes     If yes, display errors to terminal
format=ansi/terminal       ansi   Input file format
hold_cursor=yes/no         no     *If yes, hold OraCursor (don't reassign)
host=<host_language>              C, Cobol, Cob74, Fortran, Pascal, PLI
iname=<input_filename>            Input filename
include=<include_path>            *Pathname for EXEC SQL INCLUDE files
inline=yes/no              yes     If yes, generate inline code (no AM)
ireclen=<integer>          80     Input file record length
litdelim=apost/quote       quote  *Cobol literal delimiter
lname=<list_filename>             List filename
lreclen=<integer>          132    List file record length
ltype=none/long/short      long   *List type
maxliteral=<integer>              *Max len of literal string
maxopencursors=<integer>   10     *Max nr of OraCursors in Cursor Cache
oname=<output_filename>           Output (generated code) filename
oraca=yes/no               no     *Use ORACA
oreclen=<integer>          80     Output file record length
pagelen=<integer>          66     List file page length
program=<AM_ID>                   Access Module Identifier
rebind=yes/no              yes    *If yes, rebind on every FETCH/USING
release_cursor=yes/no      no     *If yes, release OraCursor after execute
select_error=yes/no        yes    *If yes, generate FOUND error on SELECT
userid=<usr>/<pwd>         /       Oracle logon user id and password
xref=yes/no                yes    *If yes, generate xref for PCC symbols


"*" indicates this option legal via EXEC ORACLE OPTION
```

Figure 13.11: PCC.EXE options displayed

You can use more than one INCLUDE if your files are spread around the disk.

The LNAME function is also a useful option. If you specify a file name, with extension .CON for the console or .PRN for the printer with this option, LNAME outputs a documentation listing based on your program listing formatted for output similar to the Microsoft C Compiler listing. This has row numbers assigned, row locations of the host variables, SQL identifier definitions, the current precompile option settings, and compile statistics. Figure 13.12 shows an excerpt from the list file PRODADD.LST.

```
Pro*ORACLE 1.1.9(-)
Options: INAME=PRODADD.PC LNAME=PRODADD.LST

Host Variables
..............

cost                        Short Float     Def: Line   9 in PRODADD.PC
                                            Ref: Line  41 in PRODADD.PC
dscrpt                      Varchar(30)     Def: Line   8 in PRODADD.PC
                                            Ref: Line  41 in PRODADD.PC
password                    Varchar(20)     Def: Line   6 in PRODADD.PC
                                            Ref: Line  28 in PRODADD.PC
prodno                      Varchar(10)     Def: Line   7 in PRODADD.PC
                                            Ref: Line  41 in PRODADD.PC
qiw                         Short Integer   Def: Line  11 in PRODADD.PC
st                          Varchar(1)      Def: Line  10 in PRODADD.PC
                                            Ref: Line  41 in PRODADD.PC
userid                      Varchar(20)     Def: Line   5 in PRODADD.PC
                                            Ref: Line  28 in PRODADD.PC

SQL Identifiers
...............
MSDOS           DEFINE                          Pre-defined symbol


Statistics
..........

Return code: 0
Number of messages at severity I: 0
Number of messages at severity W: 0
Number of messages at severity E: 0
Number of messages at severity S: 0
Number of messages at severity U: 0
Number of input lines: 134
Number of host variables declared: 7
Number of cursor names: 0
Number of statement names: 0
Maximum bytes used: 3380
```

Figure 13.12: LNAME =PRODADD.LST statistics excerpt

If you prefer including these options as part of your program code or want to alter them within the program execution, you can embed them in your Pro*C code with the command syntax

```
EXEC ORACLE OPTION (option=option value)
```

The first method results in a file named PRODADD.C in which all of the EXEC SQL statements are converted to C program statements.

COMPILING INTO PRODADD.OBJ

Once you have the standard C source, you have to compile it with a Microsoft C version 4 compiler. This compiler includes five memory models—SMALL, COMPACT, MEDIUM, LARGE, and HUGE—for handling different application sizes. Pro∗C is compatible with the Microsoft LARGE memory model. To compile Pro∗C with the LARGE model, type

```
MSC /AL PRODADD.C
```

The /AL option tells the compiler to use the LARGE memory model. This compiling produces the file PRODADD.OBJ, which contains the object module for PRODADD. If you want, you can add options to produce a listing similar to the excerpt in Figure 13.12 and an object .COD listing.

LINKING

The final step in this process is called linking, which links in the library functions and generates an executable program. To do this, type

```
LINK PRODADD,,,C:\ORACLE5\PRO\SQLMSC /SE:512 /STACK:10000
```

SQLMSC is the library of C functions that Oracle created to call the database. This library is specific to Microsoft C version 4. The linking step will fail if you are using an earlier version of the Microsoft compiler or another compiler. The /SE:512 option tells the linker to use 512 segments and the /STACK:10000 option tells the linker to increase the number of stack elements to 10000. These options are needed to handle the complexity of the application.

The previous statement creates the file PRODADD.EXE, which you can execute directly from the operating system prompt, as shown in Figure 13.4.

USER-EXITS

User-exits are compiled much as are stand-alone Pro*C programs. You can use the EXEC SQL commands within your Pro*C file (.pc). In addition, to pass parameters back and forth between the form and the exit, use the commands

```
EXEC IAF GET variable1 INTO :variable2
```

and

```
EXEC IAF PUT variable VALUES(expression)
```

You then use PCC to precompile the user-exit. Currently, only the Lattice compiler can create compiled user-exits.

At some point, you have to run the GENXTB form to add your new user-exit information to the database. Do so by typing

```
username/password
```

The form shown in Figure 13.13 will come up.

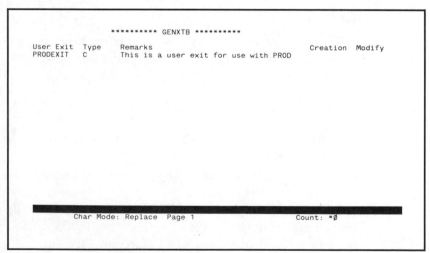

```
********** GENXTB **********

User Exit  Type   Remarks                                    Creation  Modify
PRODEXIT   C      This is a user exit for use with PROD




















                Char Mode: Replace   Page 1                      Count: *Ø
```

Figure 13.13: The GENXTB form

Enter your exit name, the code for the language it's in (C, COB, FOR, PL1, PAS), and any comments you want, and then commit it to the database table IAPXTB.

Once you have the new exit information in the database, run

```
GENXTB username/password filename
```

and the GENXTB utility creates an assembly language source file (.ASM) which you must compile with an assembler. Now you have your exit object code and the object code generated from the GENXTB utility. You have to link those two objects into the IAP object (RUNFORM.EXE) to create a new version of RUNFORM, in which you must run all of your forms with that user-exit.

As you can see, this is no easy process. It involves many different components, including a Microsoft or IBM Assembler and a Lattice C Compiler.

SUMMARY

This chapter discussed the steps required to create C language programs that access the Oracle database. With the Pro*C precompiler furnished with Oracle, you can embed high-level SQL commands into code and generate native C code. You can then compile this code and link it to executable programs.

Embedded SQL commands are an excellent way to structure updates to the database. Oracle provides several language alternatives for you to choose from. Given the proper tools, you can quickly learn to use this powerful interface to the database.

14

ORACLE UTILITIES: EXP, IMP, ODL, AND SQL*LOADER

THIS CHAPTER DESCRIBES HOW TO USE THE
Oracle utilities Export (EXP), Import (IMP), Oracle Data
Loader (ODL) and SQL*Loader. Export allows you to save
(archive) Oracle database information (tables, table creation
statements, grants, space definitions, and so on) in host operating system files. This allows you to move databases from one
computer platform to another. The Import utility loads Oracle
databases from host operating system files that are created by
Export. ODL and SQL*Loader permit you to move data from
non-database files to Oracle, providing a bridge between dissimilar software products. Collectively, the utility programs
allow you to move data between host operating systems and foreign data files.

EXPORTING AND IMPORTING ORACLE DATABASE INFORMATION

You can use the Import and Export utilities together to copy data in a database to a backup, host operating system file and restore exported data to an Oracle database. Any Professional Oracle user with CONNECT privilege can execute the Export and Import utilities. Together, Export and Import can perform the following tasks:

- Store Oracle database information (table definitions, table data, grants, synonyms, view definitions, space definitions, and indexes)

- Free up fragmented database space

- Store older or temporary data

- Move data between Oracle databases

- Translate data between ASCII (microcomputers and minicomputers) and EBCDIC (IBM minicomputers and mainframes)

- Convert databases from older Oracle versions to the latest version

- Move data from one Oracle user to another

EXPORTING ORACLE DATABASE INFORMATION

The Export utility copies database tables and associated information to an operating system file. Once it is exported, you can import the information on to other machines or save it for archive or "cold backup" purposes. You should back up your valuable database information periodically in case your host fails.

The amount and type of information you can export depends on your system privileges. If you have DBA and RESOURCE privileges, you have the greatest number of Export options. With RESOURCE privileges (CONNECT is assumed), you can exercise fewer Export options. The three *Export modes*—Table, User, and Entire Database—are shown in Table 14.1.

Table 14.1: Export Modes and Objects

	EXPORT MODES		
WHAT IS EXPORTED	**TABLE**	**USER**	**ENTIRE DATABASE**
Table definitions	X	X	X
Table data	X	X	X
Space definitions	X	X	X
Clusters		X	X
Indexes		X	X
Grants		*	X
Views			X
Synonyms			X
Others' table definitions			X
Others' table data			X
* First-level grants			

You can export only objects that you own unless you hold the DBA system privilege, in which case you can export or import tables belonging to any user and can perform a full database export or import operation. Non-DBA users can only choose the TABLE or USER export mode.

Invoking Export

The Oracle Protected Mode Executive (PME) must be loaded before you can invoke the Export utility. Execute Export by typing **EXP** at the DOS prompt.

```
C:\ORACLE5\DBS>EXP
```

If you like, you can enter a username and password (separated by a slash) on the same line before pressing Enter.

```
C:\ORACLE5\DBS>EXP PERRY/STIRLING
```

If you omit the username or password, Export will prompt you for them. Whichever method you use, Export validates your username and password and displays a series of prompts to which you respond. Although the number and type of prompts depend on your system privileges and responses to prior prompts, the first few prompts are always displayed.

The first prompt asks you to specify the amount of memory for the Export *fetch buffer,* an area of memory set aside for exported table rows. Unless you are exporting unusually large rows, the suggested default of 1024 bytes is fine, so simply press Enter. Otherwise, type an integer larger than any row of any table you are exporting. This number represents the maximum number of characters of memory to hold any row of any table being exported. Press Enter after typing a new buffer size. The prompt looks like this:

```
Enter array fetch buffer size (default is 1024)>
```

Specifying the Host Operating System File Name

The second Export prompt requests that you specify the host operating system export file name. The suggested default file name is EXPDAT.DMP, but you can type any valid DOS file name (with a path, if needed). For example, the following example specifies the export file MYTABLES to be located on drive C.

```
Export file: EXPDAT.DMP > C:\MYTABLES
```

You can use any legitimate extension. If you omit the extension, DMP is automatically assigned. Always press Enter to go to the next Export step after you finish typing your response.

Choosing an Export Mode

The next Export prompt requests that you choose from three export modes. A user with DBA privilege can choose the *Table, User,*

or *Entire Database* modes. A user with only RESOURCE and CON-
NECT privileges can choose either Table or User mode (see Table
14.1). The prompt displayed for a DBA user is:

```
E(ntire Database), U(sers), or T(ables): U >
```

Enter E, U, or T and press Enter to indicate your choice. Pressing
Enter selects the suggested default value (U in the preceding
example). If you supply a username that does not have DBA system
privilege, the Export mode prompt is limited to Users or Tables:

```
U(sers) or T(ables): U >
```

Exporting Grants

If you are in Entire Database or Users mode, the following prompt
appears.

```
Export Grants (Y/N): N >
```

The prompt does not appear if you are exporting specific tables
(Table mode), no matter what system privilege you hold. Press Y to
export tables and grant information (for example, GRANT
SELECT ON MYTABLE TO SMITH). Otherwise, press Enter or
type N and press Enter.

Exporting Table Rows

The next prompt allows you to export or not export the rows of
various tables. Pressing Enter or typing Y and pressing Enter will
export the table rows to the DOS file. Pressing N will write only the
table definition statements (CREATE TABLE) to the export file.
Normally, you want the Export-suggested default of Y. In this case,
all rows for any eligible tables are written out to the export file. The
prompt looks like this:

```
Export the rows (Y/N): Y >
```

Compressing the Exported Rows

If you indicated in the previous prompt that the rows were to be exported, you would see the message

```
Compress extents (Y/N): Y >
```

This prompt does not appear if you indicate that no rows are to be exported. Type Y or simply press Enter to compress extents. Otherwise, type N and press Enter to omit extent compression. Usually, you should indicate Y to compact the rows exported into as few *extents* as possible. Numerous deletion and insertion operations can store a database's rows in disparate locations on several disk extents. By compressing the database rows, you can reclaim unused "holes" within disk extents. Otherwise, rows that are fragmented across several extents can slow database processing. Compression does not actually take effect until you import the compressed database back into the Oracle-managed disk file. The "Compress extents" message is the last Export prompt. Subsequent Export actions depend on your responses to the previous questions.

EXPORT EXAMPLES

Several examples of exporting database tables, users, and the entire database are shown here. Pay particular attention to the invoking user's system privileges as well as to the export mode.

Exporting the Entire Database

Remember that you must have the DBA system privilege to export the entire database. Make sure that there is enough space in the export file to hold the entire database on your hard disk. Since exporting the whole database system to floppy disks (no matter how much information your floppies hold) can be a long and arduous task, you should export to a fixed disk. To invoke Export, type

```
C:\ORACLE5\DBS>EXP username/password
```

substituting your own username and assigned password. Figure 14.1 shows the Export prompts and user-supplied responses for the full

```
C:\ORACLE5\DBS>EXP PERRY/STIRLING

Export: Version 5.1.17.4 - Production on Wed Mar 15 18:00:00 1989

Copyright (c) 1986, Oracle Corporation, California, USA.  All rights reserved.

Connected to: ORACLE V5.1.17.4 - Production

 Enter array fetch buffer size (default is 4096)>

Export file: EXPDAT.DMP > C:\PERRY
E(ntire Database), U(sers), or T(ables): U > E

Export Grants (Y/N): N > N

Export the rows (Y/N): Y > Y

Compress extents (Y/N): Y > Y

Exporting the entire data base.
. Exporting user definitions.
. Exporting all space definitions.
. Exporting all clusters.
. Exporting user SYSTEM
. Exporting table AUDIT_ACTIONS        49 Rows exported
. Exporting table DTAB            44 Rows exported
. Exporting table DUAL            1 Rows exported
...
...
C:\ORACLE5\DBS>
```

Figure 14.1: Exporting the entire database

database export. The names of exported tables, views, and so on have been shortened for brevity. Ellipses indicate tables omitted from the figure.

You may want to export the entire database periodically to provide an emergency backup copy of the database. The frequency with which you produce full database exports depends, among other things, on the frequency of database changes. If your databases are frequently altered, full database exports should be frequent. Relatively static databases need not be exported as frequently.

Exporting an Entire User

You can export an entire user—all of his or her tables, views, grants, and so on—with the User export mode. If you have DBA privilege, you can export any user's tables, views, and grants; if you do not, you can export only database tables that you own. Figure 14.2 shows the prompts and responses that follow when you choose User mode.

```
C:\ORACLE5\DBS>EXP PERRY/STIRLING

Export: Version 5.1.17.4 - Production on Wed Mar 15 18:00:00 1989

Copyright (c) 1986, Oracle Corporation, California, USA.  All rights reserved.

Connected to: ORACLE V5.1.17.4 - Production

 Enter array fetch buffer size (default is 4096)>

Export file: EXPDAT.DMP > C:\PERRY
E(ntire Database), U(sers), or T(ables): U > U

Export Grants (Y/N): N > N

Export the rows (Y/N): Y > Y

Compress extents (Y/N): Y > Y

Exporting Specified Users.
User to be exported: PERRY > LATEER

. Exporting user LATEER
. Exporting table PROPSUMM          35 Rows exported
. Exporting table PAYABLES         548 Rows exported
. Exporting table MAILLIST        3245 Rows exported
C:\ORACLE\DBS>
```

Figure 14.2: Exporting an entire user

Exporting Selected Users' Tables

A user with DBA privilege can export tables owned by any user, while a non-DBA user can export only tables he or she owns. Figure 14.3 shows the prompts and responses for a DBA user. Whenever a new user is specified with the username prefix, Export indicates a change of user with the message

```
Current user changed to:
```

When you have finished exporting all desired tables, press period (.) and Enter or just Enter to terminate the table export operation.

```
C:\ORACLE5\DBS>EXP PERRY/STIRLING

Export: Version 5.1.17.4 - Production on Wed Mar 15 18:00:00 1989

Copyright (c) 1986, Oracle Corporation, California, USA.  All rights reserved.

Connected to: ORACLE V5.1.17.4 - Production

 Enter array fetch buffer size (default is 4096)>

Export file: EXPDAT.DMP > C:\PERRY
E(ntire Database), U(sers), or T(ables): U > T

Export the rows (Y/N): Y > Y

Compress extents (Y/N): Y > Y

Exporting Specified Tables.

Table Name: >  LATEER.PROPSUMM
Current user changed to: LATEER

. Exporting table PROPSUMM        35 Rows exported
Table Name: >  CORDELL.ROYALTY
Current user changed to: CORDELL

.Exporting table ROYALTY         587 Rows exported
Table Name: >  RATE

.Exporting table RATE             68 Rows exported
Table Name: >  .

C:\ORACLE5\DBS>
```

Figure 14.3: Exporting selected tables of several users

After you switch to a new user, any subsequent table names not prefixed by a username (followed by a period) are assumed to be from
the most recent user. For example, since the RATE table in Figure
14.3 is specified as simply RATE, Export assumes that the table
belongs to the latest user, CORDELL. Remember, if you have only
RESOURCE or CONNECT privileges (or both), you can export
only your own tables; Figure 14.4 shows what happens when you try
to export a table you do not own.

Notice the error message

```
Sorry, can't change users continue
```

displayed when user LATEER attempts to export CORDELL's
tables. LATEER does not have the DBA privilege.

```
C:\ORACLE5\DBS>EXP LATEER/LAZARETTI

Export: Version 5.1.17.4 · Production on Wed Mar 15 18:00:00 1989

Copyright (c) 1986, Oracle Corporation, California, USA.  All rights reserved.

Connected to: ORACLE V5.1.17.4 · Production

 Enter array fetch buffer size (default is 4096)>

Export file: EXPDAT.DMP >
U(sers), or T(ables): U > T

Export the rows (Y/N): Y > N

Exporting Specified Tables.

Table Name: >  SALES_RECEIPTS
Error: SALES_RECEIPTS is not valid or does not exist
Table Name: >  TIMECARD

. Exporting table TIMECARD
Table Name: >  CORDELL.SALES_RECEIPTS
Sorry, can't change users continue
Table Name: >  .

C:\ORACLE\DBS>
```

Figure 14.4: Attempting to export another user's table

IMPORTING ORACLE DATABASE INFORMATION

The Import utility reads data from *export files*—files created by the Export utility program. With Import, you can selectively load data (or table definitions) from an export file. Tables, clusters, and space definitions are automatically created from information contained in the exported file. Because the file is encoded in a special way, do not edit it in any way.

An important use of the Export and Import utilities is moving data between different types of databases. The exporting machine can use either EBCDIC (Extended Binary Coded Decimal Interchange Code) or ASCII (American Standard Code for Information Interchange). Since Import automatically translates between coding bases when necessary, you could export a database from an IBM mainframe computer (EBCDIC) and import it on to an ASCII-based computer like VAX.

Anyone with RESOURCE and CONNECT access to Oracle can import database tables and related information. Furthermore, the person doing an import need not be the person who created the export file. If you have only CONNECT system privileges, you cannot execute the Import utility. If you attempt to invoke Import in this situation, the following error message is issued and the Import utility is terminated:

```
Error: Insufficient Oracle privileges for operation
       IMPORT terminated due to error
```

Because users with at least CONNECT privilege can export database information, certain combinations of Export and Import are not allowed. For example, only a user with DBA privilege can import a file created by a DBA privilege holder. Moreover, if you have RESOURCE and CONNECT privileges, you can import only files created by users with RESOURCE or CONNECT privileges. Table 14.2 summarizes the valid and invalid Export and Import user privilege combinations. The vertical axis lists the highest system privilege held by the exporter; the top row of the table lists the highest system privilege held by the importer. A "NO" in the intersection of a row and column indicates that the Export/Import combination is not allowed. A "YES" indicates the Export/Import pair is allowed.

Table 14.2: Export/Import Combinations by System Privilege

IMPORT PRIVILEGE:	CONNECT	RESOURCE	DBA
CONNECT	No	Yes	Yes
RESOURCE	No	Yes	Yes
DBA	No	No	Yes

(EXPORT PRIVILEGE: on the vertical axis)

Invoking Import

As with Export, the Oracle Protected Mode Executive must be loaded before you can execute Import. If it is not, an error message such as the one in Figure 14.5 is generated. Simply load the PME and reexecute Import.

To execute Import, type **IMP** and then type in your username and password. If you do not supply your username or password before pressing Enter, Import prompts you for the missing information. The two methods of logging on to Import are:

```
C:\ORACLE5\DBS>IMP
```

or

```
C:\ORACLE5\DBS>IMP username/password
```

where you substitute a valid username and password for *username* and *password.* After your username and password are validated, Import asks a series of questions to which you respond. The information imported depends on the information contained in the export file and your answers to the Import prompts.

```
C:\ORACLE5\DBS>IMP PERRY/STIRLING

Import: Version 5.1.17.4 · Production on Wed Mar 15 18:25:32 1989

Copyright (c) 1986, Oracle Corporation, California, USA.  All rights reserved.


Oracle Error: Oracle error 003121 osd error 0000000000

IMPORT terminated due to error
C:\ORACLE5\DBS>
```

Figure 14.5: Attempting to import without loading the PME

Choosing an Import File Name

Import first requests the name of the host operating system file name to be imported. Press Enter to accept the default, or type in the full file specification of the file to be imported (with path and drive, if necessary). The prompt and sample response are

```
Import file: EXPDAT.DMP >C:\ARCHIVE\PERRY.SAV
```

In the preceding example we did not choose the proposed default file name EXPDAT.DMP but instead told Import to import the file PERRY.SAV in subdirectory C:\ARCHIVE.

Specifying the Import Buffer Size

Specifying the Import buffer size allocates space in memory for the largest rows you will import. The prompt reads

```
Enter insert buffer size(default is 10240, minimum is 4096) >
```

Type the appropriate size and press Enter, or just press Enter to accept the suggested default.

The next message indicates what version of Oracle was used to perform the Export operation and does not require a response from you.

```
Export created by ORACLE version EXPORT:V05.01.22
```

Listing the Contents of the Import File

The next prompt asks if you want to list the contents of the import file. To display a list of the table names and space definitions, type Y and press Enter. However, to import files and related data, press Enter to accept the proposed default when you see this prompt:

```
List contents of import file only (Y/N): N >
```

If you answer yes, Import asks more questions, determining whether to display the entire export file or selected parts of it.

The Ignoring Create Errors Option

If you import table rows by answering no to the previous option, this prompt appears:

```
Ignore create errors due to object existence (Y/N): Y >
```

If you indicate yes by pressing Enter or Y and Enter, Import will import rows of tables even if those tables already exist. Because the import file contains CREATE TABLE statements, Import will attempt to create a new table into which to import the rows. Attempting a CREATE TABLE on existing tables will cause an error, but Import can ignore the error if you so indicate. Note that choosing Y means that if the imported tables already exist in the database, the imported rows are *added* to the database. That is, the table is not emptied before imported rows are inserted. Be careful not to duplicate table rows by mistake when using Import.

Importing Grants

The next prompt asks whether you wish to import any GRANT commands that might have been exported to the DOS file. If you respond yes, any grants that were exported will be imported. Otherwise, no grants (whether exported or not) will be included in the import operation. If export was done in User mode, only first-level grants are exported and imported. If export was done in Entire Database export mode (see Table 14.1), *all* grants are imported. The prompt appears as:

```
Import Grants (Y/N): Y >
```

Importing Database Rows

The next prompt allows you to import data rows or to create a table with no data rows. By default, Import expects you to import the table rows:

```
Import the rows (Y/N): Y >
```

If you respond no by typing N and pressing Enter, only the data definition statements in the import file are run (statements such as CREATE TABLE and CREATE VIEW). The associated data are not inserted into the base tables. Pressing Enter causes the rows to be imported (inserted) into the corresponding tables.

Selecting How Much Data to Import

The next prompt allows you to choose which tables are imported from the import file. By default, the entire collection of tables is imported into the database. If you answer no to the prompt

```
Import of entire import file requested (Y/N): Y >
```

Import will prompt you for the username and for the tables to import. In this way, you can choose to import specific tables from selected users. Press Y and Enter or simply press Enter to import all tables and views.

Importing Files from Earlier Versions of Oracle

Oracle Version 5 Import utility will accept a Version 4 export file. It will not, however, accept any export file produced prior to Version 4. If you are importing a Version 4 export file, you cannot selectively import individual tables; you must import the entire file. You can then selectively drop tables that you do not need. In addition, because Version 5 does not support ALTER CLUSTER, it imports clustered tables in unclustered form.

IMPORT EXAMPLES

The following sections present a few of the most used Import options. The usernames indicate the user's system privileges. Similarly, the exported files have names that reveal their creators' system privilege. File CONNECT.DMP was created by a user with only CONNECT privilege; RESOURCE.DMP was created by someone with CONNECT and RESOURCE privileges; and file DBA.DMP was created by someone with all three system privileges.

Who can Import Files

Recall that if you have only CONNECT privilege you cannot import any files. If user CONNECTUSER executes the Import utility, enters the insert buffer size, and specifies the import file name, an error message is generated and Import is terminated, as shown in Figure 14.6.

Notice the warning and error messages that Import displays. The warning message simply recognizes that the exporting user and the

```
C:\ORACLE5\DBS>IMP CONNECTUSER/CONNECTUSER

Import: Version 5.1.17.4 - Production on Wed Mar 15 10:30:00 1989

Copyright (c) 1986, Oracle Corporation, California, USA.  All rights reserved.

Connected to: ORACLE V5.1.17.4 - Production

Import file: EXPDAT.DMP >C:\CONNECT.DMP

Enter insert buffer size(default is 10240, minimum is 4096) >

Export created by ORACLE version EXPORT:V05.01.17
Warning: the data was exported by PERRY, not by you
Error: Insufficient Oracle privileges for operation
IMPORT terminated due to error
C:\ORACLE5\DBS>
```

Figure 14.6: A CONNECT user import attempt

importing user are different. However, the error message

```
Error: Insufficient Oracle privileges for operation
```

indicates that with only CONNECT privilege you cannot execute Import.

Recall also that only DBA users can import files exported by DBA users. In Figure 14.7, user RESOURCEUSER attempts to import a file that a DBA user exported.

```
C:\ORACLE5\DBS>IMP RESOURCEUSER/RESOURCEUSER

Import: Version 5.1.17.4 - Production on Wed Mar 15 10:30:00 1989

Copyright (c) 1986, Oracle Corporation, California, USA.  All rights reserved.

Connected to: ORACLE V5.1.17.4 - Production

Import file: EXPDAT.DMP >C:\DBA

Enter insert buffer size(default is 10240, minimum is 4096) >

Export created by ORACLE version EXPORT:V05.01.17

Error: Only a DBA can import what another DBA exported
IMPORT terminated due to error
C:\ORACLE5\DBS>
```

Figure 14.7: A CONNECT/RESOURCE user import attempt

Importing an Entire File

A DBA user can import any export file. In particular, he or she can import a DBA-produced export file. Figure 14.8 shows how to import the entire file exported by user KING.

```
C:\ORACLE5\DBS>IMP DBAUSER/DBAUSER

Import: Version 5.1.17.4 - Production on Wed Mar 15 10:30:00 1989

Copyright (c) 1986, Oracle Corporation, California, USA.  All rights reserved.

Connected to: ORACLE V5.1.17.4 - Production

Import file: EXPDAT.DMP >C:\DBA.DMP

Enter insert buffer size(default is 10240, minimum is 4096) >

Export created by ORACLE version EXPORT:V05.01.17

List contents of import file only (Y/N): N > N

Ignore create errors due to object existence (Y/N): Y > Y

Import Grants (Y/N): Y > Y

Import the rows (Y/N): Y > Y

Import of entire import file requested (Y/N): Y > Y
. Importing user KING
. . Importing table "BOOKS"                         242 Rows imported
. . Importing table "PUBLISHERS"                     58 Rows imported

C:\ORACLE5\DBS>
```

Figure 14.8: Importing the entire export file

Because the response Y is given to the question "Import of entire import file requested," all tables in the file are imported.

Importing Selected Tables

If you want only selected tables from an import file, answer no when Oracle asks if you want to import the entire import file. Import prompts you for a username, which is located in the export file, and you can then select all or some of the tables owned by that user.

For example, suppose that you choose to import only KING's files. Furthermore, you want only the table BOOKS. Import prompts you for one or more table names. After entering each table name and pressing Enter, the prompt

```
Enter table name or . if done:
```

reappears. When you have entered all table names, press period (.) to terminate the process. Import then imports all selected tables. To import all tables belonging to a user, simply press Enter when asked for the names of tables to be imported.

To abort the Import process entirely, press the abort key (Ctrl-C in Professional Oracle). Import will immediate halt the Import operation and return control to the host operating system.

Figure 14.9 shows one way to import selected tables from the export file.

```
C:\ORACLE5\DBS>IMP DBAUSER/DBAUSER

Import: Version 5.1.17.4 - Production on Wed Mar 15 10:30:00 1989

Copyright (c) 1986, Oracle Corporation, California, USA.  All rights reserved.

Connected to: ORACLE V5.1.17.4 - Production

Import file: EXPDAT.DMP >C:\DBA.DMP

Enter insert buffer size(default is 10240, minimum is 4096) >

Export created by ORACLE version EXPORT:V05.01.17

List contents of import file only (Y/N): N > N

Ignore create errors due to object existence (Y/N): Y > Y

Import Grants (Y/N): Y > Y

Import the rows (Y/N): Y > Y

Import of entire import file requested (Y/N): Y > N

Username: KING

Enter list of table names. Null list means all tables for user
Enter table name or . if done: BOOKS

Enter table name of . if done: .
. Importing user KING
. . Importing table "BOOKS"                          242 Rows imported

C:\ORACLE5\DBS>
```

Figure 14.9: Importing selected tables

If the export file contains no tables with the names you have indicated, then no message appears and Import halts immediately. Likewise, if you enter a username that is not found in the export file to be imported, Import halts.

LOADING DATA
FROM FOREIGN FILES: ODL

The Oracle Data Loader (ODL) utility program allows you to import data into the Oracle database system from a non-Oracle source. For example, you could use ODL to load a database table from a data file produced by dBASE IV or from SuperCalc5 spreadsheet data. ODL provides the needed bridge between all other data sources and Oracle databases.

Import expects data to be in a format produced by the Export utility and does not recognize data files produced by other software packages. ODL handles most formats of "raw" data. The requirements for the data to be loaded by ODL are

- The file may be in any record format that is recognized and handled by the host operating system.

- All records in the raw data file must be the same, fixed length except for the last data value, whose length may vary.

- Not all data contained in the raw data file need be loaded. You can omit one or more "columns" from the source file.

- Records in the data file must be wholly contained in one physical block of the host operating system disk (usually not a problem for MS-DOS or OS/2 users).

- Only one table may be loaded during one execution of ODL.

ODL also requires that any tables to be loaded must exist before you execute ODL. That is, ODL does not first create Oracle tables and then load them with data. Any user with CONNECT privilege can run ODL. Clearly, however, you must have RESOURCE privilege to create any needed tables before running ODL.

FEATURES

ODL users can do the following:

- Load all the data from a host operating system file into an Oracle table

- Select and load partial data from a data file

- Load selected columns in a table, omitting chosen columns, including NOT NULL columns

- Use any Oracle function to generate unique, integer keys for each record inserted into a table

- Load only a selected number of records beginning from any arbitrary starting record in the raw data file

- Indicate the error "tolerance level"—how many errors to ignore before halting the data loading process

OVERVIEW

ODL requires two input files and produces two output files (in addition to the loaded Oracle database table). The requisite input files are called the *control file* and the *raw data file* (see Figure 14.10).

The control file contains general directions for performing the loading operation. It names the host operating system file containing the raw data, the Oracle table to be created, the columns of the Oracle table to be loaded, and shows ODL exactly where to file data in the raw file. This mapping information allows ODL to determine the start and end of fields to be loaded into Oracle table columns.

The raw data file contains data from a source other than an Oracle database that is to be loaded into an Oracle table. This file can be from a word processing program, some other database software system, or from an on-line timesharing system.

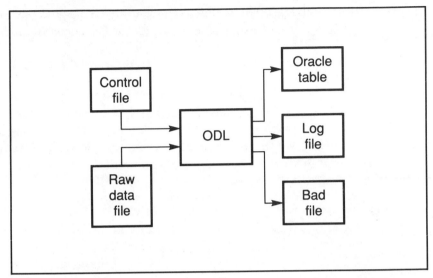

Figure 14.10: ODL input and output files

When ODL is loading data from the data file source into an Oracle table, it produces two output files: the *log file* and the *bad file*. The log file is a host operating system file (ASCII or EBCDIC) in plain text form. It contains the number of records read, loaded, and rejected as well as any error messages generated during the loading operation. The bad file is created whenever incorrect records are encountered during the load process. For example, if a raw data record contains a character string that corresponds to an Oracle column declared as NUMBER, the record is written to the bad file. Loading continues with the record in the raw data file after the one in error. Later, you can edit the record written into the bad file and use ODL to insert it into your table.

INVOKING ODL: THE COMMAND LINE

To invoke ODL, type **ODL** at the DOS prompt and then type the name of the control file followed by the name of the log file. You can include your username and password on the same line followed by a series of ODL options. If you omit your username and password, ODL prompts you for them. The syntax for the ODL command line is

```
ODL control-file-name log-file-name [username/password] [-options]
```

where *control-file-name* is the DOS control file name, *log-file-name* is the DOS log file name, *username/password* is the optional username and password pair, and *–options* are additional ODL options that determine how ODL reacts to various conditions it may encounter during execution. Here is an example with names and options specified:

```
ODL ACCT.CTL ACCT.LOG LATEER/LAZARETTI -S200 -C15 -E10
```

ACCT.CTL is the name of the control file, ACCT.LOG is the name of the log file, LATEER/LAZARETTI is the invoking user's username and password, and the ODL options are – S200, – C15, and – E10.

OPTIONAL ODL COMMAND LINE PARAMETERS

Five optional parameters can follow the username and password. Because they are options, you can omit them altogether, in which case they take on their default values. Table 14.3 lists the options and their meanings.

The command line that you type to invoke ODL refers to two files whose names follow the ODL command. ODL needs these two files to execute. The examples in the rest of this chapter refer to the PROPERTY database shown in several earlier chapters. Here is an ODL command that you might use to load the PROPERTY table from a flat file:

```
C:\ORACLE5\DBS>ODL PROPERTY.CTL PROPERTY.LOG PERRY/STIRLING
```

PROPERTY.CTL is the required DOS file containing the control file. PROPERTY.LOG is a log file that is created by ODL when ODL is executed. The invoking user has username PERRY and password STIRLING. Because no ODL optional parameters have been written, the options take on their default values.

Table 14.3: ODL Optional Parameters

PARAMETER	MEANING
B	Tells the number of characters of memory to be used for internal processing and input buffers. The default is 16K. If you are loading wide tables, you may wish to increase this value. The maximum value depends on your machine's internal memory. Specify this argument with a minus sign, the letter B, and an integer. For example, – B50.
C	The value following C tells ODL how often to execute a COMMIT command. Specifying – C50 indicates that ODL should commit after every 50th inserted record. The default is 100. – C0 means that ODL should commit all inserted records only after the whole table is loaded.
E	The value following E tells ODL how many errors (bad records) should be tolerated before ODL halts processing. The default value is 50. If you omit this parameter, ODL will stop processing if more than 50 errors occur.
L	This parameter indicates how many input records should be loaded into the table. If you specify – L60 for example, only 60 records will be loaded. If L is omitted, ODL will load all records. The default (– L0) is to load the entire file.
S	This parameter indicates how many input records to skip before loading the table. Writing the value – S30 tells ODL to skip the first 30 records (begin with the 31st input record) before loading the Oracle table. The default is to skip no records.

THE ODL CONTROL FILE

The ODL control file contains the *script,* or instructions, that ODL uses to load the raw data into a database table. This control file consists of the following three parts:

- the DEFINE RECORD statement
- the DEFINE SOURCE statement
- the FOR EACH statement

You must enter each of the preceding statements into the ODL control file for ODL to execute correctly. They specify, respectively, the raw data file structure, the raw datafile name, and the correspondence between raw data file field names and table column names. Figure 14.11 shows a sample ODL control file (for clarity, each field description is on a separate line).

```
DEFINE RECORD RAWDATAFILE AS
     RPARCELNO       (CHAR(7)),
       RSKIP1        (CHAR(1)),
     RPRICE          (CHAR(6)),
     RDATE           (CHAR(8)),
       RSKIP2        (CHAR(1)),
     RSQFT           (CHAR(4)),
       RSKIP3        (CHAR(2)),
     RBEDROOMS       (CHAR(1)),
       RSKIP4        (CHAR(1)),
     RBATHROOMS      (CHAR(3)),
     RZIPCODE        (CHAR(5));
DEFINE SOURCE FILE
     FROM PROP14.TXT
     LENGTH 41
     CONTAINING RAWDATAFILE ;
FOR EACH RECORD
     INSERT INTO PROPERTY
     (PARCEL, PRICE, SALEDATE, SQFT, BR, BA, ZIP) VALUES
     (RPARCELNO, RPRICE, NULL, RSQFT, RBEDROOMS,
      RBATHROOMS, RZIPCODE)
     NEXT RECORD
```

Figure 14.11: Contents of a typical ODL control file

The DEFINE RECORD Statement

To understand the control file, look at the raw data file that is referred to by the control file shown in Figure 14.11. The raw data file, or flat file, consists of seven fields per row (see Figure 14.12).

```
1035975 14650003/24/88 1600  3 2.092040
1040816 20750002/25/88 2108  3 2.592016
1050601 13650001/04/88 1100  3 2.092048
1081295 13840005/24/88 1332  3 2.092048
1083767 16550001/27/88 1500  3 2.092048
1151541 21450002/25/88 2700  4 2.792016
1216019 14100001/03/87 1750  3 2.592048
1233117 10350003/16/88 1288  3 2.092012

 . . .     . . .  . .   . . .    . . .
6842703 10250004/22/88 1300  3 2.092028
7005958 14150006/05/88 1350  3 2.092048
7141094 21550005/25/88 2600  4 2.092016
7354304 21950005/15/88 3350  4 3.092016
7372020 29650007/06/88 2475  4 3.092044
```

Figure 14.12: The PROPERTY raw data file

In the DEFINE RECORD portion of the control file, you describe the structure of the raw data file. The description resembles a data structure in several high-level programming languages such as COBOL. It names the record to be loaded and the fields of the record to be loaded, associates a data type with each field, and specifies the location of each field in the raw data record. Beginning with the phrase

```
DEFINE RECORD record-name AS
```

where *record-name* is an arbitrary name, the raw data file structure description consists of pairs of field names and data types. The last field description is terminated with a semicolon. The field name and data type for each field has the syntax

```
field-name ({FLOAT|INTEGER|CHAR} [(size)] [,LOC (field-loc)])
```

where *field-name* refers to the raw data field, *size* is the length of the field, and *field-loc* is the position of the field in the raw data record. *Field-loc* can be expressed as + *number,* – *number,* or *number.* An integer without any sign indicates the field's absolute location from the beginning of a record. A signed integer indicates a field's location relative to the end of the last field. LOC(– 5) means that the current field is 5 positions toward the beginning of the record from the end of the current field. Similarly, LOC(+ 12) indicates that the current field is 12 positions toward the end (to the right) of the end of the last field defined. The first position of a record is position 0 (zero).

A few examples of individual field descriptions are

```
PARCEL      (CHAR(20))

COST        (INTEGER, LOC(12))

IDENT       (CHAR(10), LOC(-4))
```

PARCEL is a character field of length 20. Because the optional parameter LOC was omitted, PARCEL's beginning column in the raw file is computed from the beginning positions and lengths of all raw data fields that precede it in the DEFINE RECORD statement. COST is an INTEGER field is located in position 13 of the raw input file (this is called the *absolute* position from position 0, the first position in a record). IDENT is 10 characters long and is located 4 positions to the left of the end of the last field defined.

None of the fields shown in Figure 14.11 contain the optional LOC phrase and are therefore written in the same order as their occurrence (left-to-right) in the raw data file. Moreover, every field has the data type designation CHAR. Because all of the fields in the PROPERTY table being filled are either CHAR or NUMBER data types, and the raw data file consists entirely of ASCII representations of numbers, you can specify the field data type as CHAR. Oracle handles the conversion to numeric format from ASCII. On the other hand, if a field in the raw data file requires either internal floating point or binary representation rather than ASCII, either FLOAT or INTEGER would be specified in the DEFINE RECORD statement.

Notice that some field names in Figure 14.11 are indented slightly (RSKIP1, RSKIP2, and so on). These are fields that are not loaded into the Oracle table but whose existence must be noted. Because the four RSKIP fields occupy space in the input raw data file, ODL must be informed of their position. Omitting them would cause the correspondence between field names and data locations to be misaligned. If you use the LOC optional parameter for all field descriptions in the DEFINE RECORD statement, you can omit these "dummy" fields altogether.

The DEFINE SOURCE Statement

The DEFINE SOURCE statement of the ODL control file defines the input media, the name of the host operating system file holding the raw data, and the record name. It also indicates the record length. The syntax of the DEFINE SOURCE statement is

```
DEFINE SOURCE      source-name
       FROM        file-name1 [,file-name2,...file-namex]
       LENGTH      length
       CONTAINING  record-name ;
```

Source-name is a placeholder for the actual source file. It can be any identifier, but FILE or TAPE are typical identifiers for this parameter. *File-name* is the host operating system file name containing the raw data. If you include more than one file name, each separated by a comma, the files are treated as one file consisting of the individual files logically concatenated. *Length* is an integer that is the length of each (and every) raw data record. If your raw data file contains records of varying lengths, this value should be the maximum record length. In Professional Oracle, because each record is normally terminated with a carriage return/linefeed, the length should be the actual record length plus 2. For example, if your raw data records have a maximum length of 57 characters, specify a length of 59. Otherwise, ODL will not load your data correctly and errors will occur.

The DEFINE SOURCE statement shown in Figure 14.11 (the PROPERTY raw data file) is

```
DEFINE SOURCE FILE
    FROM PROP14.TXT
    LENGTH 41
    CONTAINING RAWDATAFILE ;
```

The DOS raw data file is MLS14.TXT. If you count the number of characters in any record in Figure 14.12, the length is 39. Since the length written in DEFINE SOURCE is two greater than the record length, type **41**. The last phrase in the previous example and Figure 14.12 indicate that the record name, internal to the control file, is RAWDATAFILE. Notice that the DEFINE SOURCE statement ends with a semicolon.

The FOR EACH Statement

The FOR EACH statement reads each raw data record and inserts it into the specified table. It is the action portion of the control file; it executes a series of SQL INSERT statements to load the data from the raw data file into the table. The syntax of FOR EACH is

```
FOR EACH RECORD
    INSERT INTO table-name (column-name,...,column-name)
    VALUES (field-name,...,field-name)
    NEXT RECORD
```

Table-name can be an Oracle database table that you created or a synonym for a table that someone else created. You cannot refer to someone else's table without using a synonym. For example, you cannot specify the name LATEER.ACCOUNTS. *Column-name* stands for the table's column names. You need not supply all column names; only the columns specified are loaded with data from the raw data file. In Figure 14.11, the FOR EACH RECORD statement is

```
FOR EACH RECORD
    INSERT INTO PROPERTY
    (PARCEL, PRICE, SALEDATE, SQFT, BR, BA, ZIP) VALUES
    (RPARCELNO, RPRICE, NULL, RSQFT, RBEDROOMS,
      RBATHROOMS, RZIPCODE)
    NEXT RECORD
```

Notice that you can split the FOR EACH RECORD phrase across lines but you can't break a word. The preceding example has the NULL value in the list of raw data file names. You can use NULL whenever you want the NULL value to be placed in the corresponding table column. Although the raw data file contains dates (in character form), NULL is placed in that column of the PROPERTY table. There are a few additional possibilities; the following data can be inserted in the VALUES portion of the FOR EACH statement:

- The name of a field in a raw data file
- A character string
- A number (sometimes called a literal value)
- NULL

- The GENSEQ function which generates a different integer for each record (see Chapter 7)

You need the NEXT RECORD phrase to terminate the ODL insert operation.

OUTPUT FILES PRODUCED BY ODL: LOG AND BAD

ODL produces either one or two output files besides the loaded Oracle database table. It always produces a log file, which you indicate in your ODL command line. If one or more errors occur during execution, ODL also creates a bad file to hold the rejected records. The bad file has the same name as the log file, but with the extension .BAD.

The Log File

As ODL executes, it creates a log file and writes information into it. This information includes the number of records loaded and statistics and error messages resulting from the load operation. Specify the log file's name in the ODL command line. Since it has no default extension, you should specify an extension such as .LOG:

```
ODL PROP.CTL PROP.LOG PERRY/STIRLING
```

Do not use the extension .BAD for the log file because ODL uses it for the bad file. Figure 14.13 shows the log file produced when ODL loaded the PROPERTY database. Refer back to Figure 14.11 and Figure 14.12 to relate the log file messages to the raw data loaded and the control file.

The Bad File

Any errors that occur when ODL loads a table are recorded in the bad file, whose extension is .BAD and whose primary name is taken from the user-specified primary name for the log file. Errors are recorded when ODL cannot insert a record into the database table. This can occur for many reasons. For example, an input record could be rejected if one or more of its fields do not match the table column

```
ORACLE DATA LOADER: Version 5.1.17.4 - Production on Wed Mar 15 06:43:45 1989

Copyright (c) 1986, Oracle Corporation, California, USA.  All rights reserved.

LOGGED INTO ORACLE V5.1.17.4 - Production
          16384 TOTAL BIND SPACE
            207 MAXIMUM BIND ARRAY DIMENSION
           7890 MAXIMUM BIND ARRAY SIZE IN BYTES
            207 ACTUAL BIND ARRAY DIMENSION LIMITED BY MEMORY
           7890 ACTUAL BIND ARRAY SIZE IN BYTES
LOGGED OUT FROM ORACLE
STATISTICS
           1214 BYTES ALLOCATED
              0 RECORDS SKIPPED
             37 RECORDS READ
              0 RECORDS REJECTED
             37 ROWS LOADED
              0 ERRORS
END ORACLE DATA LOADER  Wed Mar 15 06:43:49 1989
```

Figure 14.13: Log file produced when the PROPERTY file is loaded

definitions. When an erroneous input record is detected, it is written to the bad file. Processing resumes with the next record in the raw data file. If an excessive number of errors occur (controlled by the E parameter described in Table 14.3), ODL halts further processing and control returns to the host operating system. If an error occurs on the first raw data file record, ODL terminates without loading any records.

Figure 14.14 shows an example of the log and bad files when errors are detected and noted. Three records are in error. The log file notes the three records and indicates the total number of errors. In each case, erroneous records contain character information where numbers are expected. Edit the raw data file to correct the mistakes. Then, rerun ODL to reload the table.

ODL ERROR MESSAGES

Three kinds of errors can occur during ODL processing:

- Control file errors
- ODL fatal errors
- Oracle errors

```
The Log file:

ORACLE DATA LOADER: Version 5.1.17.4 - Production on Wed Mar 15 09:19:14 1989

Copyright (c) 1986, Oracle Corporation, California, USA.  All rights reserved.

LOGGED INTO ORACLE V5.1.17.4 - Production
        16384 TOTAL BIND SPACE
          207 MAXIMUM BIND ARRAY DIMENSION
         7890 MAXIMUM BIND ARRAY SIZE IN BYTES
          207 ACTUAL BIND ARRAY DIMENSION LIMITED BY MEMORY
         7890 ACTUAL BIND ARRAY SIZE IN BYTES
RECORD 9 REJECTED
EXEC ERROR: ORA-1722:  invalid number
RECORD 14 REJECTED
EXEC ERROR: ORA-1722:  invalid number
RECORD 22 REJECTED
EXEC ERROR: ORA-1722:  invalid number
LOGGED OUT FROM ORACLE
STATISTICS
         1214 BYTES ALLOCATED
            0 RECORDS SKIPPED
           38 RECORDS READ
            3 RECORDS REJECTED
           35 ROWS LOADED
            3 ERRORS
END ORACLE DATA LOADER  Wed Mar 15 09:19:19 1989


The Bad file:

1248361 21150005/05/88 2789  A 3.092016
1939567    32650003/31/88 2650  3 2.09204
4753652 16550002/14/88 165S  3 2.092048
```

Figure 14.14: Example log and bad files

Control Statement Error Messages

Control statement error messages help you to find errors in the control file. These messages have three formats. The first is

```
message ON LINE # COLUMN #-
```

where *message* is one of the following:

```
Number too large
String too large
Bad number
Missing exponent
Identifier too large
Illegal character
Quoted literal not ended
```

The second format for control file error messages is

`SYNTAX ERROR LINE # ON INPUT ` <u>`symbol`</u>`·`

where *symbol* identifies the location of the detected error. The third format is

<u>`symbol`</u> ` : ` <u>`message`</u> ` ON OR ABOUT LINE #·`

where *symbol* and *message* are shown in Table 14.4.

TABLE 14.4: Components of Control Statement Errors

SYMBOL	MESSAGE
<rec field>	Field name is ambiguous
<rec field>	Field is improperly aligned
<rec field>	Inconsistent rec field definition
<rec field>	Field location too negative
<rec field>	Bad location field expression
<rec field>	Inconsistent location field
<rec field>	Unsupported field length
<rec name>	Record too large for source
<rec name>	Multiple records not supported
<source>	Source from clause is missing
<source>	Source length clause missing
<source>	Multiple sources not supported
<source>	Bad source length clause
<symbol>	Not a record field
<symbol>	Undefined record field
<symbol>	Previously defined
<symbol>	Record name expected
<symbol>	Undefined record name
<table>	Table col/field count mismatch
<table>	Multiple tables not supported

Fatal Error Messages

Fatal errors are more serious than control statement errors. They occur, for example, when ODL does not have enough memory in which to operate. The syntax of this class of error messages is

```
ODL FATAL ERROR : message
```

where *message* can be one of these three:

```
Out of parse stack space
Out of heap space
Out of table space
```

You can correct the last two messages by linking ODL with more memory.

Oracle Errors

Oracle errors should be *rare*. If one occurs, contact Oracle Corporation. The syntax of this error is

```
call ERROR : message
```

where *call* is the name of the Oracle interface subroutine that failed and *message* is one of the numbered messages listed in the Oracle manual entitled *Oracle Error Messages and Codes Manual*. Consult the Oracle documentation for details about Oracle error messages, of which there are literally hundreds.

LOADING DATA FROM FOREIGN FILES: SQL*LOADER

Like the ODL utility, the Oracle SQL*Loader utility program allows you to import data from non-Oracle files into the Oracle database. SQL*Loader can do everything that ODL can, and far more. Scheduled to replace ODL, SQL*Loader has been introduced for the first time in Oracle Version 5.1B. This section gives an overview of SQL*Loader's features and capabilities. If you have never used either ODL or SQL*Loader, you will find SQL*Loader easier to use than ODL. Furthermore, SQL*Loader can accomplish more tasks with greater ease than ODL.

SQL*Loader has many features of IBM's DB2 Load Utility from IBM Corporation and also includes several additional features. SQL*Loader can load data from files in a variety of formats, perform filtering, and load multiple tables simultaneously. Like ODL, SQL*Loader produces a detailed log file with information about the load operation and may produce a bad file of records that have been rejected. SQL*Loader can also produce a *discard file* containing records from the raw data file that were not loaded into Oracle database tables because they did not meet user-specified selection criteria.

SQL*Loader can do the following:

- Load data from multiple source data files of different file types

- Load fixed format, delimited format, and variable length records

- Support a wide range of data types, including DATE, BINARY, and PACKED DECIMAL

- Load multiple tables during one run with selected records loaded into each table

- Create a table row from multiple physical records

- Create multiple table rows from a single physical record, which eliminates repeated columns and multiple records

- Use your operating system's file or record management system to access input data files to be loaded

- Use your existing DB2 Load Utility control files to load data (including files produced by IBM's DXT utility)

- Provide thorough and informative error reports

- Generate unique sequential key values in specified table columns as data is being loaded

To load data from host operating system files into an Oracle database, you must provide SQL*Loader with the data itself, and the control information that tells SQL*Loader how to interpret the data and perform the load operation.

The control file describes the data to be loaded, including

- The names of data files

- The format of the data files

- The location and type of each data field in those files

- How to load the data—which tables and columns to load

The data to be loaded and the control file describing that data can be in one file or in separate files. SQL*Loader uses a data loading language that is compatible with the IBM DB2 Loader program. If you have a control file for the DB2 Load Utility, SQL*Loader can use it.

As SQL*Loader loads data into your Oracle tables, it creates up to three files: the log file, the bad file, and the discard file. As you know, the log file contains useful information about the results of the load operation. The bad file contains any records that were not loaded due to errors detected in the input data. The discard file contains any records that were rejected due to selection conditions that you placed in the control file.

SQL*Loader provides many ways to load data into Oracle tables. In the next sections we'll demonstrate two of those methods by loading the PROPERTY database using the SQL*Loader.

LOADING THE PROPERTY TABLE

In our first example, ten property records are loaded into the PROPERTY database table where the data to be loaded is in the control file. The POSITION phrase indicates where the input fields are found in the input data. No selection criteria is typed in the control file, so no records are omitted (except any that might be erroneous).

The Control File

The control file must be present before you can execute SQL*Loader. Besides information about the data to be loaded, this file can hold the data to be loaded. Figure 14.15 illustrates how to load the PROPERTY database from a host operating file (sometimes called a flat file).

```
LOAD DATA
INFILE *
REPLACE
INTO TABLE PROPERTY
(PARCEL      POSITION (01:07) INTEGER EXTERNAL,
 PRICE       POSITION (09:14) INTEGER EXTERNAL,
 SALEDATE    POSITION (15:22) DATE     "MM/DD/YY",
 SQFT        POSITION (24:27) INTEGER EXTERNAL,
 BR          POSITION (30:30) INTEGER EXTERNAL,
 BA          POSITION (32:34) DECIMAL EXTERNAL,
 ZIPCODE     POSITION (35:39) INTEGER EXTERNAL)
BEGINDATA
1035975 14650003/24/88 1600  3 2.092040
1040816 20750002/25/88 2108  3 2.592016
1050601 13650001/04/88 1100  3 2.092048
1081295 13840005/24/88 1332  3 2.092048
1083767 16550001/27/88 1500  3 2.092048
1151541 21450002/25/88 2700  4 2.792016
1216019 14100001/03/87 1750  3 2.592048
1233117 10350003/16/88 1288  3 2.092012
1248361 21150005/05/88 2789  4 3.092016
1297183 20150004/07/88 1760  4 2.092040
```

Figure 14.15: Loading the PROPERTY database using SQL*Loader

Notice the word "REPLACE" in the control file. This keyword tells SQL*Loader that input data is to replace any existing records in the database table. If the table being loaded already contains records, these records are removed before the new data is loaded. Two other keywords may be written: "INSERT" and "APPEND." INSERT, which is used by ODL, requires that the table to be loaded be empty. If it is not, error messages are issued and the load process is halted. APPEND loads the input data after any existing data in the table. For example, if the table being loaded already contains 30 records, SQL*Loader loads the input records after the 30 existing records. If the table is empty, APPEND functions identically to REPLACE.

The phrase INTO TABLE PROPERTY tells SQL*Loader which table is to be loaded. Following this phrase (see Figure 14.15) is a description of the column names and the corresponding positions of the data fields in the input file. For example, the phrase

```
SALEDATE POSITION (15:22) DATE   "MM/DD/YY",
```

indicates that the table column name SALEDATE is to be loaded from data found in columns 15 through 22 from the input data. Following each of the input data column indicators is a description of the input data type (the data type of the data in the file, not necessarily the data type of the column in the table being loaded). If you omit the data type, CHAR is assumed. The data types permitted are: CHAR, DATE, VARCHAR, SMALLINT, INTEGER, FLOAT, DOUBLE, DECIMAL, GRAPHIC, VARGRAPHIC, and numeric EXTERNAL. For the EXTERNAL, you can substitute INTEGER, DECIMAL, or FLOAT for "numeric" to yield data types INTEGER EXTERNAL, DECIMAL EXTERNAL, or FLOAT EXTERNAL. In the example shown in Figure 14.15, INTEGER EXTERNAL indicates a numeric value without a decimal point whereas DECIMAL EXTERNAL indicates a numeric value with a decimal point.

The keyword BEGINDATA indicates that the data to be loaded is in the control file, not in a separate data file. Ten records are listed in Figure 14.15. Because they are the data to be input, they immediately follow BEGINDATA. SQL*Loader knows to expect the data in the control file because of the * character following the keyword INFILE (see line 2 of Figure 14.15). The characters following INFILE indicate where the data file can be found. For example, typing

```
INFILE PROPERTY.DAT
```

tells SQL*Loader that the data to be loaded is found in the host operating system file called PROPERTY.DAT, not in the control file.

Invoking SQL*LOADER: The SQLLOAD Command

Assuming that the control file has the name PROPERTY.CTL, you can execute SQL*Loader by typing

```
SQLLOAD USERID=username/password, CONTROL=PROPERTY
```

at the operating system prompt. You can write several arguments to the right of SQLLOAD, either in a predefined order from left to right (called *positional*) or in any order and using a keyword to identify each argument, as shown in the previous example.

Only two arguments are required: the username and password pair and the name of the control file. You write a keyword parameter with the keyword followed by an equal sign and the associated argument. In the preceding example, the USERID keyword is followed by the username and password pair. Arguments, either keyword or positional, are separated by commas. The second argument names the control file; if you omit the secondary name, it is assumed to be CTL. In this example, the control file name is PROPERTY.CTL and is written as CONTROL = PROPERTY.

A series of messages is displayed during execution. Once SQL*Loader has completed its job, a final message indicates that the work has been committed to the database:

```
SQL*Loader: Version 1.0.16.5 - Production on Wed Mar 15 09:01:11
1989

Copyright (c) 1987, Oracle Corporation, California, USA. All
rights reserved.

Commit point reached - logical record count 10
```

The Log and Bad Files

SQL*Loader produces two output files, the log file and the bad file. Their form is slightly different than the same files in the ODL utility. Figure 14.16 shows the log file produced for the PROPERTY database example. The figure indicates that ten records were loaded and no errors occurred. The log file also shows the structure of the input data (as does DESCRIBE *tablename* in SQL*Plus) and the number of records discarded (zero in our example). Any records in error (rejected records) are placed in the bad file.

```
SQL*Loader: Version 1.0.16.5 - Production on Wed Mar 15 09:01:11 1989

Copyright (c) 1987, Oracle Corporation, California, USA.  All rights reserved.

Control File:   PROPERTY.CTL
Data File:      *
  Read Mode:    System Record
  Bad File:     PROPERTY.bad
  Discard File: none specified

Number to load: ALL
Number to skip: 0
Errors allowed: 50
Bind array:     64 rows, maximum of 64000 bytes
Record Length:  84 (Buffer size allocated per logical record)
Continuation:   none specified

Table PROPERTY, loaded from every logical record.
Insert option in effect for this table: REPLACE

Column Name                   Position   Len  Term Encl Datatype
---------------------------   --------   ---- ---- ---- --------------------
                   PARCEL       1:7       7                    CHARACTER
                    PRICE       9:14      6                    CHARACTER
                 SALEDATE      15:22      8         DATE MM/DD/YY
                     SQFT      24:27      4                    CHARACTER
                       BR      30:30      1                    CHARACTER
                       BA      32:34      3                    CHARACTER
                  ZIPCODE      35:39      5                    CHARACTER

Table PROPERTY:
  10 Rows successfully loaded.
  0 Rows not loaded due to data errors.
  0 Rows not loaded because all WHEN clauses were failed.
  0 Rows not loaded because all fields were null.

Space allocated for bind array:    3072 bytes (64 rows)
Space otherwise allocated:         6996 bytes

Total logical records skipped:        0
Total logical records read:          10
Total logical records rejected:       0
Total logical records discarded:      0

Run began on Wed Mar 15 09:01:11 1989
Run ended on Wed Mar 15 09:01:18 1989

Elapsed time was:      00:00:00.07
CPU time was:          00:00:00.00    (May not include Oracle CPU time)
```

Figure 14.16: A SQL*Loader log file

LOADING THE CENSUS FILE

In this example, a CENSUS table is loaded with typical Census Bureau data. The data includes information about cities in the United States with populations over 25,000. The raw input file contains data for over 900 U.S. cities. Data fields include a unique city/ state identification, city name, state abbreviation, population (1980), per capita income, value of new construction (by permit), and per capita retail sales.

This example illustrates the following SQL*Loader features:

- The control file loads data from a separate data file.

- Fields of the census data to be loaded are separated from one another by commas, and character data are enclosed in quotation marks (data are not in particular columns or fixed positions in the input file).

- The control file contains a phrase that directs SQL*Loader to load only records that meet a specified criteria.

- Records are *inserted* into the CENSUS database table; therefore, SQL*Loader assumes that the table definition exists and that the table is empty.

- Comments in the control file document the control program and the data it accesses.

The Control File

Figure 14.17 shows the control file. The first three rows, beginning with double hyphens, are control file comments, which are ignored by

```
-- Loads data from census information only for the state of Indiana.
-- Input data fields are terminated by commas and character fields
-- are enclosed in quotation marks.

LOAD DATA
INFILE CENSUS.TXT
DISCARDMAX 999
INTO TABLE CENSUS
WHEN STATE = 'IN'
FIELDS TERMINATED BY ',' OPTIONALLY ENCLOSED BY '"'
(IDENT, CITY, STATE, POPULATION, INCOME, CONSTRUCTION, SALES)
```

Figure 14.17: Loading the CENSUS database

SQL*Loader. The control file begins with the phrase LOAD DATA. The INFILE statement names the data file (CENSUS.TXT). The DISCARDMAX 999 phrase tells SQL*Loader that any number of discard (rejected) records is acceptable. (Remember that records that do not satisfy user-specified criteria are discarded.)

The name of the database table to be loaded follows the INTO clause (CENSUS). A WHEN clause follows the INTO clause:

```
WHEN STATE = 'IN'
```

The WHEN clause establishes the acceptance criteria that must be satisfied for input data records to be loaded into the table. STATE is one of the CENSUS table column names, and IN is a state abbreviation from the raw input file. In English, the preceding acceptance criteria means

> Load a record only if the value of the state abbreviation is equal to IN; reject all other records.

The line beginning

```
FIELDS TERMINATED BY ',' OPTIONALLY ENCLOSED BY '"'
```

tells SQL*Loader about the form of the input data (data fields are separated by commas, and character data are enclosed in quotation marks). Finally, the parenthesized list names table columns, indicating the ordering of the incoming data with respect to the table to be loaded. Figure 14.18 shows a portion of the 958 census records. The records shown are the only ones that will be loaded into the CENSUS table.

Invoking SQL*LOADER: The SQLLOAD Command

As before, you invoke SQL*Loader by typing the following at the host operating system prompt:

```
SQLLOAD USERID=PERRY/STIRLING, CONTROL=CENSUS.CTL
```

```
180065, "Anderson", "IN", 61020, 10173, 3720, 6582
180195, "Bloomington", "IN", 52500, 8513, 25257, 7298
180515, "Columbus", "IN", 30890, 12005, 8215, 8345
180680, "East Chicago", "IN", 36950, 7905, 60, 2458
180740, "Elkhart", "IN", 44180, 10194, 14028, 11455
180775, "Evansville", "IN", 129480, 10048, 8157, 7433
180825, "Fort Wayne", "IN", 172900, 10276, 49863, 6813
180905, "Gary", "IN", 136790, 7488, 0, 2516
181040, "Hammond", "IN", 86380, 9845, 248, 4390
181080, "Highland town", "IN", 24160, 11945, 1341, 8500
181145, "Indianapolis", "IN", 719820, 10836, 0, 5848
181255, "Kokomo", "IN", 45610, 10714, 6752, 8775
181285, "Lafayette", "IN", 44240, 10272, 3634, 9516
181340, "Lawrence", "IN", 26480, 10850, 8585, 4006
181470, "Marion", "IN", 35810, 9265, 2642, 7658
181536, "Merrillville town", "IN", 26530, 11514, 3760, 13798
181550, "Michigan City", "IN", 35600, 8852, 1154, 6982
181610, "Mishawaka", "IN", 41400, 10037, 14507, 9301
181735, "Muncie", "IN", 72600, 8979, 5730, 6489
181760, "New Albany", "IN", 37260, 9499, 9164, 4930
182080, "Portage", "IN", 28420, 10139, 1454, 2907
182140, "Richmond", "IN", 39030, 9126, 0, 8133
182375, "South Bend", "IN", 107190, 10154, 0, 5647
182505, "Terre Haute", "IN", 57920, 8643, 0, 9007
```

Figure 14.18: A portion of the raw census data

where the table is owned by username PERRY whose password is STIRLING. The control file shown in Figure 14.17 is stored in the file called CENSUS.CTL. When executed, SQL*Loader produces a set of messages like those shown before, except that the "logical record count" is 958.

The Log, Bad, and DSC Files

As in the previous example, the log and bad files are produced automatically, as is the discard file, which holds all records that do not pass the selection criterion contained in the control file. (In this example, records whose state abbreviation is IN are discarded.) The discard file has the same name as the input file, with a .DSC extension (that is, CENSUS.DSC).

The log file is similar to the one shown in Figure 14.16, except that the file data structure is different, and the discarded records are listed by number (order of occurrence) in the log file. Figure 14.19 shows a partial listing of the log file that differs significantly from Figure 14.16. This partial file indicates that 24 records were successfully loaded (none was in error) and that 934 records were not loaded because of the WHEN clause criteria in the control file. Figure 14.20 shows the resulting Oracle table, CENSUS.

```
    . . .
  Table CENSUS, loaded when STATE = 'IN'
  Insert option in effect for this table: INSERT

  Column Name            Position   Len  Term Encl Datatype
  ------------------     ---------- ----- ---- ---- ----------------
              IDENT      FIRST       *    ,   O(")     CHARACTER
               CITY      NEXT        *    ,   O(")     CHARACTER
              STATE      NEXT        *    ,   O(")     CHARACTER
         POPULATION      NEXT        *    ,   O(")     CHARACTER
             INCOME      NEXT        *    ,   O(")     CHARACTER
       CONSTRUCTION      NEXT        *    ,   O(")     CHARACTER
              SALES      NEXT        *   WHT  O(")     CHARACTER

  Rejected logical records and errors:

  Data File CENSUS.TXT ·

  Record 1: Discarded - failed all WHEN clauses.
  Record 2: Discarded - failed all WHEN clauses.
  Record 3: Discarded - failed all WHEN clauses.
    . . .
  Record 955: Discarded - failed all WHEN clauses.
  Record 956: Discarded - failed all WHEN clauses.
  Record 957: Discarded - failed all WHEN clauses.
  Record 958: Discarded - failed all WHEN clauses.

  Table CENSUS:
    24 Rows successfully loaded.
    0 Rows not loaded due to data errors.
    934 Rows not loaded because all WHEN clauses were failed.
    0 Rows not loaded because all fields were null.
```

Figure 14.19: A portion of a log file

```
IDENT CITY                 ST POPULATION   INCOME CONSTRUCTION   SALES
------ --------------      -- ----------  -------- ------------  --------
180065 Anderson           IN     61,020  $10,173       $3,720    $6,582
180195 Bloomington        IN     52,500   $8,513      $25,257    $7,298
180515 Columbus           IN     30,890  $12,005       $8,215    $8,345
180680 East Chicago       IN     36,950   $7,905          $60    $2,458
180740 Elkhart            IN     44,180  $10,194      $14,028   $11,455
180775 Evansville         IN    129,480  $10,048       $8,157    $7,433
180825 Fort Wayne         IN    172,900  $10,276      $49,863    $6,813
180905 Gary               IN    136,790   $7,488           $0    $2,516
181040 Hammond            IN     86,380   $9,845         $248    $4,390
181080 Highland town      IN     24,160  $11,945       $1,341    $8,500
181145 Indianapolis       IN    719,820  $10,836           $0    $5,848
181255 Kokomo             IN     45,610  $10,714       $6,752    $8,775
181285 Lafayette          IN     44,240  $10,272       $3,634    $9,516
181340 Lawrence           IN     26,480  $10,850       $8,585    $4,006
181470 Marion             IN     35,810   $9,265       $2,642    $7,658
181536 Merrillville town  IN     26,530  $11,514       $3,760   $13,798
181550 Michigan City      IN     35,600   $8,852       $1,154    $6,982
181610 Mishawaka          IN     41,400  $10,037      $14,507    $9,301
181735 Muncie             IN     72,600   $8,979       $5,730    $6,489
181760 New Albany         IN     37,260   $9,499       $9,164    $4,930
182080 Portage            IN     28,420  $10,139       $1,454    $2,907
182140 Richmond           IN     39,030   $9,126           $0    $8,133
182375 South Bend         IN    107,190  $10,154           $0    $5,647
182505 Terre Haute        IN     57,920   $8,643           $0    $9,007
```

Figure 14.20: Loaded CENSUS table

SUMMARY

This chapter described four Oracle utility programs: Export (EXP), Import (IMP), Oracle Data Loader (ODL), and SQL*Loader. Export permits you to archive Oracle database files and related information in host operating system files. These files are saved in a special format so that you can load them back into an Oracle database on another computer with the Import utility. You can export your Professional Oracle database to a file, move to a minicomputer or mainframe computer, and then import your data to another platform. This facilitates moving databases between machines of dissimilar architecture—portability in its purest form.

ODL and SQL*Loader permit you to port data from other software products into an Oracle RDBMS table. These utilities provides a bridge between dissimilar software products, allowing you to load dBASE IV data into Oracle tables and providing a gateway between IBM's IMS system and Oracle.

ORACLE FOR 1-2-3

ORACLE FOR 1-2-3 IS AN ADD-IN PRODUCT THAT pops up in Lotus 1-2-3 when you press a specified hot key. If you have used 1-2-3, the Oracle database management menus will look familiar. Oracle extends 1-2-3 data management capabilities far beyond the Data command. While 1-2-3 requires that all database records be present in the memory-resident spreadsheet cells (a limit of approximately 8192 records), Oracle can access databases containing literally millions of records stored on disk. Oracle provides a full structured query language interface (SQL) within Lotus 1-2-3. You can summarize information, display a subset of the database, sort retrieved information, join two or more tables together, and much more.

The first section of this chapter describes how to install Oracle for 1-2-3. The remaining sections lead you through an application that retrieves detailed and summary information from a central database and places it into a 1-2-3 spreadsheet. You will use familiar spreadsheet commands, functions, and operators to prepare a spreadsheet for accumulating database-retrieved summary information. You will learn how to log on to Oracle, query large databases, pull data into spreadsheets, create new database tables, store data into tables, delete database rows, and commit or revoke the most recent database changes. You will see how Oracle for 1-2-3 permits several spreadsheet users to share data from a single, consistent, and up-to-date source.

The application in this chapter is a large real estate information database. Capable of holding tens of thousands of records, the Multiple Listing-like database contains information about recent real estate sales (usually single family homes). Table columns include a unique identification number, sale price, square footage, number of bedrooms, number of bathrooms, zip code, date of sale, and length of time the property was on the market. Figure 15.1 shows a representative sample of the database rows that you will later retrieve and summarize in various ways.

Parcel Number	Sale Price	Square Feet	BR	BA	Zip-code	Sale Date	Mkt. Time
8727232	96500	1650	4	2	92035	04-DEC-87	25
8723735	211500	1650	3	2	92015	29-JAN-88	191
8723900	146500	1550	3	2.5	92015	13-JAN-88	131
8712831	223500	2100	3	2	92060	02-DEC-87	265
8715512	166000	1815	4	1.7	92060	04-DEC-87	280
8719187	106500	1100	3	1.5	92020	22-NOV-87	216
8719249	240500	2530	4	2.5	92015	08-JAN-88	266
8719784	116500	1500	3	1.5	92050	28-NOV-87	215
8722523	221500	2570	3	2.7	92020	30-NOV-87	198
8722794	155500	1050	2	1	92050	05-JAN-88	171
8723601	526500	4200	5	3	92050	08-FEB-88	283
8728621	61500	500	2	1	92050	07-OCT-88	122
8727249	157500	1150	2	1	92050	27-NOV-87	74
8724200	231500	2400	5	2.5	92015	07-JAN-88	213

Figure 15.1: Sample listing of real estate database rows

INSTALLING ORACLE FOR 1-2-3

You should follow a few, simple procedures before installing Oracle for 1-2-3 on your computer. You only need to perform these "pre-installation" steps once, and they ensure that that the installation process will go smoothly.

PRE-INSTALLATION STEPS

You should create backup copies of your Oracle software and use the *copies* to install Oracle for 1-2-3. If you have 5¼-inch Oracle disks and drives, obtain unused disks for backup purposes. If you have 3½-inch Oracle disks and drives, you will need two disks on which to copy Oracle for 1-2-3. The disk copying procedure described here applies to either the 3½-inch or 5¼-inch versions of the software. There is one method for a single-floppy disk system and another for a double-floppy disk system. Both methods assume that you also have a hard disk, which Oracle for 1-2-3 requires that you have.

To properly create backup copies of the original software, use the DOS command DISKCOPY. Since the installation procedure checks the disk labels to ensure that you have inserted the correct disk for each step, you cannot create backup copies of the software with the DOS COPY command, which does not copy the disk label. Using DISKCOPY instead of COPY guarantees that your backup copies of Oracle for 1-2-3 will have the correct disk labels as well as the correct software files.

Creating Backup Copies in a Single-Floppy Disk System

If you have a double floppy-disk system and a hard disk, follow the procedures described in the next section. Otherwise, follow these steps to create backup copies of Oracle for 1-2-3:

1. Type **DISKCOPY A: A:** and press Enter. DOS will display the message

   ```
   Insert SOURCE diskette in drive A:
   Press any key when ready . . .
   ```

2. Insert the *original* Oracle for 1-2-3 disk in drive A and press Enter. If you are using 5¼-inch disks, DOS will display the message

```
Copying 40 tracks
9 Sectors/Track, 2 Side(s)
```

3. When the DOS prompt

```
Insert TARGET diskette in drive A:
```

appears, insert the unused, backup disk in drive A and press Enter. Once the original disk is completely copied to the backup disk, the message

```
Copy another diskette (Y/N)?
```

is displayed.

4. To copy the remaining Oracle disks to backup disks, press Y and follow steps 2 and 3 repeatedly until you have copied the complete set of Oracle for 1-2-3 disks.

Creating Backup Copies in a Double-Floppy Disk System

If you have a double-floppy disk system (that is, you have two 5¼-inch disk drives or two 3½-inch disk drives), the copying process is somewhat easier. The steps are as follows:

1. Type **DISKCOPY A: B:** and press Enter. DOS display the messages:

```
Insert SOURCE diskette in drive A:
Insert TARGET diskette in drive B:
Press any key when ready . . .
```

2. Place the *original* Oracle for 1-2-3 disk in drive A, place the backup disk in drive B, and press Enter. When the disk has been completely copied, you'll see this DOS message

```
Copy another diskette (Y/N)?
```

3. To continue copying disks, press Y. Press N to halt the copying process.

INSTALLING ORACLE FOR 1-2-3

Easy-to-follow screen prompts guide you through the Oracle for 1-2-3 installation process. You begin by making the hard disk the current drive. For example, if you plan to install Oracle for 1-2-3 on drive C, make it the current drive by typing **C:** and pressing Enter.

Early in the installation process, Oracle checks that the two DOS system files AUTOEXEC.BAT and CONFIG.SYS contain certain information, making changes if necessary. If the install program changes those files, however, you will have to reboot your system and reinitiate the installation. Chapter 2 shows you how to make these changes *before* you start installing Oracle.

Once you have made your hard disk the current drive, place the first Oracle for 1-2-3 disk into drive A, type

A:INSTALL

and press Enter. The first screen displayed is shown in Figure 15.2. Press C to acknowledge the copyright screen and continue.

```
                ORACLE database add-in for Lotus 1-2-3



                        Installation Program

                (c) Copyright Oracle Corporation, 1987.

                        All Rights Reserved.

        This install program sets up the ORACLE database add-in for Lotus
        1-2-3 by creating its directories on your hard disk and copying
        its files.  In addition, this install will ask for information to
        properly configure ORACLE for 1-2-3.

        Please refer to the chapter "Installing the ORACLE database
        add-in for Lotus 1-2-3" in "Getting Started."

    Press <C> to Continue, <Q> to Quit.
```

Figure 15.2: The copyright screen

On the next screen, you need to indicate whether you are installing Oracle for 1-2-3 by itself or with previously installed copies of Professional or Networkstation Oracle. Toggle between the three choices by using ↑ or ↓ until your choice appears. Figure 15.3 displays this screen with the Professional Oracle choice.

```
The ORACLE database add-in for Lotus 1-2-3 includes a complete ORACLE
relational database for 1-2-3 users.  You will have the option to install
ORACLE for 1-2-3 with its own database or use your existing Professional
ORACLE 5.1A database or your remote ORACLE Database using Networkstation
ORACLE.


          Select how you wish to install ORACLE for 1-2-3:


          ORACLE for 1-2-3 with Professional ORACLE 5.1A


              Use ↑ ↓ to select and press <Enter>
```

Figure 15.3: Choosing the environment

If you have not installed Professional Oracle or Networkstation Oracle, select Oracle for Lotus 1-2-3. After you press Enter to finalize your choice, additional full-screen displays prompt you for information regarding:

- The default directory for Oracle for 1-2-3

- The default directory for Oracle for 1-2-3 options

- The directory containing Lotus 1-2-3

- The name of your Lotus 1-2-3 driver set

Press Enter after answering each of the preceding prompt screens.

The remaining installation steps are equally easy. You are prompted at various points to insert each of the remaining installation disks. Insert the indicated disk at each prompt.

ATTACHING ORACLE FOR 1-2-3 TO LOTUS

The next phase of installation involves attaching Oracle to Lotus. You do this by invoking the Lotus 1-2-3 Add-in Manager. You can attach Oracle to Lotus in two ways, depending on convenience and how often you will invoke Oracle from Lotus. You can have Oracle *always* available automatically when you invoke Lotus. Alternately, you can attach Oracle during each 1-2-3 session, which allows you to decide each time whether or not you want to use Oracle. You will probably want to make Oracle available automatically, since this way you don't have to repeatedly invoke steps to attach Oracle.

Attaching Oracle for 1-2-3 for Session-By-Session Use

If you use Oracle with Lotus infrequently, follow these steps to attach Oracle on a session-by-session basis. First, invoke Lotus by typing **123** and pressing Enter. The remaining steps are

1. Press Alt-F10 by holding down the Alt key and pressing the F10 function key. This key sequence brings up the Lotus Add-in manager.

2. Choose the Attach option from the menu (Figure 15.4a) by pressing A or the Enter key.

3. Type or choose **ORA123A.ADN** (Figure 15.4b).

4. Choose the Alt key combination (known as the *hot key*) with which you will invoke Oracle. F7 is chosen in the example shown in Figure 15.4c, and is used as the hot key throughout this chapter. To invoke Oracle, press this key with the Alt key.

5. Choose Attach from the displayed menu (see Figure 15.4d).

6. Type or choose **ORA123B.ADN** (see Figure 15.4e).

7. Choose Quit to leave the Add-in Manager and return to Lotus Ready mode (see Figure 15.4f).

Oracle for 1-2-3 is now available for session-by-session use. Note that the preceding steps attach Oracle to Lotus for 1-2-3 for one session only; you must repeat them each time you wish to use Oracle. You can attach Oracle for 1-2-3 permanently to Lotus (you can unattach it later) to save time and effort.

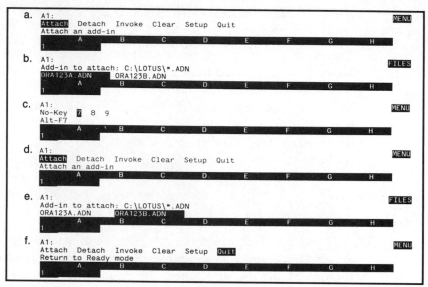

Figure 15.4: Attaching Oracle for session-by-session use

Attaching Oracle for 1-2-3 For Automatic Use

You will probably prefer to have Oracle automatically available during each Lotus 1-2-3 session. If so, follow the seven steps just described. Then, proceed with the following steps:

8. Press Alt-F10 to invoke the Add-in Manager again.

9. Choose Setup from the menu (see Figure 15.5a).

10. Choose Set from the menu (see Figure 15.5b).

11. Choose an unused slot for ORA123A (choose 1, for example).

12. Type or choose **ORA123A.ADN** (see Figure 15.5c).

13. Choose No when asked about automatically invoking the add-in (see Figure 15.5d).

14. Choose Set from the menu again (see Figure 15.5b).

15. Choose an unused slot for ORA123B (2, for example).

16. Choose or type **ORA123B.ADN** (see Figure 15.5e).

Once you complete steps 8 through 16, you need to update a special file called ADN.CFG that holds information about Lotus 1-2-3

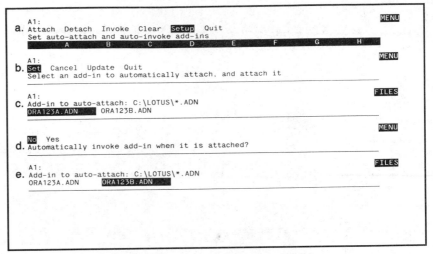

Figure 15.5: Attaching Oracle for automatic use—initial steps

add-in files. To update this file and complete the attach process, follow these steps:

17. Choose Update from the menu to save all of this information in the file ADN.CFG (see Figure 15.6a).

18. Choose Quit twice to leave the Add-in Manager (see Figure 15.6b and 15.6c).

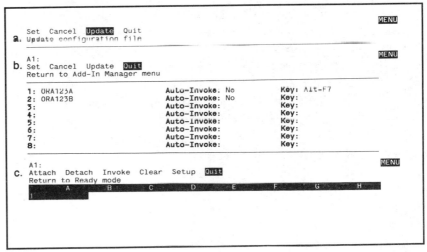

Figure 15.6: Attaching Oracle for automatic use—final steps

Having completed these steps, you can invoke Oracle from Lotus by pressing the selected hot key, Alt-F7 in this example. From here, you invoke Lotus by typing

ORA123

instead of **LOTUS** or **123**.

The remaining sections in this chapter describe how to use Oracle from within Lotus 1-2-3. Oracle and Lotus together provide powerful and convenient database and spreadsheet tools for all types of business analysis.

MANAGING DATA IN 1-2-3

Oracle for 1-2-3 provides a powerful database inside of Lotus 1-2-3 (version 2.01 or later) that follows the time-tested SQL standard. With Oracle, you can retrieve information from a database containing millions of records, select a subset of columns, select a subset of rows, sort database rows, and summarize groups of data to obtain statistics about aggregate information. In addition, you can create new database tables in Lotus and store them in Oracle. You can modify tables and insert new data into databases. When you are through with a table, you can remove it or delete one or more rows.

Oracle for 1-2-3 provides inherent data sharing and data consistency. Because data can be stored in an Oracle-managed database, various spreadsheet users can pull information into 1-2-3 from a single, up-to-date source. Keeping important information in the database rather than in a single user's spreadsheet makes it possible to share data.

You access Oracle through an extensive set of easily-understood menus and prompts that appear in the top two lines of the screen. The structure will be familiar to previous 1-2-3 users. Once you have loaded Lotus by typing

ORA123

you can invoke Oracle from Ready mode by pressing the hot key you assigned during installation (in this case, Alt-F7). You then formulate database retrieval operations by navigating through a small number of Oracle menus—as in Lotus. The next section illustrates data retrieval using the real estate database.

INVOKING LOTUS

Because you attached Oracle to Lotus, you invoke Lotus by typing **ORA123**, not **LOTUS** or **1-2-3** as you normally would. Oracle will be loaded into memory and a few seconds later 1-2-3 will be loaded. You can now use all the normal 1-2-3 commands and data entry capabilities.

INVOKING ORACLE

Press Alt-F7 (the hot key assigned during installation) to display the Oracle for 1-2-3 main menu. You can leave the Oracle main menu by pressing the Escape key (Esc). Figure 15.7 shows Oracle's main menu displayed above the spreadsheet. The back endpapers of this book contain an Oracle for 1-2-3 command tree summary, a "road map" that you can refer to as as you read this chapter.

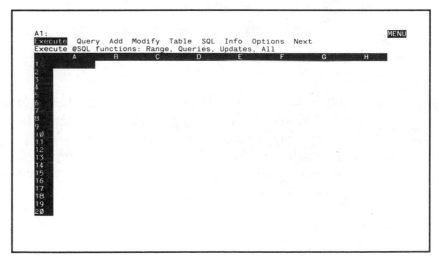

Figure 15.7: Oracle main menu

RETRIEVING DATA

The main menu specifies the first level options available in Oracle. You retrieve data from a database through this menu. The retrieved information is put into the Lotus spreadsheet. As with ordinary Lotus 1-2-3 commands, you can execute Oracle for 1-2-3 commands by either typing their first letter or by using → and ← to highlight the desired command and pressing Enter.

Select Query to begin retrieving data (see Figure 15.7). Oracle for 1-2-3 will display the menu shown in Figure 15.8.

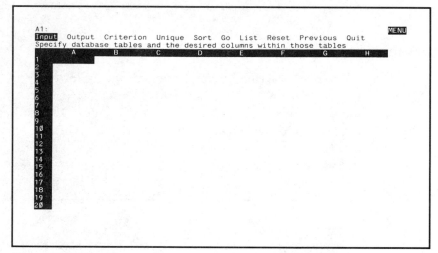

Figure 15.8: The Query menu

The Query menu contains the options you need to form SQL query formulas for retrieving data. You only need three of these options to retrieve data: Input, Output, and Go. Use the Input option to specify the data you wish to retrieve. Then complete the requested information for the Output option. Finally, execute the Go option to execute the database retrieval operation. As you become familiar with Oracle, you will want to refine your database retrieval commands further with other Query options. However, the Input option is the first step.

The Input Option

Assume that you are analyzing real estate sales in the past year for your office. You can begin by retrieving all sales data. Later, you can refine the query to select only sales data with certain characteristics, narrowing your focus until you generate summary information or retrieve a selected subset of the rather large database.

Start by forming a retrieval function that retrieves all sales data. First, specify the database containing the sales data with the Input option.

Select the Input option by pressing Enter (the option is highlighted) or by pressing the letter I. Oracle for 1-2-3 prompts you for the table names containing the data:

```
Enter table(s):
```

Type **PROPERTY** to indicate the name of the database and press Enter. Oracle then asks which table columns from that database are to be returned:

```
Enter columns:
```

Press Enter to select all database columns (later, you will specify fewer than all columns). After you press Enter, the Query menu is displayed again.

The Output Option

After you have specified the database from which to retrieve data and the columns to be retrieved, you must tell Oracle where to place the retrieved data. Select the Output option (see Figure 15.9) by pressing O or highlighting the option and pressing Enter.

You control where retrieved data is placed in your spreadsheet when Oracle prompts you for the cells in which to place the data:

```
Enter range for query output: A1
```

A1 is the Oracle-proposed location; however, you can enter an address of any Lotus cell range. Type A2 to change the proposed output range to one whose upper-left corner is A2. Clearly, one cell is

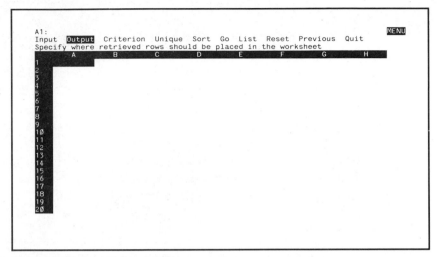

Figure 15.9: Specifying the Output option

not enough to hold many rows and columns of retrieved data. Oracle automatically adjusts that cell range according to the number of rows and columns required to retrieve the data.

After you enter the range for query output, the Query menu is redisplayed. Now you need to tell Oracle to execute the query—to retrieve the data using the SQL query you just created.

The Go Option

Select the Go option to execute your query by pressing G or highlighting the Go option and pressing Enter (see Figure 15.10).

Because you may want to reexecute this query later, all the query information is stored in a spreadsheet cell. In this way, you can build and save many queries that you can either reexecute or refine at a later time. Oracle will ask you where the query information should be stored in the spreadsheet:

```
Enter cell in which to store @SQL function: A1
```

Press Enter to accept the default location (A1, in this case) or type in another cell address. Since A1 is outside the retrieved data cell range, press Enter to store the query in cell A1.

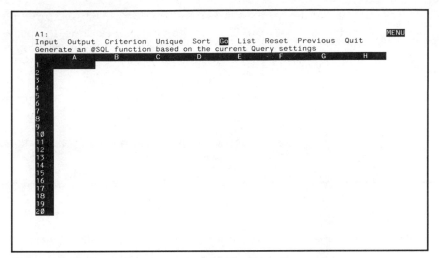

Figure 15.10: Executing the query with the Go option

Because Oracle is designed to support multiple database users, it protects all data and databases with usernames and user passwords. You must log on to Oracle before you can access any information. Our example uses username SCOTT and password TIGER. The next prompt requests that you enter a username. You need do this only once during a Lotus session (see Figure 15.11).

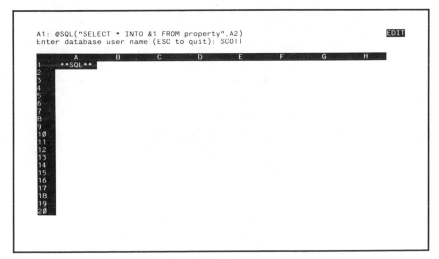

Figure 15.11: Logging on to Oracle with a username

Enter the preestablished username **SCOTT** and press Enter. Next, enter the password **TIGER**. For security reasons, the password is not displayed on the screen as you type it. Be careful to enter it correctly (see Figure 15.12).

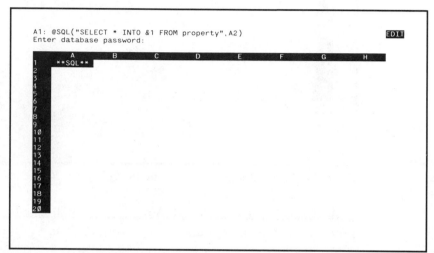

Figure 15.12: Entering a user password

Due to certain default conditions, Oracle recognizes that the retrieved data will not fit in the single column (cell A2) specified for the output range. Oracle indicates this *column overflow* condition, then asks you what to do (see Figure 15.13). Press Enter to select the Overwrite option. This allows extra columns to overwrite columns to the right of the specified output range. Selecting Stop would abort the retrieval operation.

Oracle then recognizes that more database rows will be retrieved than can fit into the specified single-cell output range. This condition, termed *row overflow*, is signaled by the prompt shown in Figure 15.14.

Of the four options for dealing with row overflow, select Overwrite by pressing Enter or the letter O. Rows below the output range will now be replaced (overwritten) by retrieved database rows. (If these rows contain formulas that will be destroyed, don't select this option).

Within a few seconds, the requested database information is imported into the spreadsheet and displayed. Figure 15.15 shows the first 20 rows retrieved.

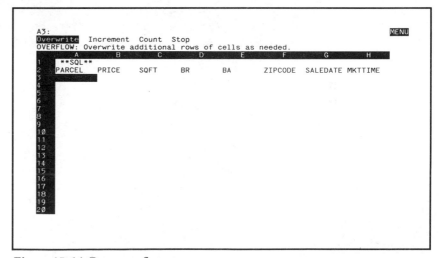

Figure 15.13: Column overflow

Figure 15.14: Row overflow

If asterisks are displayed in one or more columns, you need to widen those columns so that 1-2-3 can fully display the data. Simply exit from the Query menu (press Q or select Quit) and execute the 1-2-3 command Worksheet Column Set-Width (type **/WCS**) to widen the columns.

```
A1: @SQL("SELECT.* INTO &1 FROM property",A2..H252)                    MENU
Input  Output  Criterion  Unique  Sort  Go  List  Reset  Previous  Quit
Generate an @SQL function based on the current Query settings
         A        B        C        D       E        F        G         H
1    **SQL**
2    PARCEL    PRICE    SQFT      BR      BA      ZIPCODE  SALEDATE  MKTTIME
3    8727232    96500    1650     4       2       92035  04-Dec-87      25
4    8723735   211500    1650     3       2       92015  29-Jan-88     191
5    8723900   146500    1550     3       2.5     92015  13-Jan-88     131
6    8712831   223500    2100     3       2       92060  02-Dec-87     265
7    8715512   166000    1815     4       1.7     92060  04-Dec-87     280
8    8719187   106500    1100     3       1.5     92020  22-Nov-87     216
9    8719249   240500    2530     4       2.5     92015  08-Jan-88     266
10   8719784   116500    1500     3       1.5     92050  28-Nov-87     215
11   8722523   221500    2570     3       2.7     92020  30-Nov-87     198
12   8722794   155500    1050     2       1       92050  05-Jan-88     171
13   8723601   526500    4200     5       3       92050  08-Feb-88     283
14   8728621    61500     500     2       1       92050  07-Oct-88     122
15   8727249   157500    1150     2       1       92050  27-Nov-87      74
16   8724200   231500    2400     5       2.5     92015  07-Jan-88     213
17   8724304   127000    1312     3       2       92060  12-May-88     215
18   8725589   151500    1500     4       2       92060  30-Nov-87      51
19   8725791   118400    1390     2       2       92050  31-Dec-87     188
20   8726582   207500    1717     3       2       92020  17-Feb-88     229
```

Figure 15.15: Retrieved database sales information

When dealing with large databases, it is unlikely that you will retrieve the entire database into the spreadsheet. The next section describes how to focus your queries on smaller portions of a database, selecting both column and row subsets for retrieval.

RETRIEVING SELECTED ROWS AND COLUMNS

Oracle for 1-2-3 enables you to tailor your queries to specific columns and rows of the database. Suppose you want to see only the five columns associated with sales price, square footage, number of bedrooms, number of bathrooms, and number of days the property was on the market. Furthermore, suppose that you are interested only in data from a certain section of town—a particular zip code area. Recall that retrieving only certain columns of information is *projection*. Retrieving only certain records from the database is *selection*.

Retrieving Specific Columns

Beginning with a blank spreadsheet, press Alt-F7 (your selected hot key) to invoke Oracle, select Query to build a query, and press I to change your database specification. When Oracle prompts you for table names, PROPERTY will be redisplayed because it was the last table you queried (Oracle remembers the previous query definition as long as you do not leave 1-2-3). Query information is maintained so that you can build queries step by step, adding refinements until you retrieve exactly the information you want.

Oracle prompts you to specify column names. Because you pressed Enter to select all columns in your previous query, no suggested column names are displayed. Now you can change your query to include only selected columns. Because column names are sometimes difficult to remember, Oracle has a way to view any database's table definition and column names, types, and sizes. Oracle provides *context sensitive* help; you can obtain help on virtually any topic by pressing function key F1. If you press F1 while the Enter columns prompt is displayed, information about the Query Input option is displayed on the first screen. Information about columns of the PROPERTY table is displayed on the second help screen. Figure 15.16 shows the second screen of the display presented after you press F1.

```
A1:                                                              HELP
Enter columns:

Columns for table property:
COLUMN                    TYPE      WIDTH  DECIMAL    VALUE REQUIRED?
PARCEL                    NUMBER      7                NO
PRICE                     NUMBER      6                NO
SQFT                      NUMBER      4                NO
BR                        NUMBER      1                NO
BA                        NUMBER      2        1       NO
ZIPCODE                   NUMBER      5                NO
SALEDATE                  DATE                         NO
MKTTIME                   NUMBER      3                NO




     Press any key to return to worksheet
Help   90
```

Figure 15.16: Help display for table column names

Press any key to leave help. Then type the column names separated by commas following the Enter columns prompt and press Enter:

```
PRICE, SQFT, BR, BA, MKTTIME
```

Selecting Specific Rows: The Criterion Option

Because the database is quite large, you may only want to retreive selected rows. The Criterion option of the Query menu lets you specify which rows are to be retrieved into the spreadsheet and which are to be ignored. In this example, let's select only rows whose zipcode field equals the value 92035.

Press C to select the Criterion option. Oracle prompts you for the column name. Type in **zipcode** and press Enter (see Figure 15.17a). Next, Oracle wants to know the exact restriction on zipcode. Enter = **92035** and press the Enter key (see Figure 15.17b).

So far, the criterion—the test that must be passed by each record that is retrieved—is that the field zipcode equals 92035. Because this is the only criteria by which rows are to be selected, press Enter again when the Column prompt reappears (see Figure 15.17c). The Query menu will reappear. You can enter other query options. Then you need to tell Oracle that the retrieved information should be sorted (ordered) in a certain way.

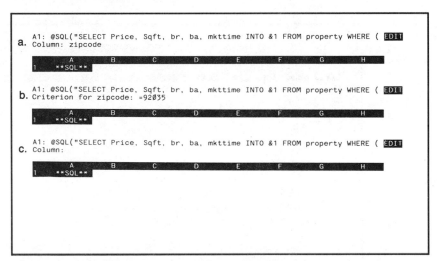

Figure 15.17: Establishing the selection criteria

Organizing the Results: The Sort Option

Database rows are in no particular order. They needn't be in order because you can retrieve any row if you know key information about it. However, reports and other output results are usually more informative if they are organized—sorted—in some significant way. In our example, you could organize the sales information in several different ways. For example, you could order the retrieved rows by the SQFT column to quickly see which homes have the largest or smallest square footage. Alternately, you might want the rows organized by the number of bedrooms.

You will organize retrieved rows by the PRICE column so that you can quickly assess price ranges in the chosen zip code area. Choose the Sort option from the Query menu by pressing S or highlighting Sort and pressing Enter. Oracle prompts you for the column on which to sort the results. Type in **PRICE** and press Enter. Press Enter again or type A to select Ascending order (see Figure 15.18a).

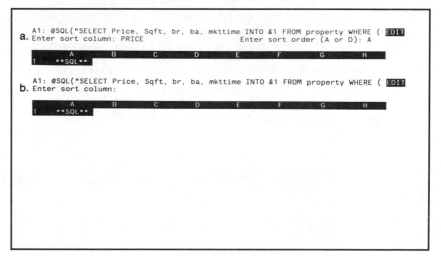

Figure 15.18: Specifying the order: the Sort option

Next, Oracle prompts you for further sort information. You can specify any number of subsidiary sort orders by repeatedly entering column names. If you enter a second column name, it will "break ties" between any matching PRICE values. Because you aren't interested in second (or third) sort orders, press Enter when the

"Enter sort column" prompt appears (see Figure 15.18b). The Query menu is redisplayed.

You have entered all of the information needed to retrieve the requested records:

- The database is called PROPERTY.

- The needed columns are PRICE, SQFT, BR, BA, and MKTTIME.

- The records returned are only those for which the condition Zipcode = 92035 is true.

Press G or highlight Go and press Enter to execute the newly built query (see Figure 15.10). The rows retrieved and placed into your spreadsheet are shown in Figure 15.19. Notice the @SQL function displayed at the top of the figure. That "formula" is stored in cell A1, just like any other formula you might write in Lotus—except that it is a database formula built by executing the Query option. Because the query is stored in the spreadsheet you can reexecute it later. You can also alter and then execute it, or copy it to other spreadsheet cells and then alter the cloned formula.

```
A1: @SQL("SELECT price, sqft, br, ba, mkttime INTO &1 FROM property WHERE ( MENU
Input  Output  Criterion  Unique  Sort  Go  List  Reset  Previous  Quit
Generate an @SQL function based on the current Query settings
        A           B          C          D          E          F          G          H
1       **SQL**
2       PRICE      SQFT        BR         BA         MKTTIME
3       79500      1200        4          2          78
4       80500      850         2          1          53
5       81900      1200        3          1.7        83
6       86500      1100        2          1.7        25
7       89500      1100        3          2          136
8       91400      1300        4          2          19
9       91500      1190        3          2          21
10      91500      1220        3          1          75
11      95500      1140        3          1.7        58
12      96000      1240        4          2          91
13      96500      1650        4          2          25
14      96500      1280        2          1          58
15      96500      1300        3          2          12
16      96500      1155        3          1.7        48
17      98000      1460        4          2          45
18
19
20
```

Figure 15.19: Rows retrieved with the Criterion and Sort options

You can format the labels in row 2 to be right-justified and can add other non-Oracle formulas to the spreadsheet by leaving the Oracle menu (press the Escape key twice) and executing various 1-2-3 commands. For example, you can form column totals below each retrieved column to compute and display maximum, minimum, and average values. Simply enter the 1-2-3 formulas **@MAX(A3..A17)**, **@MIN(A3..A17)**, and **@AVG(A3..A17)** in cells A19, A20, and A21. Then, clone the formulas into the range B19..E21 using Copy (type **/C**).

As you can see, Lotus and Oracle make a great team. Oracle provides tremendous database capabilities while Lotus provides powerful analysis and graphing tools.

RETRIEVING AND GROUPING DATABASE SUMMARY INFORMATION

Although an entire database is generally too large to fit in a 1-2-3 spreadsheet, you can easily extract summary information about all database rows. You might want to know average price, average market time, total price, and number of sales for zip code groups. If you generated this aggregate information with Oracle, you need not import the entire database into the spreadsheet before you generate column statistics. You will have Oracle compute averages, counts, and sums instead of using the Lotus @AVG, @COUNT, and @SUM functions. This avoids the difficulties of importing large amounts of data before you can compute summary statistics.

Because the next query is different from the previous one, clear out the old query information by selecting Reset (or typing R) from the Query menu to erase the previous query (see Figure 15.20a). Next, select Input (or type I) and specify the table name PROPERTY (see Figure 15.20b). When Oracle displays the columns prompt, enter the following:

```
ZIPCODE, AVG(PRICE), AVG(MKTTIME), COUNT(*), SUM(PRICE)
```

and press Enter (see Figure 15.20c).

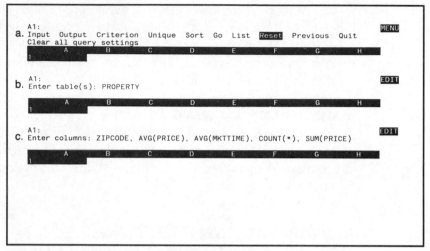

Figure 15.20: Retrieving summary information

Except for the ZIPCODE column, none of the preceding columns is found directly in the PROPERTY database. They are *derived* values computed by using database group (or *aggregate*) functions. The group function AVG(PRICE), for example, calculates the average of the (database) price column; COUNT(*) counts the number of occurrences of values in a database. In our example, the sums, averages, and counts are computed on groups of unique zip code values.

Oracle recognizes that summary information is to be retrieved whenever you use one of the group functions and include one or more database column names. (There are seven database group functions: AVG, COUNT, MAX, MIN, SUM, STDDEV, and VARIANCE. See Chapter 7 for more information on functions.) The database column names determine how groups are formed and summary statistics generated. No further query information is required, neither Criterion nor Sort options. Simply execute Go to retrieve your database rows, which are shown in Figure 15.21.

You can obtain information about the query that retrieved the preceding rows by executing the Query List option (type **/QL**). Figure 15.22 shows a representative display. It summarizes details about your most recent query, including the Input, Output, Criterion, Unique, and Sort options.

```
A1: @SQL("SELECT zipcode, avg(price), avg(mkttime), count(*), sum(price) IN MENU
Input  Output  Criterion  Unique  Sort  Go  List  Reset  Previous  Quit
Generate an @SQL function based on the current Query settings
          A          B        C        D         E        F       G       H
 1     **SQL**
 2    ZIPCODE   AVG(PRICEAVG(MKTTICOUNT(*) SUM(PRICE)
 3     92010 107133.3     60        3    321400
 4     92015 217607.4 120.1111      27   5875400
 5     92020   166935   78.475      40   6677400
 6     92035 91186.66 55.13333      15   1367800
 7     92050 130862.2 84.98611      72   9422080
 8     92055 112089.7       71      43   4819860
 9     92060   143666    64.46      50   7183300
10
11
12
13
14
15
16
17
18
19
20
```

Figure 15.21: Summary information about all database rows

```
A1: @SQL("SELECT ZIPCODE, AVG(PRICE), AVG(MKTTIME), COUNT(*), SUM(PRICE) IN STAT
INPUT:
    Tables:   PROPERTY
    Joins:    (none)
    Columns:  ZIPCODE, AVG(PRICE), AVG(MKTTIME), COUNT(*), SUM(PRICE)
    Groups:   ZIPCODE

OUTPUT:
    Range:    (A2..E9)

CRITERION:    (none)

UNIQUE:       No

SORT:         (none)



Press any key to return to worksheet

Query Parameters List
```

Figure 15.22: Query information: The List option

The results that were shown in Figure 15.21 are a little confusing. You can leave Oracle by pressing Escape twice and use 1-2-3 format commands and functions to make things clearer. Figure 15.23 shows the enhanced display of retrieved results. Notice that the Lotus function @SUM has been placed in cells D12 and E12 to display grand totals for the number of units sold and total value of all sales. New, right-justified labels (entered manually) replace the column headings returned by Oracle in rows 2 and 3.

```
A1: @SQL("SELECT ZIPCODE, AVG(PRICE), AVG(MKTTIME), COUNT(*), SUM(PRICE) IN READY

        A          B        C         D           E           F        G
1   **SQL**
2   Zipcode    Average  Average    Units        Total
3              Price    Mkt. Time  Sold         Value
4     92010    $107,133    60        3        $321,400    ⎫
5     92015    $217,607   120       27      $5,875,400    ⎪
6     92020    $166,935    78       40      $6,677,400    ⎬  Oracle generated
7     92035     $91,187    55       15      $1,367,800    ⎪  database rows
8     92050    $130,862    85       72      $9,422,080    ⎪
9     92055    $112,090    71       43      $4,819,860    ⎪
10    92060    $143,666    64       50      $7,183,300    ⎭
11                                  ----    -----------
12                                  250     $35,667,240  ⎫
13                                                       ⎬
14                                                       ⎭
15                                 Lotus 1-2-3 functions
16
17
18
19
20
```

Figure 15.23: Database information and Lotus functions

The results are quite impressive. You have accomplished what would be difficult with Lotus alone: you summarized information from a rather large collection of data. Although Lotus could handle this example database of only 250 records, it can not handle larger databases. Imagine trying to use Lotus to create this spreadsheet for all real estate sales in New York city for the past year! Without Oracle's database capabilities, the number of rows would be too great for Lotus to handle.

MODIFYING A DATABASE

So far, you have retrieved and performed analyses on data from existing database tables. Oracle for 1-2-3 can also easily *create* Oracle database tables by transferring them from your spreadsheet to the database. Storing important information in the database rather than exclusively in your 1-2-3 spreadsheet permits data sharing. It is easier for other users to access vital company information from the database than from another user's spreadsheet. What is more, using database tables as the source of spreadsheet analysis encourages people to share accurate and up-to-date information.

You can alter, update, and delete data stored in the database once you transfer it from a spreadsheet. Later sections in this chapter describe how to update, delete, and insert data and how to remove unwanted tables.

CREATING A TABLE

You will now create a new database table called SALESUMM that lists by zip code the number of homes sold (year to date) and the sales quota for the 12 month period for each zip code area. Erase the worksheet (type **/WEY**) and type the labels and numeric data into the spreadsheet cells as follows:

	A	B	C
1			
2		Units	Units
3	Zipcode	Sold	Quota
4	92010	3	20
5	92015	27	45
6	92020	40	70
7	92035	15	30
8	92050	72	90
9	92055	43	60
10	92060	50	45

To transfer the three column spreadsheet into a new database table, press the Oracle hot key (in this case, Alt-F7) and select Table. Then select Create and enter **SALESUMM** when prompted for a table name.

Next, you are asked for a range of cells that includes both the column names and the associated data. Type the range or (better yet) use the arrow keys to "paint" the range. Press Enter to complete the table creation operation. Figure 15.24 shows the display just before you press Enter.

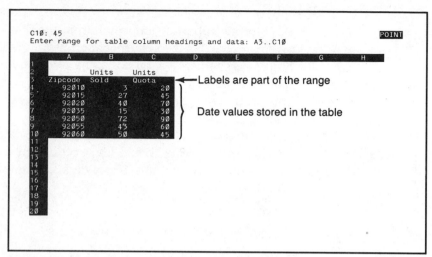

Figure 15.24: Creating a table: indicating the label/data range

Lay out the spreadsheet table carefully. You might follow spreadsheet conventions, putting dashes immediately under the column labels and putting data below the dashes, as follows

```
         A        B        C
 1
 2               Units    Units
 3     Zipcode   Sold     Quota
 4     ........ ........ ........
 5      92010        3       20
 6      92015       27       45
 7      92020       40       70
 8      92035       15       30
 9      92050       72       90
10      92055       43       60
11      92060       50       45
```

But, if you do so, the database table will contain an extra row of hyphens. Similarly, placing a blank line between spreadsheet column labels and the data rows will create an extra database row containing all *null* values. You should place labels immediately above the first data row when creating a database table from a spreadsheet.

The SALESUMM information is now stored in the database and can be accessed by other Lotus 1-2-3 users. You can clear the spreadsheet and retrieve the table to verify that it exists.

INSERTING ROWS INTO A TABLE

You use the Oracle Add command to insert rows into a database. Suppose you want to add two rows—containing actual year to date sales of homes and associated annual quotas for zipcodes 92025 and 92041—to the SALESUMM database. Enter the missing data rows into the spreadsheet in the usual way by moving to cell A11 (see Figure 15.24) and typing the following two rows of data:

92025	32	50
92041	14	30

Next, press the assigned Oracle hot key (Alt-F7 in this example), select Add, type **SALESUMM** (the name of the table to which data is added), and press Enter. Now that Oracle knows you want to add data to the SALESUMM table, you either type in the cell range of the spreadsheet data to be inserted or use the arrow keys to highlight the rows to be inserted. Press Enter to complete the Add operation. Figure 15.25 shows the display before you press Enter.

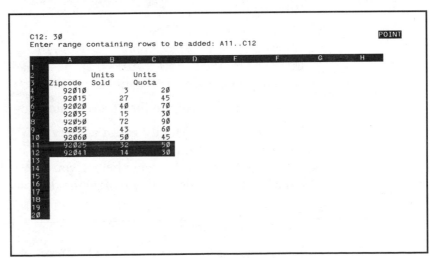

Figure 15.25: Inserting data into the SALESUMM database

Don't be concerned that the added rows are not in zip code order. Relational databases such as Oracle disregard the order of rows within database tables. If the displayed result of a database access (for a report, for instance) must be in order by a particular column, be sure to specify the Sort option of the Oracle Query command.

UPDATING A TABLE

It's important to maintain accurate and up-to-date information in a database. Before altering database values, you must first query the database. Once Oracle has retrieved database rows, you can then alter values in the spreadsheet and save those changes.

Suppose you notice that the sales quota for homes in zip code 92010 (the first data row in Figure 15.24) should be *13* instead of *20* (its present value). To change that value and place the change back in the database, follows these steps:

1. Clear the spreadsheet with the 1-2-3 Worksheet Erase command (type **/WEY**).

2. Press the Oracle hot key (Alt-F7) and execute the Query command (type Q).

3. Query the entire SALESUMM table (table: SALESUMM, columns: zipcode, sold, quota) and store the query (@SQL function) in a cell. This ensures that the spreadsheet data is current and matches data found in the database.

4. Press Escape to return to the Oracle main menu.

5. Select the Oracle Modify command (type M). You must select this command before modifying data in spreadsheet cells. Changes to cells made before you select the Modify command cannot be used to update the database.

6. Type in the address of the cell containing the @SQL function and press Enter.

7. When the choices Update and Delete appear at the top of the spreadsheet, select Update.

8. Use the arrow key to move to the cell to be modified (cell C3 in the example), type in the new value, **13**, and press Enter.

9. Press Escape if you are making no more changes. If you are making additional changes, follow steps 8 and 9 repeatedly and press Escape after the last change.

10. When the Commit and Rollback menu choices appear, select Commit to confirm all changes and have Oracle permanently change the database. The Rollback option allows you to undo your changes if you have made a mistake.

After you have executed step 10, the changes are made to the database. Figure 15.26 shows the display before you execute step 10.

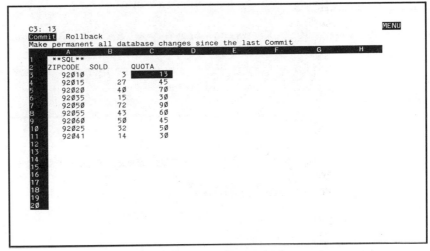

Figure 15.26: Altered value prior to update commit

DELETING ROWS FROM A TABLE

You can remove database rows from a table by executing steps much like those for updating rows in a table. Before you can remove rows, you must query the database to ensure that the spreadsheet copy of the table matches the database copy. Execute steps 1 through 6 shown previously for updating a database. Then do the following:

7. When the choices Update and Delete appear at the top of the spreadsheet, select Delete (type D).

8. When Oracle prompts you for the cells in the spreadsheet containing the rows to be deleted, type in a cell range or point to the rows. You only need to enter one cell of each row to be deleted (that is, A3..A4 will delete the entire row for both rows 3 and 4 from the database). Now press Enter.

9. Repeat step 8 to delete additional rows. Press Escape when you are done.

10. The Commit and Rollback menu choices appear. Select Commit to confirm all row deletions and make the changes permanent. The Rollback option allows you to "undelete" rows if you have made a mistake.

Figure 15.27 shows the status of your SALESUMM data just before you press Enter in step 8. All columns of both rows have been highlighted for emphasis. Remember, you only need to designate a single cell of each row to delete an entire row.

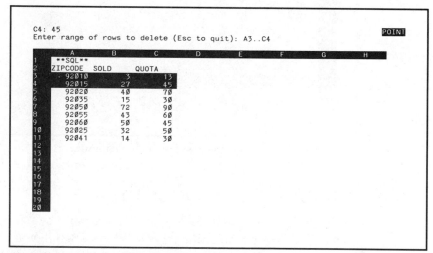

Figure 15.27: Rows to be deleted

REMOVING A DATABASE TABLE

If you no longer need a table that you originally created, you can use the Delete option to remove it from the database. Before removing a table, you can review the names of tables that you have created by executing the My-Tables option of the Info command. Press **IM** from the main Oracle menu to display the names of tables stored and managed by Oracle.

The steps for deleting a database table are as follows:

1. Press the Oracle hot key and select the Table command (type T).

2. After the Create and Delete choices are displayed, select Delete (type D).

3. Type in the name of the table to be deleted (in this case, **SALESUMM**) and press Enter.

4. Confirm your choice when the No Yes prompt appears by selecting Yes (type Y).

Oracle for 1-2-3 will delete the table you named in step 3. You can verify that the table has been removed by executing the My-Tables option of the Info command. Once a table has been deleted, you cannot recall it.

RETRIEVING RELATED DATA FROM SEVERAL TABLES

Collecting and relating data from several tables with Lotus 1-2-3 is often referred to as "consolidation," or "linking spreadsheets." It can be difficult and complicated to build and maintain spreadsheets of related information or even a single spreadsheet containing separate tables of related information.

Oracle for 1-2-3 has a terrific solution to this problem. You can keep related data in distinct database tables. Then you can pull together these different elements of a larger, consolidated spreadsheet with Oracle's joining facilities. By keeping tables in separate databases, you can easily maintain different kinds of data (sales quotas, sales by region, and so on); yet you can build, graph, and save an overview of the big picture (sales by all regions in July, for example) when needed.

INTRODUCTION TO THE APPLICATION

This section continues with the real estate sales example. You will combine the data from the PROPERTY database with that of a new table called AGENTSALES to provide summary information. This summary information will give you an overview of the sales productivity of each real estate agent. The newly introduced table, created and maintained independently of the PROPERTY database, contains two columns: PARCEL and SALESID. The SALESID column contains a sales agent's identification number for the associated property's PARCEL number. That is, the AGENTSALES table indicates which sales agent sold which properties. Furthermore, the PARCEL number from the AGENTSALES table links it to the PROPERTY database.

The two tables—individually or together—can produce a variety of informative reports. For example, you can query the AGENTSALES table to display the number of properties each agent has sold. Or, you can join both tables to display the total sales volume per agent, average market time for all sales by each agent, or preferred sales territories (zip code areas) for each agent (called a "farm" in real estate lingo).

Clearly, you could eliminate the AGENTSALES table if sales agent identification numbers were included in the PROPERTY table. However, it is easier to maintain a separate record of sales by agents. Moreover, having a separate table of agents and properties hides certain proprietary information from general users. For example, were the tables combined an agent could learn which agents sold the most properties or how much commission Fred Smith made last year.

JOINING TWO TABLES: THE CONCEPT

Suppose you want to build a report that summarizes total sales per sales agent for the year. You must join the PROPERTY and AGENTSALES tables. Two columns will be displayed, the sales agent's identification number (SALESID) and the sum of the properties he or she has sold. The SALESID field is retrieved from the AGENTSALES table, while the total value of an agent's sales is extracted from the PROPERTY table. The value of an agent's sales is a virtual value because it is calculated from a "real" database column—the PRICE column.

How are the two tables related to one another? There is a field common to both of them: the property's parcel number (PARCEL). The parcel numbers for each agent are retrieved from the AGENT-SALES table. Then, an agent's parcel numbers are used to retrieve the sales prices (by matching the PARCEL numbers) of each property he or she has sold (PRICE) from the PROPERTY table. These values are summed. The next (unique) sales agent's PARCEL numbers are retrieved from the AGENTSALES table, and this process is repeated. The result is the desired table listing sales agent identification numbers and total sales per agent.

JOINING TWO TABLES: THE IMPLEMENTATION

Begin constructing the Sales Volume by Sales Person report by clearing the display (type **/WEY**). Next, invoke the Oracle database manager (press Alt-F7) and tell Oracle to exclude database column names from retrieved tables by executing Options Query Headings Exclude (type **OQHE**). Press Alt-F7 to reinvoke Oracle, select Query, and select Reset to clear out any previous queries. You can now create sales volume summary information.

Select Input (type I) and enter the table names as follows:

```
Enter table(s): PROPERTY, AGENTSALES
```

Oracle will prompt you for the common column name that links these two tables with the prompt

```
Enter join condition(s):
```

Type in **PARCEL** and press Enter. (Recall that PARCEL is the column that relates the two tables.)

Next, enter the columns to be retrieved:

```
Enter columns: SALESID, SUM(PRICE)
```

and press Enter. If you cannot remember the column names, simply press F1. A full-screen display will list database file names and their associated column names. Press any key to redisplay the Enter Columns prompt after noting the requisite column names.

Select Output and enter **A6** when prompted for the output range. Finally, execute the query by selecting the Go option (press G or highlight Go and press Enter). Store the query in cell C6 when prompted for the @SQL function storage location.

Oracle quickly searches both tables and relates and summarizes the information. After the results are placed in the spreadsheet, you can clean up the report (format currency for dollar amounts, add a title at the top of the spreadsheet, and add more descriptive column labels). Figure 15.28 displays the final result.

```
C6: @SQL("SELECT salesid, sum(price) INTO &1 FROM property, agentsales WHER READY

        A            B           C        D        E        F        G
1   Sales Volume By Salesperson
2
3      Sales-     Total Sales
4      Person    Volume (YTD)
5   --------------------------
6       1001        $872,500    **SQL**
7       1002      $3,753,900
8       1004      $2,333,150
9       1005      $2,253,400
10      1007      $5,748,800
11      1008      $2,412,900
12      1009      $1,450,050
13      1010      $2,178,850
14      1011      $1,920,400
15      1012      $5,666,790
16      1013      $3,401,100
17      1014      $1,375,900
18      1015      $2,299,500
19
20
```

Figure 15.28: Joining two tables and summarizing results

Once the data has been retrieved, you can use the Lotus 1-2-3 Graph command to build the graph shown in Figure 15.29.

ORACLE UTILITY PROGRAMS

Special Oracle utilities help to keep your Oracle database functioning smoothly. The Oracle for 1-2-3 software package includes a special Lotus 1-2-3 spreadsheet, *ORACLE.WK1,* that implements

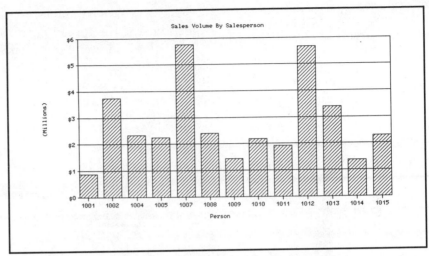

Figure 15.29: Lotus graph of Oracle-retrieved sales summary

Oracle utility and maintenance functions. Oracle for 1-2-3 provides two types of utilities. One group performs user management and performance enhancement functions such as

- Creating table definitions
- Changing user passwords
- Creating indexes for faster data retrieval

The second group performs disk management functions such as

- Expanding the size of the database to create additional free space
- Compressing the contents of the current database to combine small, unused portions into larger blocks of free space and to combine occupied database blocks into larger, contiguous blocks

OVERVIEW OF THE ORACLE UTILITY SPREADSHEET

To execute the utility programs, you must retrieve the special worksheet ORACLE.WK1 that comes with Oracle for 1-2-3. To do so, execute the Lotus 1-2-3 File Retrieve command (type **/FR**) and type **ORACLE.WK1**. A good deal of the spreadsheet (the first 185 rows or so) contains documentation and useful comments.

You invoke Oracle utilities by executing a macro stored in this worksheet. The macro is invoked by pressing Alt-Z (hold down the Alt key and press Z). After you enter a valid username and password, the Utility main menu appears (see Figure 15.30).

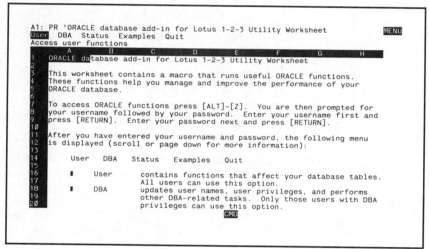

Figure 15.30: Utility program main menu

The Main Menu

The five menu options in the main menu are User, DBA, Status, Examples, and Quit. As in standard Lotus 1-2-3 menus, you execute one of the displayed options either by typing its first letter or by moving the cursor to the command and pressing Enter. The Status option shows the last SQL command that was executed, and the Examples option creates the sample tables described in the *Introduction and User's Guide*, which accompanies Oracle for 1-2-3. The User and DBA options are of particular interest. You can perform certain utility operations only through the DBA choice, while you can perform others by executing the User choice.

The User Menu

Anyone can execute User; you do not need the DBA privilege to execute any of the User commands. When you select User, the next menu offers seven command choices: Index, Table, Rename, Synonym, Access, Password, and Quit.

The Index command improves the efficiency of retrieval operations and enforces *database integrity*. An index based on one of the table columns helps Oracle locate information much faster. Database integrity means that an index on a given column guarantees that a value entered for that column (for example, the PARCEL column of the PROPERTY database) is unique.

The Table command affects the columns of an existing table. With this command, you can add a new column to a table, alter the width of a current column, and permit or disallow empty (Null) values in a column.

Rename allows you to rename a table. Synonym creates or removes synonyms. You can assign a synonym that only you can access, such as SALES, as an alias to the database PROPERTY. Then, you can refer to that table by either name, SALES or PROPERTY.

Using the Access command, you can allow (GRANT) or disallow (REVOKE) other users' access to tables that you have created. The degrees of access (called table access privileges) that you can grant or revoke are SELECT, INSERT, UPDATE, DELETE, ALTER, INDEX, or ALL to include all of the preceding privileges. SELECT permits retrieval only, whereas INSERT, UPDATE, and DELETE privileges permit other users to change the data to varying degrees. ALTER allows other users to add new columns to your table; the INDEX privilege lets other users index your table.

PASSWORD allows you to change your own password or, if you have the DBA system access privilege, to change any user's password. Without DBA privileges, you can change only your own password.

Press Q or highlight Quit and press Enter to exit the User command. Do not press the Escape key.

The DBA Menu

If you choose DBA from the Utility main menu, you must have DBA privilege to execute any of the commands that follow.

The DBA functions are displayed as the menu choices Username, Privileges, Synonym, and Quit. These functions allow you to update user names and privileges, and to create public synonyms. Through this menu, you can also add new usernames and passwords, drop users, assign or revoke privileges (CONNECT, RESOURCE, or DBA), create synonyms, and assign synonyms to the special user, PUBLIC (see Chapters 3 and 11 for a discussion of the special user PUBLIC).

If you are using Professional Oracle for microcomputers, you are the database administrator and will use the DBA function more frequently than the others.

The Username DBA menu command permits you to Add, Delete, or List usernames. By selecting Add, you can create new usernames and then set privileges for each. Delete removes one or more usernames from the system, preventing removed users from accessing Oracle. List can list all of the current usernames and their privileges. Figure 15.31 shows a representative listing displayed when you execute Username List (type **/UL**).

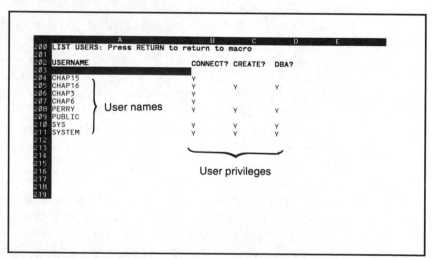

Figure 15.31: List of user names and privileges

Execute the DBA Privileges command whenever you want to either give (GRANT) or remove (REVOKE) any user's DBA and/or RESOURCE privileges. DBA privileges allows a user to a great deal of power and should be given sparingly. The RESOURCE privilege allows users to create tables and indexes. Without the RESOURCE privilege, a user can only view tables that others have created.

The Synonym command allows you to create public synonyms for any table or view in the system. Unlike the Synonym option of the User command, the DBA Synonym command does not restrict you to creating synonyms for tables and views that you have created.

Like the User Quit option, the DBA Quit option exits the DBA command and returns to the Utilities main menu. Remember to press Q rather than Escape to leave.

SOME IMPORTANT USER MANAGEMENT UTILITIES

This section describes a subset of the utility programs you can invoke using the ORACLE.WK1 spreadsheet. Two functions of particular interest are adding or deleting users and altering existing users' passwords. Oracle for 1-2-3 software has three important usernames already in place: SYS, SYSTEM, and SCOTT. One of the first things you should do is change the password for SYS and SYSTEM.

Changing Passwords of Existing Users

Two built-in usernames, SYS and SYSTEM, maintain system-sensitive and critical Oracle databases and system tables. Because everyone purchasing Oracle for 1-2-3 knows the default passwords for SYS and SYSTEM, you should change those passwords to protect you system. The password for username SYS is CHANGE_ON-_INSTALL, and the password for username SYSTEM is MAN-AGER. You should use the SYS account only once: to change its password. You should do all other work requiring the DBA privilege with the username (account) SYSTEM.

To change the SYS password, invoke Oracle for 1-2-3 (type **ORA123** at the DOS prompt) and follow these steps:

1. Retrieve the ORACLE.WKS spreadsheet with the File Retrieve command (type **/FR**).

2. Invoke the Oracle Utility Program by pressing Alt-Z.

3. Log on to Oracle with the username **SYS** and the password **CHANGE_ON_INSTALL** when prompted for each one.

4. Select User from the Utilities main menu.

5. Select Password.

6. Type in the username **SYS** and press Enter.

7. Type in a new password (for example, **SHERLOCK**)—of up to 30 characters and press Enter.

8. Press Q to quit.

Repeat the preceding steps to change the password for username SYSTEM. Be sure to write down the new passwords. There is *no way* to display passwords if you forget them!

Adding and Deleting Usernames

As your own Professional Oracle database administrator, you may find it helpful to organize different database applications under different usernames. For example, you might maintain customer names and addresses under username CUSTOMER_NAMES, accounting applications under username ACCOUNTS, and so on.

It is easy to create new users and corresponding passwords. Load the Utility worksheet ORACLE.WK1 and press Alt-Z to begin the process. Then follow these steps:

1. Select the DBA option from the Utility main menu by typing D.

2. Select the Username option.

3. Select Add, type in the new username, and press Enter.

4. Type in the password for the new username and press Enter.

5. When you are prompted with

```
Grant Create privileges? (Y/N):
```

type either Y or N and press Enter. Y allows the new user to create tables and views; N does not.

6. The phrase

```
Grant DBA privileges? (Y/N):
```

appears next. Type Y or N and press Enter to either allow or disallow DBA privileges. Be sparing with DBA privileges. You should probably create only one username with DBA privilege in addition to the SYS and SYSTEM usernames.

7. Finally, press Q to exit this procedure and return to the worksheet.

Recall that you can review usernames and associated privileges with the Utility worksheet command DBA Username List (type **DUL**). Check the list and make any necessary adjustments.

You can remove usernames even more easily than you can add them. However, *never* remove either SYS or SYSTEM. These two usernames are essential to the Oracle system. Should you inadvertently remove either of them, you must reinstall Oracle for 1-2-3.

Once you have loaded the ORACLE.WK1 worksheet and pressed Alt-Z, follow these steps to remove one or more usernames:

1. Select the DBA option.

2. Select the option Username.

3. Select Delete and type in the username to be deleted when the prompt "Enter or more user names:" appears. Then press Enter.

4. Select Quit to complete the process and return to the worksheet.

To remove several usernames at once, simply type them at the appropriate prompt, separated by commas, and press Enter.

ALTERING THE 1-2-3 DRIVER SET

You may find it necessary to change the 1-2-3 driver set (123.SET) in order to alter selected equipment such as the type of printer or console that you are using. Whenever you do this, all of the 1-2-3 add-in programs will be lost, including Oracle for 1-2-3. Whenever you change the driver set, you must reload Oracle for 1-2-3 by executing the procedure ADD_MGR. After changing your 1-2-3 driver set, type

```
C>ADD_MGR 123.SET
```

and press Enter at the DOS prompt to add Oracle for 1-2-3 back into the driver set.

DETACHING ORACLE FROM LOTUS

To detach (de-install) Oracle for 1-2-3 from Lotus 1-2-3, follow these steps:

1. Invoke Lotus as usual, by typing **ORA123** at the DOS prompt and pressing Enter.

2. Press Alt-F10 (*not* Alt-F7) to invoke the Lotus Add-in Manager menu.

3. Select Clear if Oracle for 1-2-3 is the only add-in product attached to Lotus. Otherwise, select Detach; ORA123A can be detached, but you will not be able to detach ORA123B using this menu.

4. Select Setup.

5. Select Cancel to detach the two Oracle files ORA123A and ORA123B. An error message will appear, but ignore it.

6. Select Update and then select Quit; control returns to the Add-in Manager.

7. Select Quit to return to the Lotus Ready mode.

SUMMARY

This chapter covered Oracle for 1-2-3, starting with installation and proceeding through data management in 1-2-3. You saw how to retrieve selected rows and/or columns from your database and how to organize the results using the Sort option. You also learned how to modify a database using Oracle for 1-2-3 and how to join related data from different databases. Finally, the chapter explored the Oracle Utility programs.

16

USING THE
SPREADSHEET:
SQL*CALC

SQL*CALC IS A FULL FUNCTION SPREADSHEET
that is similar to Lotus 1-2-3. If you have used 1-2-3, you
already know how to use much of SQL*Calc. However,
SQL*Calc's database manipulation capabilities go far beyond
those of 1-2-3. While 1-2-3 requires all database records to be
present in the memory-resident spreadsheet cells (a limit of
approximately 8192 records), SQL*Calc can access massive
databases containing literally millions of records. Furthermore,
SQL*Calc is identical on *all* hardware platforms, including
large IBM mainframes, VAX minicomputers, and IBM PS/2
microcomputers, among others. In fact, the machine running
SQL*Calc is transparent to a user. Lotus 1-2-3, as you know,
runs on microcomputers only.

Because SQL*Calc has a rich set of commands facilitating
database access, it emphasizes database (SQL) commands
rather than the "usual" spreadsheet commands. Since you are
probably already familiar with most of the spreadsheet commands, functions, and operators, this chapter presents the ones
common to SQL*Calc and 1-2-3 in a support role.

The first section of this chapter prepares you to use SQL*Calc. It describes how to load the Oracle executive system, how to execute SQL*Calc, and how to log on to the Oracle database system. The remaining sections help you develop a real estate sales summary spreadsheet. You will use familiar spreadsheet commands, functions, and operators to prepare a spreadsheet which you will later use to accumulate database-retrieved summary information. You will learn special database capabilities for logging on to Oracle, querying large databases, pulling data into a spreadsheet, creating new database tables, storing data in tables, deleting database rows, and committing or revoking the most recent database changes. You will see that Oracle's SQL*Calc interface permits many users to share data from a single, consistent, and current source.

A large real estate information database illustrates SQL*Calc's power and capabilities. Capable of holding tens of thousands of records, the multiple listing database contains information about recent real estate sales (usually, single family homes). Table columns include unique identification number, address (street, city, zipcode), sale price, sale date, number of bedrooms, number of bathrooms, square footage, and the length of time the property was on the market. Figure 16.1 shows a representative sample of the database rows that you will later retrieve and summarize in various ways. The address columns have been omitted for clarity.

GETTING STARTED

If you are using a microcomputer system, you will need to load the Oracle RDBMS Protected Mode Executive before using SQL*Calc. Simply type **ORACLE** at the system prompt to load the kernel (see Chapter 2). If you are on a larger, multiuser system (such as a minicomputer), the Oracle Protected Mode Executive is probably already resident in memory.

You can start SQL*Calc in one of several ways. From the DOS prompt, you can type

```
C:\>SQLCALC
```

```
  IDENT.    SALE    SALE     MKT      SQ.
  NUMBER    PRICE   DATE    TIME BR   FT.  BATH
 .......  .........  ......... ....  ..  ....... ....

 8712831  $223,500 02-DEC-87  265   3   2,100  2.0
 8715512  $166,000 04-DEC-87  280   4   1,815  1.7
 8719187  $106,500 22-NOV-87  216   3   1,100  1.5
 8719249  $240,500 08-JAN-88  266   4   2,530  2.5
 8719784  $116,500 28-NOV-87  215   3   1,500  1.5
 8722523  $221,500 30-NOV-87  198   3   2,570  2.7
 8722794  $155,500 05-JAN-88  171   2   1,050  1.0
 8723601  $526,500 08-FEB-88  283   5   4,200  3.0
 8723735  $211,500 29-JAN-88  191   3   1,650  2.0
 8723900  $146,500 13-JAN-88  131   3   1,550  2.5
 8724200  $231,500 07-JAN-88  213   5   2,400  2.5
 8724304  $127,000 12-MAY-88  215   3   1,312  2.0
 8725589  $151,500 30-NOV-87   51   4   1,500  2.0
 8725791  $118,400 31-DEC-87  188   2   1,390  2.0
 8726582  $207,500 17-FEB-88  229   3   1,717  2.0
 8726695   $89,500 20-NOV-87  136   3   1,100  2.0
 8726711  $211,500 09-FEB-88  239   3   1,750  2.0
 8727020  $191,500 19-JAN-88  148   3   1,086  1.0
 8727232   $96,500 04-DEC-87   25   4   1,650  2.0
 8727249  $157,500 27-NOV-87   74   2   1,150  1.0
 8727328  $160,500 25-NOV-87   15   3   1,600  2.0
 8727393   $69,500 25-JAN-88  194   2     700  1.0
 8727546  $221,500 11-DEC-87  149   4   2,553  2.5
 8727549  $131,480 08-JAN-88  177   2     950  1.0
 8727866  $156,000 10-DEC-87  153   3   1,940  1.7
```

Figure 16.1: Sample listing of records

to invoke SQL∗Calc without loading a spreadsheet. Or, you can type

```
C:\>SQLCALC @sheetname
```

to invoke SQL∗Calc and load a spreadsheet whose name you type immediately after the at @ sign.

To invoke SQL∗Calc and log on to the Oracle RDBMS with the name and associated password, you can type

```
C:\>SQLCALC name/password
```

Finally, you can combine the previous two methods by typing

```
C:\>SQLCALC @sheetname name/password
```

You need not be an enrolled Oracle RDBMS user to use SQL∗Calc. However, you only get the real power of SQL∗Calc when you are enrolled as a user and log on to the system. As an enrolled user, you can issue commands within SQL*Calc to query databases and manipulate tables. Whether enrolled or not, you can use all of the standard spreadsheet functions and commands without accessing any databases.

Because the examples presented in this chapter use data stored in Oracle-controlled databases, you must invoke SQL*Calc and supply a username and password. Execute SQL*Calc by typing

```
C:\>SQLCALC
```

and pressing Enter. The SQL*Calc opening screen will be displayed, and you will be asked to enter a username or press Enter. If you enter a username and press Enter, you are then asked to enter a password. Figure 16.2 shows the first SQL*Calc screen requesting that you enter a username. You need not log on to Oracle immediately—you can execute a SQL*Calc command later if you need to access a database.

```
                          SQL*Calc
                The Spreadsheet Interface to the
        ORACLE Relational Database Management System

                   Copyright (c) 1986, 1987
        Oracle Corporation, Belmont, California, USA
                     All Rights Reserved











 0% USED.  SQL*Calc V1.1.10.10 - Production, for IBM-PC/MS-DOS 2.0
 Enter your ORACLE user identification.  (Press RETURN to skip logon.)
```

Figure 16.2: The opening SQL*Calc screen

The examples in this chapter contain database information that is restricted to a small group of employees. To keep unauthorized people from viewing the information, SQL*Calc requires that database users identify themselves with a username and password. Type in your username and press Enter when requested to do so (see last line of Figure 16.2). After you have entered your username, the last line of the screen displays

```
Enter password
```

and the system pauses for your response. Type in the password associated with the username and press Enter. Once Oracle has verified your username and password, an empty SQL*Calc spreadsheet appears on the screen (see Figure 16.3).

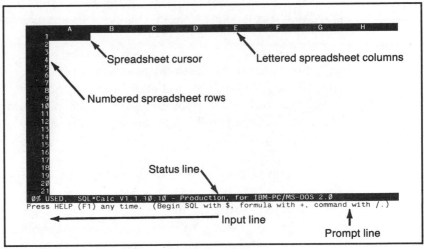

Figure 16.3: Structure of an empty spreadsheet

STANDARD SPREADSHEET ACTIVITIES

If you are a Lotus 1-2-3 user, the SQL*Calc screen will look familiar to you (Figure 16.3). Spreadsheet columns are identified by letters, and rows by numbers. The *Status Line* at the bottom of the spreadsheet displays messages and cell contents. The *Prompt Line* always displayed by SQL*Calc (but not by 1-2-3) indicates what your can do next. The last line is the data *Input Line.* You enter and edit all data, formulas, functions, and SQL commands on this portion of the screen.

ENTERING TEXT AND NUMBERS

Entering text (also called *labels*) and numbers in SQL*Calc is like entering data in 1-2-3. Enter the text title

```
Summary of Sales of Single Family Homes
```

into cell A1. Type the numeric entries **1987** and **1988** into cells B2 and D2, respectively. Place the hyphen character in cell C2 to separate the two years.

The spreadsheet cursor is initially positioned in the HOME cell, A1. Type the "Summary of Sales..." text in that cell and press Enter. Notice that text too long to fit in a single cell spills over into adjacent empty cells—as it does in 1-2-3. Using the ↓ and ← keys on the numeric key pad, position the spreadsheet cursor in cell B2 and type **1987**, but *do not* press Enter. Instead, press the → key. The cursor enters the data into cell B2 and then moves to the right. Pressing an arrow key instead of Enter saves time because it places data into a cell *and* moves to the next cell in the direction of the arrow key pressed.

The hyphen following the first date (1987) indicates to SQL*Calc that you are entering a negative numeric value or formula. If you press the hyphen key and then press Enter, you will get an error message. To "fool" SQL*Calc into accepting a numeric entry as text, prefix the hyphen with an apostrophe ('). In this way, the text entry hyphen can be placed into a cell (cell C2, in this example). After you press the → key to move to cell D2, enter the numeric value **1988**. Press Enter to finish entering this value, because the next cell to be entered is not adjacent to the current one.

To enter column names in two rows, press the GoTo key (function key F5 on an IBM keyboard) and type **B3** to move the spreadsheet cursor directly to that cell. In cells B3, C3, and D3 enter the text strings **Average**, **Avg Mkt**, and **Units**. Enter the text **Zipcode**, **Price**, **Time**, and **Sold** in cells A4 through D4. Once entered, those rows of text should look like this:

```
        Average  Avg Mkt  Units
Zipcode Price    Time     Sold
```

ENTERING REPEATING TEXT

You can input repeating text into one or more cells to visually separate column heading from data. When you enter repeating text, it fills one cell. To reproduce the text in other cells, execute the Copy command. You enter repeating text by typing a backslash (\) followed by one or more characters (numbers, alphabetics, or special characters) to be repeated. To enter repeating equal signs in the row below the column labels, move to cell A5, type \ = , and press Enter. Figure 16.4 shows the spreadsheet created so far.

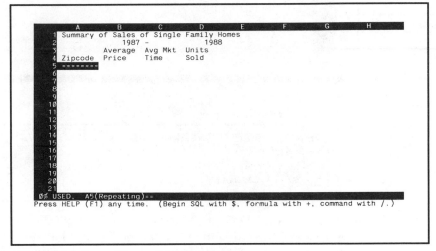

Figure 16.4: Spreadsheet with repeating text

EXECUTING THE COPY COMMAND

To replicate one or more cells in other cells, execute the Copy command. You execute all commands, including Copy, by first pressing the slash (/) key. Figure 16.5 shows the first level commands displayed on the lower portion of the spreadsheet after you press /. The Copy command will be highlighted if you press the → key twice.

Press **C** to select the Copy command; press Enter to copy from the current cell (A5). Finally, type **B5.D5** to specify the range of cells to which you want to copy cell A5. The period separates the two cell limits of the range. Press Enter to complete the Copy command.

The column labels in rows 3 and 4 (see Figure 16.5) would look better if they were on the right side of their respective cells, since numbers will be placed below them later. Text is by default left-justified in a cell. If it is unclear how to reorganize text—in Lotus 1-2-3 you execute the command / Range Format Text—on-line SQL*Calc help is available.

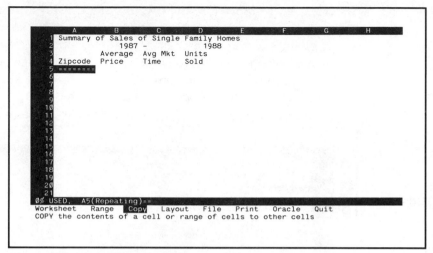

Figure 16.5: Executing SQL∗Calc commands

OBTAINING HELP

Context sensitive, on-line help is available in SQL∗Calc. For example, if you want to alter the way that text is placed in cells but are not sure which command to use, press the function key F1 to obtain general help. For help on particular commands, press the slash key to invoke the SQL∗Calc commands and then press the F1 function key.

When help is displayed on the screen, it temporarily displaces the spreadsheet. The type of helpful information displayed depends on what you have already typed on the Input Line. Figure 16.6 shows one of the help screens displayed when you press F1 after typing a slash on the Input Line.

You can obtain additional help on various SQL∗Calc topics. Figure 16.7 shows the help screen displayed when you press F1 after typing a slash and the letter L, the Layout command.

The help displayed about the Layout command makes it clear that this is the command you need to right-justify the text in rows 3 and 4.

ADJUSTING DISPLAYED VALUES: LAYOUT

To right-justify the text in the cells, position the spreadsheet cursor in the row to be adjusted (row 3). Then execute the Layout command by pressing **/LHA1** (Layout Horiz-Row Align 1). You'll see the following choices:

```
LAYOUT ALIGN:   1) Text-Right   2) Text-Left   3) Number-Right   4) Number-Left
```

```
Press ESCAPE to return to the worksheet, any other key for more help
                          SLASH COMMANDS

            SQL*Calc groups many commands and their options
            into sets, as shown below.  To see the list of
            options available in each set, type / followed
            by the first letter of the command (/W, for example).

            /W  WORKSHEET commands--global commands affecting
                all cells on the worksheet.  (For example,
                /Worksheet Erase lets you erase the entire
                worksheet.)

            /R  RANGE commands--commands affecting only a
                specified set of cells.  (For example,
                /Range Erase lets you erase a single cell
                or a block of cells.)

                                 (More slash commands on the next screen.)

 0% USED,   A5(Repeating)==
 Worksheet    Range   Copy   Layout   File   Print   Oracle   Quit
 Set options, titles or windows; insert, delete or move rows & cols; erase all
```

Figure 16.6: Typical help screen

```
Press any key to return to the worksheet
            /LAYOUT COMMAND:

            With this command you determine how text and numbers will
            be displayed in cells on the screen and on printouts or
            files you create with the /PRINT command.

       Select the scope of the LAYOUT command by typing one of these letters:

            C  -- applies to every cell in the current Column
            H  -- applies to every cell in the current Horizontal-Row
            F  -- applies to the current Field (cell)
            W  -- applies to every cell in the Worksheet

            You can also press  M  to modify a style you want
            to apply to all numbers you enter on the worksheet.

       In SQL*Calc, any layout commands that you give for an individual
       cell override any that cover a row or column.  Row and column
       layout commands override those given for the whole worksheet.

 0% USED,   A5(Repeating)==
LAYOUT:   Column    Horiz-Row   Field   Worksheet   Modify-Styles
Modify current COLUMN width, format (incl style), alignment, or decimal places
```

Figure 16.7: Detailed help on the Layout command

Choice 1 corresponds to the desired right-justified form. You can right- or left-justify additional rows of text or numbers by repeating the preceding actions. Move the spreadsheet cursor to the row, column, or individual cell to be adjusted, and then execute the Layout command. Figure 16.8 shows the newly-aligned text cells (rows 3 and 4) after you have executed the Layout command twice.

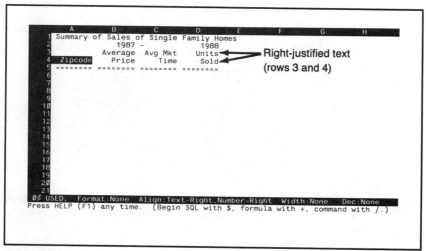

Figure 16.8: Formatting text cells right-justified

Notice that the Status Line in Figure 16.8 indicates several things about the current cell: it is right-aligned for text and numbers, and the default column width has not been altered ("Width:None"). This Status Line form appears immediately after you execute the Layout command. If you move the cursor to another cell, the Status Line message displays the contents of the cell (the value of the current cell is shown in the spreadsheet).

SAVING A SPREADSHEET

It is a good idea to save your spreadsheet periodically—even if it is not complete. This will keep you from losing data (and lots of work!) if the computer system fails while you are using SQL*Calc.

When you save a spreadsheet, it is stored on disk with a primary name of your own choosing. SQL*Calc automatically appends the extension .CAL to the file. Save a spreadsheet by executing the File Save command. Press the slash key to initiate a command, the F key to execute the File command, and the S key to indicate the Save operation. The Status and Prompt Lines then ask you to enter a file name. If you created the file from scratch (you did not load a previously-created spreadsheet), the Status Line displays the message "Current file:". Otherwise, it suggests the name of the file you last loaded. Figure 16.9 shows your spreadsheet after you pressed **/FS** but before you entered a file name.

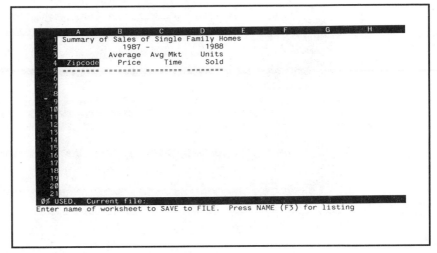

Figure 16.9: Saving a spreadsheet: /FS

Next, type in the file name to save the spreadsheet (for example, SALESUMM) and press Enter. The Prompt and Input Lines then display

```
FILE SAVE:  All   Values-only
Save all information about the spreadsheet
```

with the All option highlighted. Press Enter to save all information—you want to save cell contents as well as displayed values. The spreadsheet will be quickly stored and the Status Line will signal successful completion of the file save operation with the message

```
File operation completed
```

PRINTING A SPREADSHEET

Although your spreadsheet is not complete, you should know how to create a printed copy of it, which you can refer to as you continue to read this chapter. As with other commands, you execute the Print command by pressing the slash key. Figure 16.10 shows the Status, Prompt, and Input Lines at the bottom of a spreadsheet as you execute each step for printing a spreadsheet.

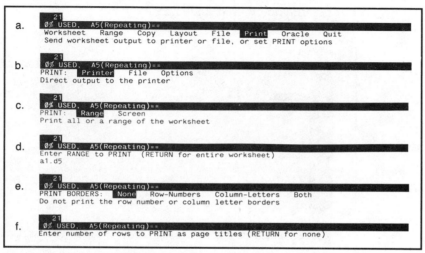

Figure 16.10: Steps for printing a spreadsheet

First, press the letter P or move the command pointer to the Print command and press Enter (see Figure 16.10a). The Prompt Line indicates that you may now print to the printer, print to a disk file, or change options (Figure 16.10b). Press Enter to select the Printer option.

You must specify a range of spreadsheet cells so that SQL*Calc knows how many of the cells to output to the printer. Pressing Enter (see Figure 16.10c) selects the Range option; next, you can enter the range of cells to be printed (Figure 16.10d). An appropriate range of cells includes the upper-left cell address followed by a period and the lower-right cell address. The cell range A1 through D5 encompasses your entire spreadsheet so far. An easy way to enter the upper-left and lower-right cell addresses is to press the Home key, type a period, and then press the End key. This guarantees that you will include the whole spreadsheet in the range (every non-empty spreadsheet cell).

After you press Enter to finalize the cell range to print, you can decide whether or not to print row-numbers, column-letters, both, or neither row numbers or column letters (None). Press Enter to accept the default choice None highlighted in Figure 16.10e.

Finally, you can choose whether or not to include page titles in the printed spreadsheet (see Figure 16.10f). If you choose not to have page titles, press Enter. The spreadsheet will immediately begin to print. If nothing happens, check that your printer is on.

SQL*Calc compares favorably with Lotus 1-2-3, but SQL*Calc *database* commands, which permit access to large, relational databases, go far beyond the capabilities of Lotus 1-2-3. Using SQL*Calc as a window to relational databases, you can access databases that contain millions of records. You can summarize database information, alter selected database records, create new database tables, and insert new records into a database—all within SQL*Calc.

The sections that follow describe the database query and manipulation commands that you can execute from within the friendly SQL*Calc environment. First, you will learn how to query a database to extract selected rows and place them into a SQL*Calc spreadsheet.

QUERYING DATABASES

In order to "link" SQL*Calc to the Oracle RDBMS, you must explicitly log on to the Oracle system. If you executed SQL*Calc by typing

```
C>SQLCALC username/password
```

at the DOS prompt, you are already linked to the Oracle RDBMS. However, if you invoked SQL*Calc by typing

```
C>SQLCALC
```

and then merely pressed Enter when prompted for your username, you can log on to Oracle from within SQL*Calc.

LOGGING ON TO ORACLE

The SQL*Calc command Oracle is the first step for logging on to Oracle. To initiate the command, type /O. Figure 16.11 shows the steps required to log on to the Oracle system. Figure 16.11a shows the Status, Prompt, and Input Lines with the Oracle command high-lighted. After pressing **/O**, select the Logon choice (see Figure 16.11b) either by pressing the letter **L** (either upper- or lowercase) or by moving the command pointer to Logon and pressing Enter.

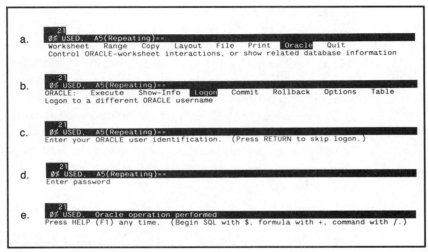

Figure 16.11: Logging on to the Oracle RDBMS from SQL*Calc

Next, enter username and press Enter (see Figure 16.11c). You are then asked to type your password (Figure 16.11d). Do so, and press Enter. Your username and password are validated by the Oracle system. If you have supplied a correct username and password, a message confirms that you are logged on to the Oracle system (see Figure 16.11e). If the username and password pair are incorrect, an error message is placed in the status line:

`Oracle msg: Invalid user username/password or Oracle not installed.`

If this message appears, you may have misspelled either your username or password. Attempt to log on again: type **/OL** and your username password and then press Enter. Then type your password and press Enter again. If the error message persists and you are on a multiuser system, contact your database administrator—perhaps your username and password are not entered in the system.

Once you have logged on, you can execute the SQL query, insert, update, delete, and create commands from within SQL*Calc.

SQL*Calc can manipulate database information because it is both a high quality spreadsheet and a versatile database tool. Because SQL*Calc can interact with Oracle-controlled databases, it can take advantage of all of the SQL database commands to query large databases, create new database tables, and alter database information. Unlike Lotus 1-2-3, SQL*Calc does not require data to be spreadsheet-resident in order to calculate averages on columns, for example. You can extract database information from large databases with the special $ SQL command. This command allows you to frame any SQL command and have the returned results inserted into your spreadsheet. The examples that follow describe the SQL database interface commands using the real estate sales database. Although the examples manipulate a database subgroup of only 250 records, interface commands operate exactly the same way for databases containing tens of thousands of records.

WRITING SQL*CALC SELECT STATEMENTS

The most often used SQL statement is SELECT. A SQL cell in a spreadsheet contains standard SQL instructions to Oracle. You begin entering a SQL SELECT statement by typing dollar sign ($) in any empty cell. Then begin the database command with the word SELECT. This statement is similar to a SQL*Calc function or formula. After the SELECT statement has been entered in a cell, information begins to appear in the current cell of your spreadsheet.

Selecting All Database Columns

There are several forms of the SELECT statement. The most basic form consists of at least two parts: a *SELECT clause* and a *FROM clause*. The SELECT clause lists the Oracle RDBMS columns that you wish to retrieve, while the FROM clause names the table or tables in which that data is found. The simplest form of the SELECT clause is

`$SELECT * FROM table-name`

The $SELECT * clause indicates that Oracle is to retrieve *all* columns of information, and the FROM *table-name* clause tells Oracle the name of the table (or view) from which the data is to be extracted. In effect, the preceding SELECT statement asks Oracle to retrieve all columns and all rows of a table. You can write all SQL*Calc SQL statements in either upper- or lowercase.

Selecting Spreadsheet Cells to Receive Information

A SQL*Calc option of the SELECT statement not found in standard ANSI SQL specifies where the retrieved data is to be placed in the spreadsheet. This optional clause is called the *INTO clause,* which controls the placement of data in your spreadsheet cells. For example, to direct Oracle to place the retrieved table rows and columns into cells B6 through D17, type

```
$SELECT * INTO &b6.d17 FROM table-name
```

Notice that the INTO clause follows the * and precedes the FROM clause. Also, the cell range in the INTO clause is always preceded by an ampersand. The cell range in the INTO clause is written in lowercase to facilitate automatic cell adjustment (described later) in case that formula is later copied to other cells.

If you do not know how many rows or columns Oracle will retrieve, it is best to omit the INTO clause. SQL*Calc will automatically determine how many spreadsheet rows and columns are needed, begin placing data in the block with the SELECT statement as the upper-left corner boundary of that block, and fill the appropriate spreadsheet rows and columns.

Retrieving Specific Table Columns

To control how many database columns are placed in a spreadsheet, you can specify table column names in the SELECT clause. This limits the number of spreadsheet columns that are filled with retrieved data. An example that specifies three columns drawn from the real estate sales database is:

```
$SELECT ZIPCODE, PRICE, MARKETTIME FROM PROPERTY
```

Three fields of the database—zipcode, price, and markettime—are the only columns of all database records that will be placed in the block beginning with the SELECT statement.

Limiting the Rows Selected

In addition to specifying the columns to be placed in the spreadsheet, you can use the SELECT statement *WHERE clause* to list the criteria for selecting database rows. You may wish to insert only rows that meet certain restrictions. For example, to retrieve all columns of the PROPERTY database for which the sales price is greater than $150,000, type the SELECT statement

```
$SELECT * FROM PROPERTY WHERE PRICE > 150000
```

All other rows would be ignored. You can also use optional SQL clauses like GROUP BY and ORDER BY to organize the retrieved results into groups or sorted order.

RETRIEVING SALES INFORMATION FROM THE PROPERTY DATABASE

The real estate sales spreadsheet being developed consists of tens of thousands of rows of information. The partial listing shown early in the chapter (see Figure 16.1) is a small fraction of the total information. In a 1-2-3 spreadsheet, memory capacity would be exceeded if you tried to use the large database. Furthermore, a 1-2-3 spreadsheet could accommodate only a subset of the sales information, even though it can (in theory) have up to 8,192 rows and 256 columns memory-resident. Lotus is not the ideal spreadsheet tool for summarizing the information from large databases.

Your first database query example will select summary information from thousands of database records and place the results in the rows below the previously created column labels. Because the database is large and you want only summary information, you will ask Oracle to compute averages of some fields before inserting the information into the spreadsheet. The SQL function AVG and the optional clause GROUP BY can compute aggregate averages and then group resulting information. Suppose you want to extract the following data

- Zipcode
- Average sale price
- Average market time

from the PROPERTY table and place it in columns A, B, and C of your spreadsheet.

Begin by placing the spreadsheet cursor in cell A6 and entering the SQL*Calc formula

```
$SELECT ZIPCODE,AVG(PRICE),AVG(MARKETTIME) FROM PROPERTY GROUP BY ZIPCODE
```

The Status, Prompt, and Input Lines are shown in Figure 16.12. After you press Enter, Oracle executes the SELECT statement and begins retrieving information.

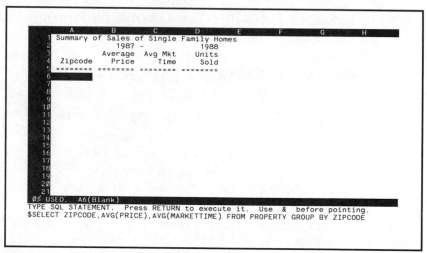

Figure 16.12: Entering a SQL*Calc SELECT statement

The SELECT statement retrieves the zipcode field, the average price, and average market time columns. The GROUP BY ZIP-CODE clause produces group averages for both price and market time—one per unique zipcode. The results are placed in the spreadsheet in groups of zipcodes in ascending order by zipcode.

Initially, only the first row is displayed in the spreadsheet. SQL*Calc then asks whether it should insert additional spreadsheet rows or overwrite existing (currently blank) spreadsheet rows to accommodate additional table rows retrieved from the database (see Figure 16.13).

Notice the message that appears in the Prompt Line:

```
OVERFLOW: 6 EXTRA ROWS. Insert   Overwrite   Stop
```

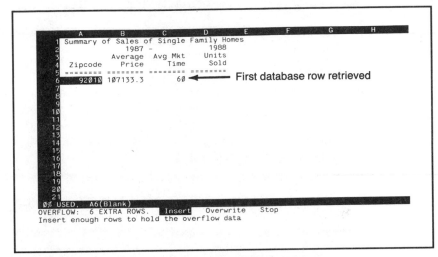

Figure 16.13: The first of several retrieved database rows

The message occurs because more than one row is to be inserted into the spreadsheet. This could destroy information already on the spreadsheet. There are three options: Insert, Overwrite, and Stop. Insert causes SQL*Calc to insert as many new lines as needed to accommodate the retrieved database rows (it is similar to the Lotus 1-2-3 spreadsheet command Worksheet Insert Row). Any rows immediately below row 6 are "pushed down." Overwrite causes existing spreadsheet rows to be replaced with incoming database rows. If there is no data in these spreadsheet rows, you can overwrite without harming existing data. The Stop option keeps you from importing more database rows into the spreadsheet—only the first row from the database remains.

To retrieve the remaining rows, press Enter to select Insert, the default (highlighted) choice (see Figure 16.13). The remaining rows (six in this example) are brought into the spreadsheet. Figure 16.14 displays the spreadsheet after all rows satisfying the SQL SELECT statement in cell A6 are retrieved.

AUTOMATING OVERFLOW AND UNDERFLOW OPTIONS

With a series of SQL*Calc commands, you can easily automate the process of choosing Insert, Overwrite, or Stop. You can alter each

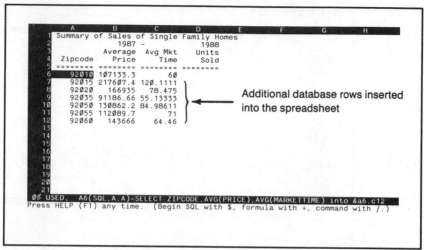

Figure 16.14: Remaining database rows retrieved

SQL SELECT statement to automatically indicate that extra database rows are to be inserted or to overwrite existing spreadsheet rows. Options for each SQL SELECT statement are displayed in the Status Line when the spreadsheet cursor is positioned on a SQL cell (a cell containing a SQL statement such as SELECT). Notice the Status Line in Figure 16.14. Displaying SQL formula option information, the indicator

```
(SQL,A,A)=
```

has three parts. The first part indicates that the cell contains a SQL formula ("SQL"). The second and third parts each contain the indicator "A"—shorthand for ask. The second indicator dictates what will take place when incoming database rows exceed the number of rows specified in the optional INTO clause in the SELECT statement. This is called the *overflow* option. The third part, also indicating "A," determines what takes place when incoming database rows are fewer than the number of spreadsheet rows that will hold them. This is called an *underflow* condition.

For SQL*Calc to automatically decide how to handle row overflow or underflow, you must change these two options for one or more $SELECT formulas in the spreadsheet, as described in the next section.

Changing the Response to Overflow

It is easy to set options to handle any overflow conditions automatically. Suppose the SELECT formula that follows were written in cell A6:

```
$SELECT * INTO &a6.a10 FROM PROPERTY
```

The number of selected rows (all records from the property database) would exceed the five rows (&a6.a10) set aside in the SELECT formula. To force SQL*Calc to "open up" the needed extra spreadsheet rows automatically, execute the SQL*Calc command **/OOO** (Oracle Options Overflow) to change the default action taken when there is overflow. Next, indicate the SQL cell or cell range for which this option applies (type A6 or a larger cell range to encompass more SQL cells) and press Enter (see Figure 16.15a, b, and c). Then select the Insert overflow option and press Y for Yes (see Figure 16.15d and e). After you press Enter to lock in your choices, the SQL SELECT formula overflow option is changed so that extra database rows are inserted into newly created spreadsheet rows; all SQL statements and other formulas in displaced rows are copied. The new SQL options indicator for the SELECT formula is

```
(SQL,IY,A)=
```

where "I" indicates Insert and "Y" indicates Yes—copy formulas and SQL statements. This changed form of the SELECT statement indicator is shown in the Status Line of Figure 16.15f.

Changing the Response to Underflow

If you execute a SELECT statement such as

```
$SELECT SUM(PRICE) INTO &a10.a19 FROM PROPERTY
```

the resulting total value of the PROPERTY table's column is placed into cell A10. Only one row (and one column, the average) will be returned by the Oracle RDBMS. However, the INTO clause specifying the spreadsheet cell range provides more cells than necessary. In this example, ten rows (cells A10 through A19) are available, but

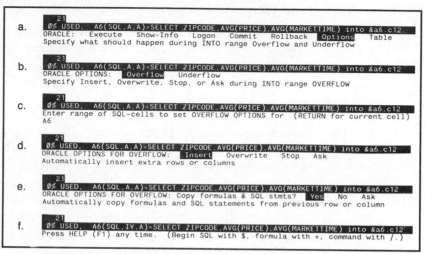

Figure 16.15: Setting SQL SELECT formula overflow options

only one row is required to hold the retrieved value. Because of this, SQL*Calc displays a message in the Status Line asking how to handle the underflow condition. You can take one of two actions. You can either delete extra spreadsheet rows in the INTO range or stop the retrieval operation without further processing, leaving the INTO range as it was originally in the SELECT statement. In either case, the extra rows (nine in our example) are blanked—that is, data previously stored in rows 11 through 19 is erased.

SQL*Calc asks which of the preceding two options it should invoke. If you place your spreadsheet cursor on the SELECT cell, the Status Line will display the selected overflow and underflow options. If the previous SELECT statement were placed in cell A6, the Status Line associated with cell A6 would display

```
A6(SQL,IY,A)=SELECT SUM(PRICE) INTO &a10.a19 FROM PROPERTY
```

The third character group inside the parentheses displays the underflow option "A." Changing this option from Ask to either Delete (D) or Stop (S) allows SQL*Calc to deal with underflow without pausing to ask you what to do. Changing this option is similar to changing the overflow option.

SQL SELECT underflow options are set by executing the SQL*Calc Oracle Options Underflow command (type **/OOU**).

When you type **/O**, this prompt line appears at the bottom of screen:

```
ORACLE: Execute  Show-Info  Logon  Commit  Rollback  Options  Table
```

Enter O for Options, and the Prompt Line changes to

```
ORACLE OPTIONS:  Overflow  Underflow
```

Enter U for Underflow, and the Prompt Line becomes

```
Enter range of SQL-cells to set UNDERFLOW OPTIONS for (RETURN for current cell)
```

Enter the cell or cell range desired (for example, A6 for the spreadsheet SQL cell shown in Figure 16.14) and press Enter. The Prompt Line will change to:

```
ORACLE OPTIONS FOR UNDERFLOW:  Delete  Stop  Ask
```

You can press D or the Delete option, S for Stop, or A for Ask. Press D to select Delete. The operation is complete, and the Status Line displays the message "Oracle operation performed." The cell contents line shown in the Status Line now displays

```
A6(SQL,IY,D)=
```

and indicates that overflow will cause insertion and SQL statements and formulas will be copied ("IY"). The underflow indicator "D" indicates that unneeded spreadsheet rows will be deleted automatically. If particular overflow and underflow options should be changed for all SELECT formulas in a spreadsheet, you can type in a large cell range as you set each option.

RETRIEVING ROWS WITH THE WHERE CLAUSE

You can restrict which rows of tables are retrieved by using the optional WHERE clause in SELECT statements. The expression that follows the word WHERE sets the criteria that determine whether or not a given row is retrieved. For example, the statement

```
$SELECT * FROM PROPERTY WHERE PRICE > 150000
```

retrieves all table columns for properties whose sale price is greater than $150,000.

To retrieve the number of properties sold in each zipcode area (and complete the Units Sold column of the sales summary spreadsheet), first position the spreadsheet cursor in cell D6. The Oracle function COUNT(*) retrieves and displays the number of rows in a selected zipcode area. An appropriate WHERE clause for restricting the count to zipcode 92010 is WHERE ZIPCODE = 92010. However, observe that zipcodes are already present in the Zipcode column of our spreadsheet, having been retrieved by a previous SQL SELECT operation. You can take advantage of this fact by creating a WHERE clause that refers to an existing spreadsheet cell: WHERE ZIPCODE = &a6.

The complete SELECT statement placed in cell D6 to count units sold in selected zipcodes is:

```
$SELECT COUNT(*) FROM PROPERTY WHERE ZIPCODE = &a6
```

Note that the zipcode cell reference (a6) is preceded with an ampersand and is written in lowercase. This is important when you create clones of this statement in cells D7 through D12, because SQL*Calc will adjust any lowercase cell references in formulas. When the D6 formula is copied to cells D7 through D12, the zipcode cell reference will be adjusted to a7, a8, and so on. If the WHERE clause were

```
WHERE ZIPCODE = &A6
```

the cell reference would not be adjusted when the entire SELECT statement were copied to other cells.

After you enter the previous SELECT statement into cell D6, press Enter. Oracle quickly computes the number of units sold in zipcode 92010 and places the result in cell D6. Figure 16.16 shows the resulting spreadsheet (see cell D6). The contents of cell D6 is the SELECT statement. Its displayed value, however, is 3. Both a cell's contents (underlying formulas or expressions) and its displayed values can co-reside in a cell.

To retrieve the remaining count values of properties in particular zipcodes, copy the SQL formula in cell D6 to cells D7 through D12.

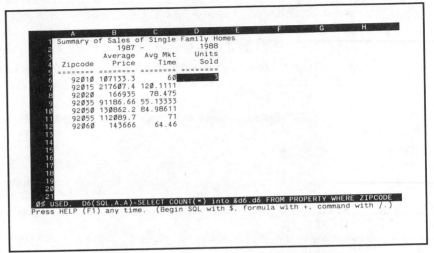

Figure 16.16: WHERE clause containing spreadsheet cell reference

COPYING SQL SELECT STATEMENTS TO OTHER CELLS

Like other cells in your spreadsheet, cells containing SQL statements can be copied to other cells. Any relative cell references contained within SQL statements are adjusted after they are copied. Relative cell references are written in lowercase. Absolute cell references are written in uppercase and are not changed. Cell D6 contains the result of the SELECT formula shown in the Status Line of Figure 16.16. The complete formula reads:

```
$SELECT COUNT(*) FROM PROPERTY WHERE ZIPCODE = &a6
```

The reference to the Zipcode column cell a6 (&a6) establishes what values are retrieved by the SELECT statement. To determine the number of units sold for other zipcodes, you can copy the SQL SELECT statement in D6 to cells D7 through D12. The copied SELECT statements will each refer to the zipcode in their row.

To copy one or more cells to other locations, execute the Copy command. After typing **/C**, enter the FROM address (the cell or cell range to be copied), press Enter, enter the to address, and press Enter again. To copy cell D6 to the cell range D7 through D12, type **/C**, enter the FROM cell range **A6** and press Enter. Then, type **D7.D12** and press Enter. The SELECT statement in cell D6 is copied to the six cells D7 through D12 after you press Enter following the to range. Figure 16.17 shows the spreadsheet after the Copy operation.

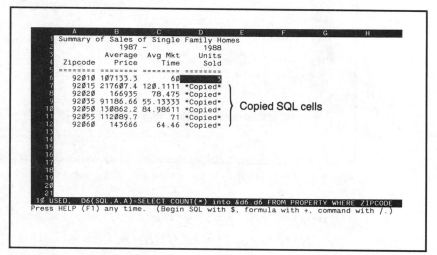

Figure 16.17: Copying SQL statements

Notice that cells D7 through D12 contain the special mark *Copied*. This always indicates cells that contain copies of SQL statements that have not been executed. In other words, even though you copied SQL statements to these cells, Oracle has not been instructed to carry them out and retrieve data. For example, cell D12 contains the statement

```
$SELECT COUNT(*) FROM PROPERTY WHERE ZIPCODE = &a12
```

However, since that SELECT statement has not been invoked SQL*Calc cannot yet display a value for the cell.

You can execute cells containing the *Copied* indicator in one of three ways. You can move the cursor to the cell, execute the edit command (press function key F2 on the PC), and then press Enter. The unchanged SQL statement is then executed by Oracle. It is more efficient, especially if there are several copied SQL statements, to execute the SQL*Calc Oracle Execute Copied command (type / **OEC**), which executes any cell containing the *Copied* indicator.

Oracle is invoked to retrieve the results for SQL SELECT cells that have been copied. The quickest way to force *Copied* cells to be executed is to press the special function key *Copied* (F10 on the IBM PC), which executes all copied SQL statements in the spreadsheet. Appendix E has a complete list of the special SQL*Calc function keys and the action that each performs.

To have Oracle retrieve data and fill cells D7 through D12, press the *Copied* function key to execute all cells containing the *Copied* indicator. Oracle will complete its work and fill in values, one by one, for D7 through D12. Figure 16.18 shows the results after the copied cells are executed.

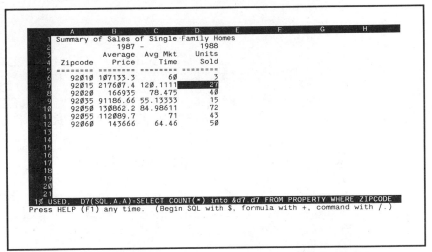

Figure 16.18: Executing copied cells with Oracle Execute Copied

To complete the sales summary spreadsheet, add one more column that shows total sales volume for each zipcode area. Place the text labels **Total** in cell E3 and **Value** in cell E4. Put the repeating text " = = = = = = = = =" in cell E5 (type \ =). Then type the SELECT statement

```
$SELECT SUM(PRICE) FROM PROPERTY WHERE ZIPCODE = &a6
```

into cell E6 and press Enter. Be careful to type the zipcode cell reference as &a6, not &A6. Copy this formula into cells E7 through E12.

Finally, instruct Oracle to execute the copied formulas by either executing the Oracle Execute Copied command (type **/OEC**) or pressing the *Copied* key. The resulting total sales by zipcode are calculated by Oracle and placed into cells E7 through E12.

Calculating Statistics with MIN, AVG, and MAX

Statistics about minimum, average, and maximum values for sale prices, market times, and units sold would be useful. You can use the Oracle database aggregate functions MIN, AVG, and MAX to calculate these statistics. Place the labels Min:, Avg, and Max: in cells A14, A15, and A15. Three SELECT statements and the cells containing them are:

CELL	SELECT STATEMENT
B14	$SELECT MIN(PRICE), MIN(MARKETTIME) INTO &b14.c14 FROM PROPERTY
B15	$SELECT AVG(PRICE), AVG(MARKETTIME) INTO &b15.c15 FROM PROPERTY
B16	$SELECT MAX(PRICE), MAX(MARKETTIME) INTO &b16.c16 FROM PROPERTY

Once these three SELECT statements are executed, the values for minimum price and market time, average price and market time, and maximum price and market time are displayed in cells B14 through C16.

Because the Units Sold column was not derived from any column of the PROPERTY table, you cannot use the AVG or MIN functions to generate its minimum, average, and maximum values. Instead, SQL*Calc functions will be used to calculate these results from the spreadsheet itself. Enter the three SQL*Calc functions **+MIN(d6.d12)**, **+AVG(d6.d12)**, and **+MAX(d6.d12)** into cells D14 through D16, respectively.

If you want to simplify the way values are displayed, make all spreadsheet values integer values (they are just summary values, after all) by executing the Layout Width Integer command (type **/LWI**). Remember to press Enter at the end of the command. All values are now displayed as rounded integers, and the spreadsheet is considerably neater and more understandable. For an overview of all of the SQL*Calc commands, see Appendix E. Also look for the *Oracle Command Map*, a handy tree-structured guide to the commands in the same appendix.

Figure 16.19 shows the completed spreadsheet with all statistics. The database-retrieved statistics are in cells B14 through C16, and similarly named SQL*Calc functions are in cells D14 through D16 with their displayed results shown.

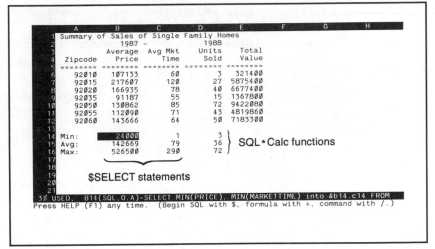

Figure 16.19: Completed single-family sales spreadsheet

STAYING UP-TO-DATE: RE-EXECUTING QUERIES

The data in Oracle RDBMS databases is continually being altered: rows are updated, values for various columns are changed, and rows are deleted. In spreadsheets, the ability to always have current data fosters the use of shareable and up-to-date information. However, you must remember to always ensure that your spreadsheet contains accurate, up-to-the-minute information.

Spreadsheets that contain one or more SELECT statements can get out of date. Once you store your spreadsheet with the File Save Command (/FS), the information it contains does not change. When you retrieve the spreadsheet to work on it later, the underlying database information will probably have changed. There is a simple and efficient way to ensure that your spreadsheet remains up-to-date.

Whenever you load in a spreadsheet with the File Retrieve command (/FR), always press the Query key to reexecute all the SELECT statements stored in your spreadsheet (press the F7 function key on an IBM PC). Alternately, you can execute the Oracle Execute Select command (type **/OES**) to reexecute all SELECT statements in your spreadsheet.

CREATING NEW DATABASE TABLES AND INSERTING DATA

Suppose that you want to copy the real estate sales summary data into another spreadsheet. SQL*Calc provides a way for different spreadsheets and users to share data. With a few simple SQL*Calc commands, you can create a database table from a SQL*Calc spreadsheet. You can then retrieve the table into another spreadsheet or make it available to other users.

You can create an Oracle table from a spreadsheet with the Oracle Table command (type **/OT**). You will do so with the spreadsheet shown in Figure 16.19. The new table, stored and maintained as a relational database by Oracle, will be called SALESUMM. Figure 16.20 shows each step involved in creating this table.

Begin by typing **/OT** to execute the SQL*Calc Oracle Table command (see Figure 16.20a). Next, enter the name of the database table to be created:

SALESUMM

and press Enter (see Figure 16.20b). The name can be up to 30 characters long. Define the cell range containing the labels in your spreadsheet. These will become the table column names. Be sure that each designated cell in the range contains a text label that is unique among the chosen names, because table column names must be unique within a given table. (All lowercase letters in the spreadsheet range of names are translated into uppercase table column names). Press Enter after typing the cell range. The values in cells A4 through E4—zipcode, price, time, sold, and value—are selected for your column names (see Figure 16.20c).

Next, designate the range of spreadsheet cells containing the data to be inserted into the table. Since cells A6 through E12 (see Figure 16.19) are the data values to be stored, type **A6.E12** and press Enter (see Figure 16.20d).

Once you have entered the table name, column name range, and data range, Oracle creates the table and fills it with rows of data from your spreadsheet. The message "Creating table SALESUMM" appears at the bottom of the SQL*Calc screen briefly during the process (see Figure 16.20e). When the message "Table created and data inserted" appears in the spreadsheet Status Line, the table is complete (see Figure 16.20f).

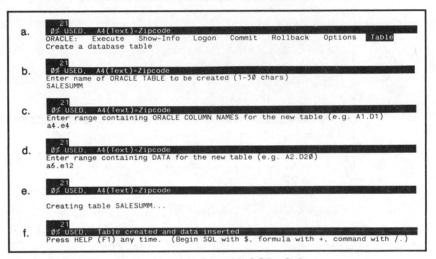

Figure 16.20: Creating an Oracle table with SQL*Calc

A quick way to check that the sales summary spreadsheet data is stored in an Oracle table is to retrieve it into an empty spreadsheet. Execute the Worksheet Erase command (type **/WE**) and place the command

```
$SELECT * FROM SALESUMM
```

in any cell to retrieve all database rows and columns.

Another test would be to erase the spreadsheet, type the incorrect SELECT statement that follows into cell A1, and press Enter:

```
$SELECT * FROM SALESUM
```

(The table name is misspelled on purpose). The error screen displaces the spreadsheet temporarily and indicates the problem: the table does not exist (see Figure 16.21). Edit the SELECT statement (press the Edit key, F2 on the IBM PC), by adding the missing "M" to the table name and press Enter to store the changed SELECT statement back into the cell.

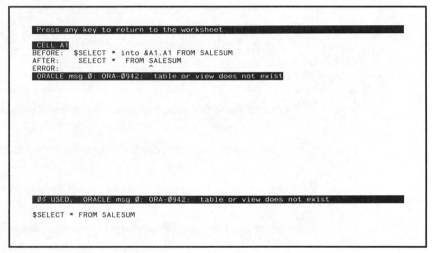

Figure 16.21: Error screen

Once you correct the SELECT statement, Oracle retrieves all data from SALESUMM and returns it to cells A1 through E8. The table is now easily retrieved. Other users can access the SALESUMM table once you grant them access to it. Furthermore, any of your spreadsheets can access the table.

UPDATING DATABASE ROWS

You can alter database information from within SQL*Calc using the standard UPDATE statement. Like the SELECT statement, the UPDATE statement is preceded by a $ so that SQL*Calc reads it as an Oracle database command. As you have learned, the syntax for the UPDATE statement is

```
UPDATE table-name SET column-name = value WHERE condition
```

The WHERE clause is optional but is part of most UPDATE statements. *Table-name* is the name of the table to be updated, and *column-name* is a column of the table whose value is to be altered to *value*.

Because the PRICE column of the SALESUMM table needs to be accurate only to the nearest thousand dollars, the PRICE column values from the spreadsheet will be rounded. Then, the rounded values will replace the unrounded values in the SALESUMM table. You do this in four steps:

1. In the spreadsheet, create a new column with rounded price values.

2. Write an UPDATE statement to replace the table value with that of the spreadsheet.

3. Copy the UPDATE formula for the other rows' price values.

4. Execute the copied UPDATE statements and thereby replace the remaining price values in the SALESUMM table with those from the spreadsheet.

Place the formula **+ INT((&b2 + 500)/1000)*1000** into cell F2. Because SQL*Calc does not have the Lotus 1-2-3 equivalent function of @ROUND, a rounded value can be calculated by the preceding formula which rounds the value in cell B2 to the nearest thousand. Copy the formula down the cell range F3 through F8.

Now that you have created the replacement values for the PRICE column, you can write the UPDATE statement in cell G2. Type the formula:

```
$UPDATE SALESUMM SET PRICE=&f2 WHERE ZIPCODE=&a2
```

in cell G2 and press Enter. Oracle executes the UPDATE statement passed to it from SQL*Calc and replaces the price value in the row of the SALESUMM table whose zipcode equals that found in cell A2 (92010).

Copy the UPDATE statement from G2 to cells G3 through G8 (see Figure 16.22). As before, the *Copied* indicator means that an unexecuted SQL statement is in the cell. Execute all of the remaining UPDATE statements (those in cells marked with *Copied*) by pressing the *Copied* key (function key F10 on the IBM PC). Oracle updates the remaining PRICE column entries for zipcodes 92015 through 92060.

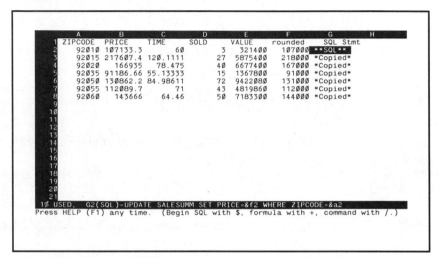

Figure 16.22: Copied UPDATE statements

Now all of the price values have been altered to contain rounded values obtained from a SQL*Calc spreadsheet. If you wish to verify the updates, type

```
$SELECT * FROM SALESUMM
```

in any empty spreadsheet cell and check the retrieved price values. A good way to practice the UPDATE statement is to round the TIME column values to the nearest integer and replace the SALE-SUMM column TIME with the new, rounded market time values.

OTHER DATABASE OPERATIONS

You can use any of the ANSI SQL statements described in the early chapters of this book in a SQL*Calc spreadsheet. These include statements such as INSERT and DELETE. Note, however, that these statements are unlike the SQL*Calc commands Worksheet Insert (/WI) and Worksheet Delete (/WD). The latter affect a spreadsheet only, whereas the former affect Oracle database tables. An example INSERT statement using the SALESUMM table is:

```
$INSERT INTO SALESUMM VALUES (&a9.e9)
```

where cells A9 through E9 contain data for a new database row (zipcode, price, time, and so on).

Deleting rows from database tables is equally easy. The general syntax for the DELETE command is:

```
$DELETE FROM table-name WHERE condition
```

where *table-name* is the Oracle table and *condition* is the selection criterion specifying which rows to delete. Be careful. If you omit the optional WHERE clause, *all* database rows will be deleted! You probably will never want to execute the statement

```
$DELETE FROM SALESUMM
```

because it deletes all of the database rows. However, if you have no more use for a particular database table, use the DROP TABLE command instead of deleting all the rows from the table:

```
$DROP TABLE table-name
```

where *table-name* is the table to be dropped (deleted entirely) from the system. You could delete The SALESUMM table by typing

```
$DROP TABLE SALESUMM
```

Should you forget what tables you have stored in the Oracle system, the SQL*Calc command Oracle Show-Info My-Tables (press /OSM) will display a list of database tables that you have created.

If you delete rows or entire tables by mistake, a SQL*Calc command, Oracle Rollback (type /OR), reverses any database activities since the last committed change. For example, if you wish to restore to a table several deleted rows, execute the Rollback command. You must execute this SQL*Calc command before too many other database commands are executed, otherwise Oracle will be unable to restore deleted records or dropped tables.

The SQL*Calc command Oracle Commit /OC makes all changes permanent. By executing the Commit command, you affirm that the changes to that point are correct and should be retained.

*LEAVING SQL*CALC*

When you execute the Quit command (type **/Q**) and then press Y to confirm, control goes back to the host operating system. Before you leave SQL*Calc, be sure to save your spreadsheet. Otherwise, you will lose any work that you have done between when you loaded it (**/FR**) and when you quit.

SUMMARY

This chapter covered the SQL*Calc spreadsheet available from Oracle. SQL*Calc is similar to Lotus 1-2-3, but can access much larger databases and run on a wider variety of machines. SQL*Calc is also capable of producing multiuser spreadsheets that are always accurate and up-to-date.

ORACLE'S
RESERVED WORDS

The following words are reserved in SQL*Plus and are not acceptable as names of database objects.

ACCESS	CREATE	FROM	LOCK	OR	START
ADD	CURRENT	GRANT	LONG	ORDER	SUCCESSFUL
ALL	DATAPAGES	GRAPHIC	MAXEXTENTS	PARTITION	SYNONYM
ALTER	DATE	GROUP	MINUS	PCTFREE	SYSDATE
AND	DBA	HAVING	MODE	PRIOR	SYSSORT
ANY	DECIMAL	IDENTIFIED	MODIFY	PRIVILEGES	TABLE
APPEND	DEFAULT	IF	MOVE	PUBLIC	TEMPORARY
AS	DEFINITION	IMAGE	NEW	RAW	THEN
ASC	DELETE	IMMEDIATE	NOAUDIT	RENAME	TO
ASSERT	DESC	IN	NOCOMPRESS	REPLACE	TRIGGER
ASSIGN	DISTINCT	INCREMENT	NOLIST	RESOURCE	UID
AUDIT	DOES	INDEX	NOSYSSORT	REVOKE	UNION
BETWEEN	DROP	INDEXED	NOT	ROW	UNIQUE
BY	EACH	INDEXPAGES	NOWAIT	ROWID	UPDATE
CHAR	ELSE	INITIAL	NULL	ROWNUM	USER
CLUSTER	ERASE	INSERT	NUMBER	ROWS	USING
COLUMN	EVALUATE	INTEGER	OF	RUN	VALIDATE
COMMENT	EXCLUSIVE	INTERSECT	OFFLINE	SELECT	VALUES
COMPRESS	EXISTS	INTO	OLD	SESSION	VARCHAR
CONNECT	FILE	IS	ON	SET	VARGRAPHIC
CONTAIN	FLOAT	LEVEL	ONLINE	SHARE	VIEW
CONTAINS	FOR	LIKE	OPTIMIZE	SIZE	WHENEVER
CRASH	FORMAT	LIST	OPTION	SMALLINT	WHERE
				SPACE	WITH

DATA DICTIONARY
VIEWS

TABLE NAME	DESCRIPTION AND COMMENTS
AUDIT_ACCESS	Audit entries for accesses to user's tables/views (DBA sees all)
AUDIT_ACTIONS	Maps auditing action numbers to action names
AUDIT_CONNECT	Audit trail entries for user logon/logoff (DBA sees all)
AUDIT_DBA	Audit trail entries for DBA activities (for DBA use only)
AUDIT_EXISTS	Audit trail entries for objects that do not exist (for DBA use only)
AUDIT_TRAIL	Audit trail entries relevant to the user (DBA sees all)
CATALOG	Tables and views accessible to user (excluding data dictionary)
CLUSTERCOLUMNS	Maps cluster columns to clustered table columns
CLUSTERS	Clusters and their tables (either must be accessible to user)
COL	Specifications of columns in tables created by the user
COLUMNS	Columns in tables accessible to user (excluding data dictionary)
DBLINKS	Public and private links to external databases
DEFAULT_AUDIT	Default table auditing options
DTAB	Description of tables and views in Oracle data dictionary
EXTENTS	Data structure of extents within tables
INDEXES	Indexes created by user and indexes on tables created by user

TABLE NAME	DESCRIPTION AND COMMENTS
PARTITIONS	File structure of files within partitions (for DBA use only)
PRIVATESYN	Private synonyms created by the user
PUBLICSYN	Public synonyms
SESSIONS	Audit trail entries for the user's sessions (DBA sees all)
SPACES	Selection of space definitions for creating tables and clusters
STORAGE	Data and Index storage allocation for user's own tables
SYNONYMS	Synonyms, private and public
SYSAUDIT_TRAIL	Synonym for SYS.AUDIT_TRAIL (for DBA use only)
SYSCATALOG	Profile of tables and views accessible to the user
SYSCOLAUTH	Directory of column update access granted by or to the user
SYSCOLUMNS	Specifications of columns in accessible tables and views
SYSDBLINKS	All links to external databases (for DBA use only)
SYSEXTENTS	Data structure of tables throughout system (for DBA use only)
SYSINDEXES	List of indexes, underlying columns, creator, and options
SYSPROGS	List of programs precompiled by user
SYSSTORAGE	Summary of all database storage (for DBA use only)
SYSTABALLOC	Data and index space allocations for all tables (for DBA use only)

TABLE NAME	DESCRIPTION AND COMMENTS
SYSTABAUTH	Directory of access authorization granted by or to the user
SYSTEM_AUDIT	System auditing options (for DBA use only)
SYSUSERAUTH	Master list of Oracle users (for DBA use only)
SYSUSERLIST	List of Oracle users
SYSVIEWS	List of accessible views
TAB	List of tables, views, clusters, and synonyms created by the user
TABALLOC	Data and index space allocations for all users' tables
TABLE_AUDIT	Auditing options of user's tables and views (DBA sees all)
TABQUOTAS	Table allocation (space) parameters for tables created by user
VIEWS	Defining SQL statements for views created by the user

SQL AND SQL*PLUS
REFERENCE

SQL COMMANDS

COMMAND	DESCRIPTION
ALTER PARTITION	Adds a file to a database partition
ALTER SPACE	Alters a space definition
ALTER TABLE	Adds a column to, or redefines a column in, an existing table
AUDIT	Audits use of a table, view, synonym, or system facility
COMMENT	Inserts into the data dictionary a comment about a table or column
CREATE CLUSTER	Creates a cluster which may contain two or more tables
CREATE DATABASE LINK	Creates a link to a user name in a remote database
CREATE INDEX	Creates an index for a table
CREATE PARTITION	Creates a new partition in the database
CREATE SPACE	Creates a space definition which then may be used to define the space allocation properties of a table
CREATE SYNONYM	Creates a synonym for a table or view name
CREATE TABLE	Creates a table and defines its columns and other properties
CREATE VIEW	Defines a view of one or more tables or other views
DELETE	Deletes one or more rows from a table or view
DROP	Deletes a cluster, database link, index, space definition, synonym, table, or view from the database
GRANT	Grants system and object database privileges to users

COMMAND	DESCRIPTION
INSERT	Adds new rows to a table or view
LOCK TABLE	Permits shared access to the table by multiple users while preserving the table's integrity
NOAUDIT	Partially or completely reverses the effect of a prior AUDIT command or of auditing options in the default table. Oracle ceases auditing the use of a table, view, synonym, or system facility
RENAME	Changes the name of a table, view, or synonym
REVOKE	Revokes database system or object access privileges from users
SELECT	Performs a query and selects rows and columns from one or more tables or views
UPDATE	Changes the values of fields in a table or view
VALIDATE INDEX	Checks the integrity of a table index

SQL COMMAND SYNTAX

DATA MANIPULATION AND RETRIEVAL COMMANDS

```
DELETE
FROM      table
[WHERE    condition];


INSERT
INTO      table [ (column [,column]...) ]
VALUES    (value [,value]...);
or
INSERT
INTO      table [ (column [,column]...) ]
query;
```

```
SELECT      [ALL | DISTINCT] {[table.]* | expression [alias],...}
FROM        table [alias] [,table [alias]]...
[WHERE      condition]
[CONNECT BY condition [START WITH condition]]
[GROUP      BY expr [,expr]... [HAVING condition]]
[ORDER      BY {expr | position} [ASC | DESC] [,{expr | position}
            [ASC | DESC]]...]
[{UNION | INTERSECT | MINUS} query]
[FOR UPDATE OF column [,column]... [NOWAIT]];


UPDATE      table [alias]
SET         column = expression [,column = expression]...
[WHERE      condition];
or
UPDATE      table [alias]
SET         (column [,column]...) = (query)
[WHERE      condition];
```

DATA DEFINITION COMMANDS

ALTER PARTITION *partition* ADD FILE *text*;

```
ALTER SPACE  [DEFINITION] sname
[DATAPAGES    ([INITIAL {5 | n}] [INCREMENT {25 | n}]
               [MAXEXTENTS {9999 | n}] [PCTFREE {20 | n}] )]
[INDEXPAGES  ([INITIAL {5 | n}] [INCREMENT {25 | n}]
               [MAXEXTENTS {9999 | n}] )]
[PARTITION {SYSTEM | pname}];


ALTER TABLE table
ADD          (column spec [NULL | NOT NULL]
              [,column spec [NULL | NOT NULL]]...);
or
ALTER TABLE table
MODIFY       (column [spec] [NULL | NOT NULL]
              [,column [spec] [NULL | NOT NULL]]...);
```

COMMENT ON {TABLE *table* | COLUMN *table.column*} IS *comment-characters*;

```
CREATE CLUSTER cluster
(column spec [,column spec]…)
[SIZE n] [SPACE space] [COMPRESS | NOCOMPRESS];

CREATE [PUBLIC] DATABASE LINK link
CONNECT TO user IDENTIFIED BY password USING 'database';

CREATE [UNIQUE] INDEX indexname
ON table (column [ASC | DESC] [,column [ASC | DESC]]…)
[COMPRESS | NOCOMPRESS]
[SYSSORT | NOSYSSORT]
[ROWS = n] [PFTREE = {20 | n}];

CREATE PARTITION name;

CREATE SPACE [DEFINITION] sname
[DATAPAGES    ([INITIAL {5 | n}] [INCREMENT {25 | n}]
                [MAXEXTENTS {9999 | n}] [PCTFREE {20 | n}] )]
[INDEXPAGES ([INITIAL {5 | n}] [INCREMENT {25 | n}]
                [MAXEXTENTS {9999 | n}] )]
[PARTITION {SYSTEM | pname}];

CREATE [PUBLIC] SYNONYM synonym FOR
[username.]table[@database];
CREATE TABLE table (column spec [NOT NULL]
                    [,column spec [NOT NULL]…] )
[[SPACE space-definition] [PCTFREE n] |
  CLUSTER cluster (column [,column]…)];
or
CREATE TABLE table (column [NOT NULL]
                    [,column [NOT NULL]…] )
[[SPACE space-definition] [PCTFREE n] |
  CLUSTER cluster (column [,column]…)]
[AS query];

CREATE VIEW view-name [(alias [,alias]…)]
AS query
[WITH CHECK OPTION];
```

```
DROP {  CLUSTER cluster                          |
        [PUBLIC] DATABASE LINK link              |
        INDEX index [ON table]                   |
        SPACE [DEFINITION] space-name            |
        [PUBLIC] SYNONYM synonym-name            |
        TABLE table                              |
        VIEW view            };
```

RENAME *old-name* TO *new-name*;

VALIDATE INDEX *index* [ON *table*] [WITH LIST];

DATA CONTROL COMMANDS

AUDIT {*option* [,*option*]... | ALL}
[ON {*table* | DEFAULT} [BY {ACCESS | SESSION}]]
[WHENEVER [NOT] SUCCESSFUL];

GRANT CONNECT [,RESOURCE] [,DBA]
TO *user* [,*user*]...
IDENTIFIED BY *password* [,*password*]...;
or
GRANT { *privilege* [,*privilege*]... | ALL}
ON *table*
TO {*user* [,*user*]... | PUBLIC}
[WITH GRANT OPTION];

LOCK TABLE *table* [,*table*]...
IN {SHARE | SHARE UPDATE | EXCLUSIVE} MODE [NOWAIT];

NOAUDIT {*option* [,*option*]... | ALL}
[ON {*table* | DEFAULT}]
[WHENEVER [NOT] SUCCESSFUL];

REVOKE [CONNECT] [,RESOURCE] [,DBA]
FROM *user* [,*user*]...;
or
REVOKE { *privilege* [,*privilege*]... | ALL}
ON *table*
FROM {*user* [,*user*]... | PUBLIC};

SQL *PLUS COMMANDS

COMMAND	DESCRIPTION
@	Runs a command file
#	Ends a sequence of comment lines begun by a DOCUMENT command
$	Executes a host operating system command line without leaving SQL*Plus (equivalent to the HOST command)
/	Runs the SQL command in the SQL buffer
/* ... */	Defines a comment within a SQL command
ACCEPT	Prompts the user for input and assigns the response as the value of a user variable
APPEND	Appends text to the end of the current line in the current buffer
BREAK	Specifies what events will cause a break and what action SQL is to perform when a break occurs
BTITLE	Makes SQL display a title at the bottom of each page of a report
CHANGE	Changes the contents of the current line of the current buffer
CLEAR	Clears break definitions, current buffer text, column definitions, and so on.
COLUMN	Specifies how a column and column heading should be formatted in a report
COMMIT	Makes permanent the changes made to the database since the last COMMIT
COMPUTE	Performs computations on groups of selected rows
CONNECT	Logs users off of and back on to Oracle (with a specified username)
COPY	Creates data from one SQL*Net database to another

COMMAND	DESCRIPTION
DEFINE	Designates a user variable and assigns it a character value
DEL	Deletes the current line of the current buffer
DESCRIBE	Displays a brief description of a table
DISCONNECT	Commits pending work to the database and logs user off of Oracle; does not terminate SQL*Plus
DOCUMENT	Begins a block of documentation in a command file
EDIT	Invokes the host system's standard text editor on the contents of the current buffer
EXIT	Terminates SQL*Plus and returns control to the operating system
GET	Loads file into the current buffer
HELP	Displays information about a SQL or SQL*Plus command
HOST	Executes a host operating system command line without leaving SQL (equivalent to the $ command)
INPUT	Adds new lines after the current line in the current buffer
LIST	Lists lines of the current buffer
NEWPAGE	Advances spooled output to the beginning of the next page (obsolete; avoid whenever possible)
PAUSE	Displays a message and then waits for Enter to be pressed
QUIT	Terminates SQL*Plus and returns control to the operating system (equivalent to the EXIT command)
REMARK	Begins a comment in a command file (similar to /*...*/)
ROLLBACK	Rolls back and discards changes made to the database since the most recent COMMIT

COMMAND	DESCRIPTION
RUN	Displays and then runs the command in the SQL buffer
SAVE	Saves the contents of the current buffer in the database or in an operating system file
SET	Sets a SQL parameter to a specified value
SHOW	Displays the setting of a SQL parameter or SQL*Plus property (such as the current release number)
SPOOL	Manages spooling of displayed output to a system file or system printer
SQLPLUS	Begins executing the SQL*Plus interface interpreter
START	Executes the contents of a command file stored as an operating system file
TIMING	Provides SQL command and command file performance analysis
TTITLE	Makes SQL display a title at the top of each page of output
UNDEFINE	Deletes the definition of a user-defined variable

SQL*PLUS BUILT-IN FUNCTIONS

ARITHMETIC FUNCTIONS

FUNCTION	DESCRIPTION
ABS (n)	Absolute value of n
CEIL (n)	Smallest integer greater than or equal to n
FLOOR(n)	Largest integer less than or equal to n
MOD(m,n)	Remainder of m divided by n
POWER(m,n)	Raise m to the nth power; n must be an integer

FUNCTION	DESCRIPTION
ROUND(n,m)	Round n to m decimal places (if m is omitted, value is rounded to zero decimal places)
SIGN(n)	If $n < 0$, then -1; if $n = 0$, then 0; if $n > 0$, then 1
SQRT(n)	Square root of n. If n is negative, NULL is returned
TRUNC(n,m)	Truncate value n to m decimal places; if m is omitted, n is truncated to zero decimal places

CHARACTER STRING FUNCTIONS

FUNCTION	DESCRIPTION
ASCII(*char*)	ASCII value of *first* character of string *char*
CHR(n)	Character with ASCII value numeric n
INITCAP(*char*)	Capitalize first character of string
INSTR(*char1*,*char2*,*n*,*m*)	Position of the *m*th occurrence of *char2* in *char1* beginning with position n; if m or n is omitted, 1 is assumed; position is given relative to the first character of *char1*, even when $n > 1$
LENGTH(*char*)	Length in characters of string
LOWER(*char*)	Force all characters of string to lowercase
LPAD(*char1*,*n*,*char2*)	Left pad *char1* to length n with the sequence of characters in *char2*; if *char2* is omitted, the padding character is blank
LTRIM(*char*,*set*)	Remove initial characters up to the first character not in the string *set*
RPAD(*char1*,*n*,*char2*)	Right pad character string *char1* to length n with sequence of characters in *char2*; if *char2* is omitted, blanks are used for padding
RTRIM(*char*,*set*)	Remove final characters after the last character not in the string *set*

FUNCTION	DESCRIPTION
SOUNDEX(*char*)	A character string representing the sound of the words in the string *char*
SUBSTR(*char,m,n*)	A substring of *char* beginning at the character *m* and that is *n* characters long; if *n* is omitted, the substring continues to the end of *char*
TRANSLATE(*char, from,to*)	Translate *char* from the character set *from* to the character set *to*
UPPER(*char*)	Force all letters in the string to uppercase
USERENV(*char*)	Return information about the user that is useful for writing an application-specific audit trail table

GROUP FUNCTIONS

FUNCTION	DESCRIPTION
AVG([DISTINCT | ALL] *n*)	Average value of *n*, ignoring null values
COUNT([DISTINCT | ALL] {* | *n*})	Number of times *n* evaluates to something other than NULL (asterisk makes COUNT count all selected rows)
MAX([DISTINCT | ALL] *expr*)	Maximum value of *expr*
MIN([DISTINCT | ALL] *expr*)	Minimum value of *expr*
STDDEV([DISTINCT | ALL] *n*)	Standard deviation of *n*, ignoring NULL values
SUM([DISTINCT | ALL] *n*)	Sum of values of *n*
VARIANCE([DISTINCT | ALL] *n*)	Variance of *n*, ignoring NULL values

CONVERSION FUNCTIONS

FUNCTION	DESCRIPTION
CHARTOROWID(*rowid*)	Converts a character value to a row ID
HEXTORAW(*char*)	Converts *char* containing a hexadecimal number to a binary value suitable for inclusion in a RAW type table column
RAWTOHEX(*raw*)	Converts *raw* to character value containing a hexadecimal number
ROWIDTOCHAR(*rowid*)	Converts a row ID to a character value
TO_CHAR(*expr, fmt*)	Converts the expression *expr* (a number or date value) to a character value in the format specified by the character string *fmt*; if *fmt* is omitted, a date is converted to default date format; a number is converted to a character value just wide enough to hold the significant digits
TO_DATE(*char, fmt*)	Converts a date from a character value to a date value; the character string *fmt* specifies the format of the character string to be converted; if *fmt* is omitted, the string *char* must be in default date format
TO_DATE(*n, fmt*)	Converts a number into a date
TO_NUMBER(*char*)	Converts the character string *char* to a number value; the string *char* must contain only digits

DATE FUNCTIONS

FUNCTION	DESCRIPTION
ADD_MONTHS(*d,n*)	Date *d* plus *n* months
LAST_DAY(*d*)	Date of last day of month containing *d*

FUNCTION	DESCRIPTION
MONTHS_BETWEEN(*d,e*)	Number of months between dates *d* and *e* (either positive or negative)
NEW_TIME(*d,a,b*)	Date and time in time zone *b* when date and time in time zone *a* is *d* (*a* and *b* are character values identifying time zones)
NEXT_DAY(*d,char*)	Date of first day of week named by character string *char* that is equal to or later than date *d*
TRUNC(*date*)	A date form in which the time of day is removed from *date*

MISCELLANEOUS FUNCTIONS

FUNCTION	DESCRIPTION
DECODE(*char,val,code,val,code,…,default*)	If *char* equals any *val*, the *code* that follows it is returned; if not, the *default* value is returned (*char* and *val* are character values; *code* and *default* are numeric values)
DUMP(*expr,radix,start-position,bytes*)	Displays the contents of Oracle internal data areas; all arguments except *expr* are optional
GREATEST(*expr,expr…*)	Returns the largest value of the list of numeric values
LEAST(*expr,expr…*)	Returns the smallest value of the list of numeric values
NVL(*x,expr*)	If *x* is null, the value of expression *expr* is returned; if *x* is not null, the value *x* is returned (*x* and *expr* may be of any type)

FUNCTION	DESCRIPTION
VSIZE(*expr*)	Returns the number of bytes in Oracle's internal representation of the expression *expr*

PSEUDO COLUMNS

LEVEL	Used in the SELECT...CONNECT BY command where 1 is the root node, 2 is the child of the root, and so on
NULL	Returns a null value; may be used in INSERT and other commands but not in logical expressions
ROWID	Returns the current row's internal row identification; ROWID is of type ROWID, not number or char
ROWNUM	Returns, beginning with 1, the order in which the current row was selected from the table
SYSDATE	Returns the current date and time
UID	Returns the numeric value identifying the current user
USER	Returns the name of the current user

——— SQL *PLUS SET SYSTEM VARIABLES ———

SYNTAX OF THE SQL *PLUS SET COMMAND

SET {? | HELP}; |

```
SET { ARRAYSIZE {20 | n}                                   |
      AUTO[COMMIT] {OFF | ON | IMM[EDIATE]}                |
      BUF[FER] buffer                                      |
      CMDS[EP] {; | c | OFF | ON}                          |
      CONCAT {. | c | OFF | ON}                            |
      COPYCOMMIT {0 | n}                                   |
      DCL[SEP] {! | c}                                     |
      DEF[INE] {& | c | OFF | ON}                          |
```

```
          DOC[UMENT] {OFF | ON}                        |
          ECH[OSET] {OFF | ON}                         |
          EMBEDDED {OFF | ON}                          |
          ESCAPE {c | OFF | ON}                        |
          FEED[BACK] {6 | n | OFF | ON}                |
          FLUSH {OFF | ON}                             |
          HEA[DING] {OFF | ON}                         |
          HEADS[EP] { | | c | OFF | ON}                |
          LIN[ESIZE] {80 | n}                          |
          LONG {80 | n}                                |
          MAXD[ATA] n                                  |
          NEWP[AGE] {1 | n}                            |
          NULL text                                    |
          NUMF[ORMAT] text                             |
          NUM[WIDTH] {10 | n}                          |
          PAGES[IZE] {14 | n}                          |
          PAU[SE] {OFF | ON | text}                    |
          SCAN {OFF | ON}                              |
          SHOW[MODE] {OFF | ON}                        |
          SPA[CE] {1 | n}                              |
          SQLC[ONTINUE] { ' > ' | char }               |
          SQLN[UMBER] {OFF | ON}                       |
          SQLPRE[FIX] {# | c}                          |
          SQLP[ROMPT] { SQL > | text}                  |
          SQLT[ERMINATOR] {; | c | OFF | ON}           |
          SUFFIX {SQL | text}                          |
          TAB {OFF | ON}                               |
          TERM[OUT] {OFF | ON}                         |
          TI[ME] {OFF | ON}                            |
          TIMI[NG] {OFF | ON}                          |
          TRIM[OUT] {OFF | ON}                         |
          TRU[NCATE] {OFF | ON}                        |
          UND[ERLINE] {- | c | ON | OFF}               |
          VER[IFY] {OFF | ON}                          |
          WRAP {OFF | ON}                            } ;
```

SQL*PLUS SET SYSTEM VARIABLE DESCRIPTIONS

ARRAYSIZE { <u>20</u> | *n* }

Sets the number of rows that may be fetched from the database at one time. Valid values are 1 to 5000. A large value increases the efficiency of queries and subqueries that fetch many rows, but requires more main memory in the host computer. ARRAYSIZE does not affect the results of SQL*Plus operations.

AUTO[COMMIT] { <u>OFF</u> | ON | IMM[EDIATE] }

ON or IMM makes SQL commit pending changes to the default database immediately after each command is executed. OFF suppresses automatic committing, so that you must commit changes manually (for example, with the COMMIT command).

BUF[FER] *buffer*

Buffer becomes the current buffer. Initially the SQL buffer is the current buffer.

CMDS[EP] { <u>;</u> | *c* | <u>OFF</u> | ON }

c sets the character used to separate multiple SQL*Plus commands entered on a line. ON or OFF controls whether multiple commands may be entered on a line.

CONCAT { <u>.</u> | *c* | OFF | <u>ON</u> }

Sets a character that may be used to terminate a user variable reference, which would otherwise be followed immediately by a character that would be interpreted as a part of the user variable name. Setting CONCAT ON resets its value to '.'.

COPYCOMMIT { <u>0</u> | n }

The COPY command will commit rows to the destination database each time it has copied this number of batches of rows. Valid values are 0 to 5000. If COPYCOMMIT is 0, COPY will perform a commit only at the end of a copy operation.

DCL[SEP] { ! | c }

Sets the character used to separate multiple operating system commands entered in SQL*Plus.

DEF[INE] { & | c | OFF | ON }

c sets the character used to prefix substitution variables. ON or OFF controls whether SQL*Plus will scan commands for substitution variables and replace them with their values.

DOC[UMENT] { OFF | ON }

ON enables the DOCUMENT command. OFF disables it. If DOCUMEMT is disabled, the DOCUMENT command is invalid and any lines following a DOCUMENT command are interpreted as commands.

ECH[OSET] { OFF | ON }

ON makes SQL*Plus display commands as they are executed from a command file. OFF suppresses the display.

EMBEDDED { OFF | ON }

OFF forces a report generated by a nonprocedural command to start at the top of a new page. ON allows such a report to begin anywhere on a page.

ESCAPE { c | OFF | ON }

c defines an escape character. OFF "undefines" the escape character. ON defines the escape character as \.

FEED[BACK] { 6 | n | OFF | ON }

n makes SQL*Plus display the number of records selected in a query when at least n records are selected. ON or OFF turns this display on or off. Turning feedback ON sets n to 1. Setting feedback to 0 is equivalent to turning it OFF.

FLUSH { OFF | ON }

OFF allows the host operating system to flush output to the user's display device while ON causes SQL*Plus to flush output to the user's display device each time SQL*Plus writes a piece of text. You should use OFF only when a command file is running non-interactively, making it unnecessary to see output and/or prompts until the command file is complete. It may improve performance by reducing the amount of I/O a program must do.

HEA[DING] { OFF | <u>ON</u> }

ON makes SQL print column headings in reports. OFF suppresses column headings.

HEADS[EP] { | | *c* | OFF | <u>ON</u> }

c sets the heading separator character, which makes SQL*Plus begin a new title line where it appears in the old forms of BTITLE and TTITLE. ON or OFF turns heading separation on or off. When heading separation is OFF, a heading separator character is printed like any other character.

LIN[ESIZE] { <u>80</u> | *n* }

Sets the number of characters that SQL*Plus will display on a line before beginning a new line. Also controls the position of centered and right-aligned text. The maximum value of n is 999.

LONG { <u>80</u> | *n* }

Sets maximum width for displaying and copying LONG values. Valid values are 1 to 32767.

MAXD[ATA] *n*

Sets the maximum total row width that SQL*Plus can process. The default and maximum values of n vary in different host operating systems. See the Oracle Installation and User's Guide for details.

NEWP[AGE] { <u>1</u> | *n* }

Sets the number of blank lines to be printed between the bottom title of each page and the top title of the next page. A value of 0 makes SQL*Plus send a form feed between pages; this clears the screen on most terminals.

NULL *text*

Sets the text that a SQL*Plus displays to represent a null value. NULL with no text makes SQL*Plus display nothing (blanks).

NUMF[ORMAT] *text*

Sets the default format for displaying number data items. *text* should be a number format.

NUM[WIDTH] { <u>10</u> | *n* }

Sets default width for displaying number values.

PAGES[IZE] { <u>14</u> | *n* }

Sets the number of lines per page. For reports printed on paper 11 inches long, a value of 54 (plus a NEWPAGE value of 6) leaves one-inch margins above and below the page.

PAU[SE] { <u>OFF</u> | ON | *text* }

ON makes SQL*Plus wait for you to press Return before displaying a new page of output. OFF suppresses the wait. text specifies text SQL*Plus should display before waiting.

SCAN { OFF | <u>ON</u> }

OFF suppresses processing of substitution variables. ON allows normal processing.

SHOW[MODE] { <u>OFF</u> | ON }

ON makes SQL*Plus display the old and new settings of a SQL parameter when it is changed with SET. OFF makes SQL*Plus display neither.

SPA[CE] { <u>1</u> | *n* }

Sets the number of spaces between columns in a table display. The maximum value of n is 10.

SQLC[ONTINUE] { '>' | char }

Sets the character sequence to be displayed as a prompt for a continuation of a SQL*Plus command line.

SQLN[UMBER] { OFF | <u>ON</u> }

ON sets the prompt for second and following lines of a SQL command to be the line number. OFF lets SQLPROMPT control the prompt.

SQLPRE[FIX] { <u>#</u> | *c* }

Sets the SQL prefix character. While you are entering a SQL∗Plus command at the SQL> prompt, you may enter a SQL command on a separate line, prefixed with the SQL prefix character. SQL will execute the SQL command immediately without affecting the SQL∗Plus command being entered.

SQLP[ROMPT] { <u>SQL></u> | *text* }

Sets the SQL command prompt that is displayed when SQLNUMBER is OFF.

SQLT[ERMINATOR] { <u>;</u> | *c* | OFF | <u>ON</u> }

Sets the character used to end SQL commands. OFF means that no SQL command terminator will be recognized; you terminate a SQL command by entering an empty line. ON resets the terminator to the default (';') even if the system variable is already ON.

SUFFIX { <u>SQL</u> | *text* }

Sets the default filename extension that SQL∗Plus uses in commands that refer to command files. For example, if you execute the command "SET SUFFIX UFI" and the command "GET EXAMPLE," SQL∗Plus will load a file named EXAMPLE.UFI instead of EXAMPLE.SQL.

TAB { OFF | <u>ON</u> }

ON makes SQL∗Plus use the tab character to format white space in output. OFF makes SQL use spaces. The default value of TAB is system-dependent. TAB is set ON for Professional Oracle.

TERM[OUT] { OFF | <u>ON</u> }

ON suppresses displayed output generated by commands executed from a file, so that output may be spooled without appearing on the screen. OFF allows output to be displayed.

TI[ME] { <u>OFF</u> | ON }

ON makes SQL*Plus display the current time before each command prompt. OFF suppresses the time display.

TIMI[NG] { <u>OFF</u> | ON }

ON makes SQL*Plus give timing statistics on each SQL command run. OFF suppresses timing of each command.

TRIM[OUT] { OFF | <u>ON</u> }

ON makes SQL*Plus trim blanks at the end of each displayed line. This can improve the speed of operations over dial-up lines. OFF allows trailing blanks to be displayed. TRIMOUT ON does not affect spooled output; it is ignored unless SET TAB ON is in effect.

TRU[NCATE] { <u>OFF</u> | ON }

TRUNCATE is the inverse of WRAP; that is, SET TRUNCATE ON is equivalent to SET WRAP OFF, and vice versa. It is better to use WRAP, because the SHOW command recognizes WRAP and does not recognized TRUNCATE.

UND[ERLINE] { <u>-</u> | c | <u>ON</u> | OFF }

c sets the character used to underline column headings in SQL*Plus reports. ON or OFF turns underlining on or off without affecting the value of c.

VER[IFY] { OFF | <u>ON</u> }

ON makes SQL*Plus display the text of a command line before and after replacing a substitution variable's reference with the value's value. OFF suppresses the display.

WRAP { OFF | <u>ON</u> }

OFF truncates the display of a data item if it is too long to fit the current line width. ON allows the data item to wrap to the next line. Use the COLUMN command's WRAPPED and TRUNCATED clauses to override the WRAP setting for specific columns.

SQL*FORMS
REFERENCE

SQL *FORMS
DEVELOPER'S FUNCTION KEYS

SQL *FORMS ACTION	IBM KEY NAME
Accept	F10
Clear Field	Ctrl-End
Create Field	F3
Cut	F5, Shift-F5
Define	F4
Delete Backward	Backspace
Delete Character	Del
Down	↓
Draw Box or Line	F7
Exit Help (Show Function Keys)	F10, Shift-F10
Exit or Cancel	Esc, Shift-F10
Help (Show Function Keys)	F1
Insert or Replace	Ins
Left	←
Next Field	Enter, Tab, Ctrl-→
Paste	F6
Previous Field	Shift-Tab, Ctrl-←
Print	Shift-F8
Redisplay Screen	Shift-F9
Resize Field	Shift-F4
Right	→
Run-Options Window	F9
Select	F2
Select Block	Shift-F2
Undo	F8
Up	↑

SQL*FORMS OPERATOR'S FUNCTION KEYS

SQL*FORMS ACTION	IBM KEY NAME
Block Menu	F5
Clear Block	Shift-F5
Clear Field	Ctrl-End
Clear Form/Rollback	Shift-F7
Clear Record	Shift-F4
Commit Transaction	F10
Count Query Hits	Shift-F2
Create Record	F6
Delete Backward	Backspace
Delete Character	Del
Delete Record	Shift-F6
Display Error	Shift-F1
Duplicate Field	F3
Duplicate Record	F4
Enter Query	F7
Execute Query	F8
Exit Help	(any function key)
Exit/Cancel	Esc, Shift-F10
Help	F2
Help (Show Function Keys)	F1
Insert or Replace	Ins
Left	←
List Field Values	F9
Next Block	PgDn
Next Field	Enter, Tab, Ctrl-→
Next Primary Key Field	Shift-F3

SQL*FORMS ACTION	IBM KEY NAME
Next Record	↓
Next Set of Records	Ctrl-PgDn
Previous Block	PgUp
Previous Field	Shift-Tab, Ctrl-←
Previous Record	↑
Print	Shift-F8
Redisplay Page	Shift-F9
Right	→

SQL *FORMS COMMAND MAP

The command map on the following pages presents an overview of the entire SQL*Forms program. You'll find this map especially useful while you are learning SQL*Forms. Refer to it whenever you need a quick reminder of the program's structure or features.

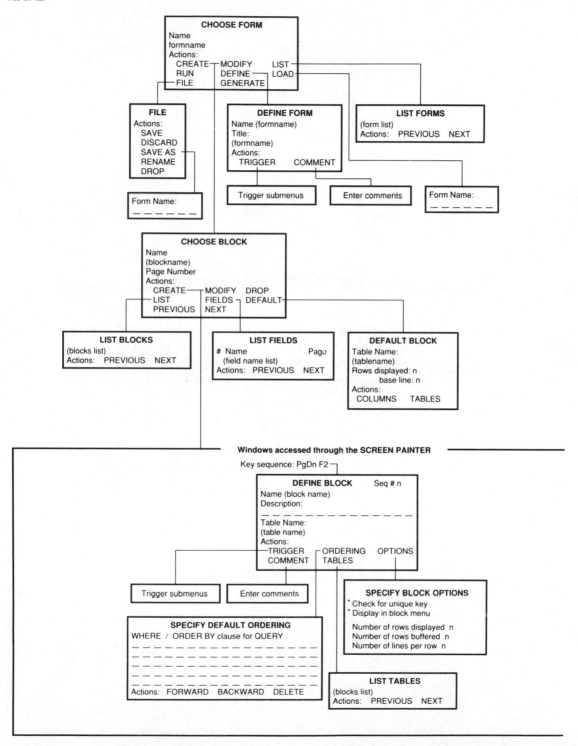

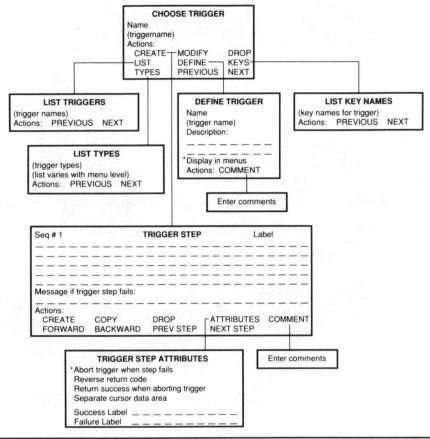

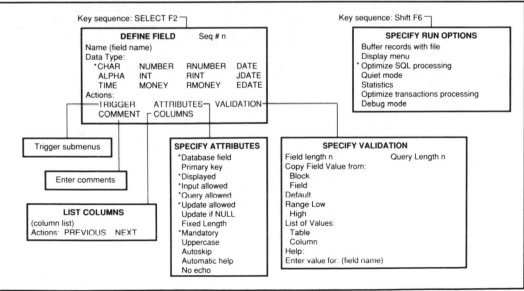

SQL*CALC
REFERENCE

*SQL *CALC FUNCTION KEYS*

SQL*CALC KEY NAME	IBM KEY	FUNCTION DESCRIPTION
Help	F1	Context-sensitive help
Edit	F2	Place content of current cell on the input line for editing
Name	F3	List all *.CAL files
GoTo	F5	Prompt for cell coordinate or name and then go to that cell
Window	F6	Switch between each spreadsheet window
Query	F7	Execute all $SELECT statements in the spreadsheet
Table	F8	List all of your database tables
Calc	F9	Recalculate spreadsheet formulas and update displayed results
Copied	F10	Execute all copied SQL statements in the spreadsheet
PageUp	PgUp	Show previous window of rows
PageDown	PgDn	Show next window of rows
Insert	Ins	Switch between insert and overwrite during cell editing
Delete	Del	Delete character at the cursor
Home	Home	Move to cell A1. When editing, move to the beginning of the Input Line
End	End	Move to cell in highest row and highest column coordinate. When editing, move to the end of the Input Line
Return	Enter	Enter data
Backspace	Backspace	Erase character to the left of the cursor
Escape	Esc	Cancel command and erase data

SQL*CALC KEY NAME	IBM KEY	FUNCTION DESCRIPTION
Up Arrow	↑	Move cursor up one cell
Down Arrow	↓	Move cursor down one cell
Left Arrow	←	Move cursor left one cell. When editing, move cursor left one character (non-destructive)
Right Arrow	→	Move cursor right one cell. When editing, move cursor right one character (non-destructive)
Exit	Ctrl-Z	Return to operating system without saving current spreadsheet

SQL*CALC FUNCTIONS

FUNCTION	YIELDS THE FOLLOWING
ABS(x)	Absolute value of x
ACOS(x)	Inverse cosine in radians of x
AND(*list*)	True if none of the items in *list* is false
ASIN(x)	Inverse sine in radians of x
ATAN(x)	Inverse tangent in radians of x
AVG(*list*)	Average value of all items in *list*
CHOOSE(x,*list*)	Item number x from the list of items
COS(x)	Cosine of angle x in radians
COUNT(*list*)	Number of numeric items in list of items
DEG(x)	Value in degrees of angle x (in radians)
E	Value of the natural logarithm base (2.718...)
ERR	Value ERR indicating a formula evaluation occurred
EXP(x)	Number E raised to the power x
FALSE	Equivalent to the value 0
IF(x,t,f)	Displays t if formula x is true; otherwise displays formula f

FUNCTION	YIELDS THE FOLLOWING
INT(x)	Truncates formula to integer
ISERR(c)	If formula evaluation error, the value 1; otherwise, value 0
ISNA(c)	If formula c is not available, the value 1; otherwise, value 0
LN(x)	Natural logarithm of formula x
LOG(x)	Common logarithm (base 10) of formula x
LOOKUP(x,r)	Value of cell next to cell which is greater than or equal to formula x in the cell range r. If range r is a partial row, the value is taken from the cell below; if range r is a partial column, the value is taken from the cell to the right
MAX(*list*)	Maximum value from *list*
MIN(*list*)	Minimum value from *list*
NA	Value N/A displayed; indicates the value of the cell is "not available"
NPV(x,r)	Net present value at rate x computer over range r
NOT(x)	Negates the formula x: if x is true, 0; otherwise, 1
OR(*list*)	Value 1 (true) if *any* item in *list* is true; 0 if *all* items in *list* are false (0)
PI	Value of pi
RAD(x)	Value, in radians, of angle x given in degrees
SIN(x)	Sine of angle x, which is in radians
SQRT(x)	Square root of formula x
SUM(*list*)	Sum of the *numeric* items in *list*. Non-numeric items (including empty cells) are treated as 0
TAN(x)	Tangent of angle x, which is in radians
TRUE	Value of 1 (true)

SQL*CALC COMMAND MAP*

This command map presents an overview of the entire SQL*Calc program. You'll find it especially useful while you are learning SQL*Calc. Refer to it whenever you need a quick reminder of the program's structure or features.

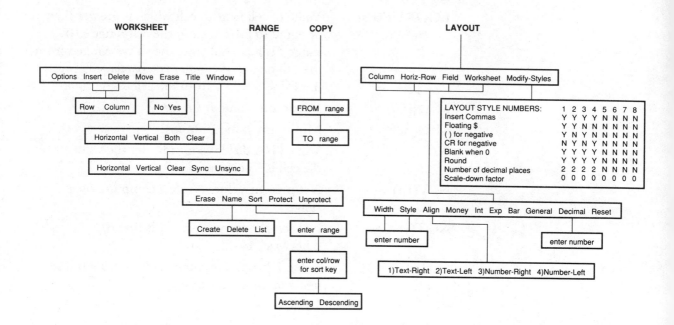

* *Within boxes, leftmost choice is default. Options are capitalized; prompts are lowercase.*

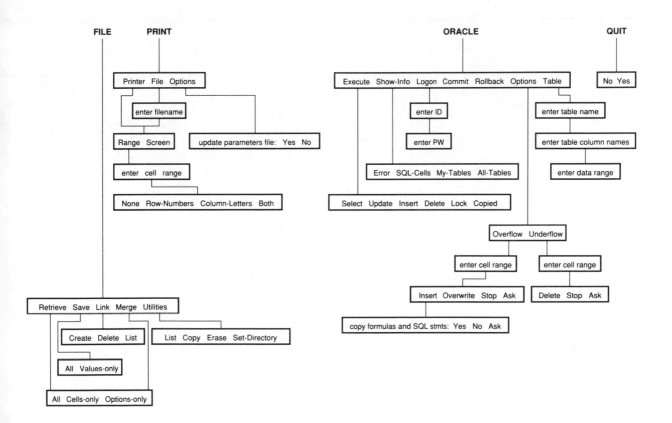

BIBLIOGRAPHY

Bass, Paul. "Selecting the Right Index." *Database Programming & Design,* February 1988, pp. 56-59.

Bell, D. E., and LaPadula, L. J. "Secure Computer Systems: Mathematical Foundations and Model." *MITRE Corporation Technical Report.* Bedford, Mass.: MITRE Corporation, 1974.

Date, C. J. *A Guide to DB2.* Reading, Mass.: Addison-Wesley Publishing Company, 1984, p. 128.

_____. *An Introduction to Database Systems.* Vol. 1. Reading, Mass.: Addison-Wesley Publishing Company, 1986, pp. 361-392.

_____. *An Introduction to Database Systems.* Vol. 2. Reading, Mass.: Addison-Wesley Publishing Company, 1983, pp. 199-201.

_____. *Relational Database Selected Readings.* Reading, Mass.: Addison-Wesley Publishing Company, 1986, pp. 417-470.

Department of Defense Computer Security Center. *Computer Security Requirements/Guidance for Applying the Department of Defense Trusted Computer System Evaluation Criteria in Specific Environments.* CSC-STD-003-85. Fort George Meade, Maryland: Department of Defense, June 1985.

_____. *Department of Defense Trusted Computer System Evaluation Criteria.* DoD 5200.2A-STD. Fort George Meade, Maryland: Department of Defense, August 1983.

_____. *Technical Rational Behind CSC-STD-003-85: Guidance for Applying the Department of Defense Trusted Computer System Evaluation Criteria in Specific Environments.* CSC-STD-004-85. Fort George Meade, Maryland: Department of Defense, June 1985.

INDEX

Selections from The SYBEX Library

SPREADSHEETS AND INTEGRATED SOFTWARE

The ABC's of 1-2-3 (Second Edition)
Chris Gilbert/Laurie Williams
245pp. Ref. 355-4

Online Today recommends it as "an easy and comfortable way to get started with the program." An essential tutorial for novices, it will remain on your desk as a valuable source of ongoing reference and support. For Release 2.

Mastering 1-2-3 (Second Edition)
Carolyn Jorgensen
702pp. Ref. 528-X

Get the most from 1-2-3 Release 2 with this step-by-step guide emphasizing advanced features and practical uses. Topics include data sharing, macros, spreadsheet security, expanded memory, and graphics enhancements.

Lotus 1-2-3 Desktop Companion (SYBEX Ready Reference Series)
Greg Harvey
976pp. Ref. 501-8

A full-time consultant, right on your desk. Hundreds of self-contained entries cover every 1-2-3 feature, organized by topic, indexed and cross-referenced, and supplemented by tips, macros and working examples. For Release 2.

Advanced Techniques in Lotus 1-2-3
Peter Antoniak/E. Michael Lunsford
367pp. Ref. 556-5

This guide for experienced users focuses on advanced functions, and techniques for designing menu-driven applications using macros and the Release 2 command language. Interfacing techniques and add-on products are also considered.

Lotus 1-2-3 Instant Reference SYBEX Prompter Series
Greg Harvey/Kay Yarborough Nelson
296pp. Ref. 475-5; 4 3/4x8

Organized information at a glance. When you don't have time to hunt through hundreds of pages of manuals, turn here for a quick reminder: the right key sequence, a brief explanation of a command, or the correct syntax for a specialized function.

Mastering Lotus HAL
Mary V. Campbell
342pp. Ref. 422-4

A complete guide to using HAL "natural language" requests to communicate with 1-2-3—for new and experienced users. Covers all the basics, plus advanced HAL features such as worksheet linking and auditing, macro recording, and more.

Simpson's 1-2-3 Macro Library
Alan Simpson
298pp. Ref. 314-7

Increase productivity instantly with macros for custom menus, graphics, consolidating worksheets, interfacing with mainframes and more. With a tutorial on macro creation and details on Release 2 commands.

Mastering Symphony (Fourth Edition)
Douglas Cobb
857pp. Ref. 494-1

Thoroughly revised to cover all aspects of the major upgrade of Symphony Version 2, this Fourth Edition of Doug Cobb's classic is still "the Symphony bible" to this complex but even more powerful package. All the new features are discussed and placed in context with prior versions so that both new and previous users will benefit from Cobb's insights.

Focus on Symphony Databases
Alan Simpson/Donna M. Mosich
398pp. Ref. 336-8
Master every feature of this complex system by building real-life applications from the ground up—for mailing lists, inventory and accounts receivable. Everything from creating a first database to reporting, macros, and custom menus.

Mastering Quattro
Alan Simpson
576pp. Ref. 514-X
This tutorial covers not only all of Quattro's classic spreadsheet features, but also its added capabilities including extended graphing, modifiable menus, and the macro debugging environment. Simpson brings out how to use all of Quattro's new-generation-spreadsheet capabilities.

Mastering Framework II
Douglas Hergert/Jonathan Kamin
509pp. Ref. 390-2
This business-minded tutorial includes a complete introduction to idea processing, "frames," and software integration, along with its comprehensive treatment of word processing, spreadsheet, and database management with Framework.

Mastering Excel on the IBM PC
Carl Townsend
628pp. Ref. 403-8
A complete Excel handbook with step-by-step tutorials, sample applications and an extensive reference section. Topics include worksheet fundamentals, formulas and windows, graphics, database techniques, special features, macros and more.

Mastering Enable
Keith D. Bishop
517pp. Ref. 440-2
A comprehensive, practical, hands-on guide to Enable 2.0—integrated word processing, spreadsheet, database management, graphics, and communications—from basic concepts to custom menus, macros and the Enable Procedural Language.

Mastering Q & A (Second Edition)
Greg Harvey
540pp. Ref. 452-6
This hands-on tutorial explores the Q & A Write, File, and Report modules, and the Intelligent Assistant. English-language command processor, macro creation, interfacing with other software, and more, using practical business examples.

Mastering SuperCalc 4
Greg Harvey
311pp. Ref. 419-4
A guided tour of this spreadsheet, database and graphics package shows how and why it adds up to a powerful business planning tool. Step-by-step lessons and real-life examples cover every aspect of the program.

Understanding Javelin PLUS
John R. Levine
Margaret Levine Young
Jordan M. Young
558pp. Ref. 358-9
This detailed guide to Javelin's latest release includes a concise introduction to business modeling, from profit-and-loss analysis to manufacturing studies. Readers build sample models and produce multiple reports and graphs, to master Javelin's unique features.

DATABASE MANAGEMENT

Mastering Paradox (Third Edition)
Alan Simpson
663pp. Ref. 490-9
Paradox is given authoritative, comprehensive explanation in Simpson's up-to-date new edition which goes from database basics to command-file programming with PAL. Topics include multiuser networking, the Personal Programmer Application Generator, the Data-Entry Toolkit, and more.

TO JOIN THE SYBEX MAILING LIST OR ORDER BOOKS
PLEASE COMPLETE THIS FORM

NAME _____ COMPANY _____

STREET _____ STATE _____ ZIP _____

☐ PLEASE MAIL ME MORE INFORMATION ABOUT **SYBEX** TITLES

ORDER FORM (There is no obligation to order)

PLEASE SEND ME THE FOLLOWING:

TITLE	QTY	PRICE
_____	____	____
_____	____	____
_____	____	____
_____	____	____

TOTAL BOOK ORDER _____ $_____

CUSTOMER SIGNATURE _____

SHIPPING AND HANDLING PLEASE ADD $2.00
PER BOOK VIA UPS _____

FOR OVERSEAS SURFACE ADD $5.25 PER
BOOK PLUS $4.40 REGISTRATION FEE _____

FOR OVERSEAS AIRMAIL ADD $18.25 PER
BOOK PLUS $4.40 REGISTRATION FEE _____

CALIFORNIA RESIDENTS PLEASE ADD
APPLICABLE SALES TAX _____

TOTAL AMOUNT PAYABLE _____

☐ CHECK ENCLOSED ☐ VISA
☐ MASTERCARD ☐ AMERICAN EXPRESS

ACCOUNT NUMBER _____

EXPIR. DATE _____ DAYTIME PHONE _____

CHECK AREA OF COMPUTER INTEREST:

☐ BUSINESS SOFTWARE

☐ TECHNICAL PROGRAMMING

☐ OTHER: _____

**THE FACTOR THAT WAS MOST IMPORTANT IN
YOUR SELECTION:**

☐ THE SYBEX NAME

☐ QUALITY

☐ PRICE

☐ EXTRA FEATURES

☐ COMPREHENSIVENESS

☐ CLEAR WRITING

☐ OTHER _____

**OTHER COMPUTER TITLES YOU WOULD LIKE
TO SEE IN PRINT:**

_____

_____

OCCUPATION

☐ PROGRAMMER   ☐ TEACHER

☐ SENIOR EXECUTIVE   ☐ HOMEMAKER

☐ COMPUTER CONSULTANT ☐ RETIRED

☐ SUPERVISOR   ☐ STUDENT

☐ MIDDLE MANAGEMENT   ☐ OTHER:

☐ ENGINEER/TECHNICAL _____

☐ CLERICAL/SERVICE

☐ BUSINESS OWNER/SELF EMPLOYED

CHECK YOUR LEVEL OF COMPUTER USE

☐ NEW TO COMPUTERS

☐ INFREQUENT COMPUTER USER

☐ FREQUENT USER OF ONE SOFTWARE

PACKAGE:

NAME _____

☐ FREQUENT USER OF MANY SOFTWARE

PACKAGES

☐ PROFESSIONAL PROGRAMMER

OTHER COMMENTS:

_____

_____

_____

_____

_____

_____

_____

PLEASE FOLD, SEAL, AND MAIL TO SYBEX

SYBEX, INC.
2021 CHALLENGER DR. #100
ALAMEDA, CALIFORNIA USA
94501

SEAL

SYBEX Computer Books are different.

Here is why . . .

At SYBEX, each book is designed with you in mind. Every manuscript is carefully selected and supervised by our editors, who are themselves computer experts. We publish the best authors, whose technical expertise is matched by an ability to write clearly and to communicate effectively. Programs are thoroughly tested for accuracy by our technical staff. Our computerized production department goes to great lengths to make sure that each book is well-designed.

In the pursuit of timeliness, SYBEX has achieved many publishing firsts. SYBEX was among the first to integrate personal computers used by authors and staff into the publishing process. SYBEX was the first to publish books on the CP/M operating system, microprocessor interfacing techniques, word processing, and many more topics.

Expertise in computers and dedication to the highest quality product have made SYBEX a world leader in computer book publishing. Translated into fourteen languages, SYBEX books have helped millions of people around the world to get the most from their computers. We hope we have helped you, too.

For a complete catalog of our publications:

SYBEX, Inc. 2021 Challenger Drive, #100, Alameda, CA 94501
Tel: (415) 523-8233/(800) 227-2346   Telex: 336311
Fax: (415) 523-2373

Oracle for 1-2-3 Command Map

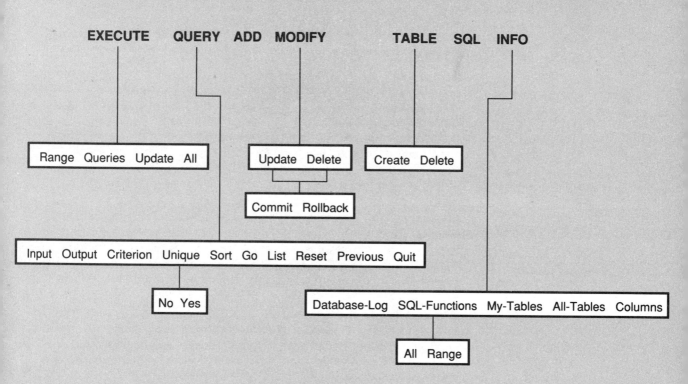